Void's Enigmatic Mansion

1

HEEEUN KIM
JIEUN HA

Yen
Press

Void's
Enigmatic
Mansion

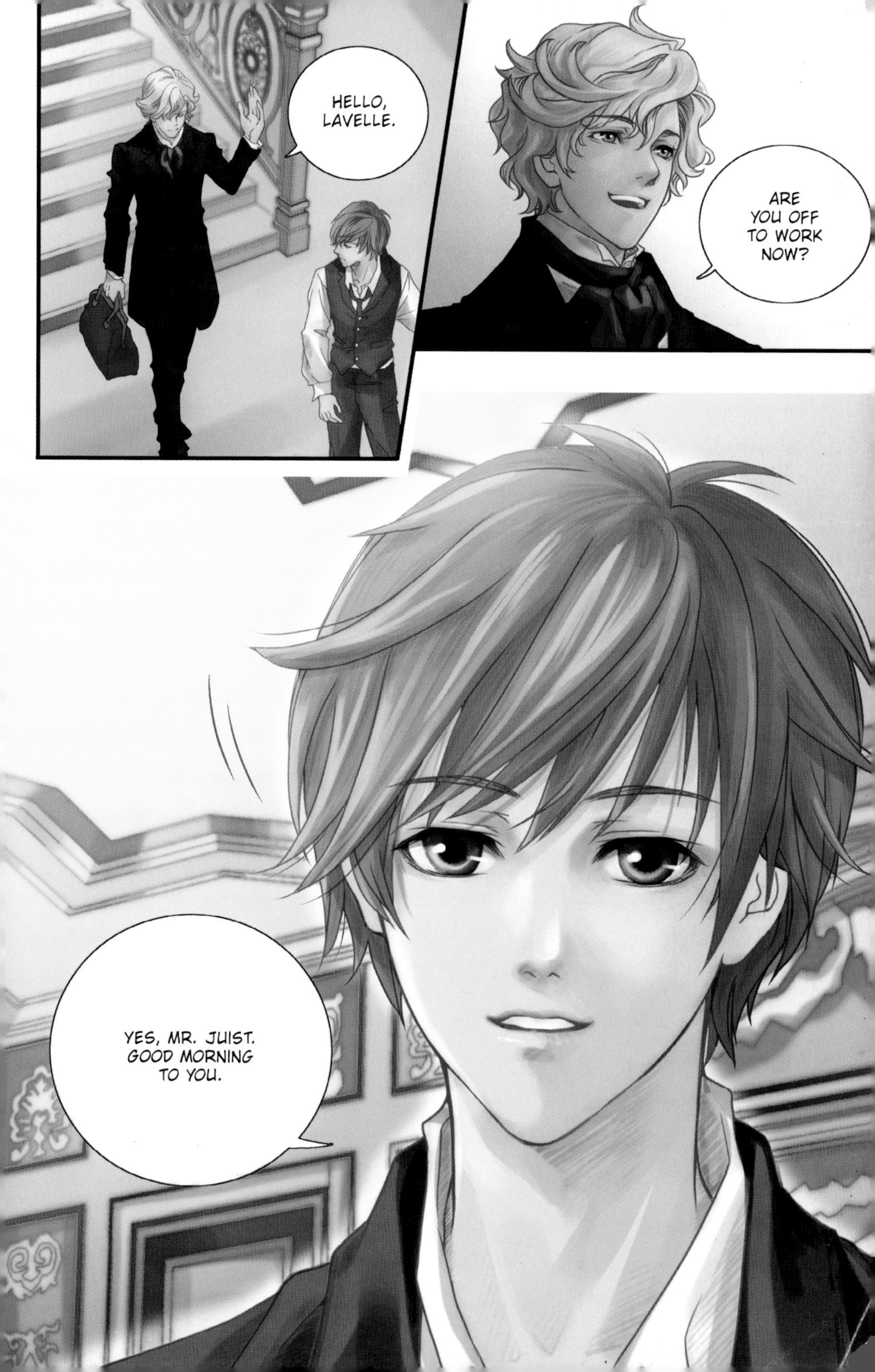
HELLO, LAVELLE.
ARE YOU OFF TO WORK NOW?
YES, MR. JUIST. GOOD MORNING TO YOU.

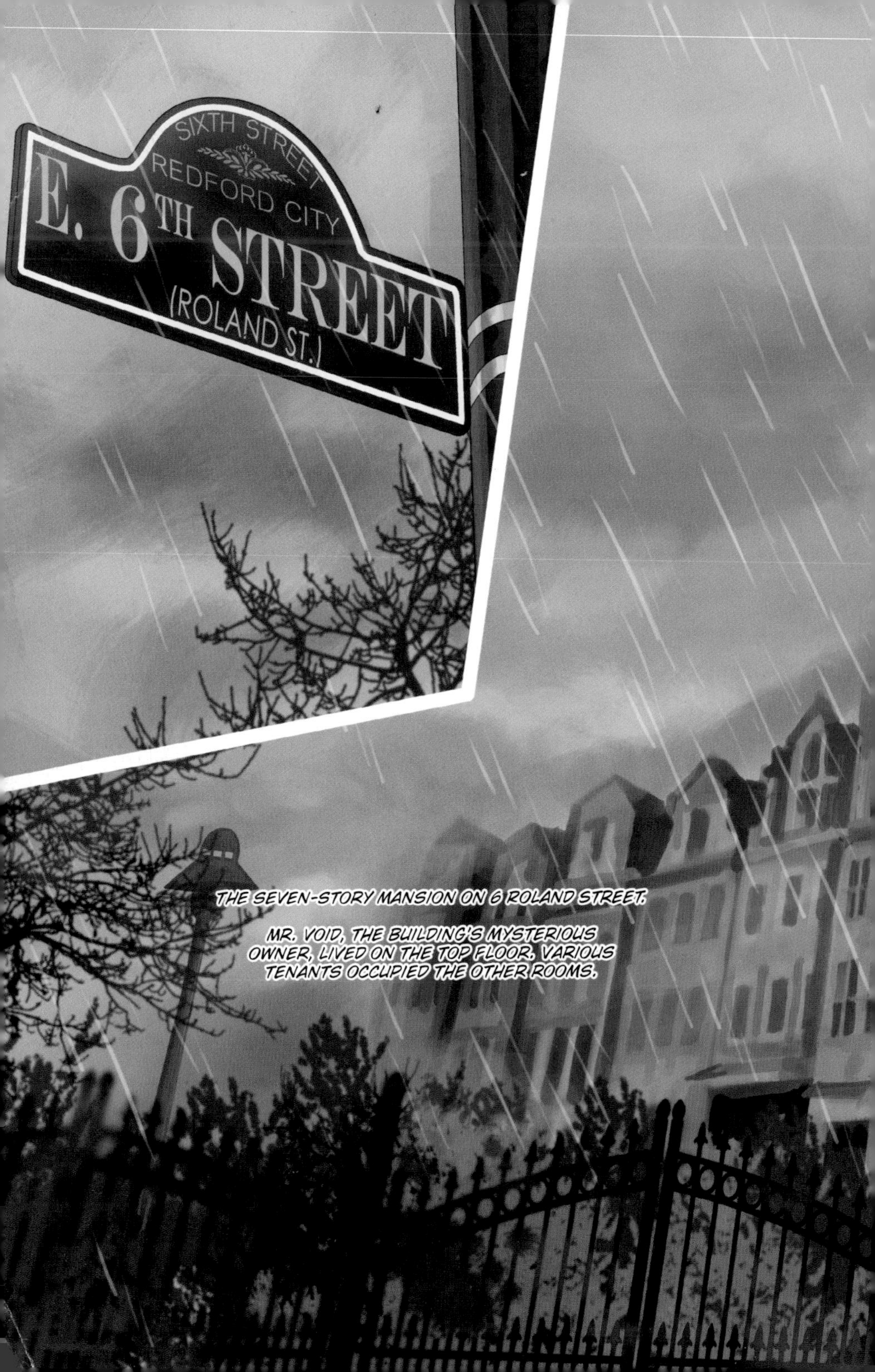
SIXTH STREET
REDFORD CITY
E. 6TH STREET
(ROLAND ST.)
THE SEVEN-STORY MANSION ON 6 ROLAND STREET.
MR. VOID, THE BUILDING'S MYSTERIOUS OWNER, LIVED ON THE TOP FLOOR. VARIOUS TENANTS OCCUPIED THE OTHER ROOMS.

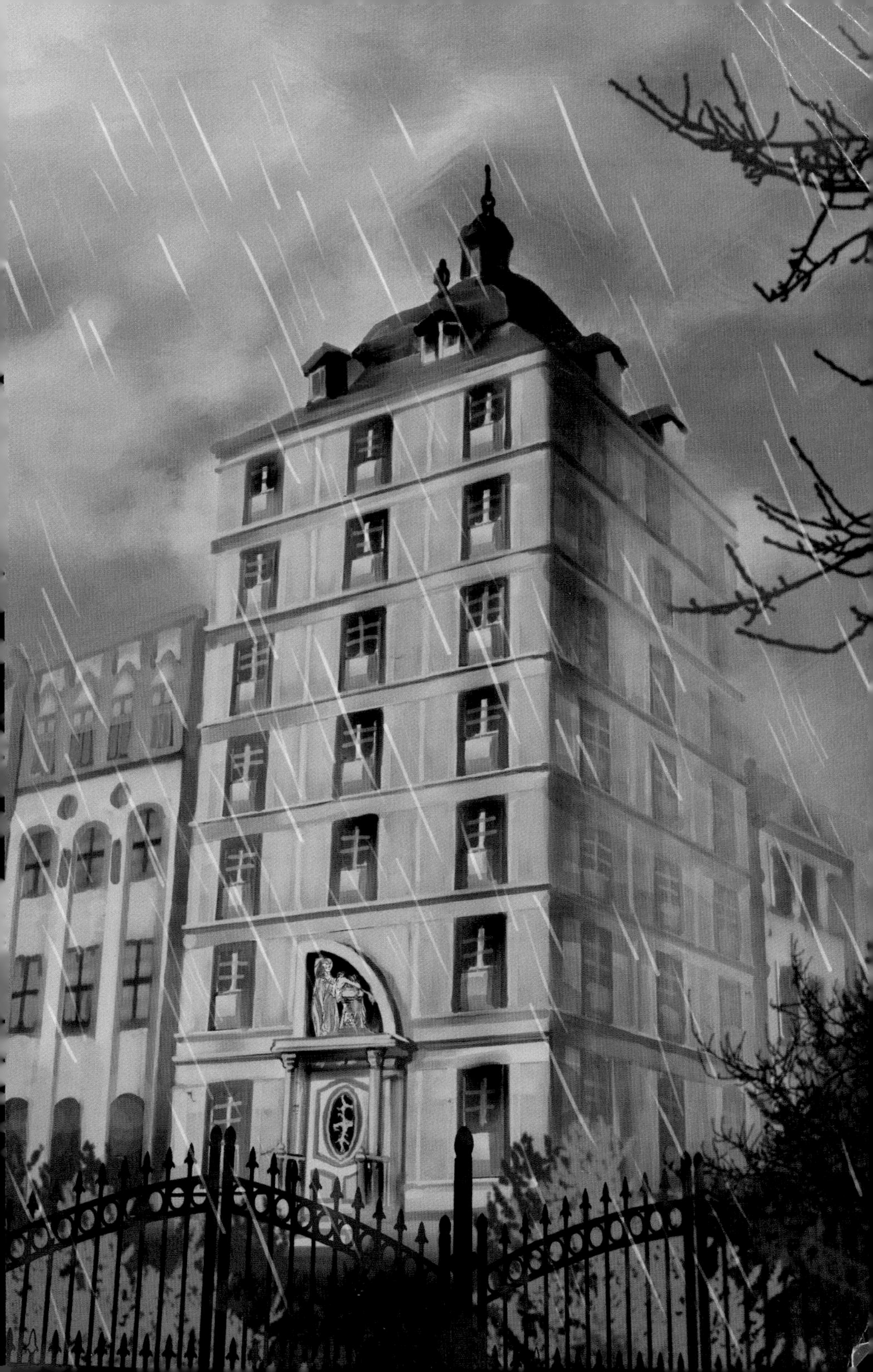

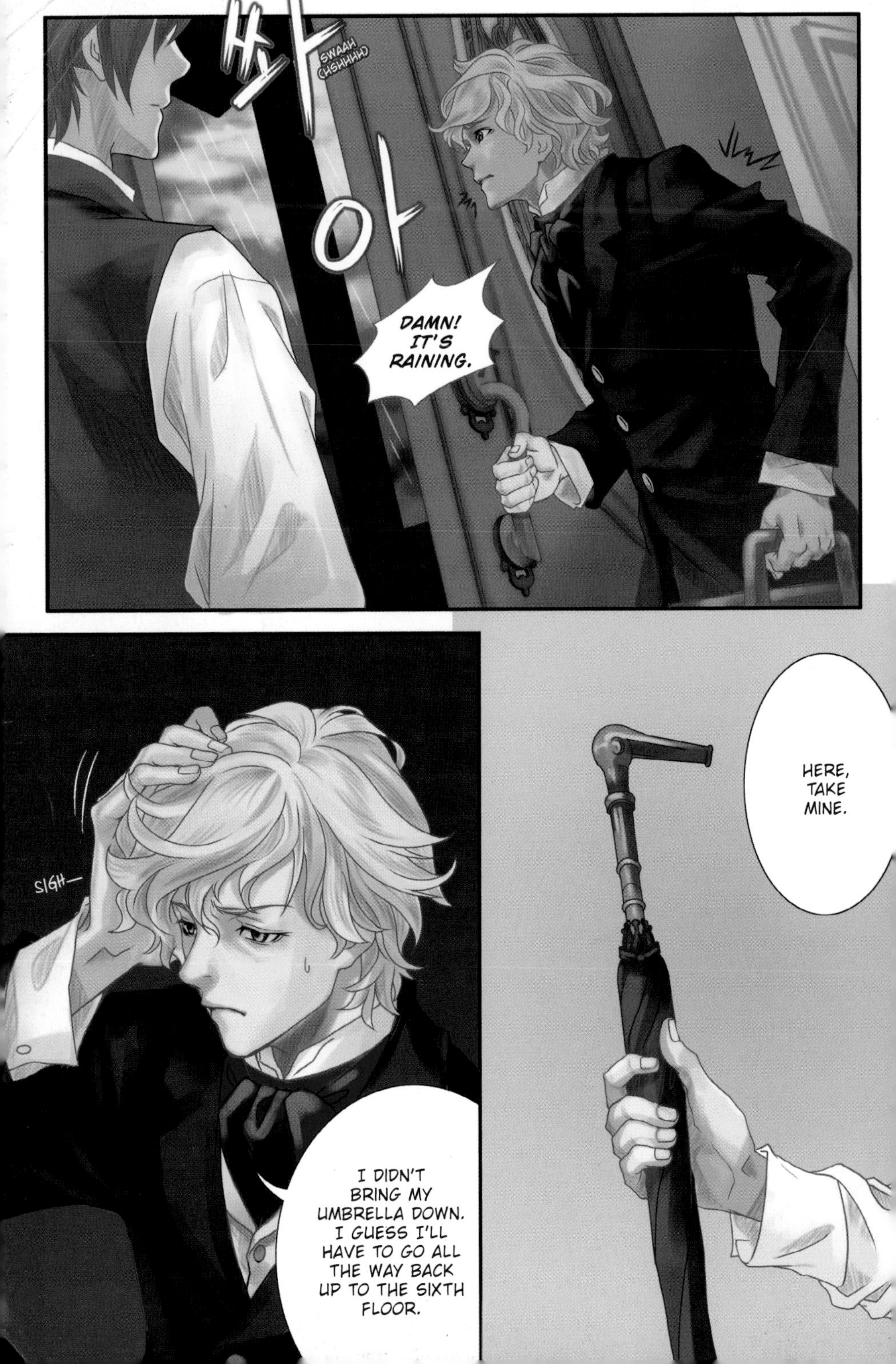
쏴아
SWAAH (SHHHHH)
DAMN! IT'S RAINING.
SIGH—
I DIDN'T BRING MY UMBRELLA DOWN. I GUESS I'LL HAVE TO GO ALL THE WAY BACK UP TO THE SIXTH FLOOR.
HERE, TAKE MINE.

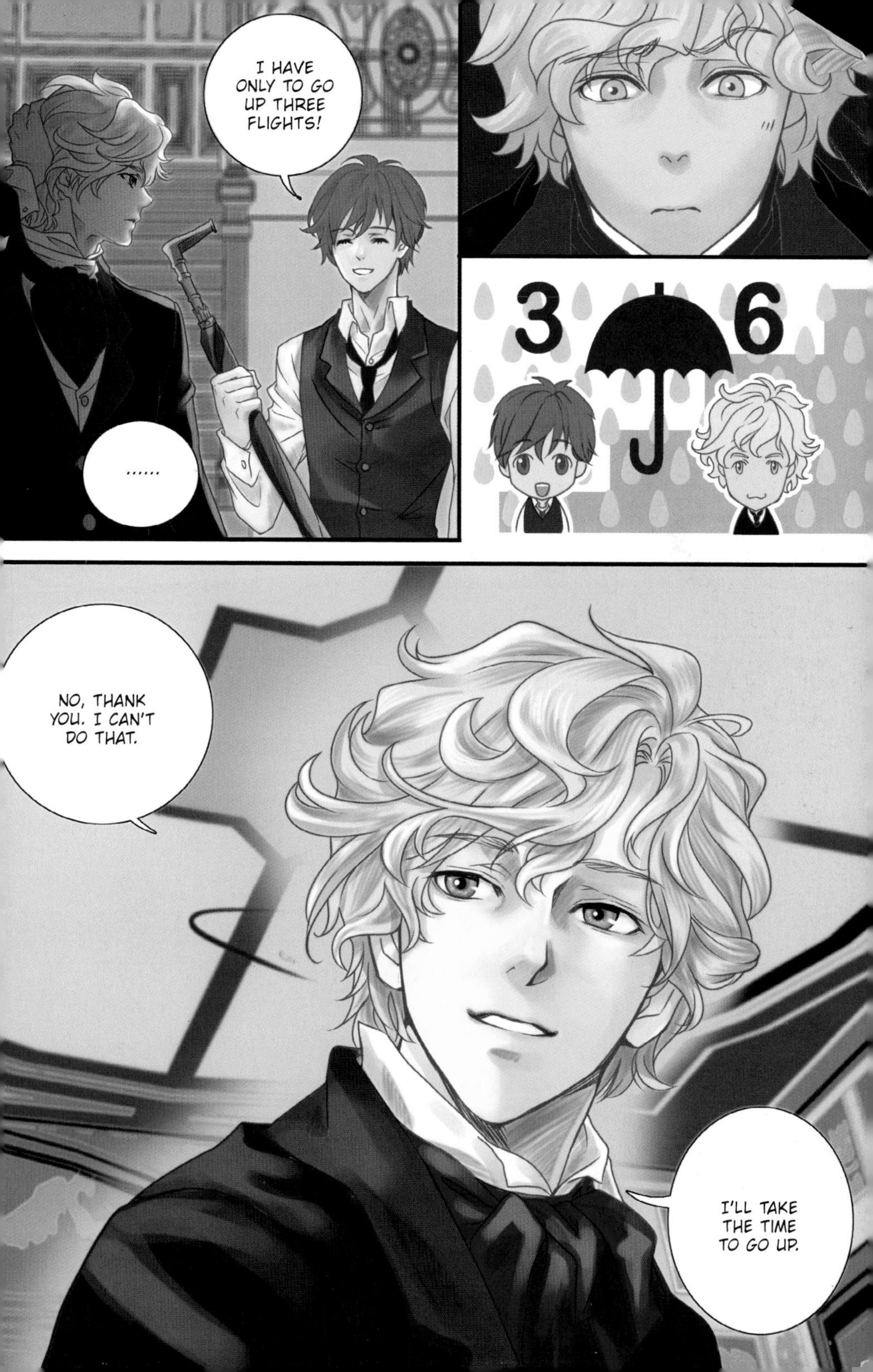
I HAVE ONLY TO GO UP THREE FLIGHTS!
......
3
6
NO, THANK YOU. I CAN'T DO THAT.
I'LL TAKE THE TIME TO GO UP.

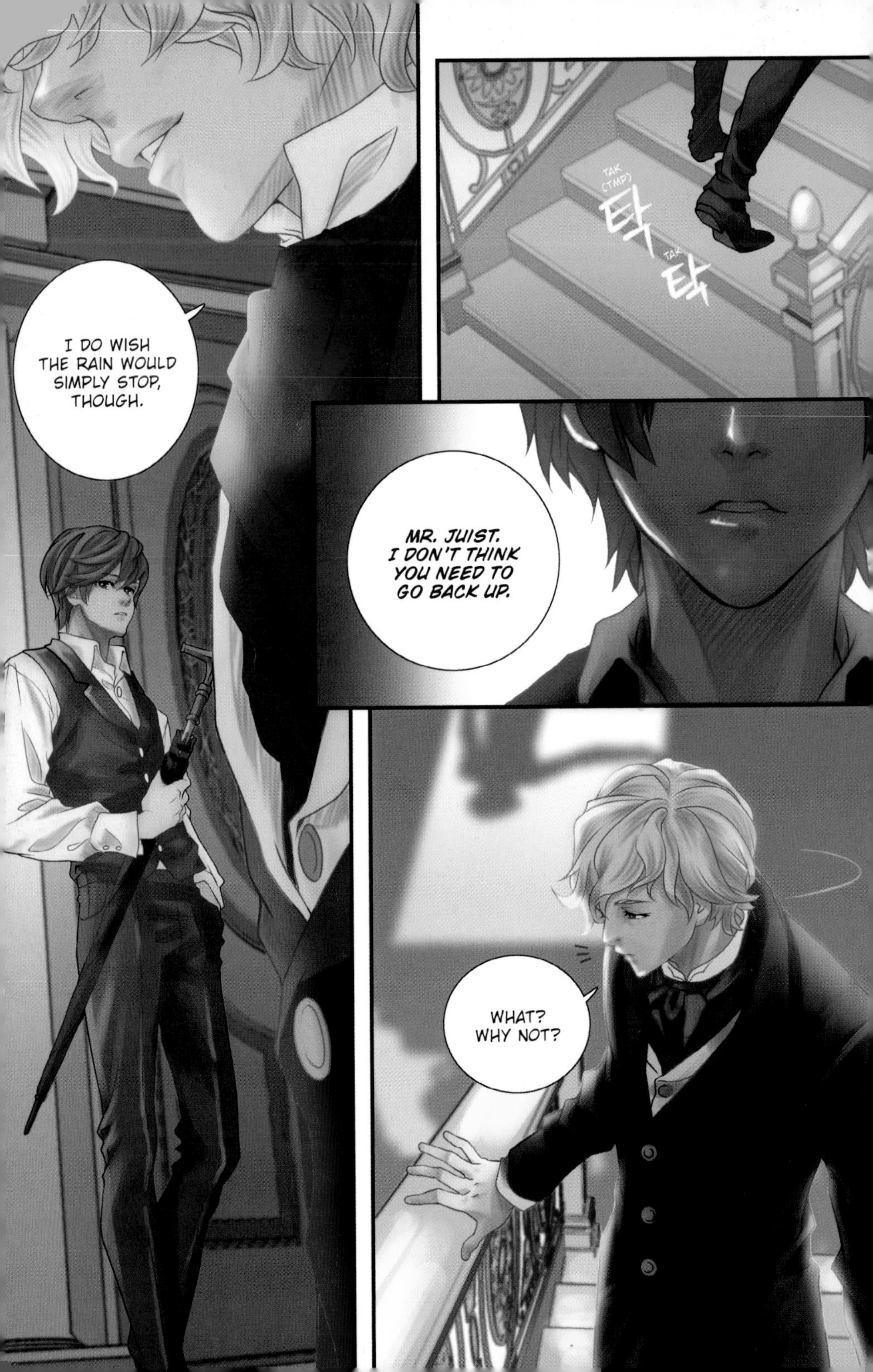
I DO WISH THE RAIN WOULD SIMPLY STOP, THOUGH.
TAK (TMP)
탁
TAK
탁
MR. JUIST. I DON'T THINK YOU NEED TO GO BACK UP.
WHAT? WHY NOT?

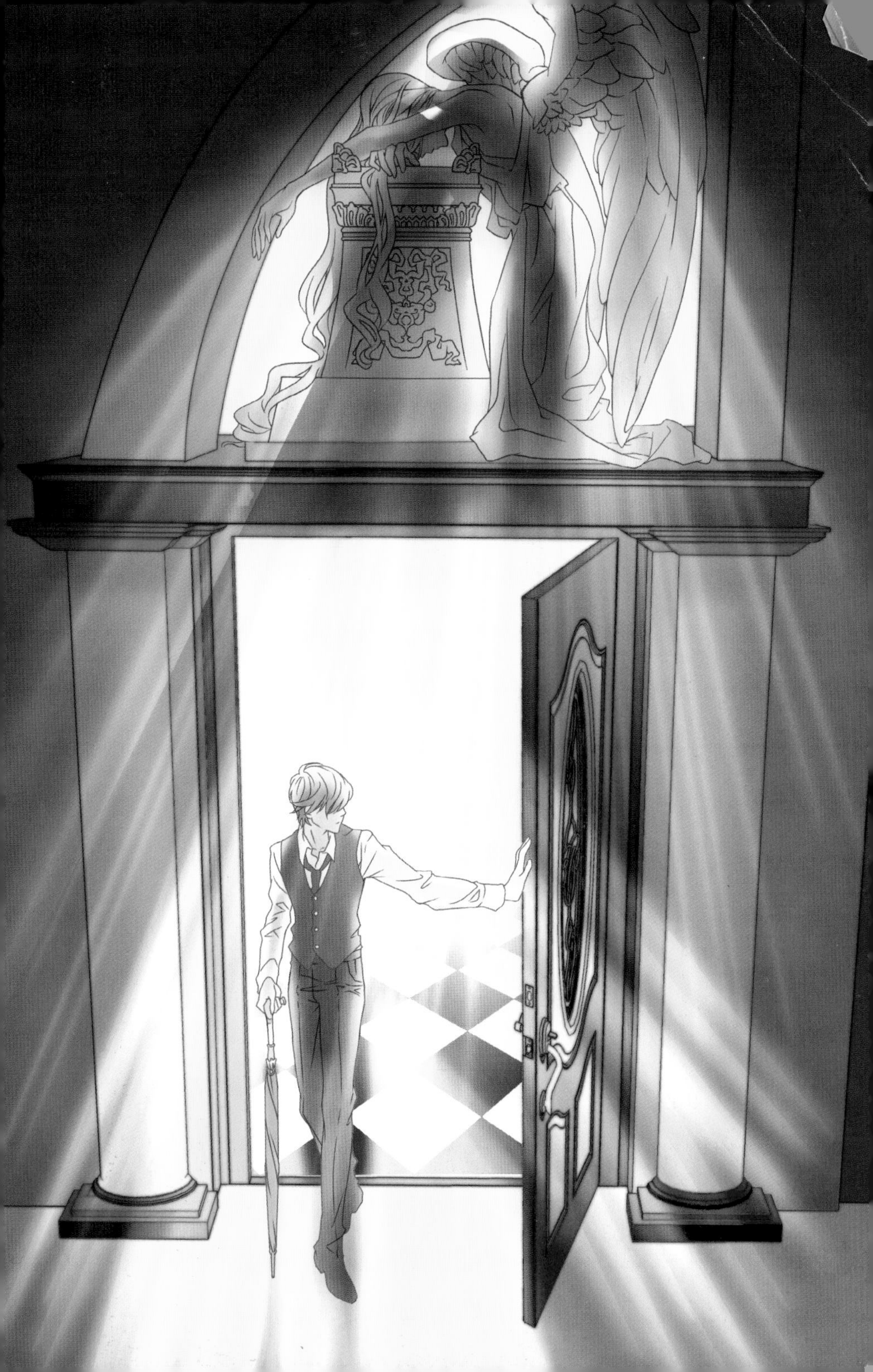

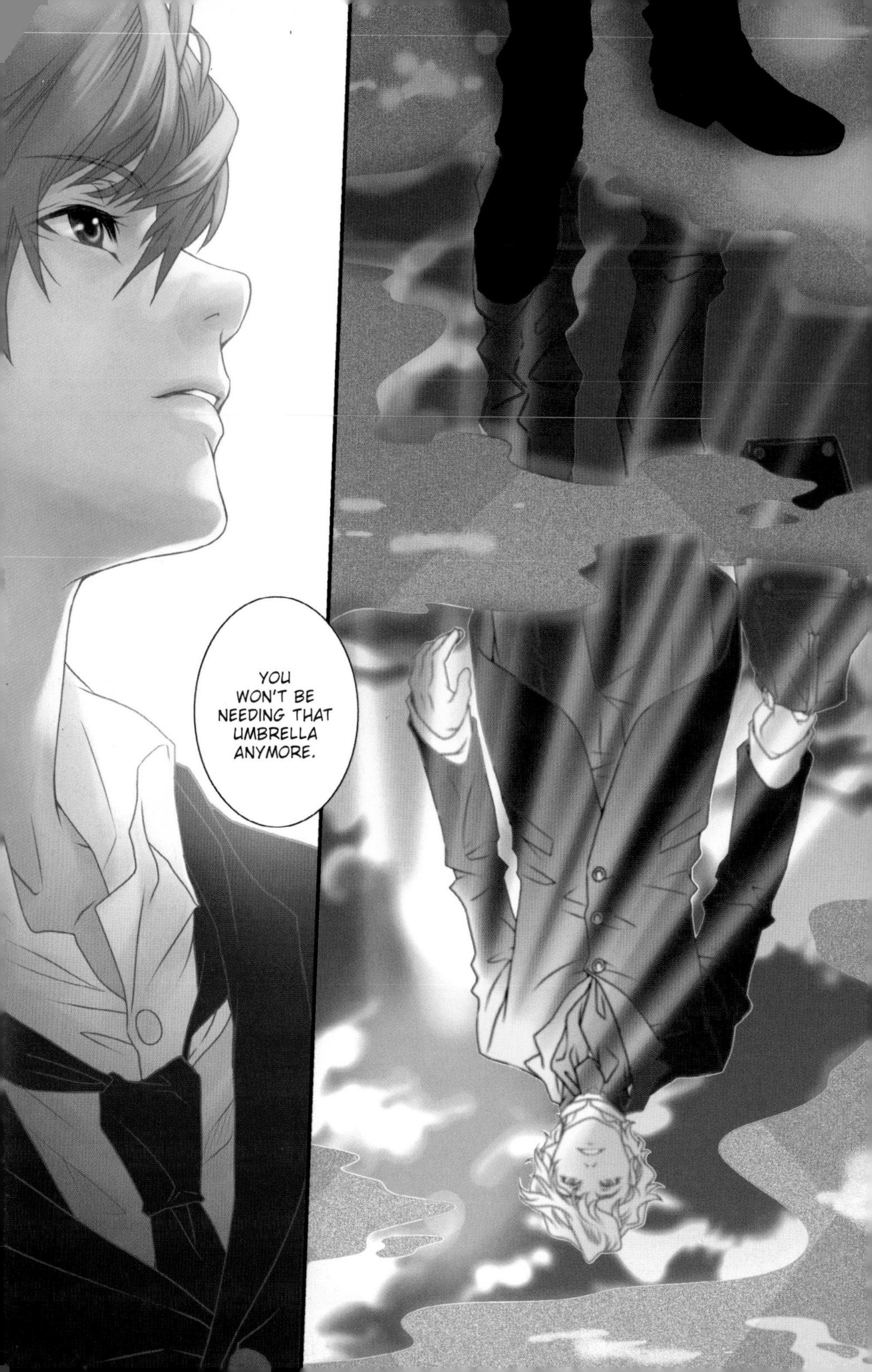
YOU WON'T BE NEEDING THAT UMBRELLA ANYMORE.

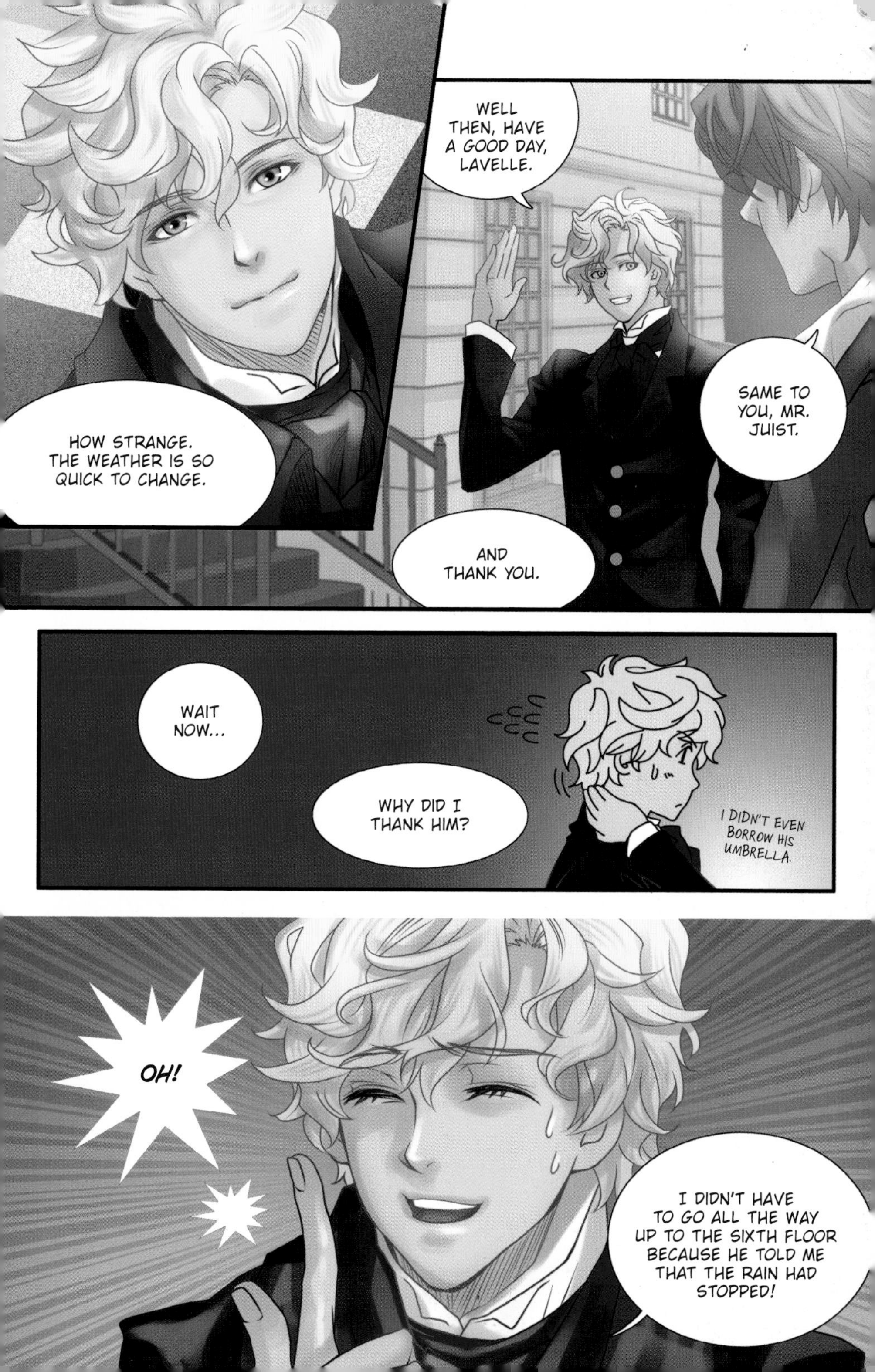
HOW STRANGE. THE WEATHER IS SO QUICK TO CHANGE.
WELL THEN, HAVE A GOOD DAY, LAVELLE.
SAME TO YOU, MR. JUIST.
AND THANK YOU.
WAIT NOW...
WHY DID I THANK HIM?
I DIDN'T EVEN BORROW HIS UMBRELLA.
OH!
I DIDN'T HAVE TO GO ALL THE WAY UP TO THE SIXTH FLOOR BECAUSE HE TOLD ME THAT THE RAIN HAD STOPPED!

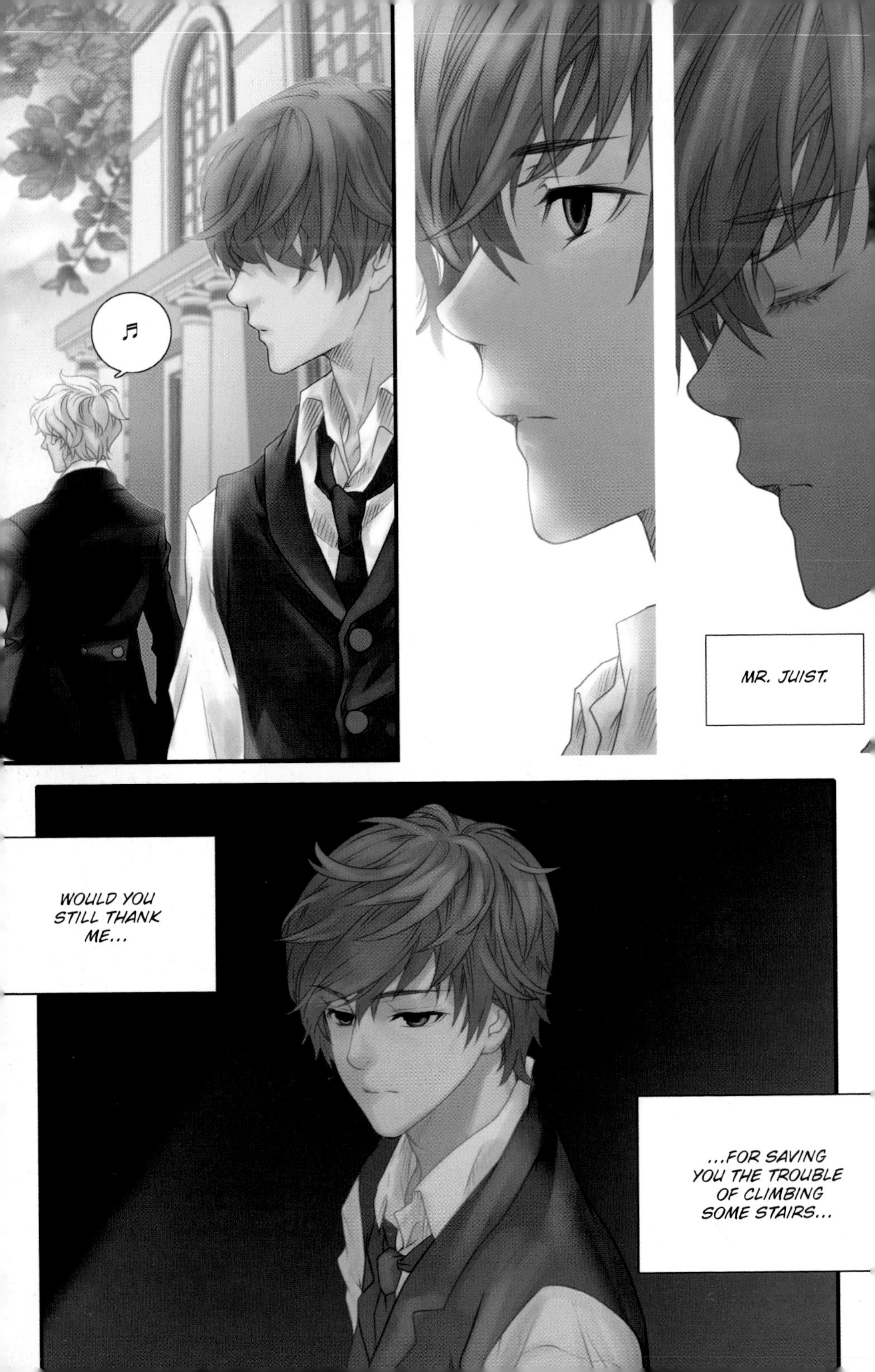
MR. JUIST.
♬
WOULD YOU STILL THANK ME...
...FOR SAVING YOU THE TROUBLE OF CLIMBING SOME STAIRS...

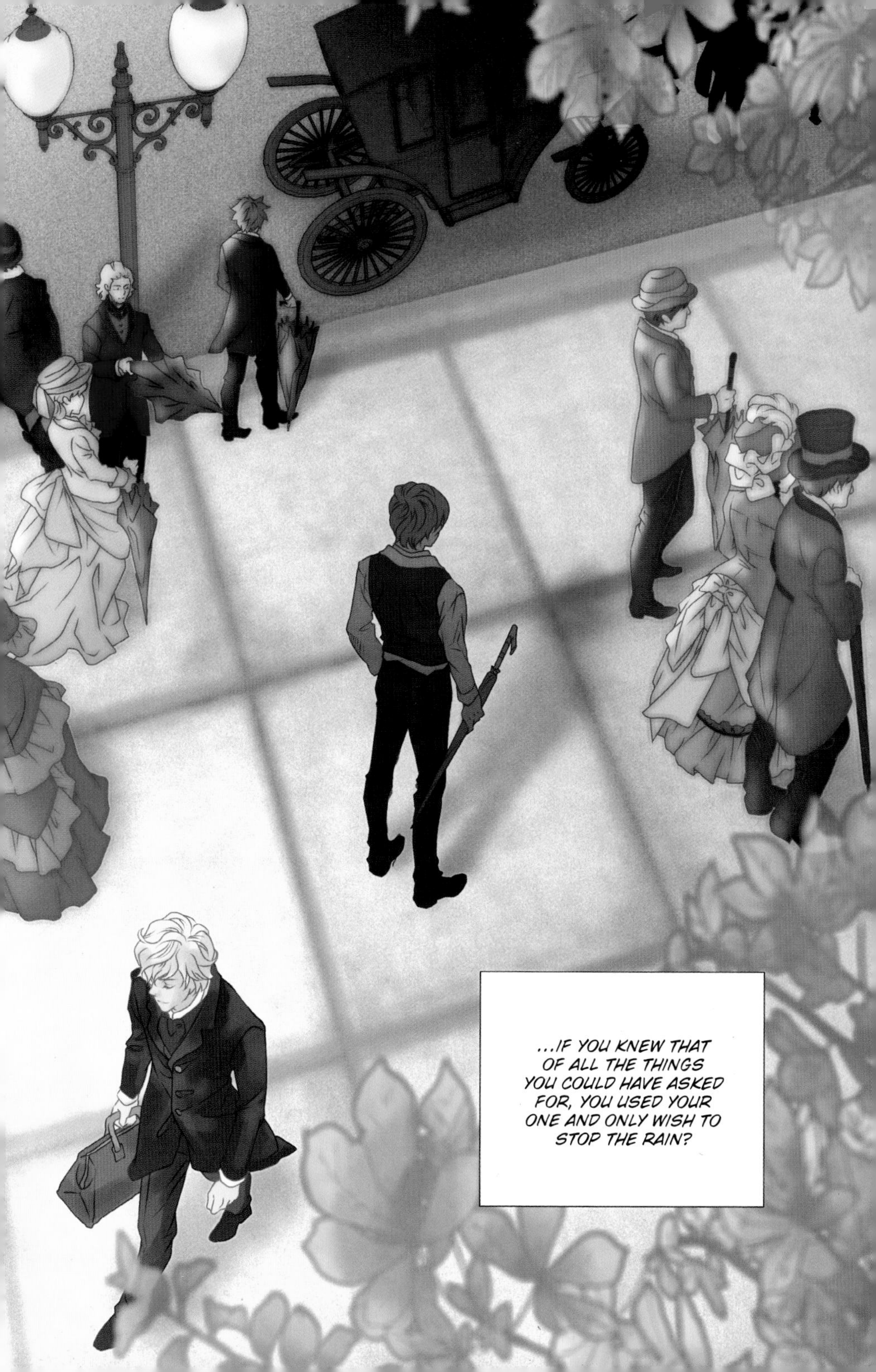
...IF YOU KNEW THAT OF ALL THE THINGS YOU COULD HAVE ASKED FOR, YOU USED YOUR ONE AND ONLY WISH TO STOP THE RAIN?

Void's Enigmatic Mansion

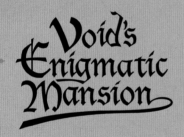

"

Do you have a wish?
Just be careful what
you wish for, child.

"

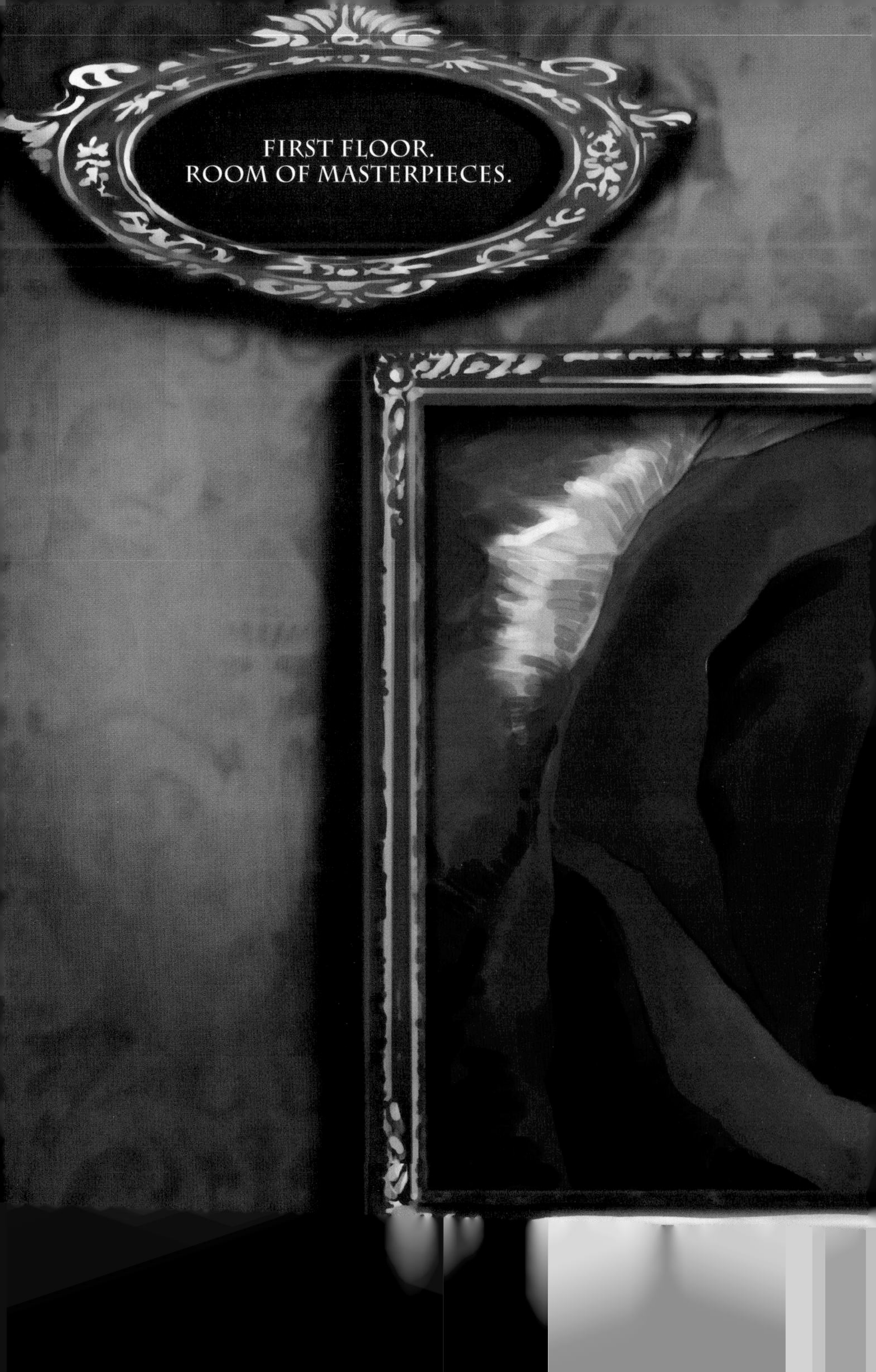
FIRST FLOOR.
ROOM OF MASTERPIECES.

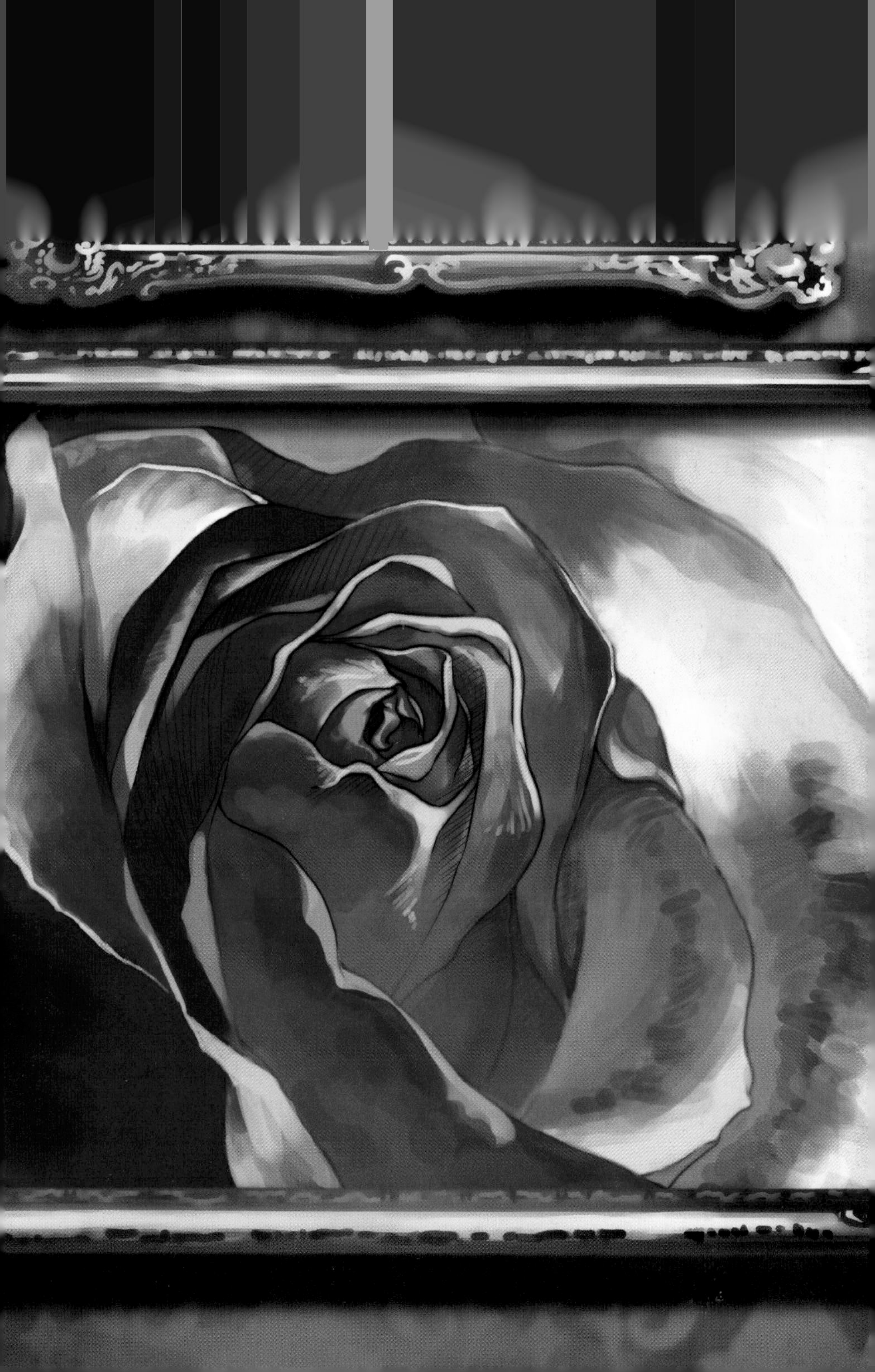

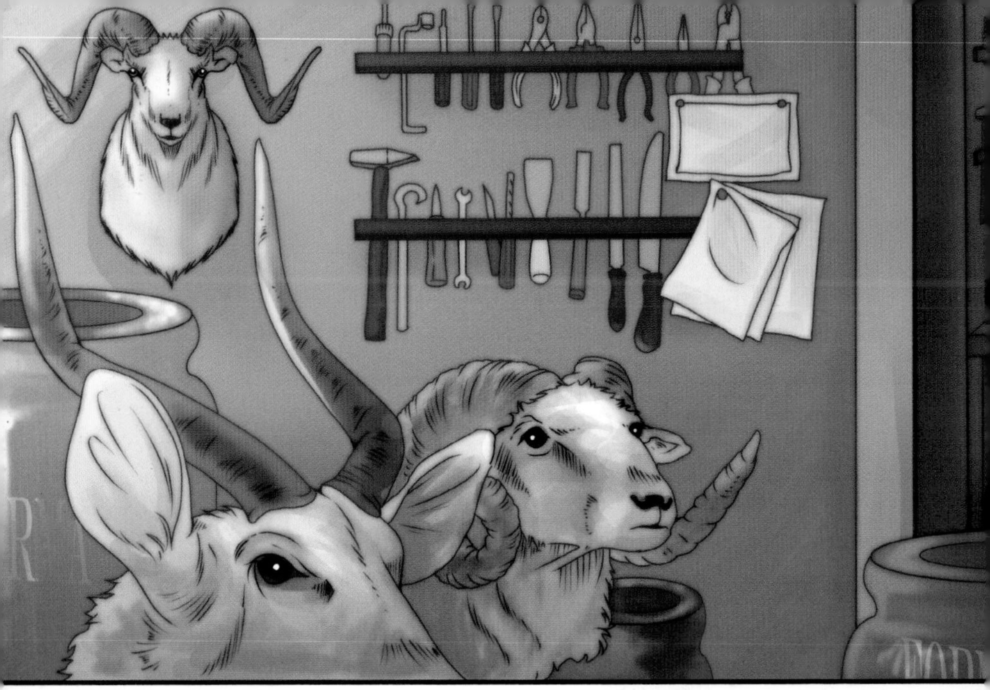

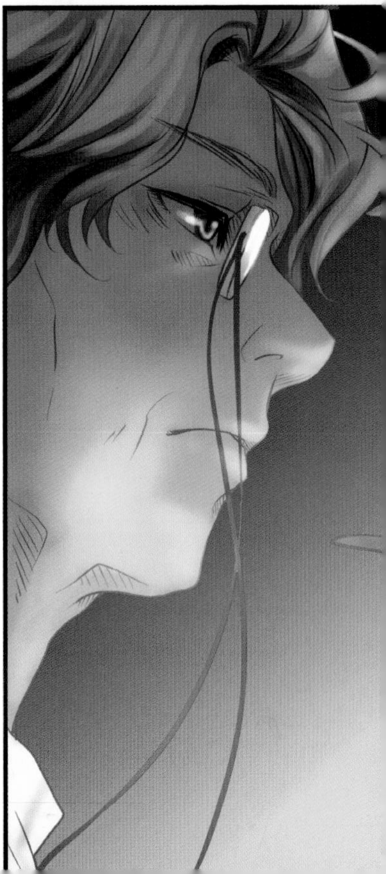

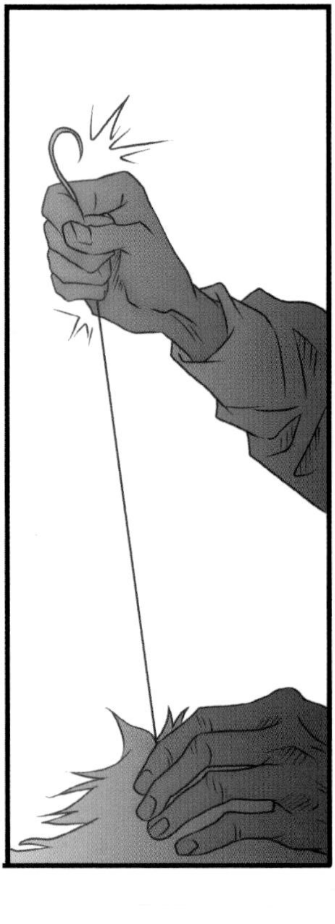

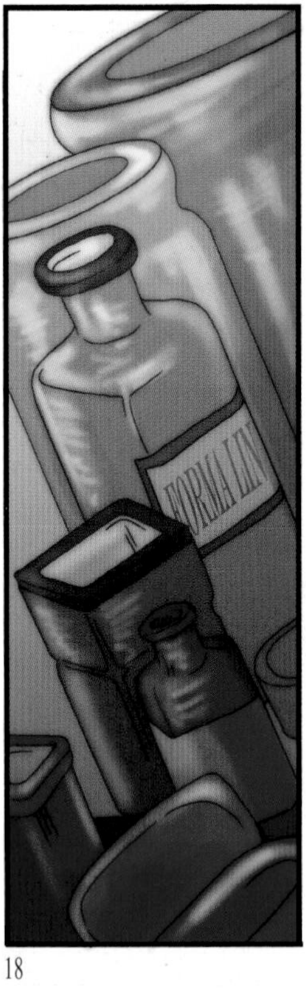
FORMALIN

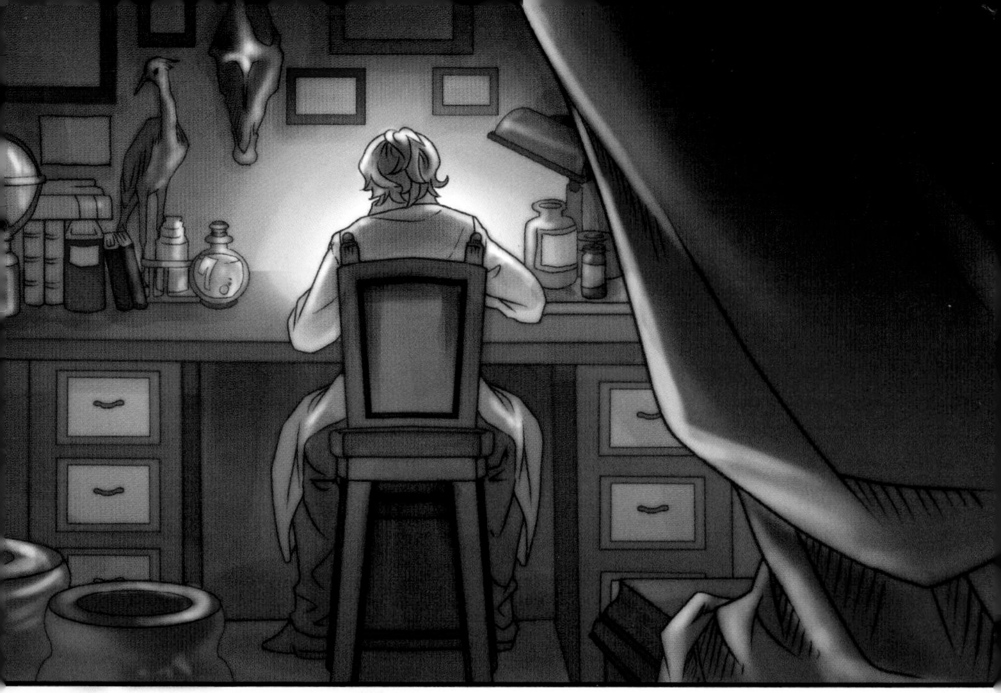
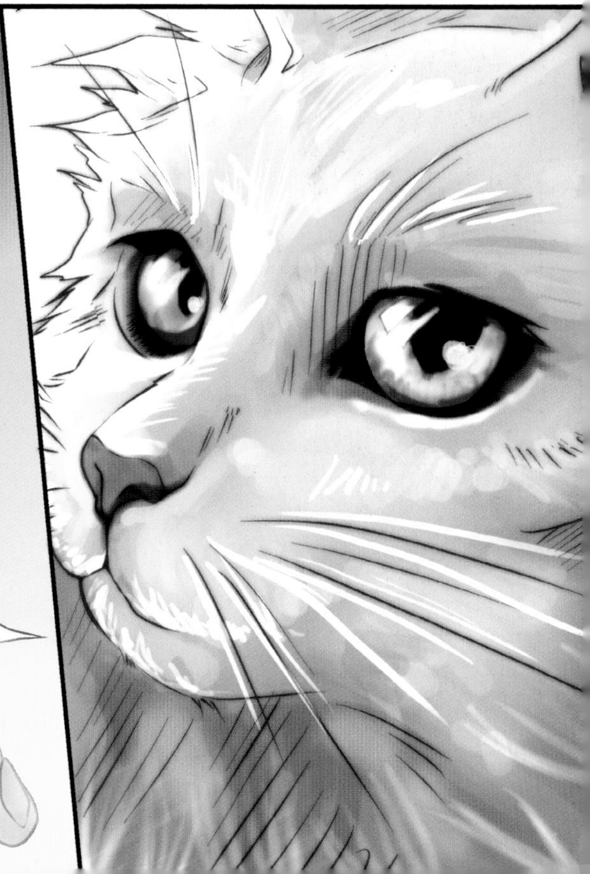
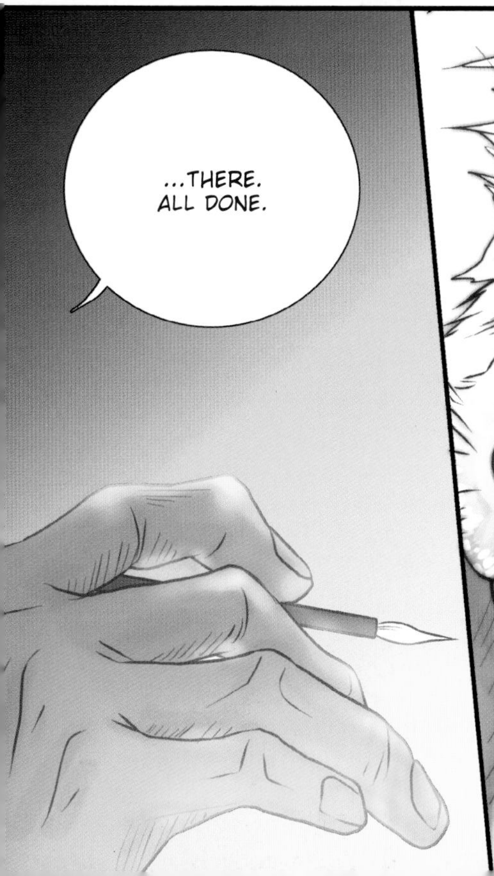
...THERE.
ALL DONE.

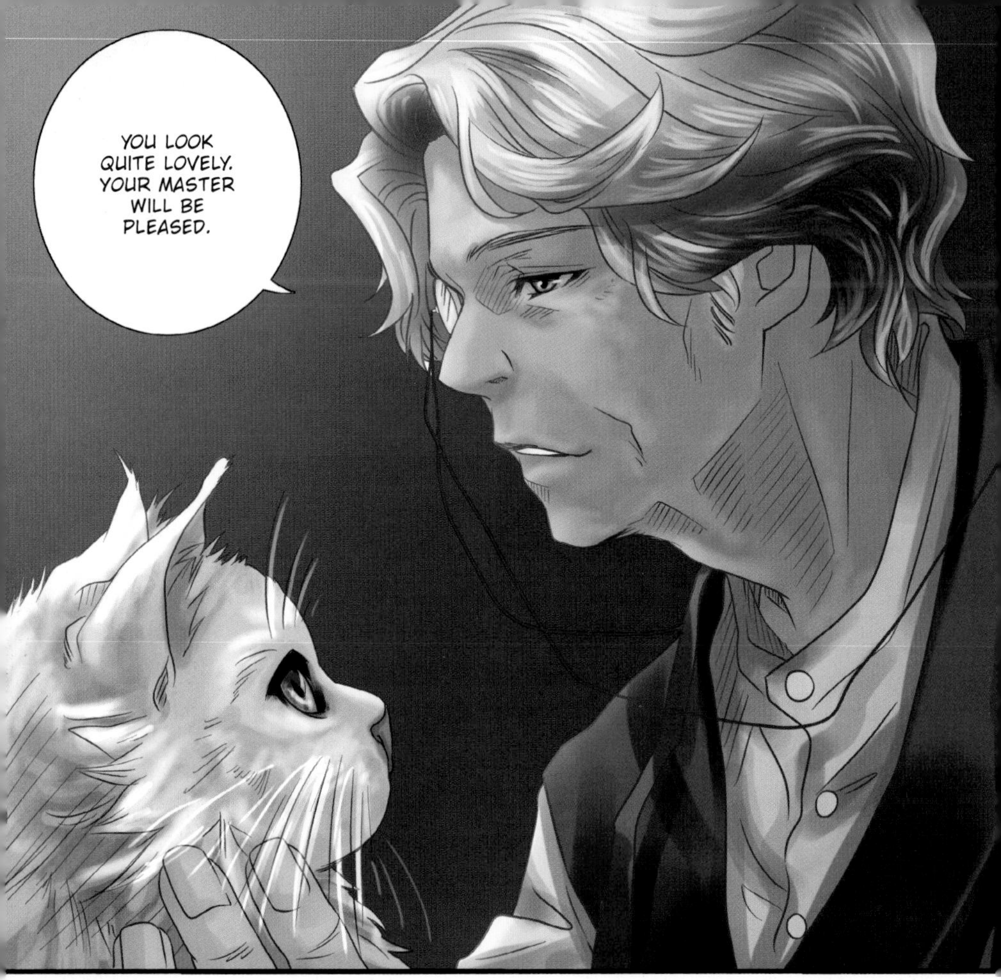
YOU LOOK QUITE LOVELY. YOUR MASTER WILL BE PLEASED.
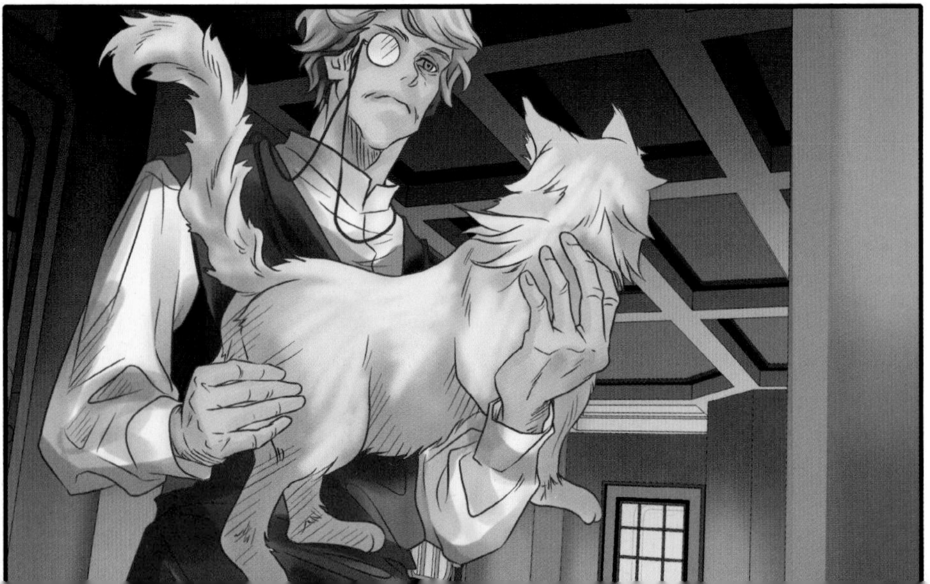

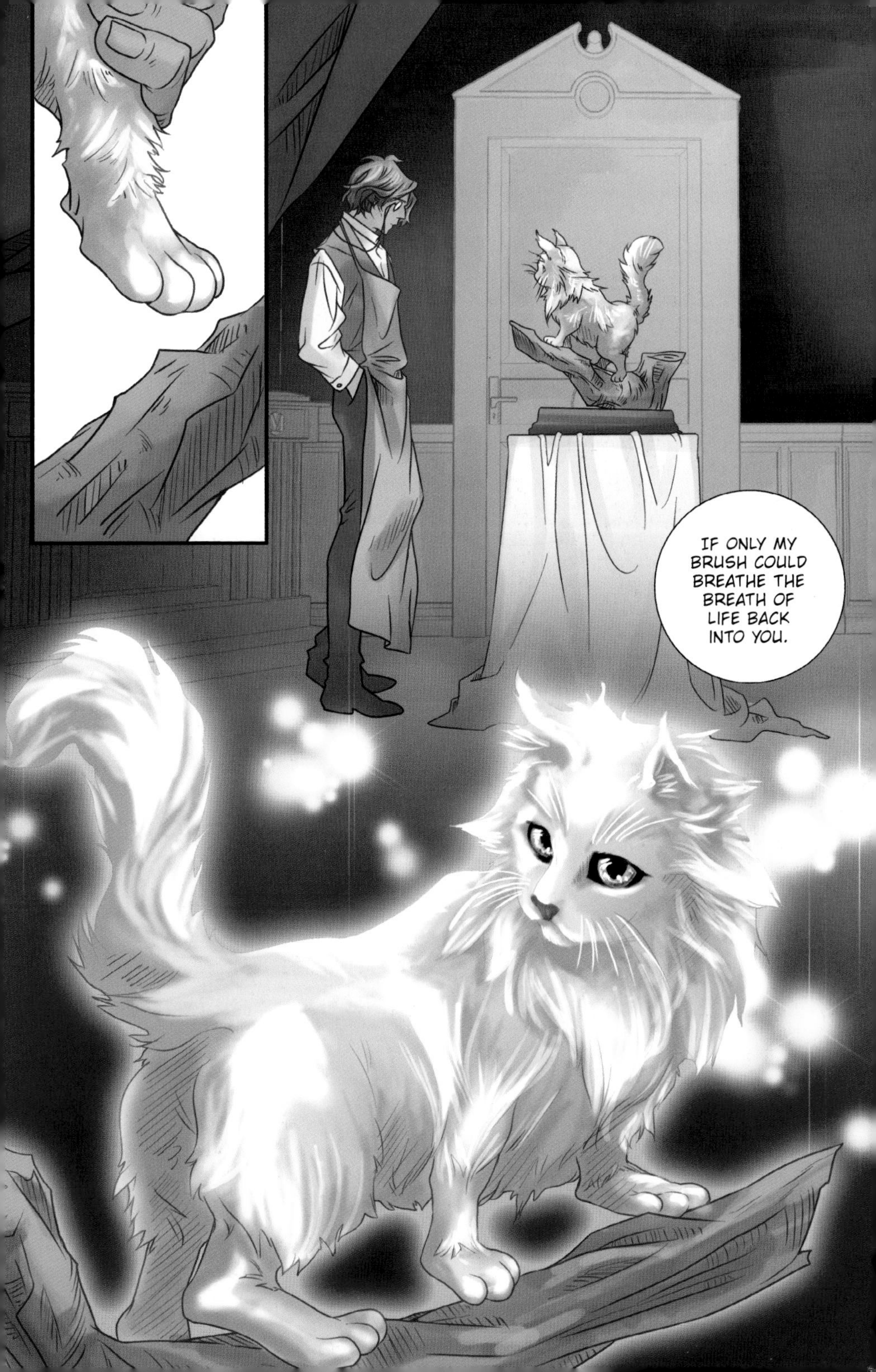
IF ONLY MY BRUSH COULD BREATHE THE BREATH OF LIFE BACK INTO YOU.

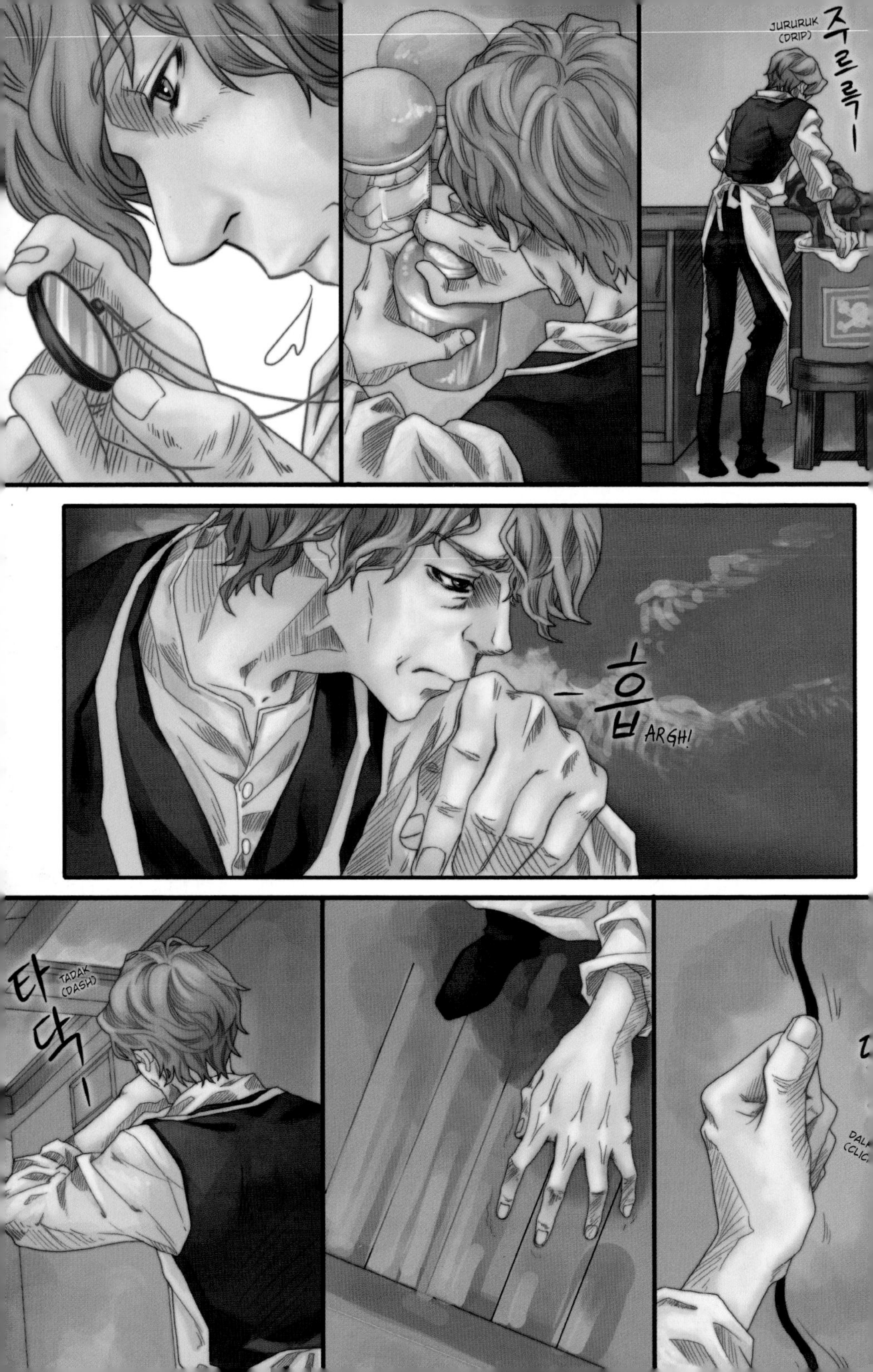
주르륵
JURURUK (DRIP)
흡
ARGH!
타닥
TADAK (DASH)

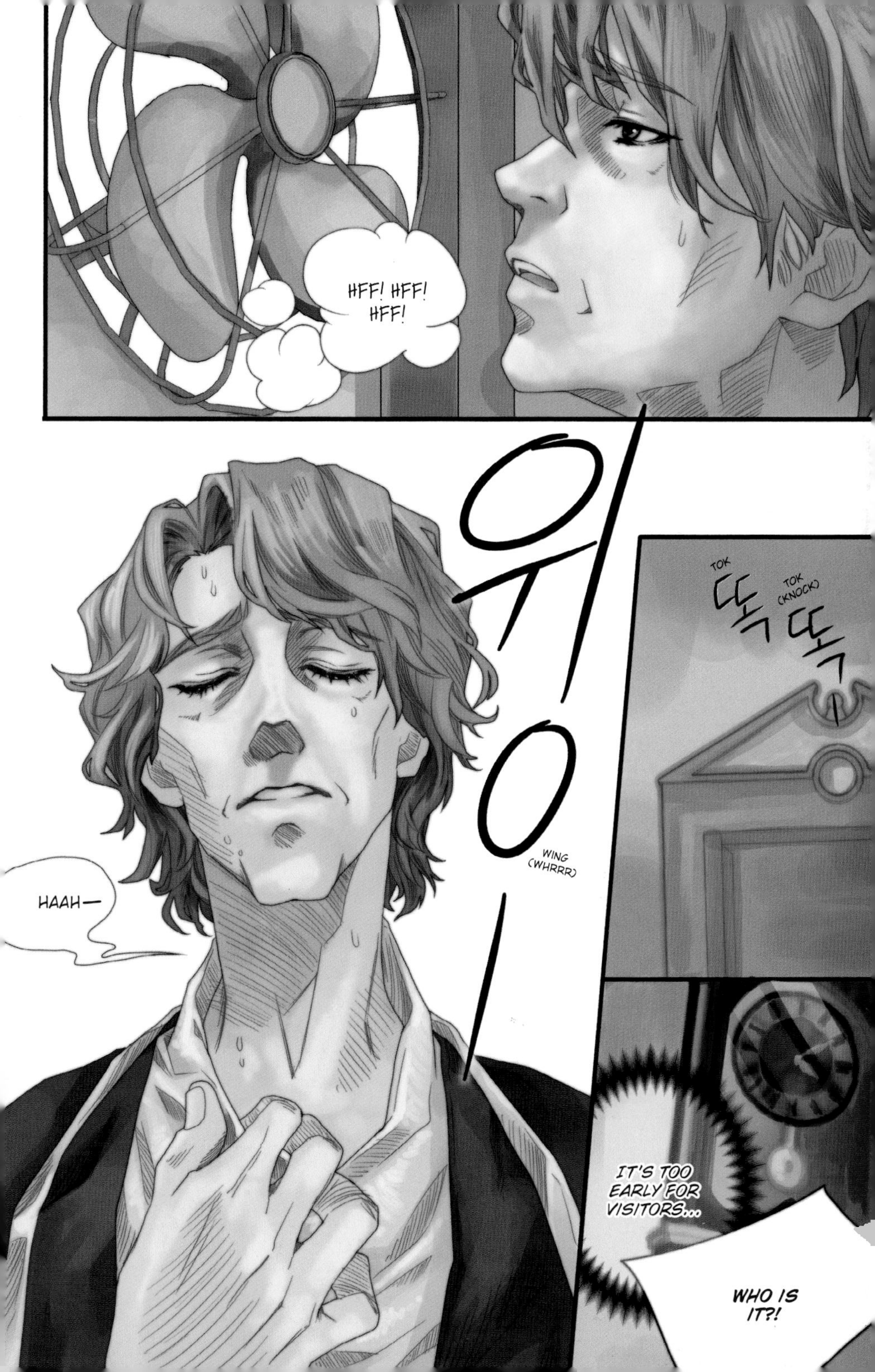
HFF! HFF! HFF!
HAAH—
WING (WHRRR)
똑 TOK
똑 TOK (KNOCK)
IT'S TOO EARLY FOR VISITORS...
WHO IS IT?!

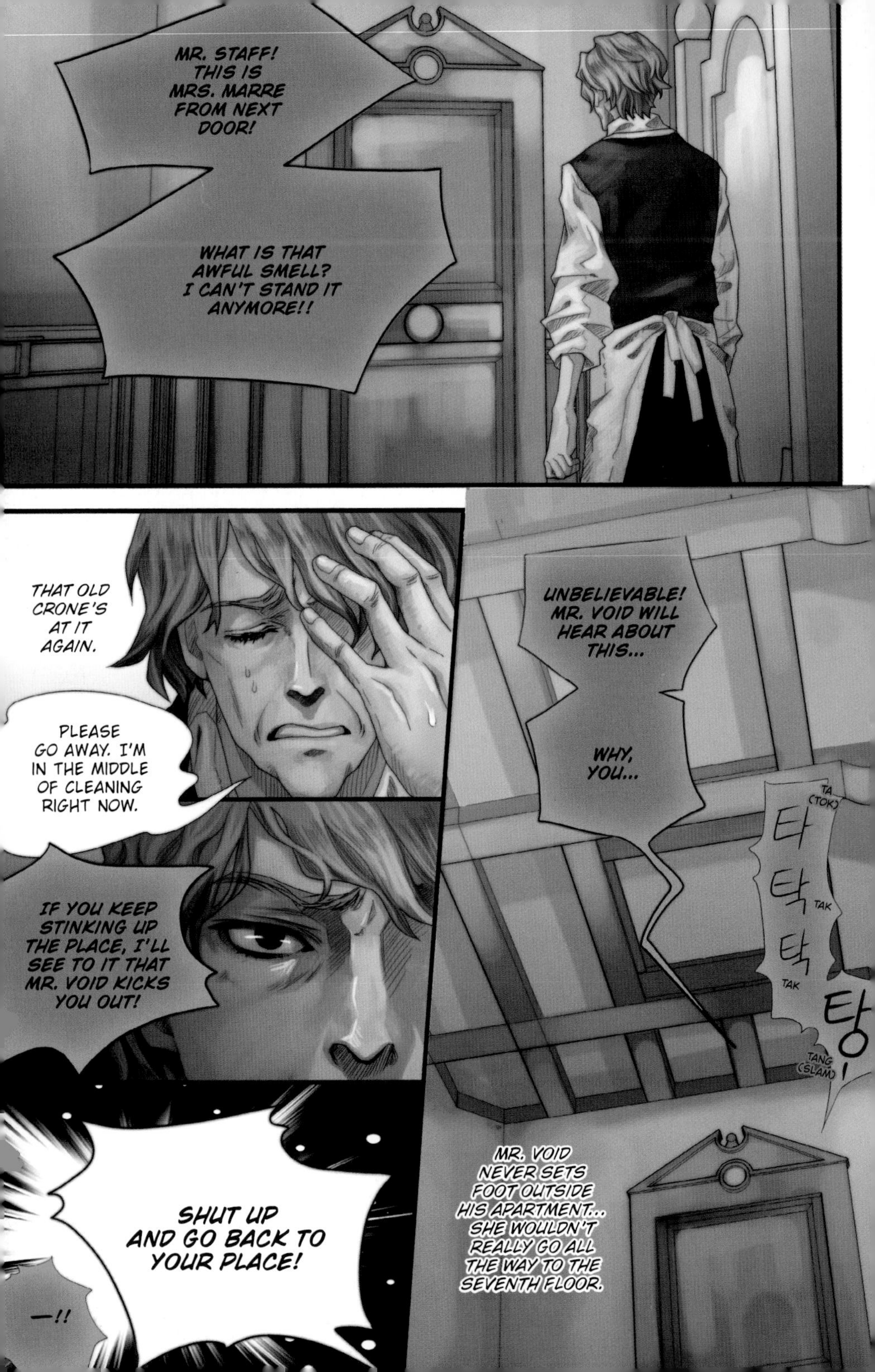
MR. STAFF! THIS IS MRS. MARRE FROM NEXT DOOR!
WHAT IS THAT AWFUL SMELL? I CAN'T STAND IT ANYMORE!!
THAT OLD CRONE'S AT IT AGAIN.
PLEASE GO AWAY. I'M IN THE MIDDLE OF CLEANING RIGHT NOW.
IF YOU KEEP STINKING UP THE PLACE, I'LL SEE TO IT THAT MR. VOID KICKS YOU OUT!
SHUT UP AND GO BACK TO YOUR PLACE!
—!!
UNBELIEVABLE! MR. VOID WILL HEAR ABOUT THIS...
WHY, YOU...
타 TA (TOK)
탁 TAK
탁 TAK
탕! TANG (SLAM)
MR. VOID NEVER SETS FOOT OUTSIDE HIS APARTMENT... SHE WOULDN'T REALLY GO ALL THE WAY TO THE SEVENTH FLOOR.

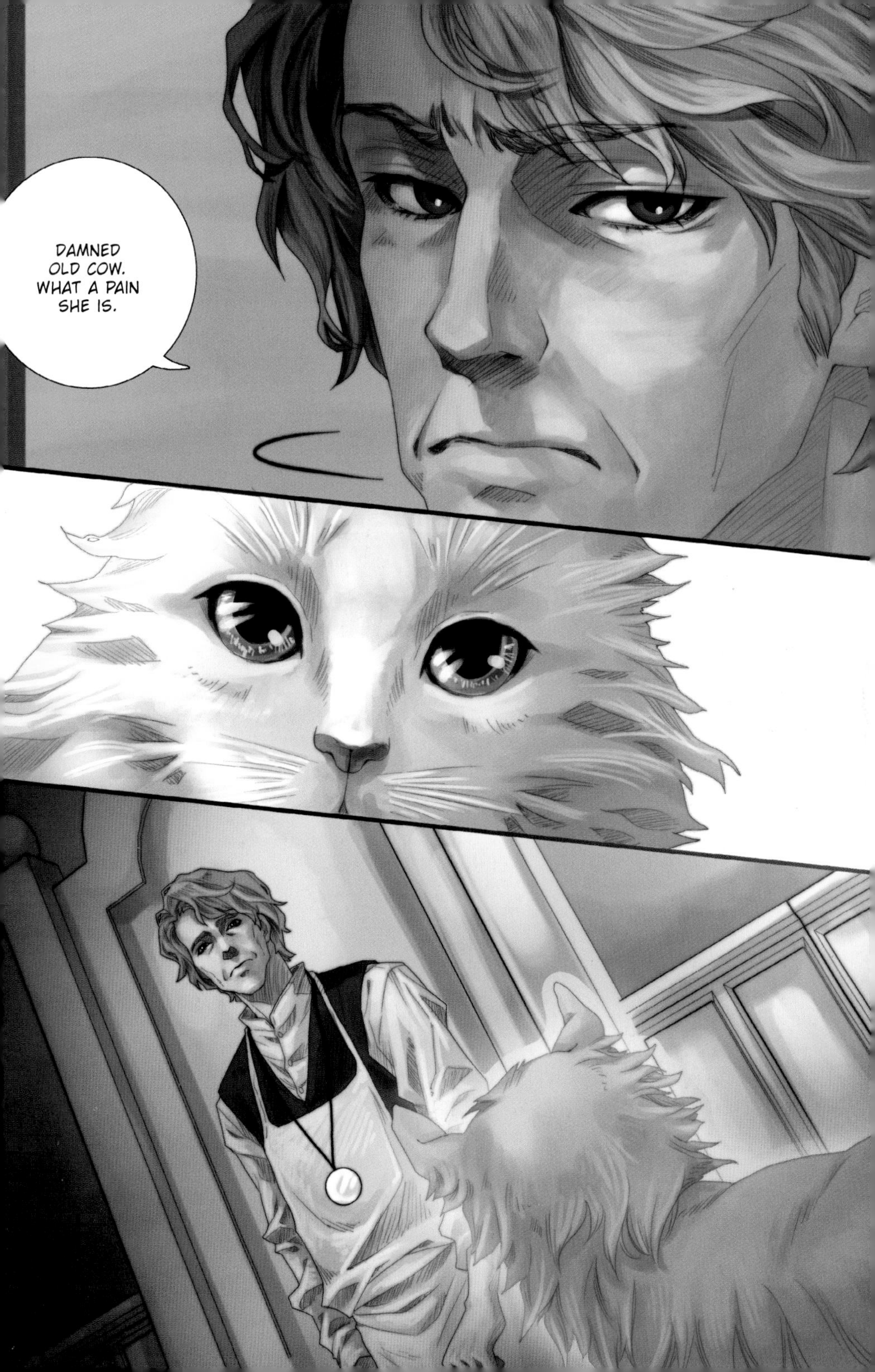
DAMNED OLD COW. WHAT A PAIN SHE IS.

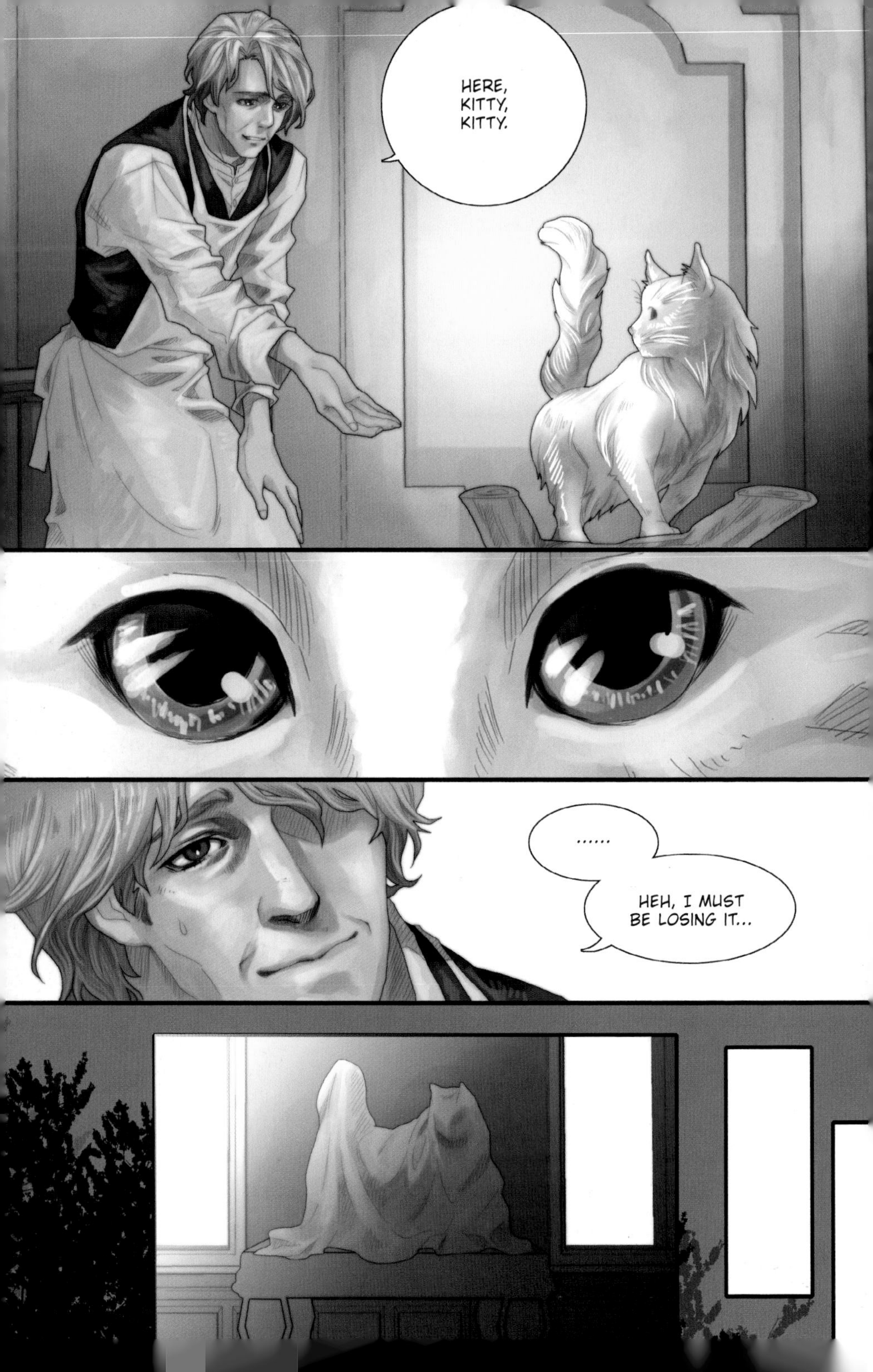
HERE, KITTY, KITTY.
......
HEH, I MUST BE LOSING IT...

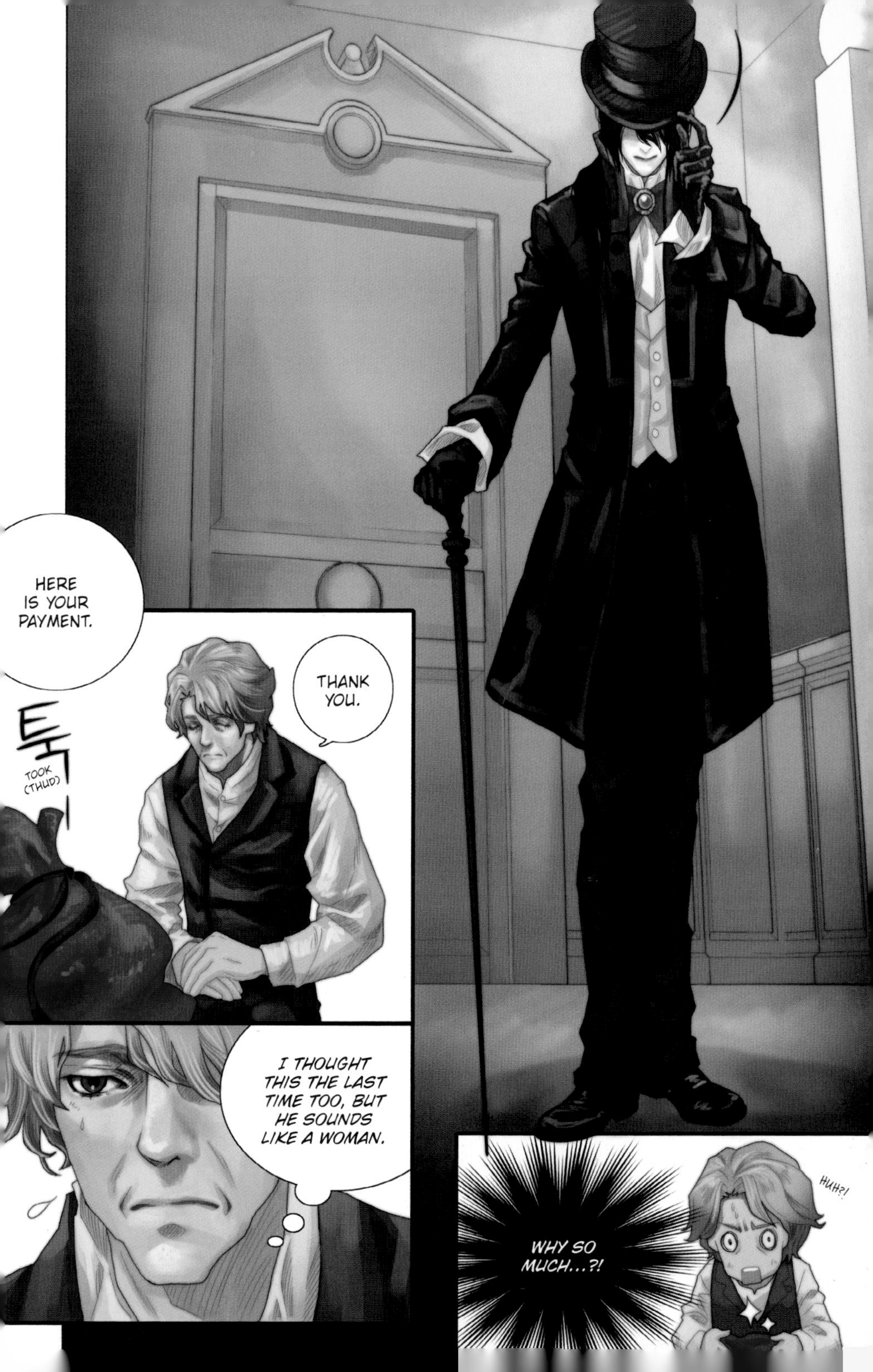
HERE IS YOUR PAYMENT.
툭
TOOK (THUD)
THANK YOU.
I THOUGHT THIS THE LAST TIME TOO, BUT HE SOUNDS LIKE A WOMAN.
WHY SO MUCH...?!
HUH?!

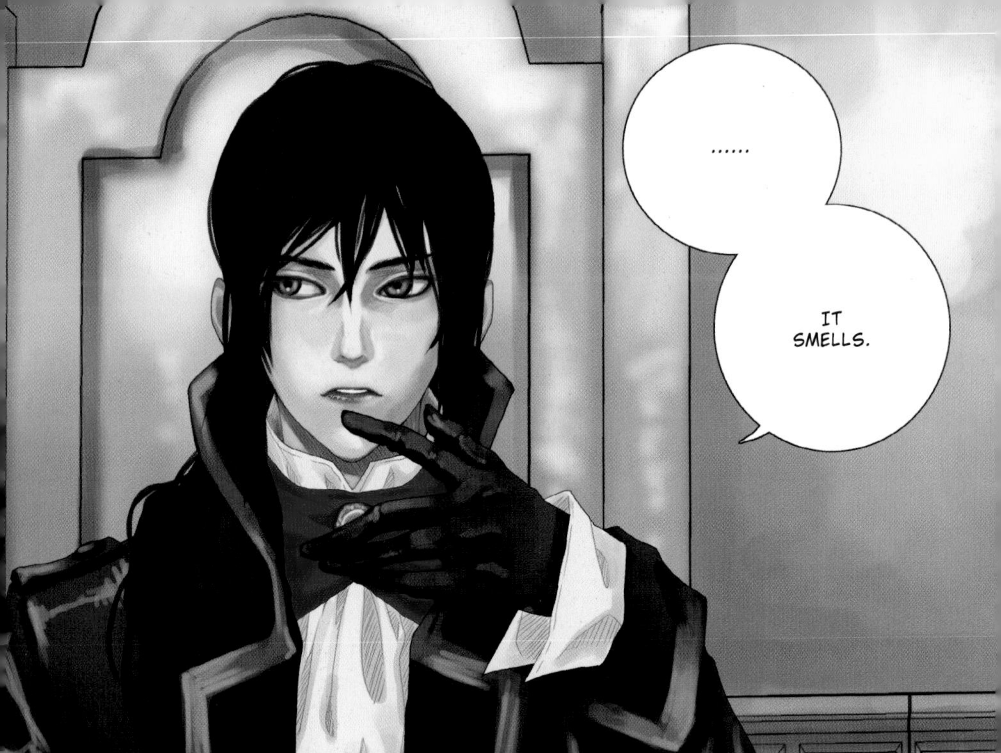
......
IT SMELLS.
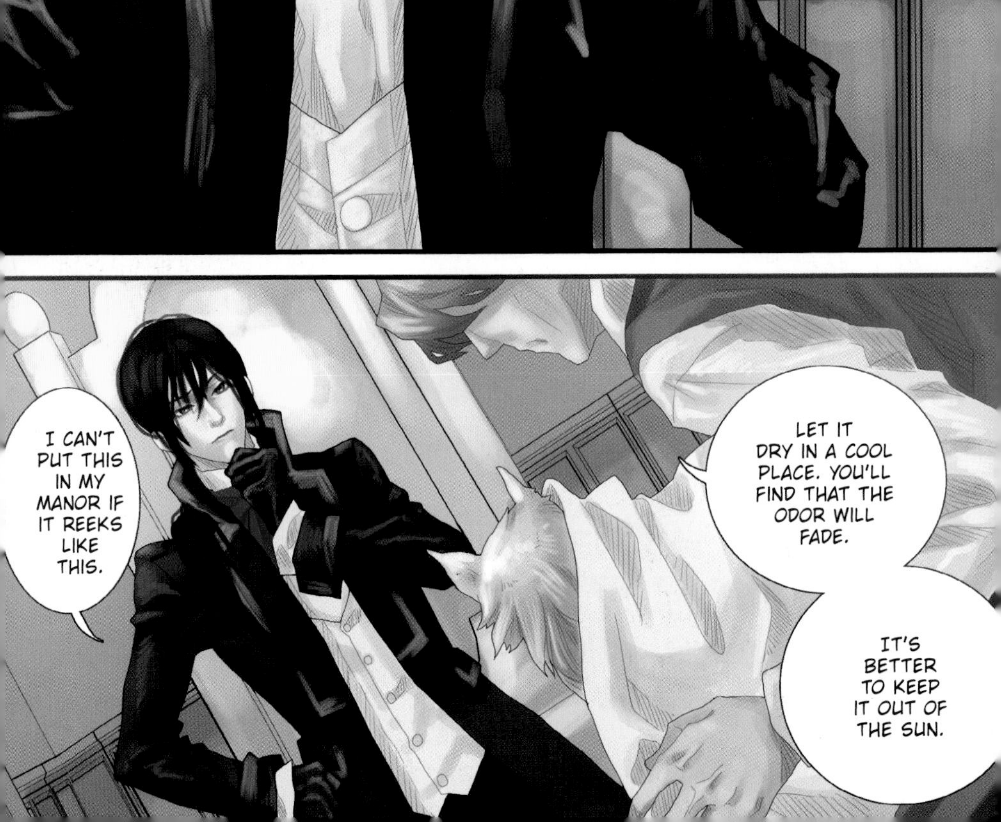
I CAN'T PUT THIS IN MY MANOR IF IT REEKS LIKE THIS.
LET IT DRY IN A COOL PLACE. YOU'LL FIND THAT THE ODOR WILL FADE.
IT'S BETTER TO KEEP IT OUT OF THE SUN.

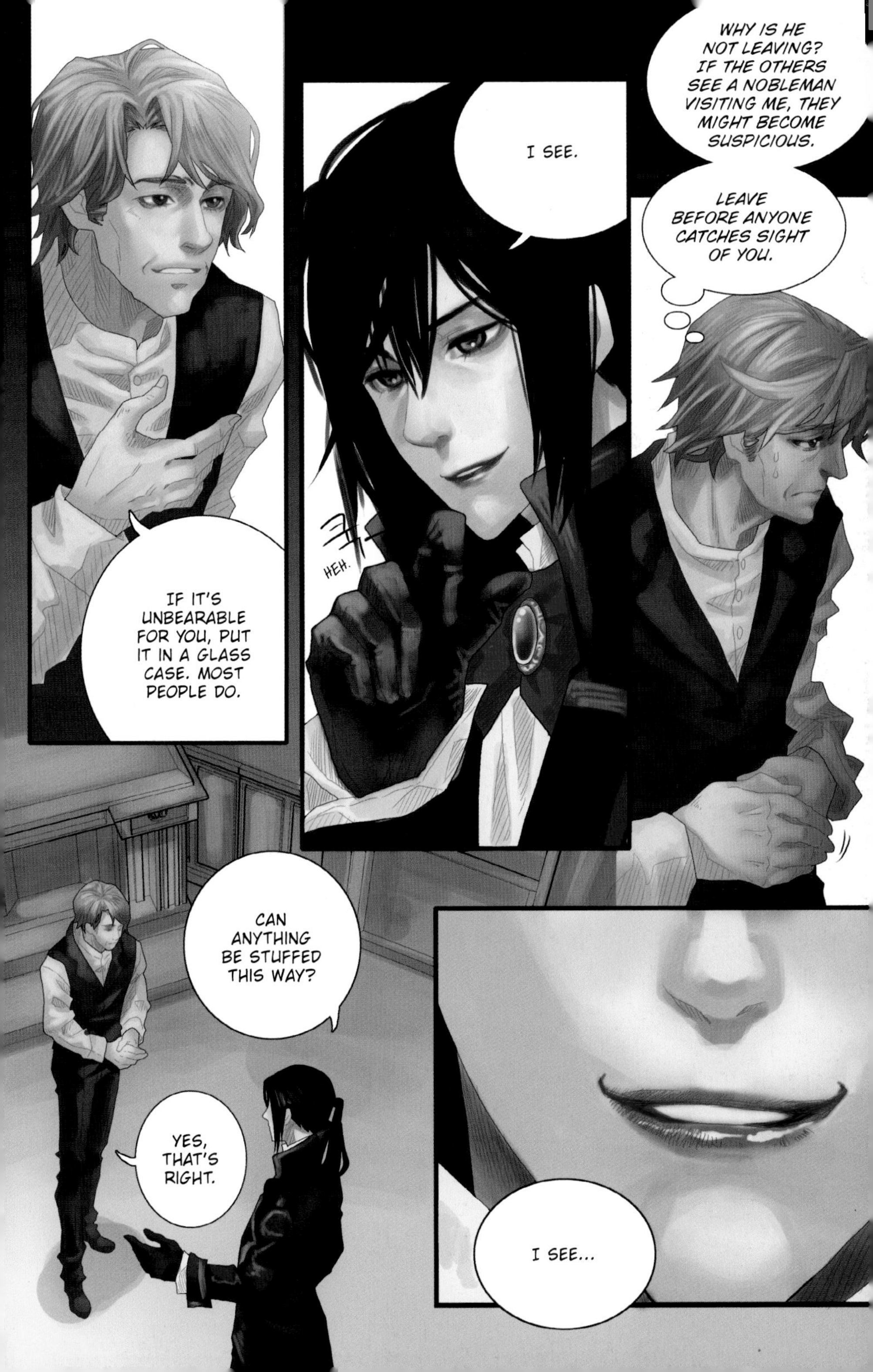
IF IT'S UNBEARABLE FOR YOU, PUT IT IN A GLASS CASE. MOST PEOPLE DO.
I SEE.
HEH.
WHY IS HE NOT LEAVING? IF THE OTHERS SEE A NOBLEMAN VISITING ME, THEY MIGHT BECOME SUSPICIOUS.
LEAVE BEFORE ANYONE CATCHES SIGHT OF YOU.
CAN ANYTHING BE STUFFED THIS WAY?
YES, THAT'S RIGHT.
I SEE...

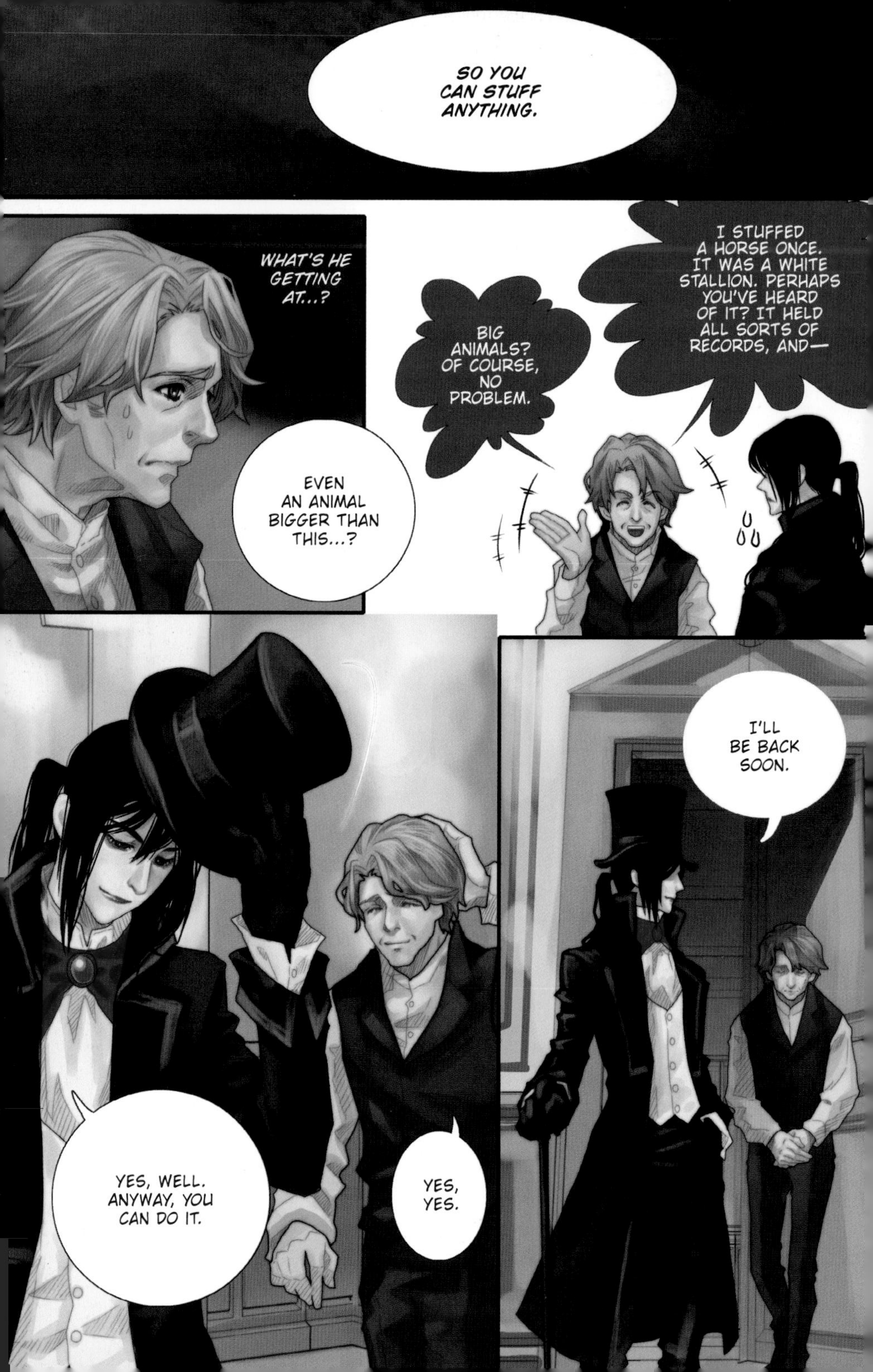
SO YOU CAN STUFF ANYTHING.
WHAT'S HE GETTING AT...?
EVEN AN ANIMAL BIGGER THAN THIS...?
BIG ANIMALS? OF COURSE, NO PROBLEM.
I STUFFED A HORSE ONCE. IT WAS A WHITE STALLION. PERHAPS YOU'VE HEARD OF IT? IT HELD ALL SORTS OF RECORDS, AND—
YES, WELL. ANYWAY, YOU CAN DO IT.
YES, YES.
I'LL BE BACK SOON.

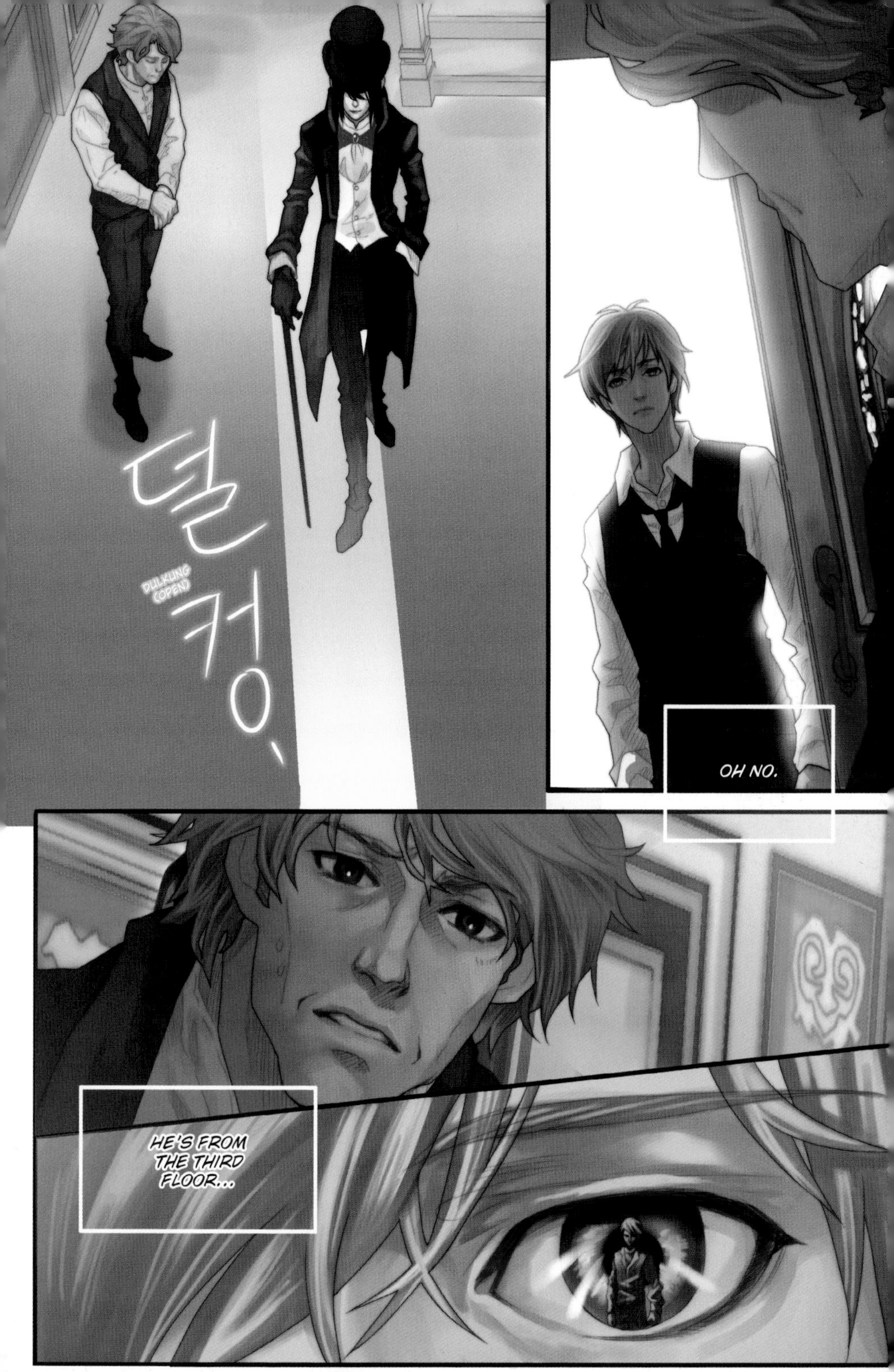
덜컹,
DULKUNG (OPEN)
OH NO.
HE'S FROM THE THIRD FLOOR...

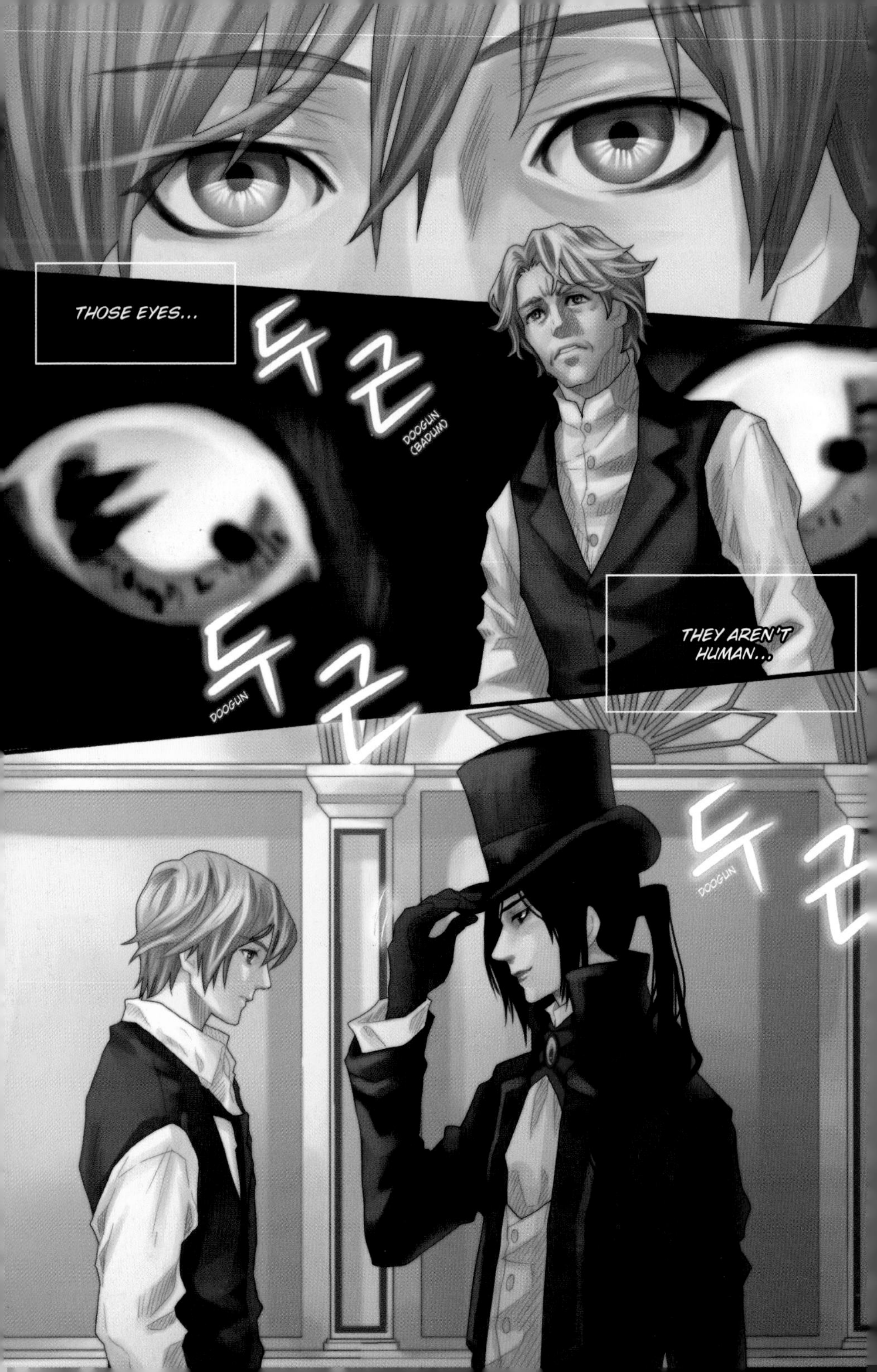
THOSE EYES...
두근
DOOGUN (BADUM)
두근
DOOGUN
THEY AREN'T HUMAN...
두근
DOOGUN

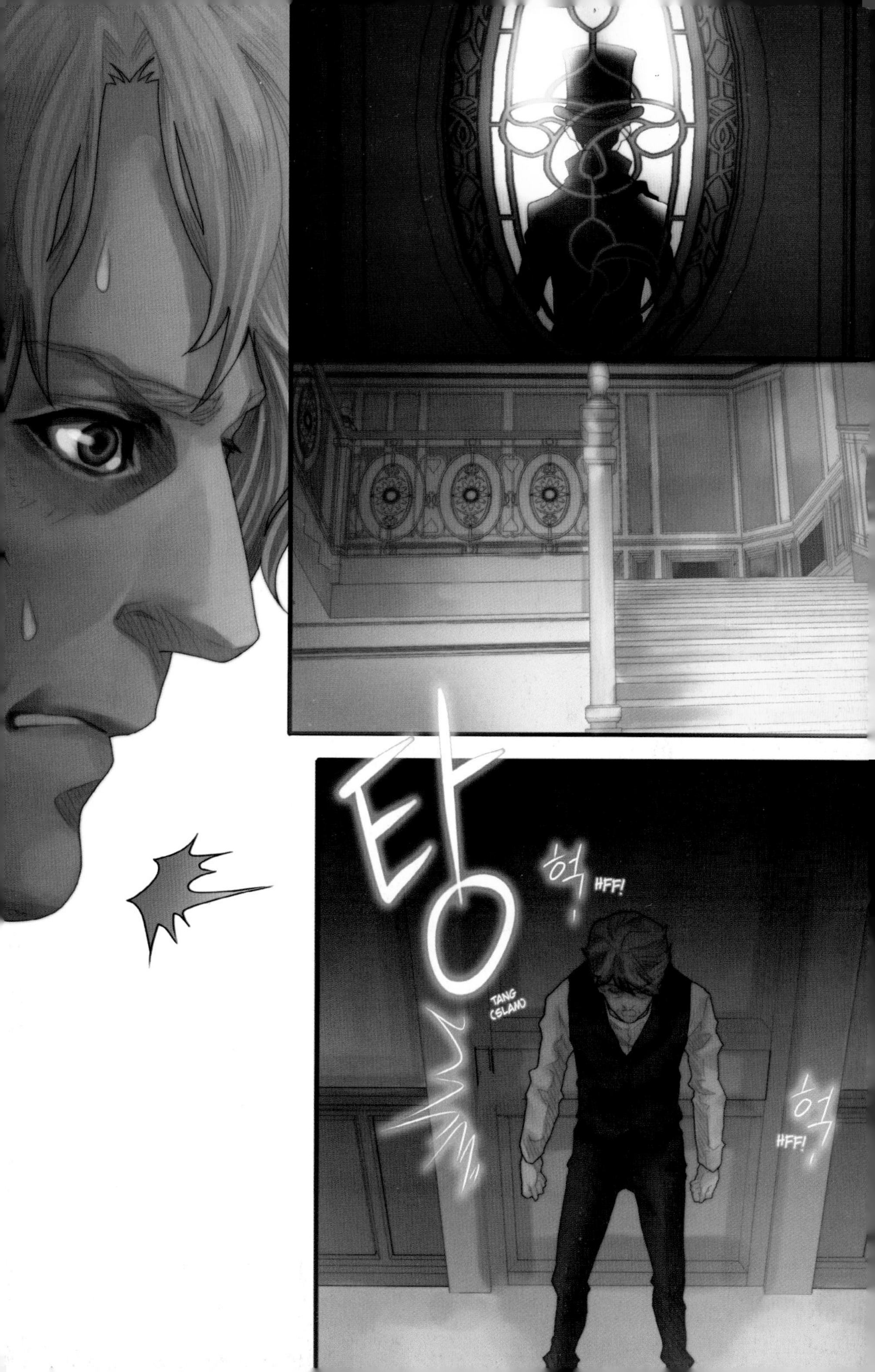
탕
TANG (SLAM)
헉
HFF!
헉
HFF!

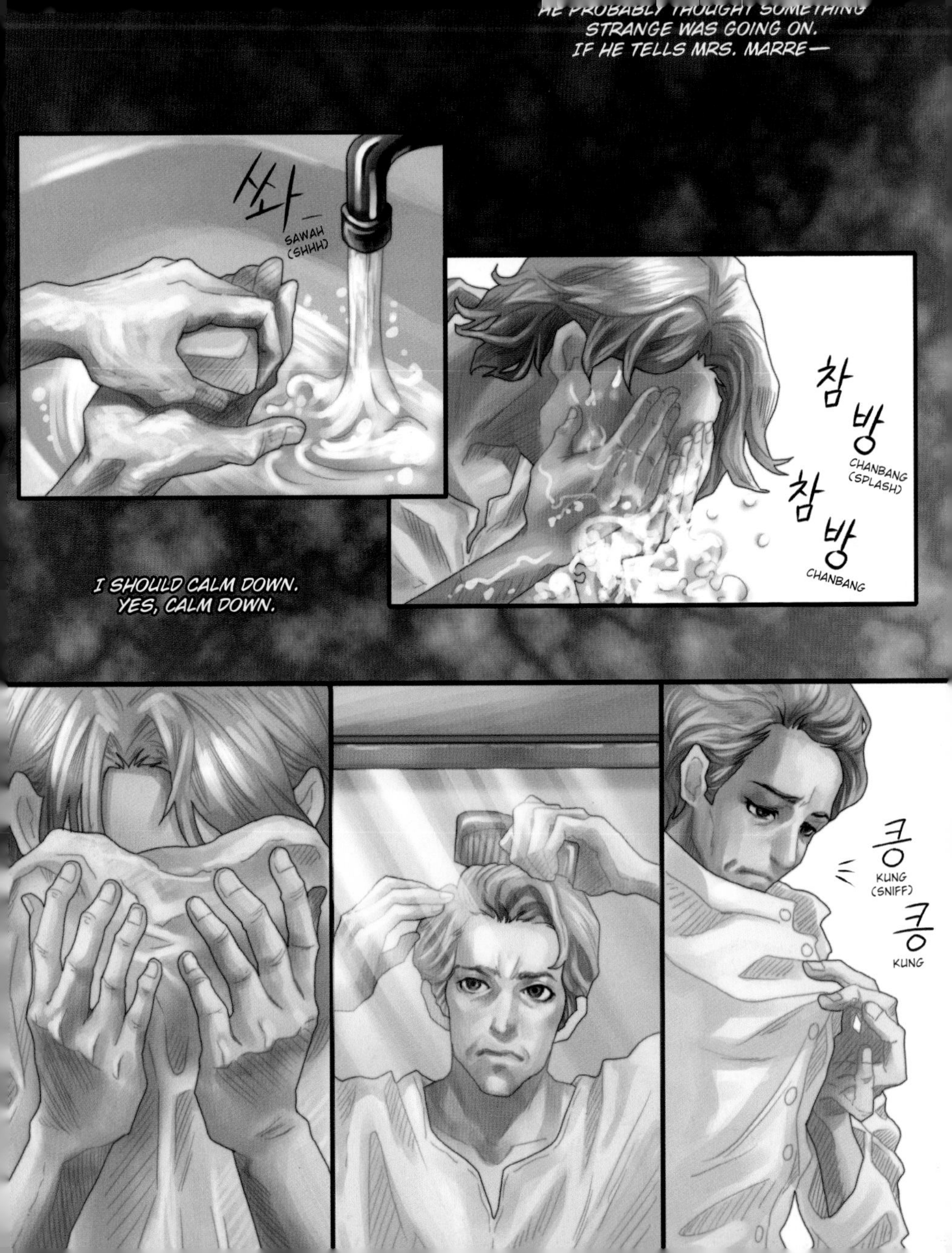
HE PROBABLY THOUGHT SOMETHING STRANGE WAS GOING ON. IF HE TELLS MRS. MARRE—
쏴
SAWAH (SHHH)
참방
CHANBANG (SPLASH)
참방
CHANBANG
I SHOULD CALM DOWN. YES, CALM DOWN.
킁
KUNG (SNIFF)
킁
KUNG

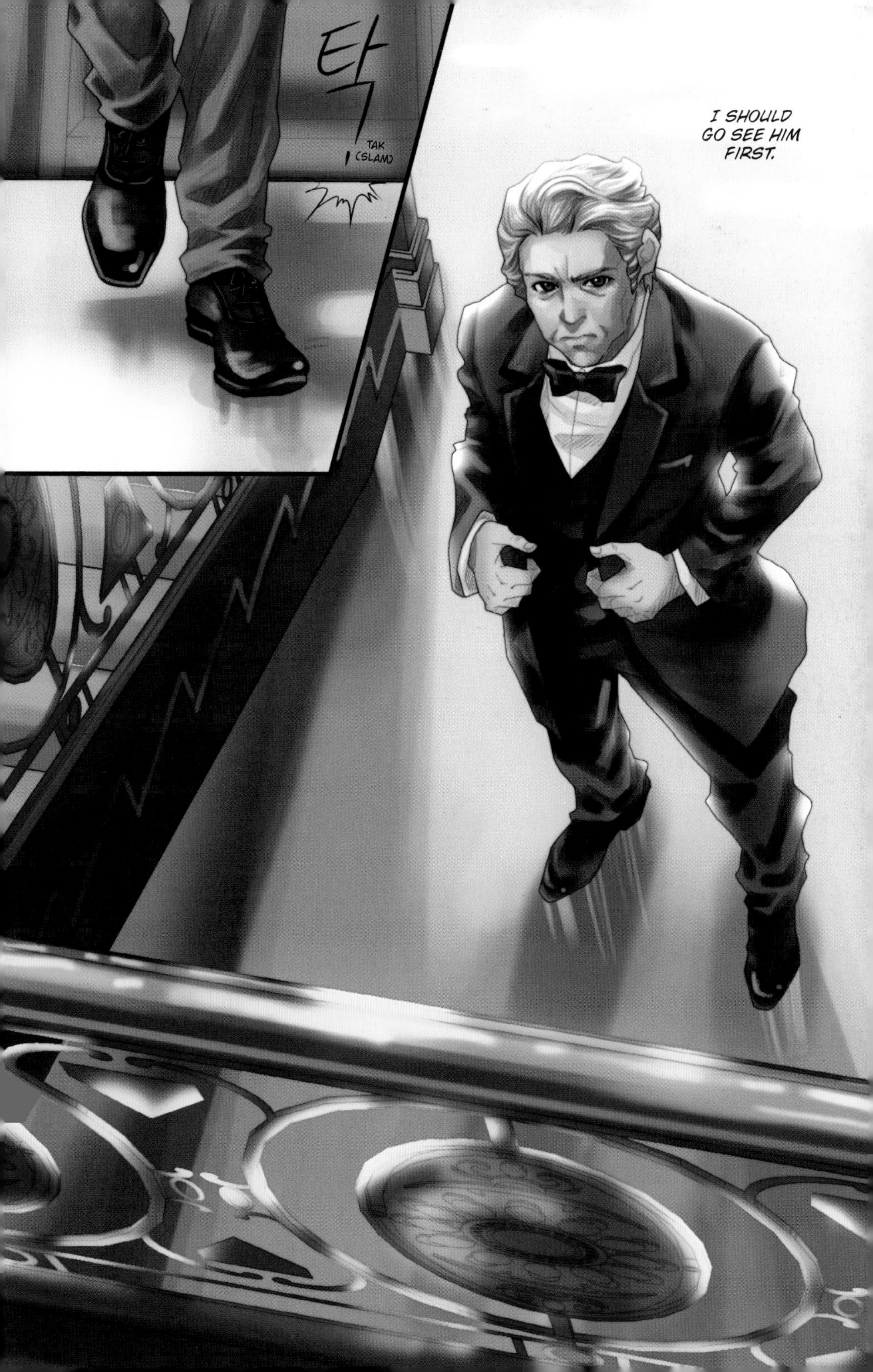
탁
TAK (SLAM)
I SHOULD GO SEE HIM FIRST.

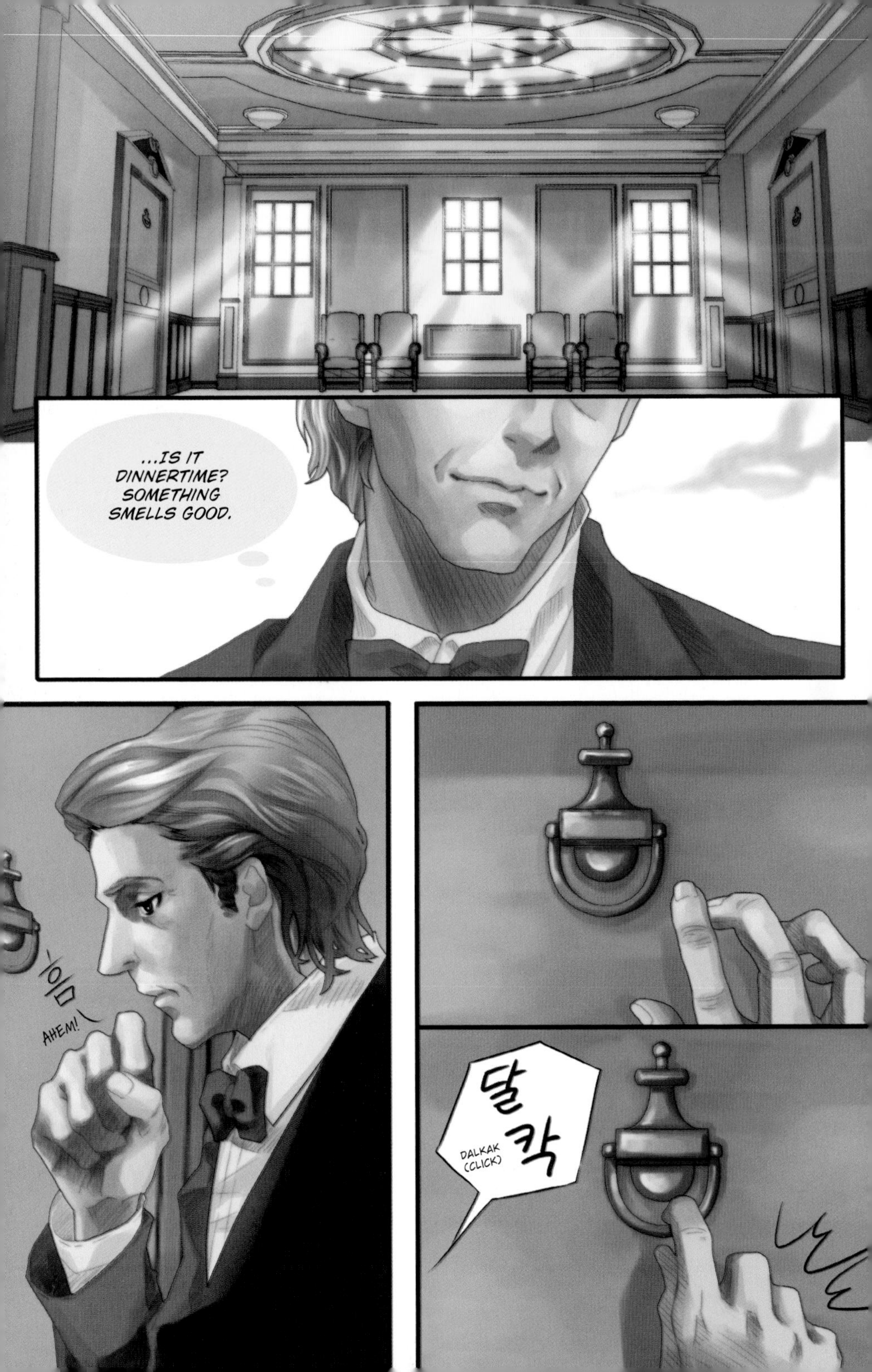
...IS IT DINNERTIME? SOMETHING SMELLS GOOD.
흠
AHEM!
달칵
DALKAK (CLICK)

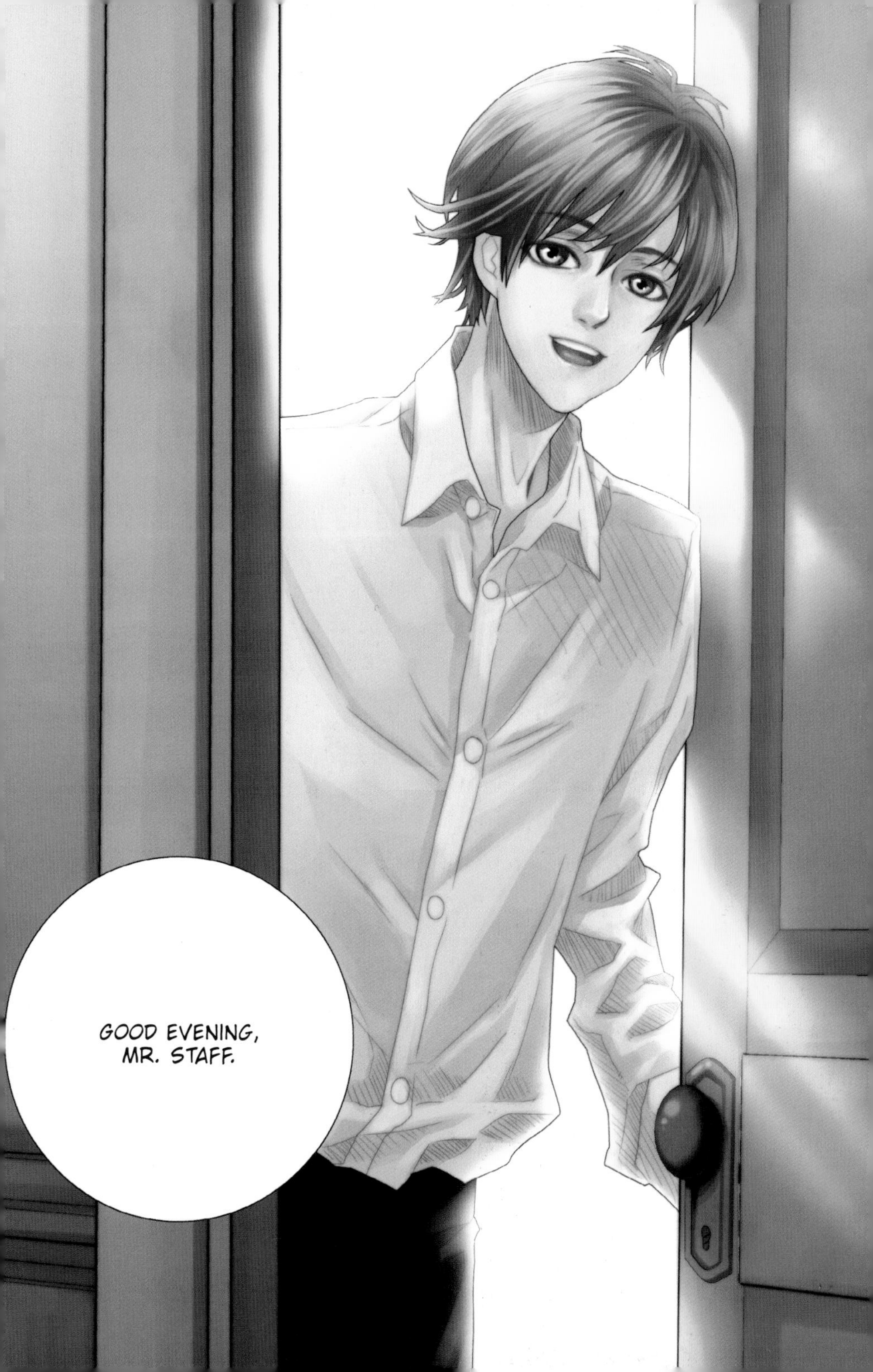
GOOD EVENING, MR. STAFF.

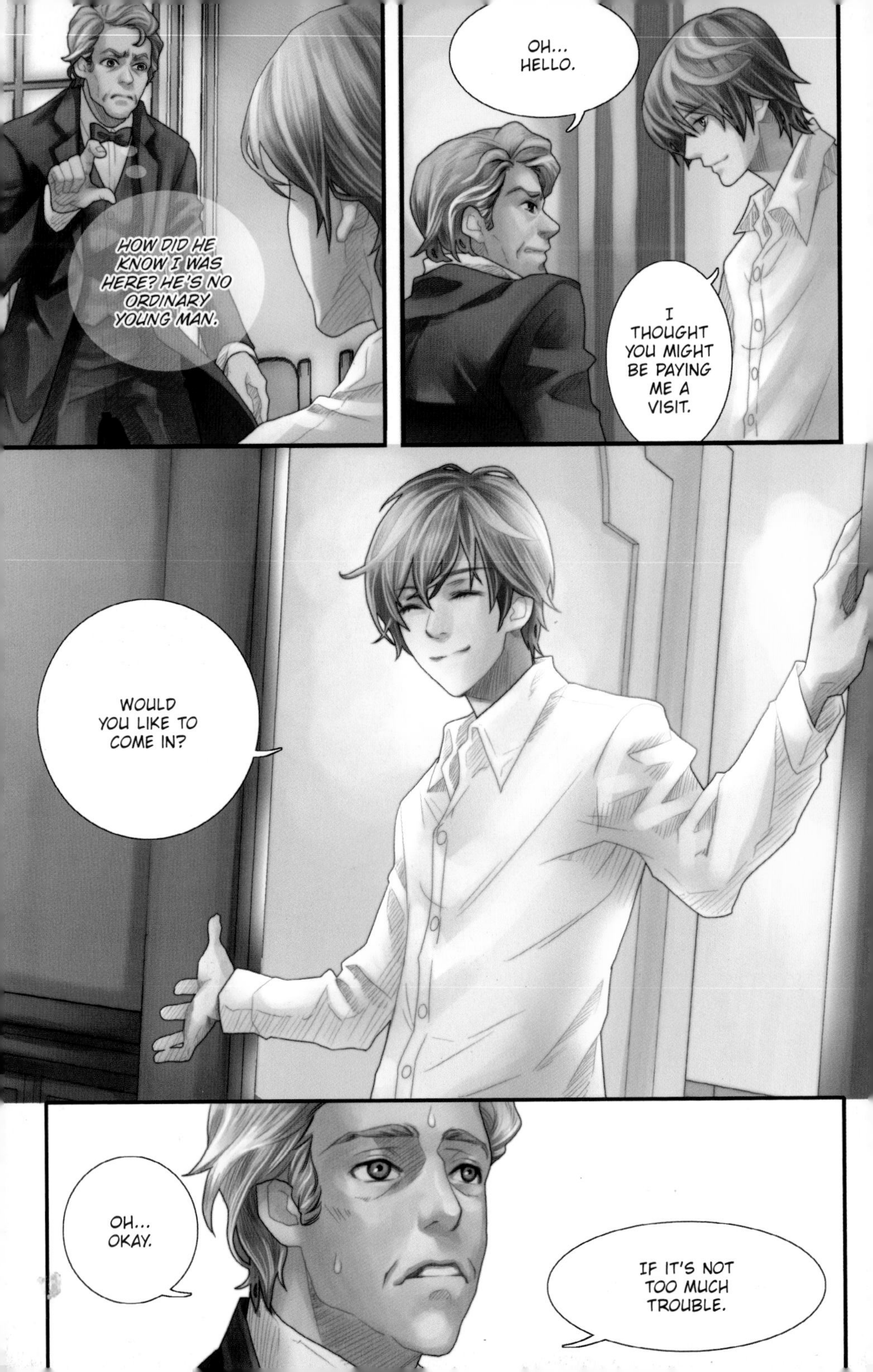
HOW DID HE KNOW I WAS HERE? HE'S NO ORDINARY YOUNG MAN.
OH... HELLO.
I THOUGHT YOU MIGHT BE PAYING ME A VISIT.
WOULD YOU LIKE TO COME IN?
OH... OKAY.
IF IT'S NOT TOO MUCH TROUBLE.

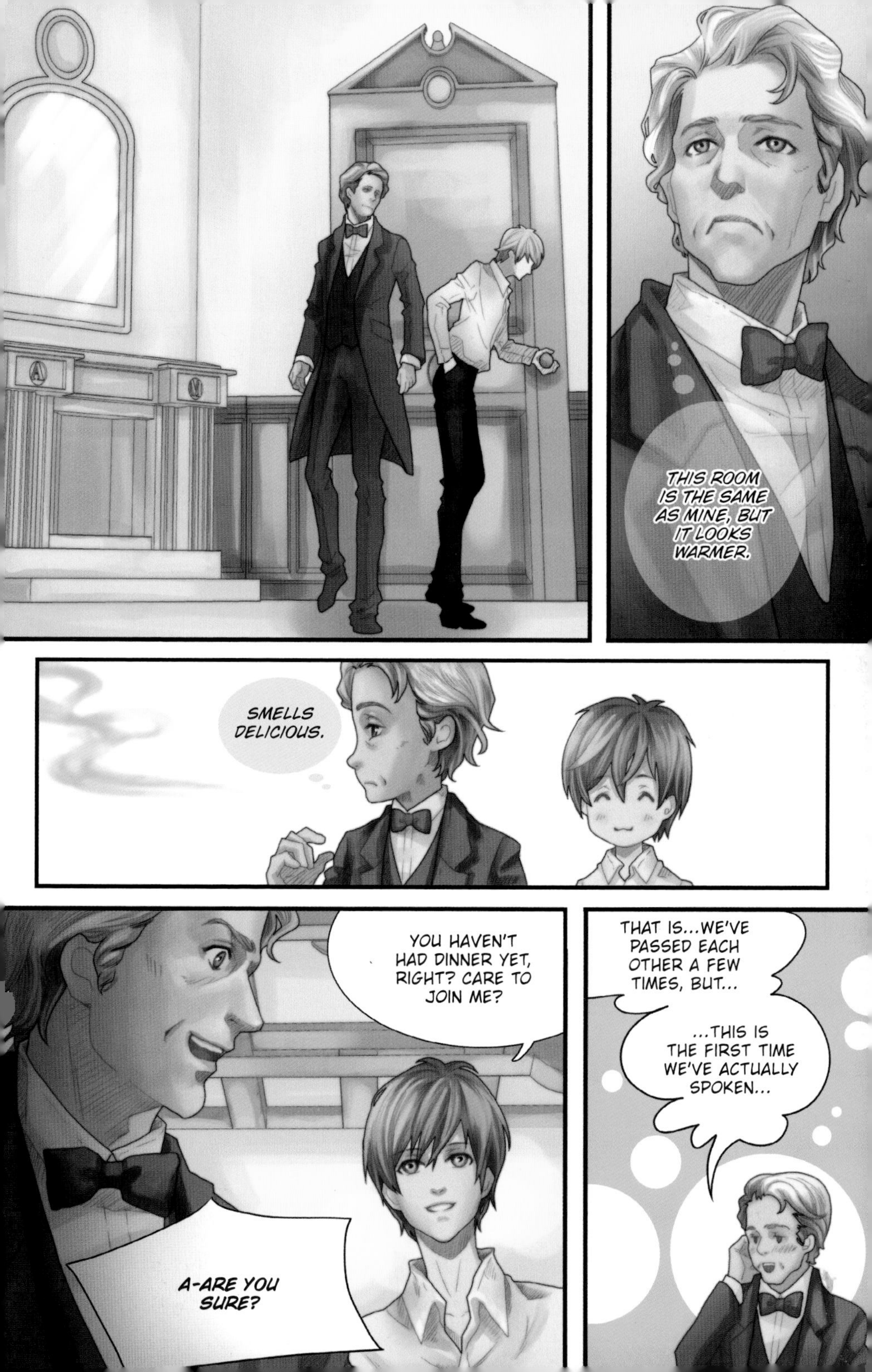
THIS ROOM IS THE SAME AS MINE, BUT IT LOOKS WARMER.
SMELLS DELICIOUS.
YOU HAVEN'T HAD DINNER YET, RIGHT? CARE TO JOIN ME?
A-ARE YOU SURE?
THAT IS...WE'VE PASSED EACH OTHER A FEW TIMES, BUT...
...THIS IS THE FIRST TIME WE'VE ACTUALLY SPOKEN...

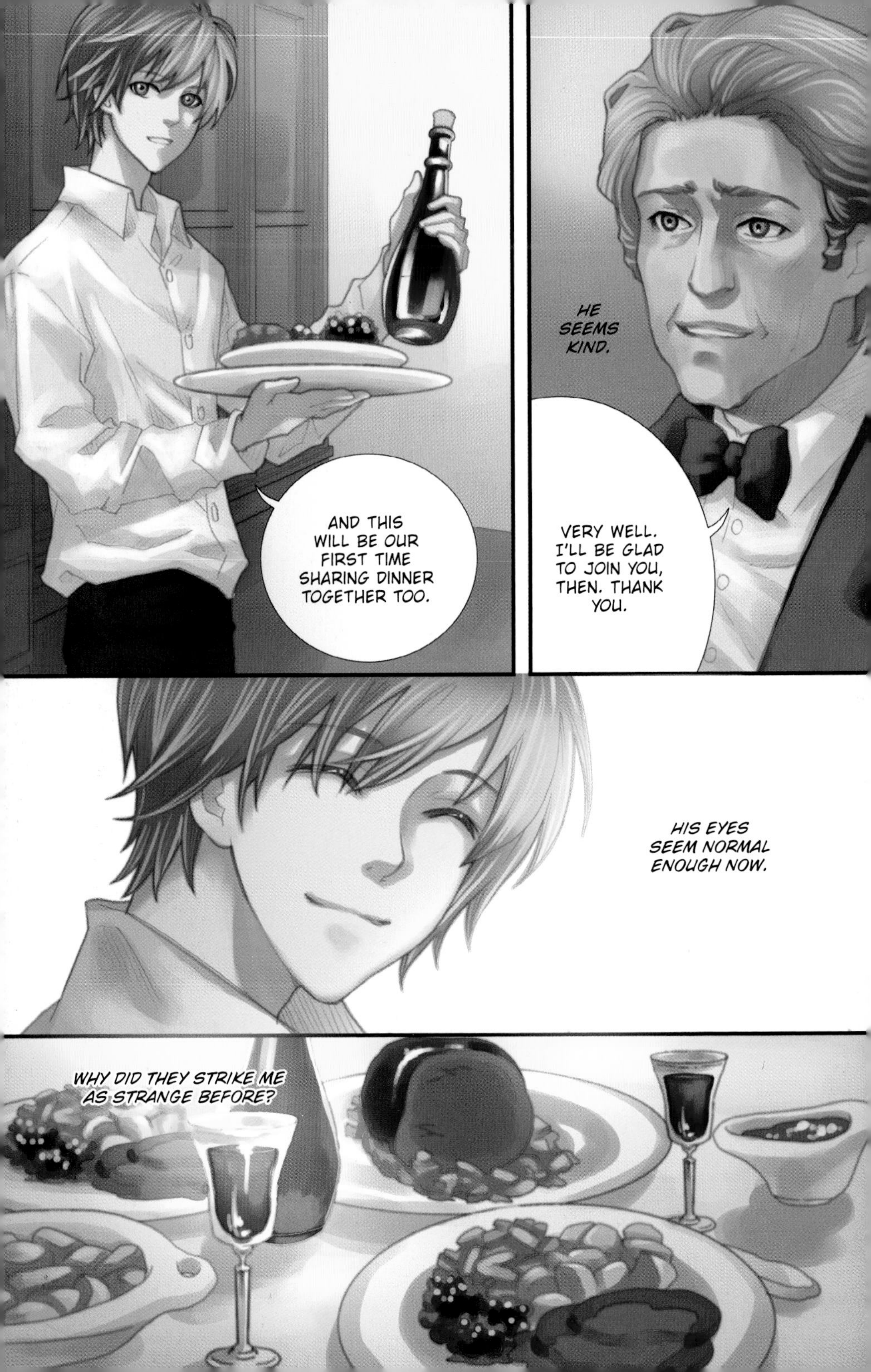
AND THIS WILL BE OUR FIRST TIME SHARING DINNER TOGETHER TOO.
HE SEEMS KIND.
VERY WELL. I'LL BE GLAD TO JOIN YOU, THEN. THANK YOU.
HIS EYES SEEM NORMAL ENOUGH NOW.
WHY DID THEY STRIKE ME AS STRANGE BEFORE?

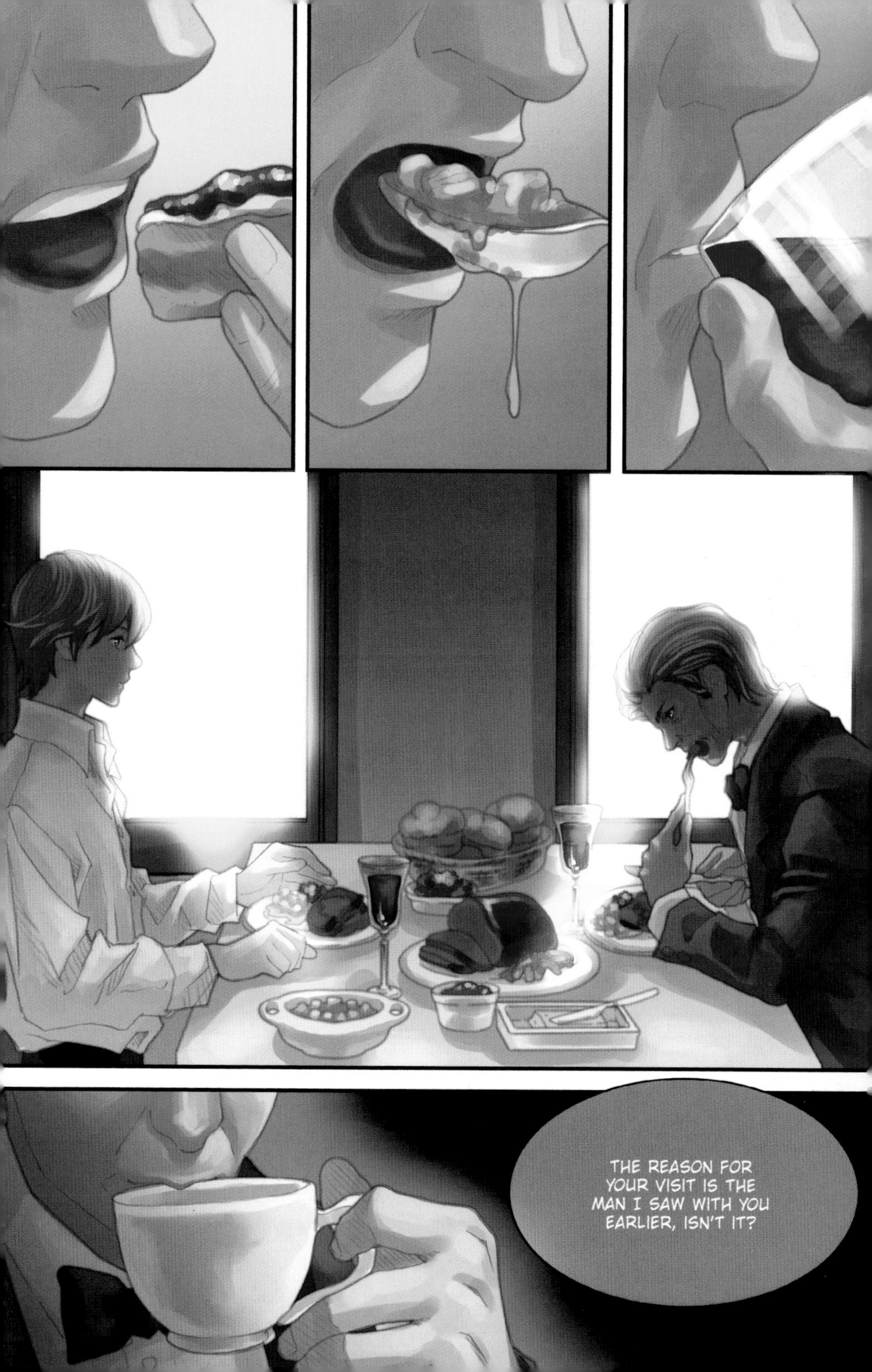
THE REASON FOR YOUR VISIT IS THE MAN I SAW WITH YOU EARLIER, ISN'T IT?

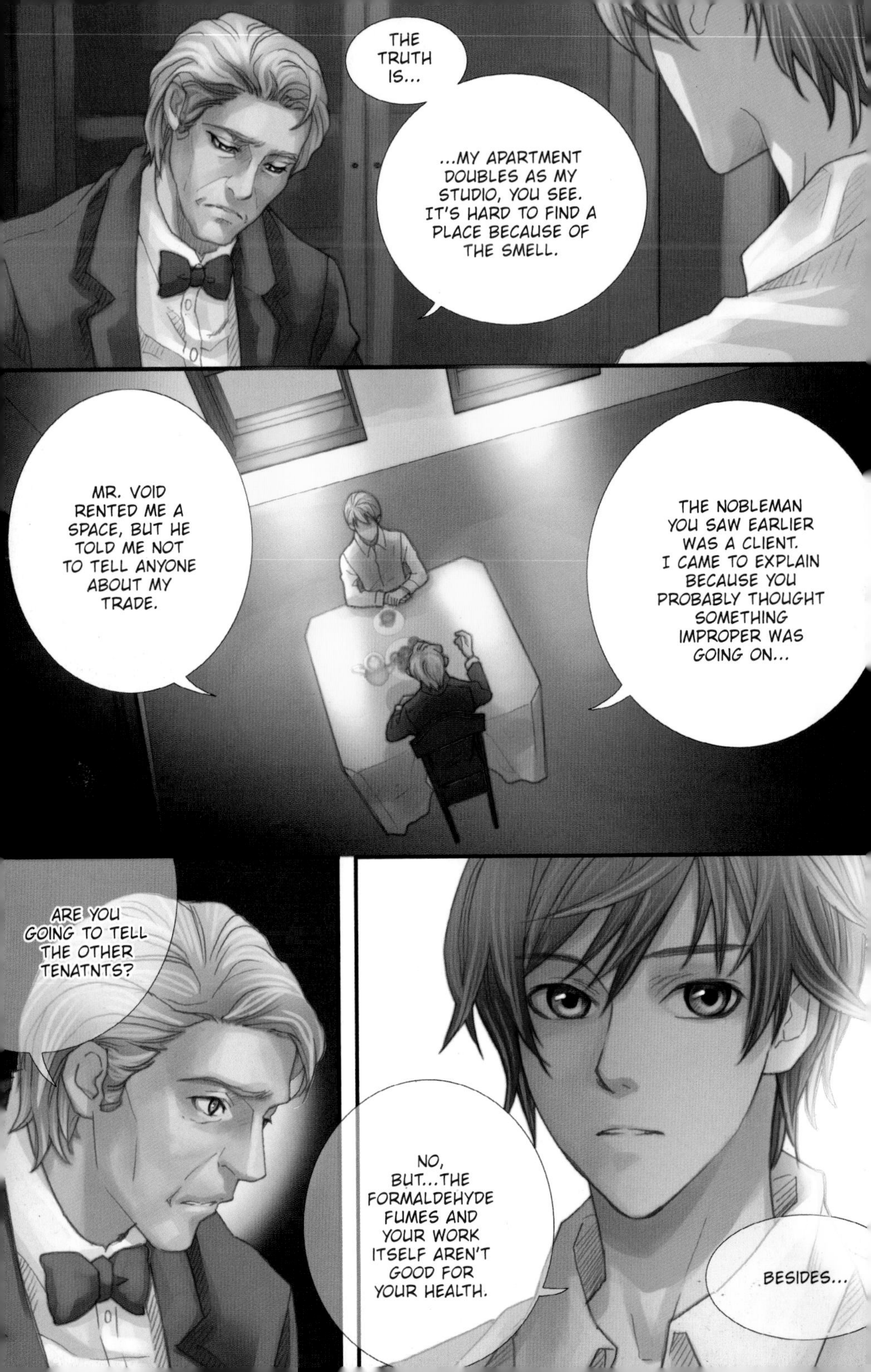
THE TRUTH IS...
...MY APARTMENT DOUBLES AS MY STUDIO, YOU SEE. IT'S HARD TO FIND A PLACE BECAUSE OF THE SMELL.
MR. VOID RENTED ME A SPACE, BUT HE TOLD ME NOT TO TELL ANYONE ABOUT MY TRADE.
THE NOBLEMAN YOU SAW EARLIER WAS A CLIENT. I CAME TO EXPLAIN BECAUSE YOU PROBABLY THOUGHT SOMETHING IMPROPER WAS GOING ON...
ARE YOU GOING TO TELL THE OTHER TENATNTS?
NO, BUT...THE FORMALDEHYDE FUMES AND YOUR WORK ITSELF AREN'T GOOD FOR YOUR HEALTH.
BESIDES...

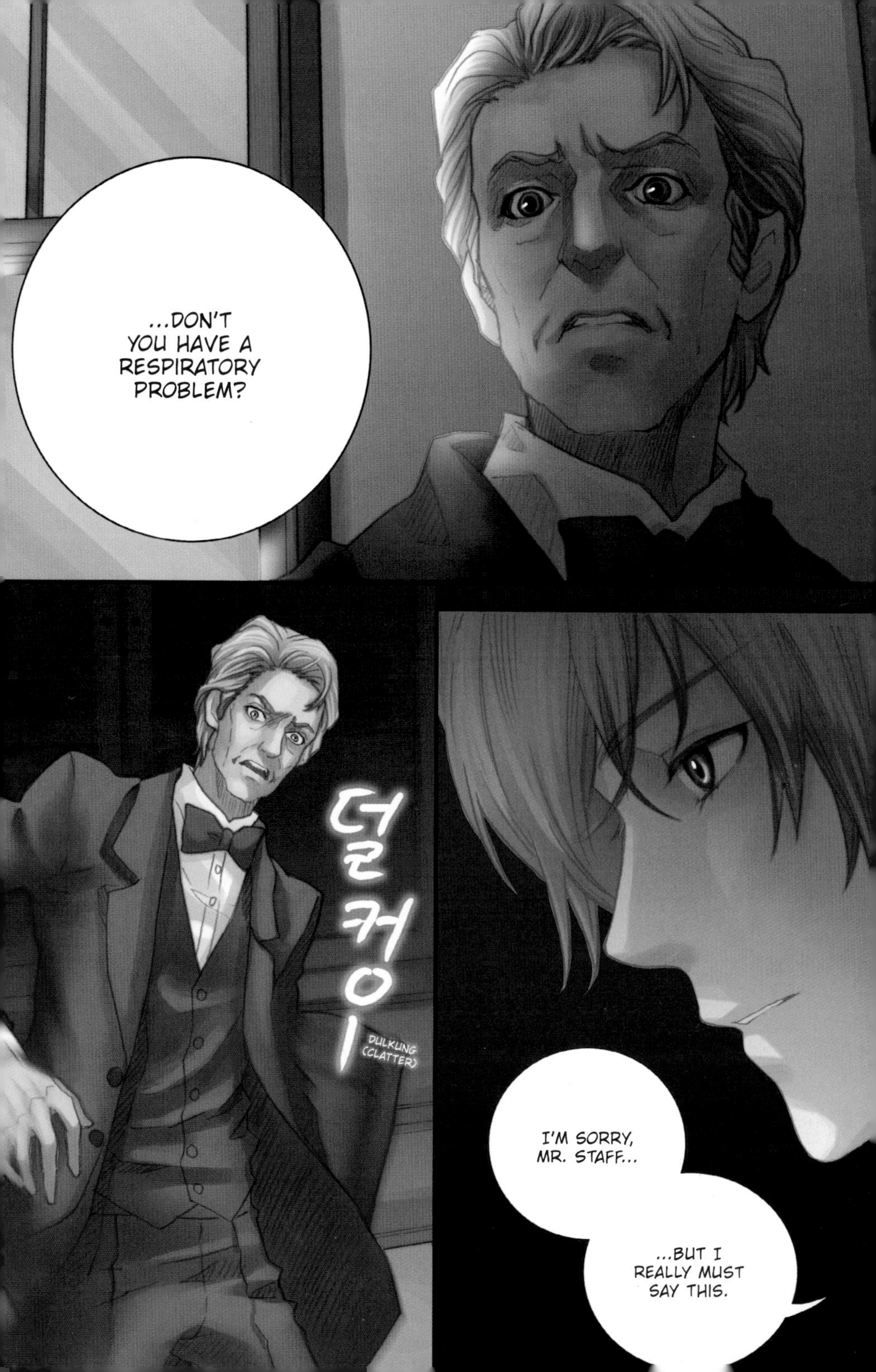
...DON'T YOU HAVE A RESPIRATORY PROBLEM?
DULKUNG (CLATTER)
I'M SORRY, MR. STAFF...
...BUT I REALLY MUST SAY THIS.

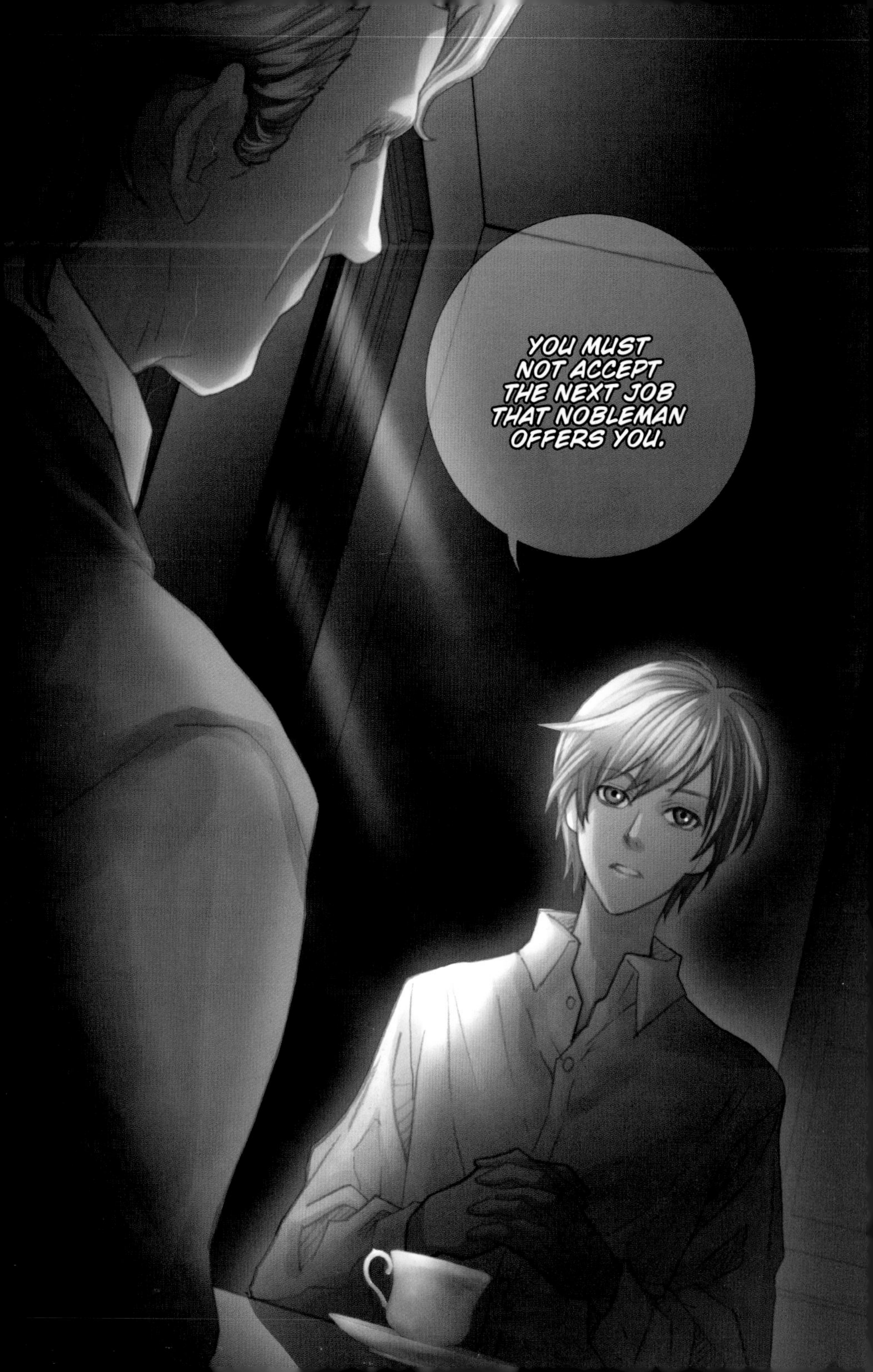
YOU MUST NOT ACCEPT THE NEXT JOB THAT NOBLEMAN OFFERS YOU.

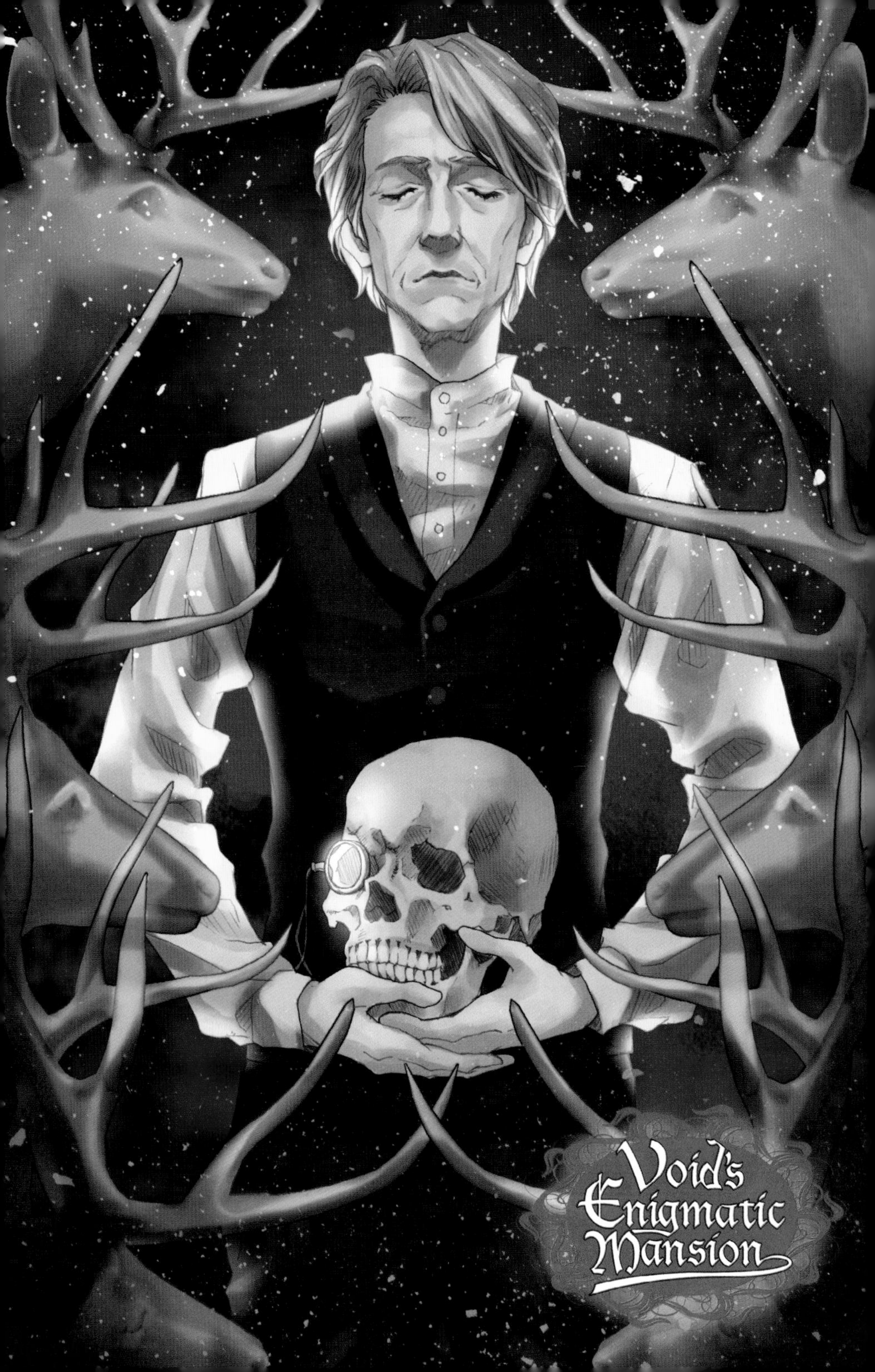
Void's Enigmatic Mansion

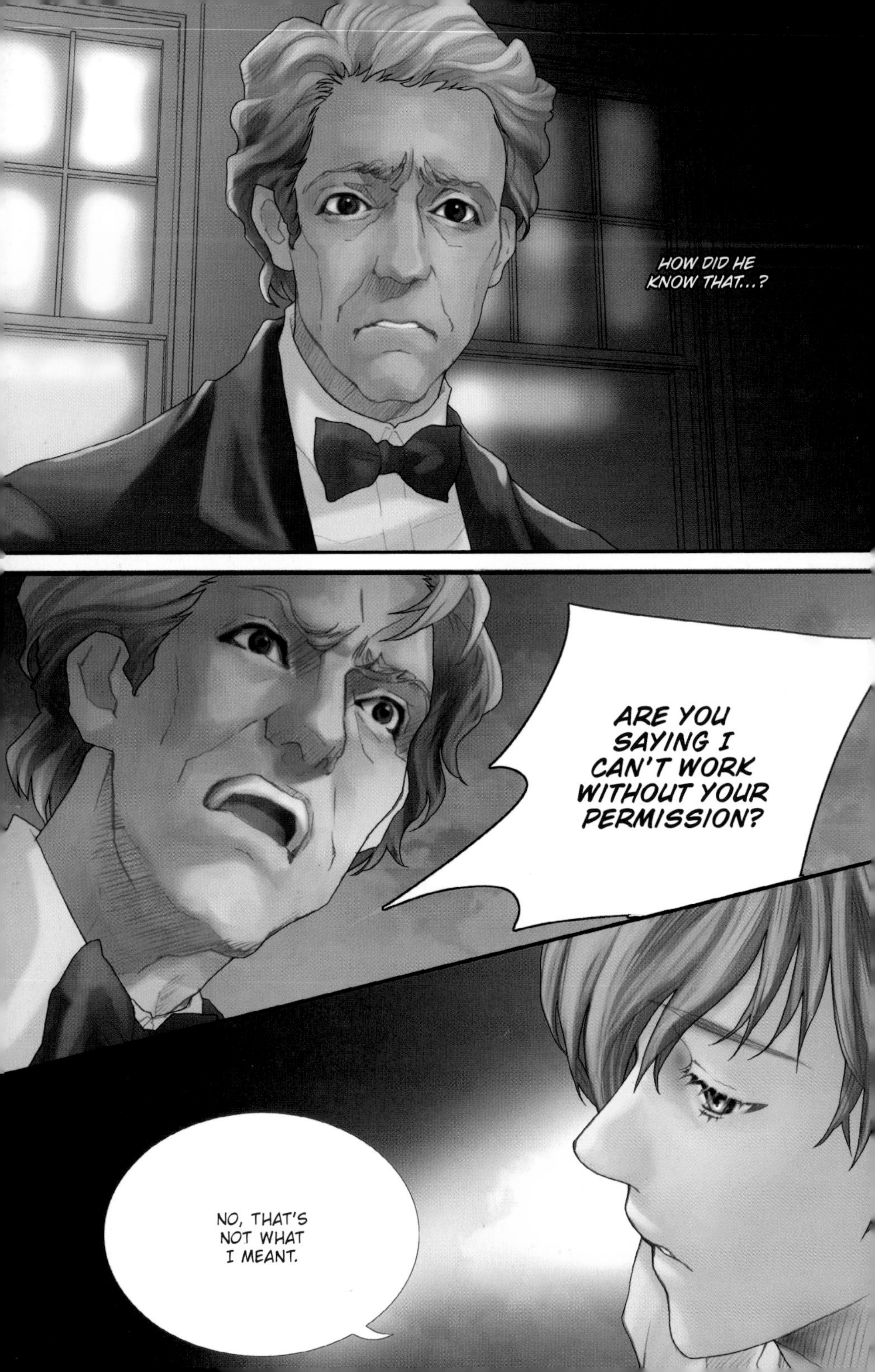
HOW DID HE KNOW THAT...?
ARE YOU SAYING I CAN'T WORK WITHOUT YOUR PERMISSION?
NO, THAT'S NOT WHAT I MEANT.

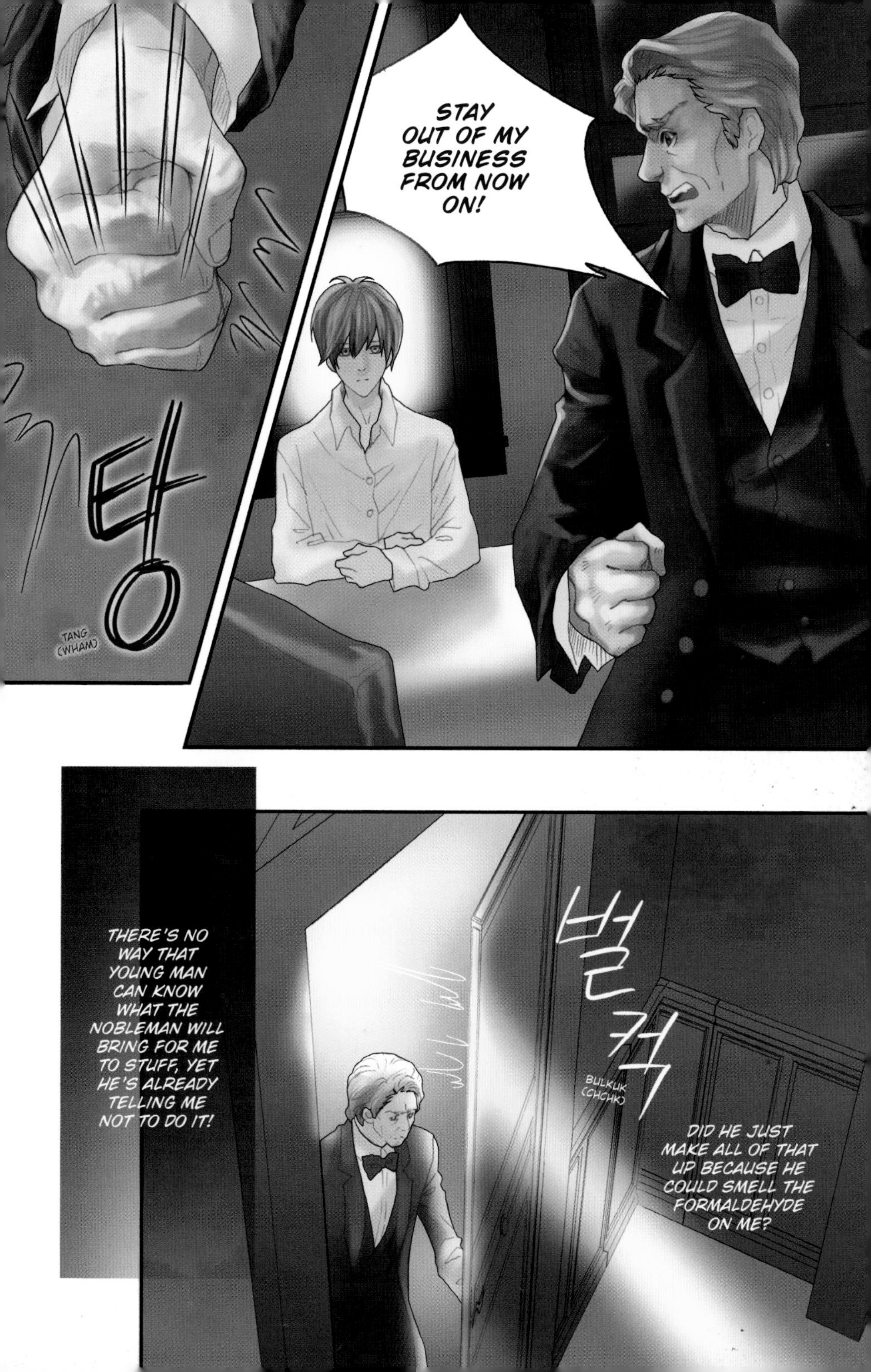
탕
TANG (WHAM)
STAY OUT OF MY BUSINESS FROM NOW ON!
THERE'S NO WAY THAT YOUNG MAN CAN KNOW WHAT THE NOBLEMAN WILL BRING FOR ME TO STUFF, YET HE'S ALREADY TELLING ME NOT TO DO IT!
벌컥
BULKUK (CHCHK)
DID HE JUST MAKE ALL OF THAT UP BECAUSE HE COULD SMELL THE FORMALDEHYDE ON ME?

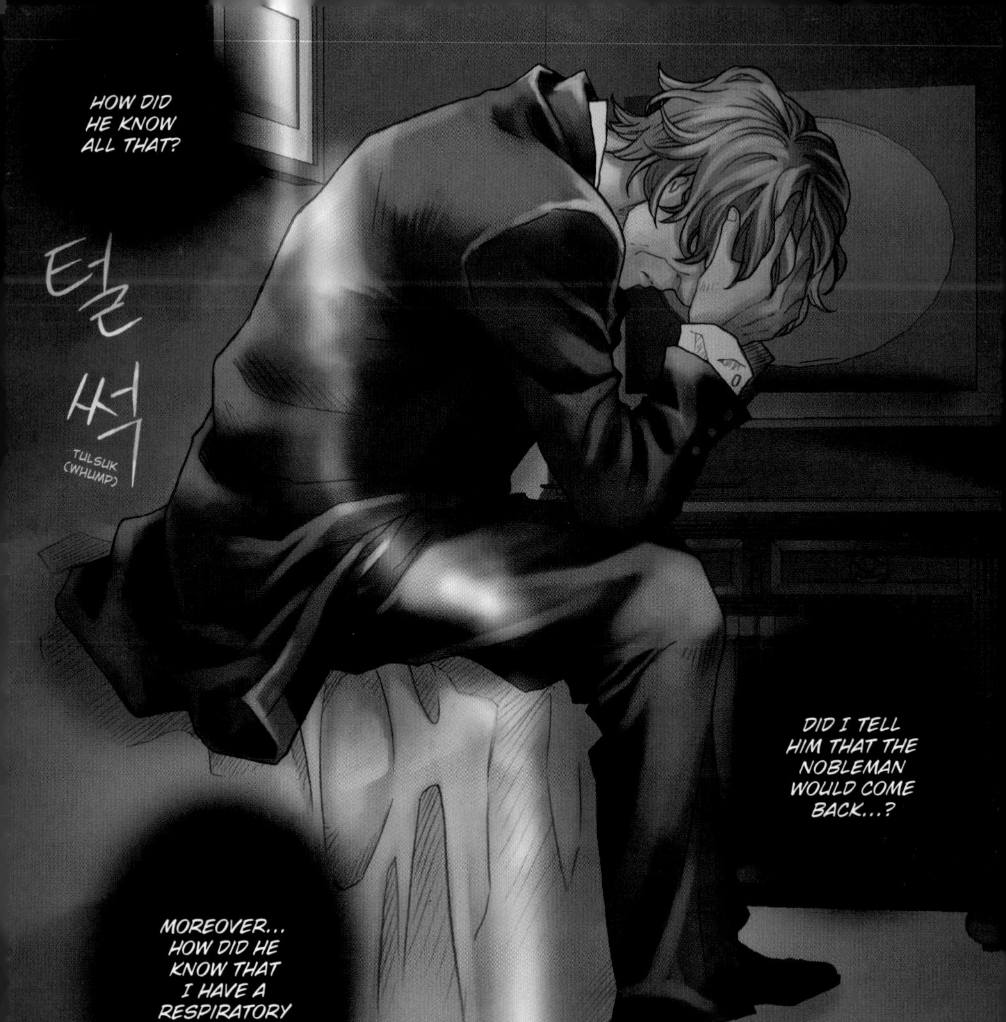
HOW DID HE KNOW ALL THAT?
털썩
TULSUK (WHUMP)
DID I TELL HIM THAT THE NOBLEMAN WOULD COME BACK...?
MOREOVER... HOW DID HE KNOW THAT I HAVE A RESPIRATORY PROBLEM?
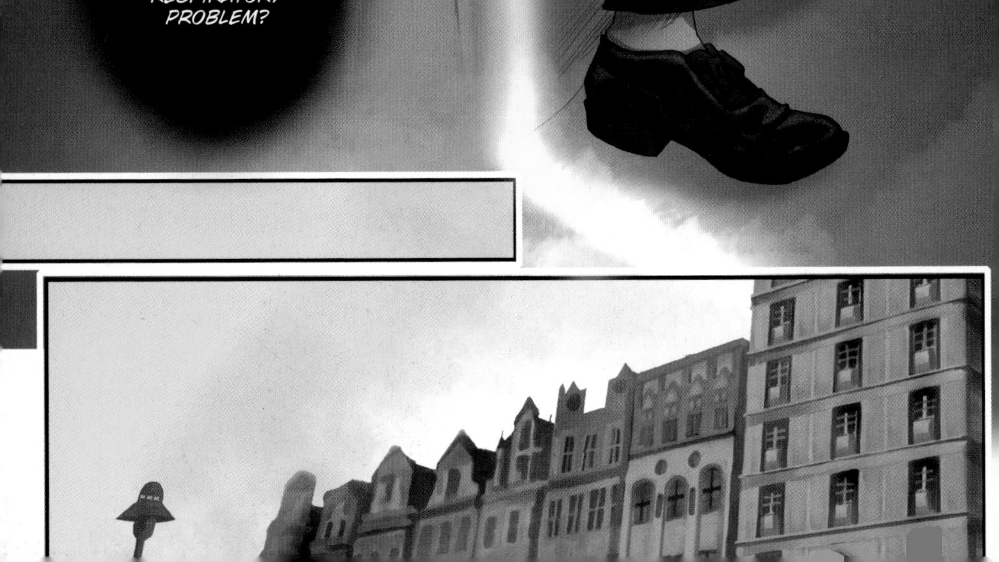

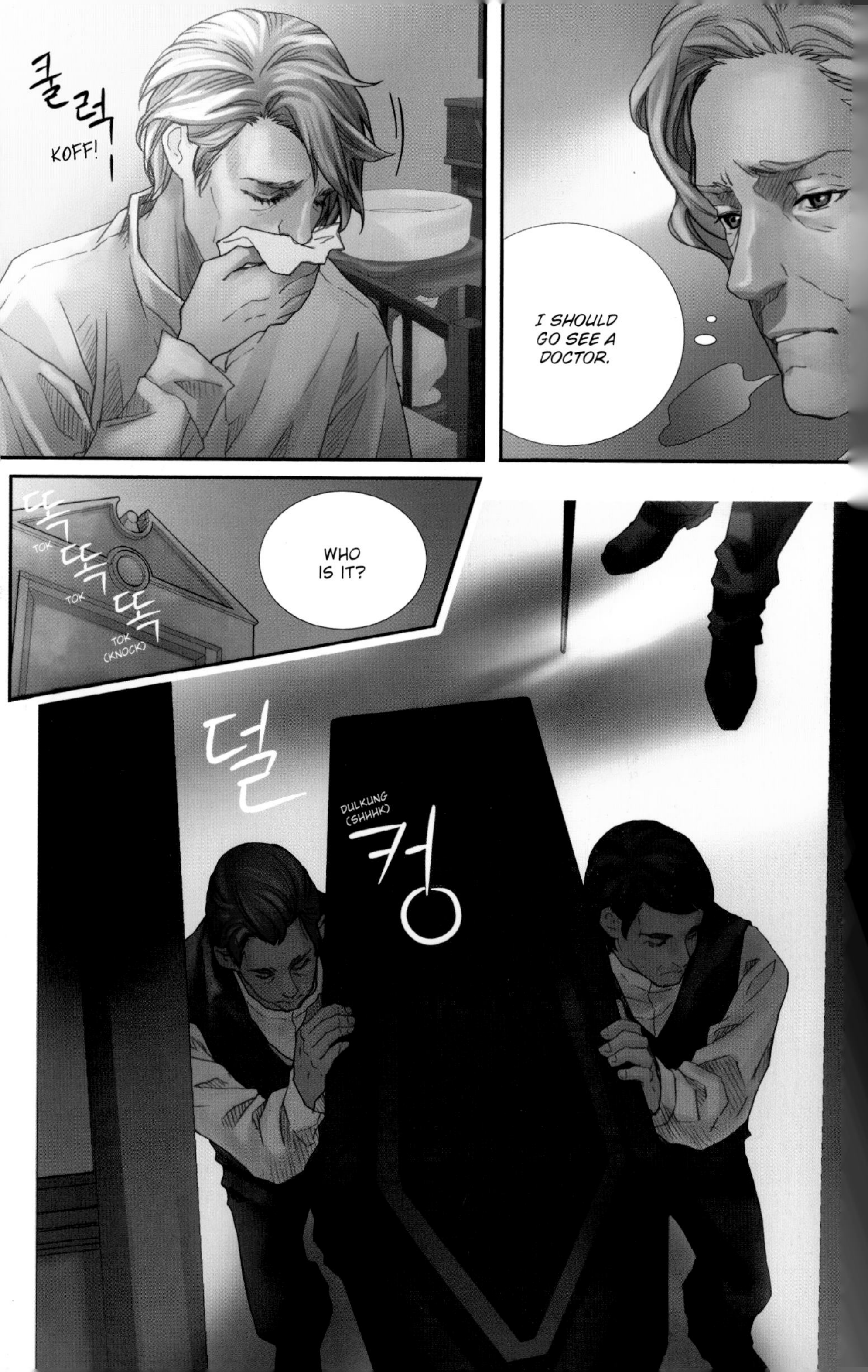
콜럭
KOFF!
I SHOULD GO SEE A DOCTOR.
똑 똑 똑
TOK TOK TOK (KNOCK)
WHO IS IT?
덜컹
DULKUNG (SHHHK)

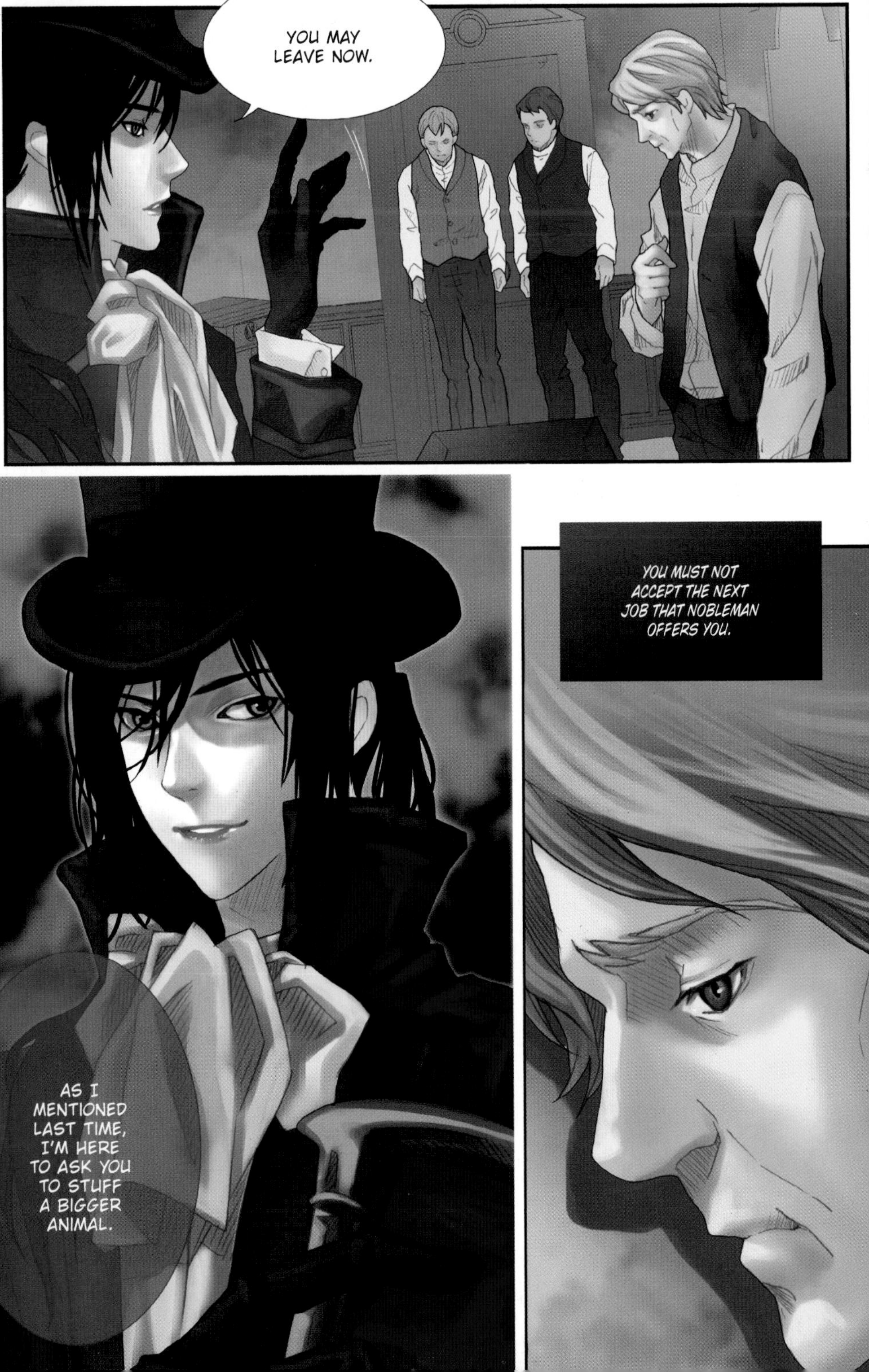
YOU MAY LEAVE NOW.
AS I MENTIONED LAST TIME, I'M HERE TO ASK YOU TO STUFF A BIGGER ANIMAL.
YOU MUST NOT ACCEPT THE NEXT JOB THAT NOBLEMAN OFFERS YOU.

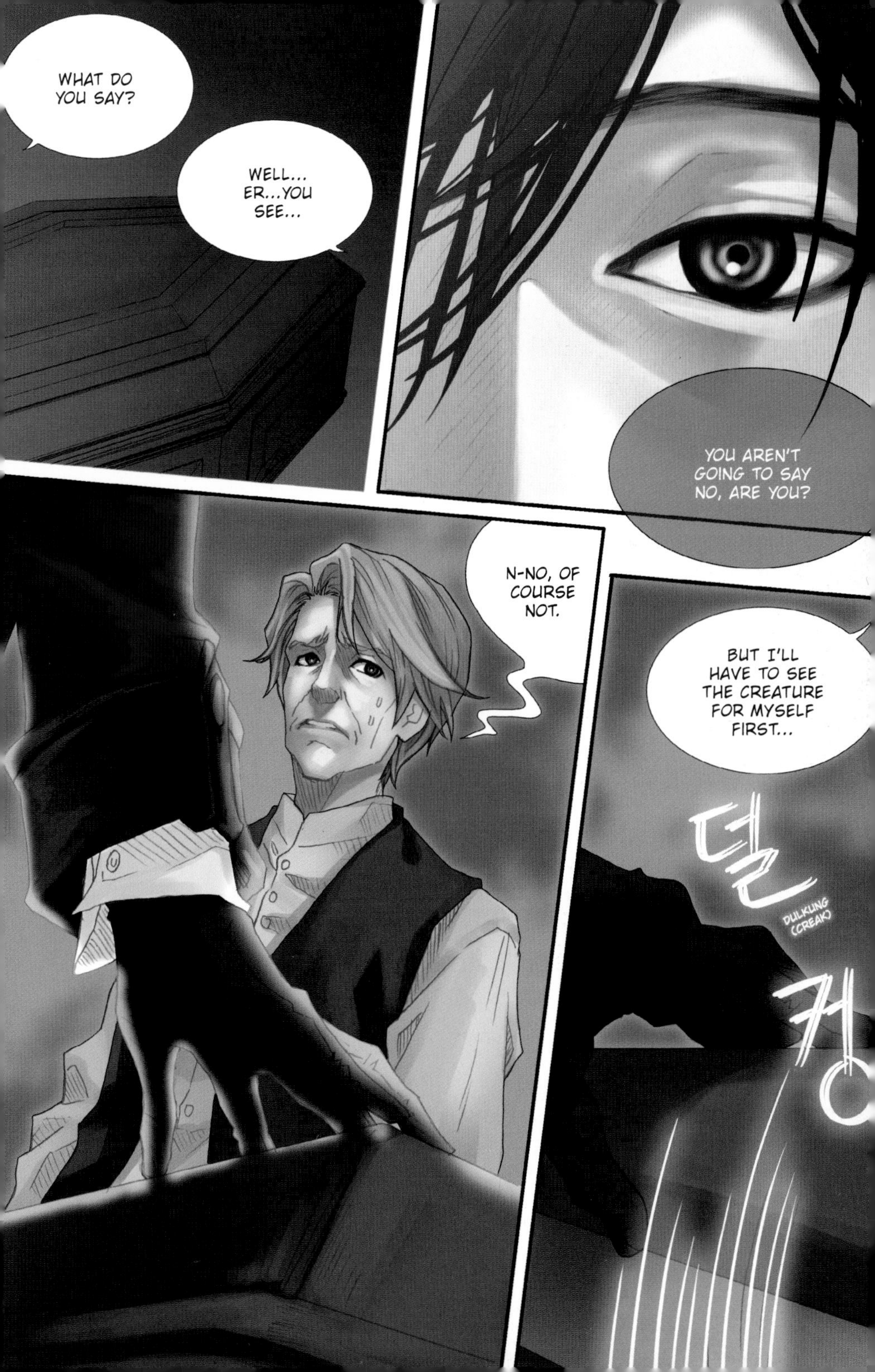
WHAT DO YOU SAY?
WELL... ER...YOU SEE...
YOU AREN'T GOING TO SAY NO, ARE YOU?
N-NO, OF COURSE NOT.
BUT I'LL HAVE TO SEE THE CREATURE FOR MYSELF FIRST...
덜컹
DULKUNG (CREAK)

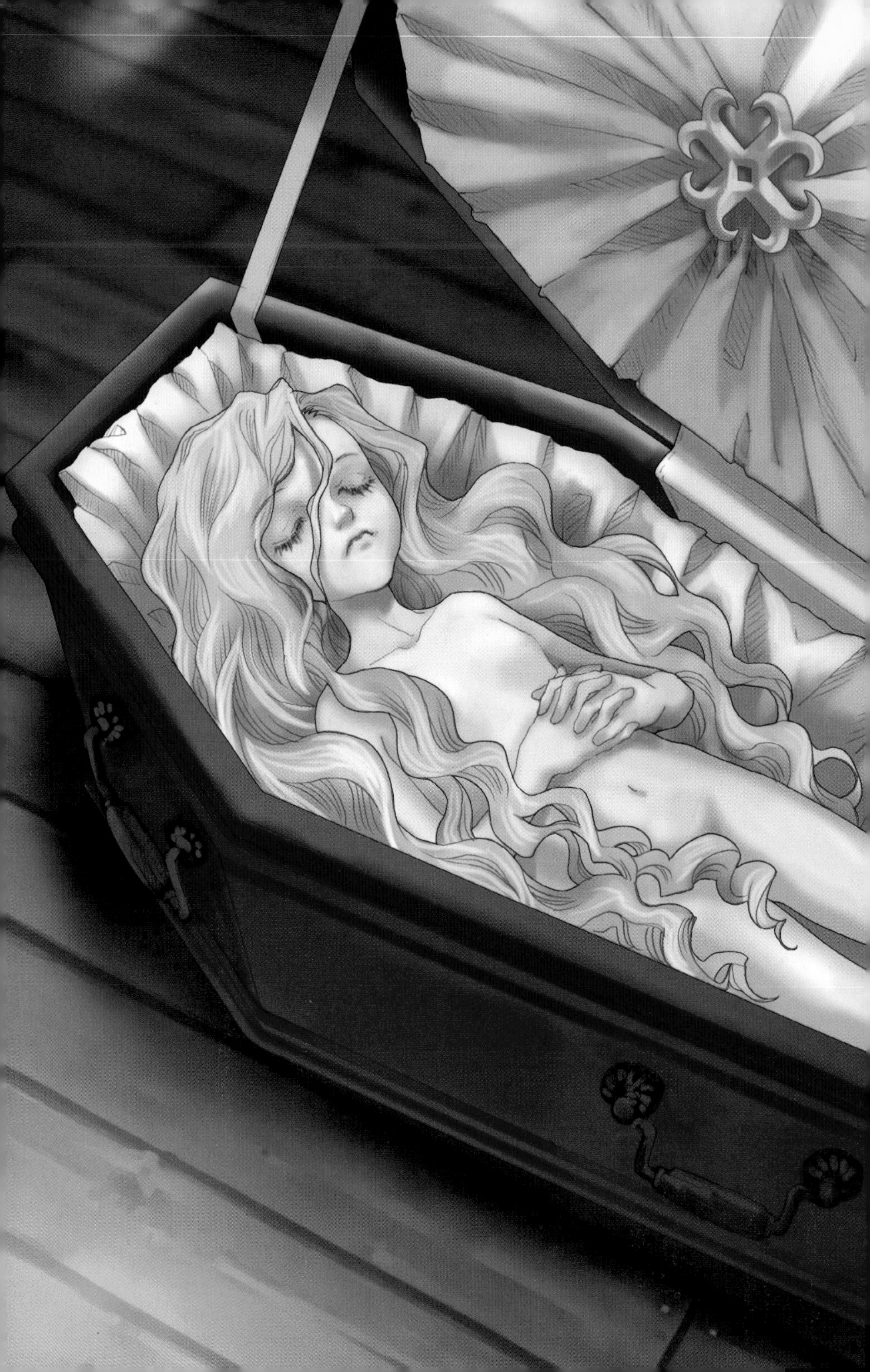

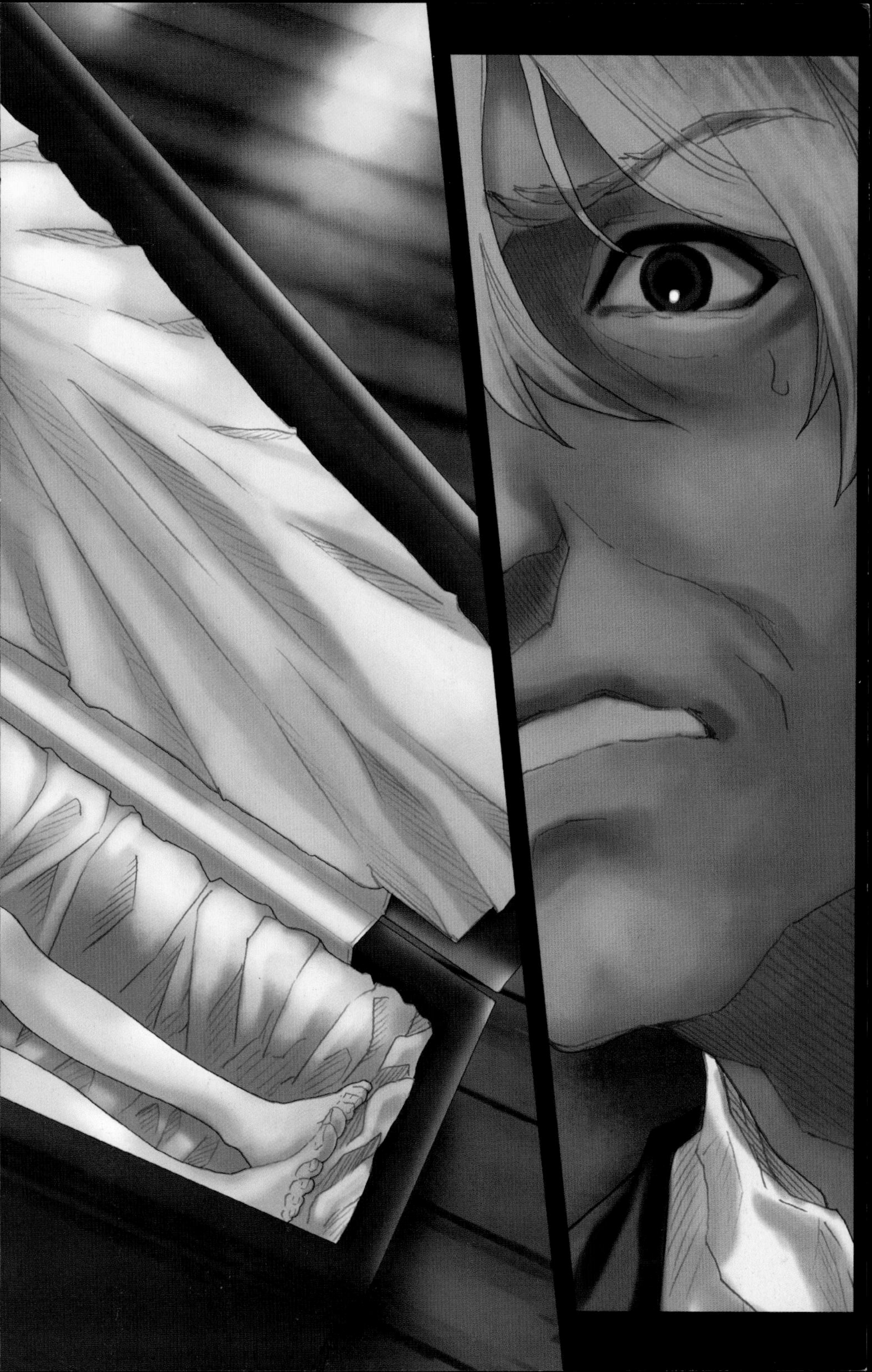

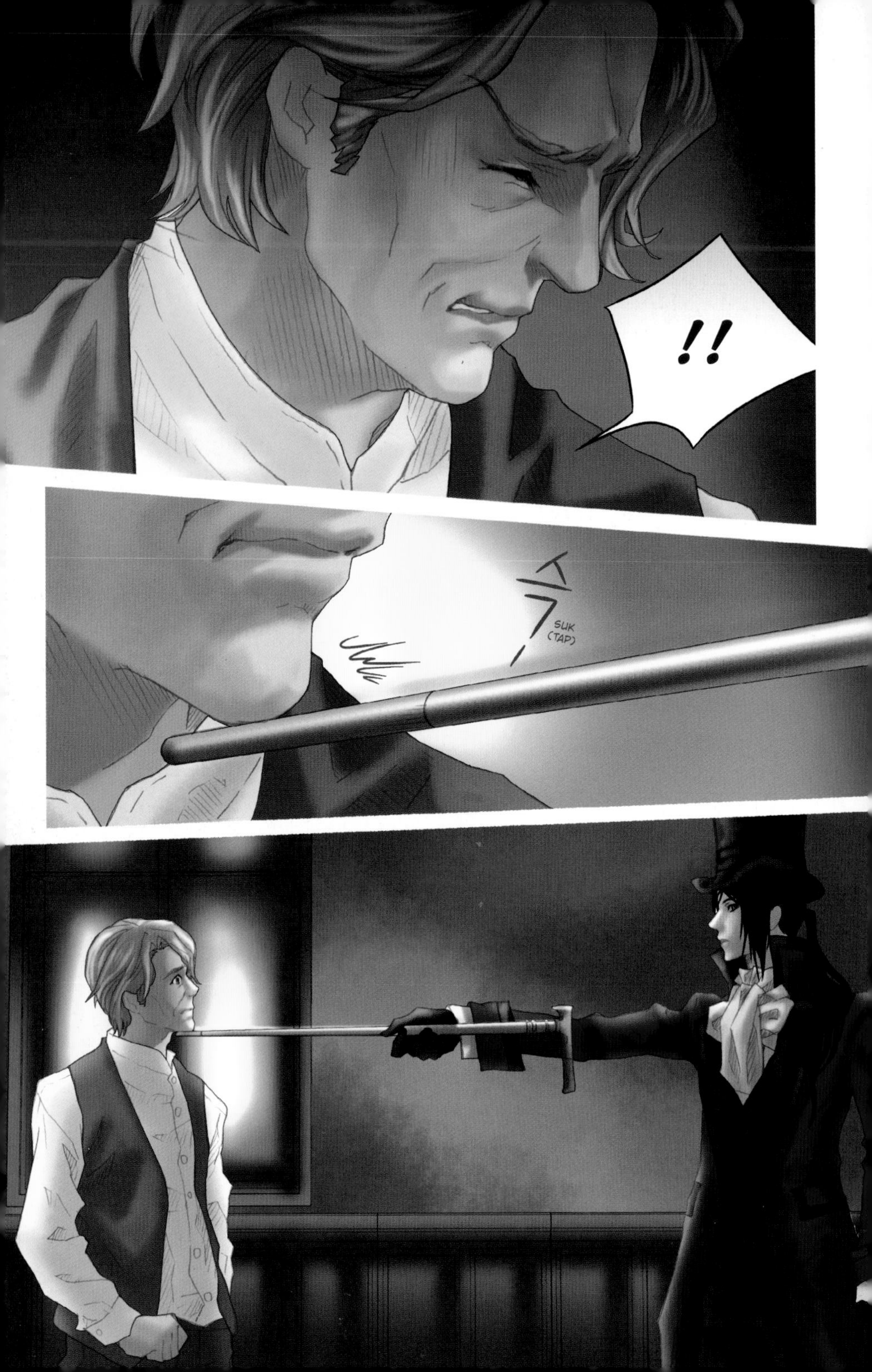
!!
SUK
(TAP)

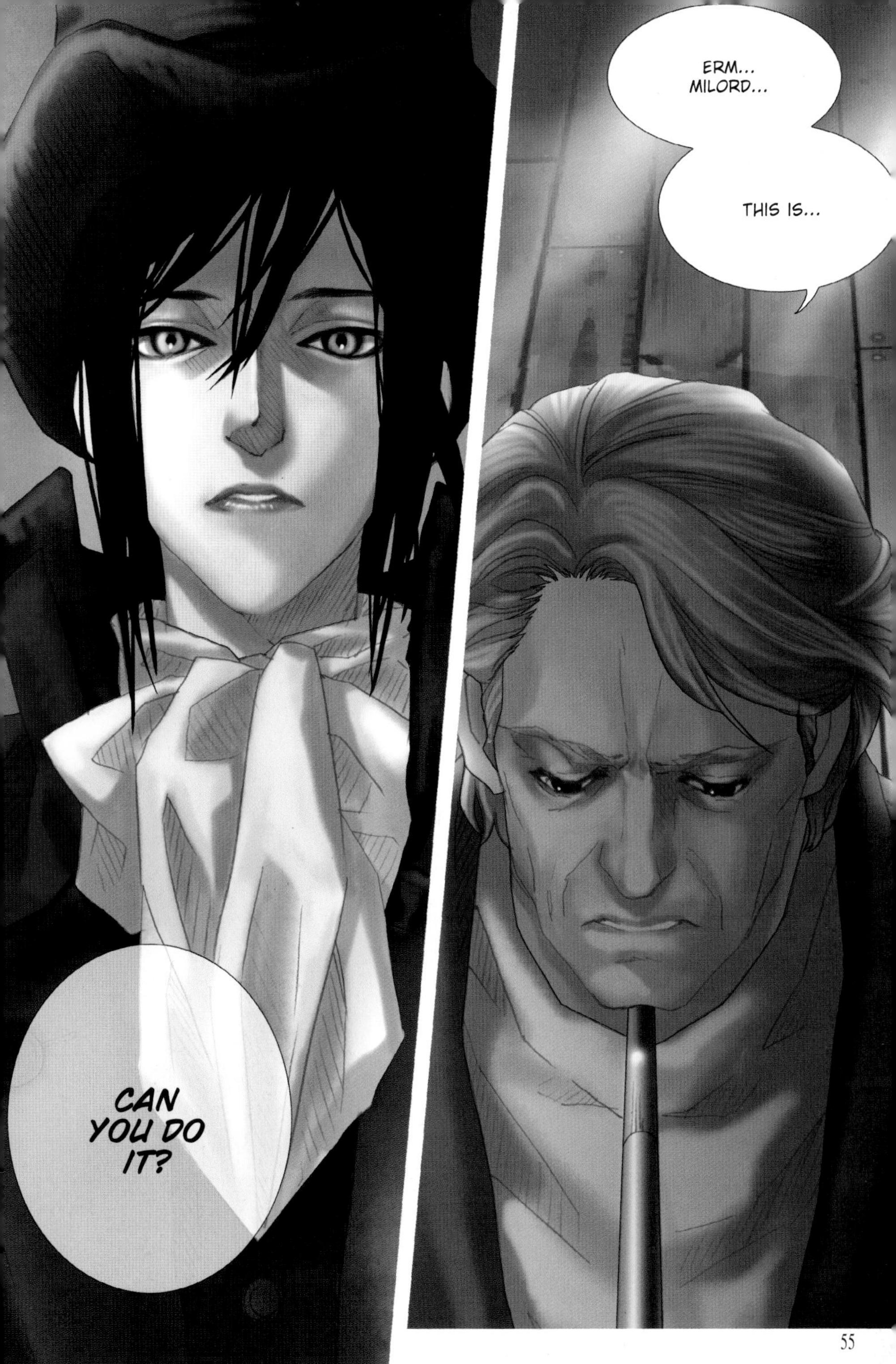
ERM... MILORD...
THIS IS...
CAN YOU DO IT?

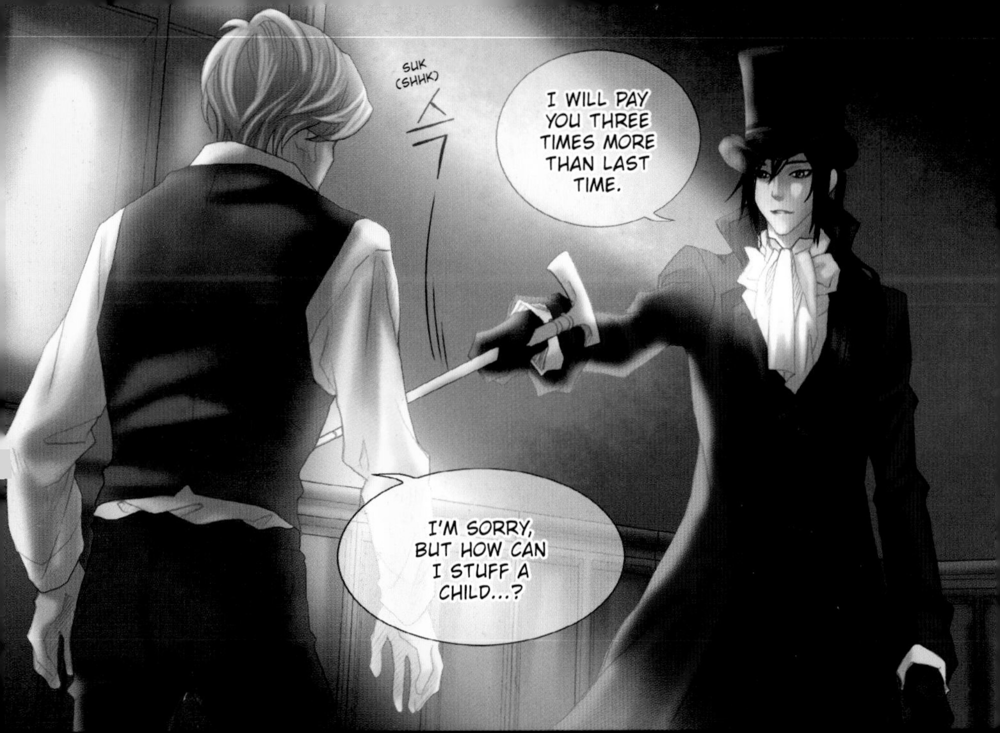
SUK (SHHK)
I WILL PAY YOU THREE TIMES MORE THAN LAST TIME.
I'M SORRY, BUT HOW CAN I STUFF A CHILD...?
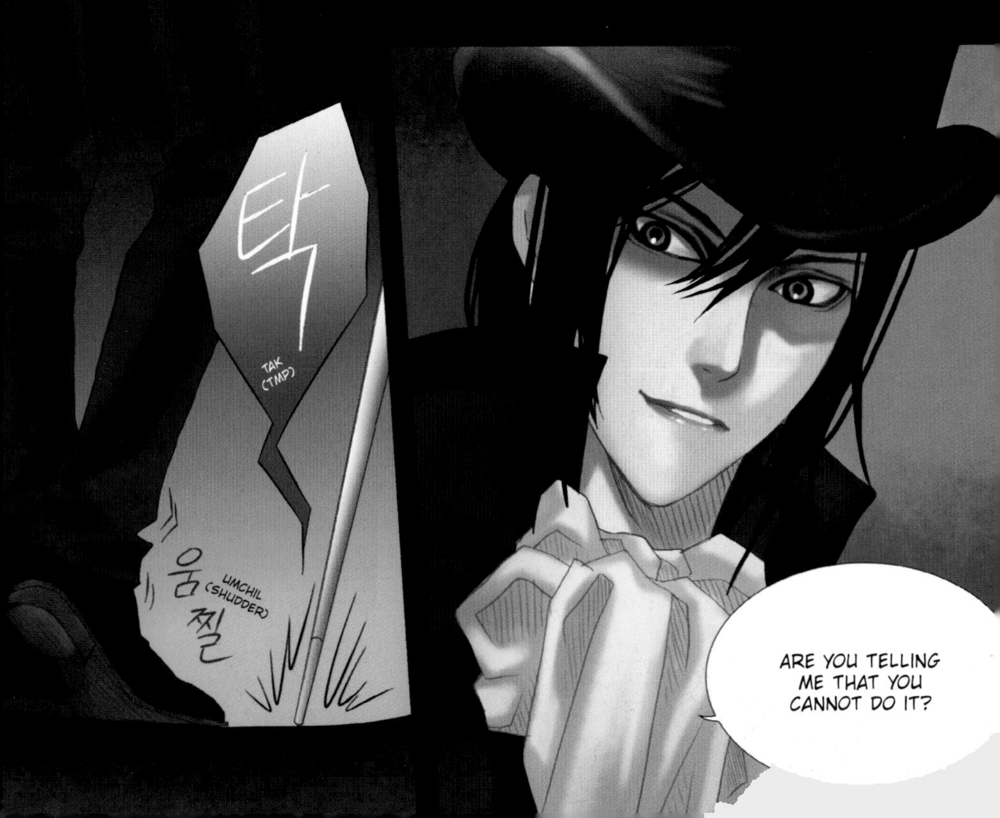
TAK (TMP)
UMCHIL (SHUDDER)
ARE YOU TELLING ME THAT YOU CANNOT DO IT?

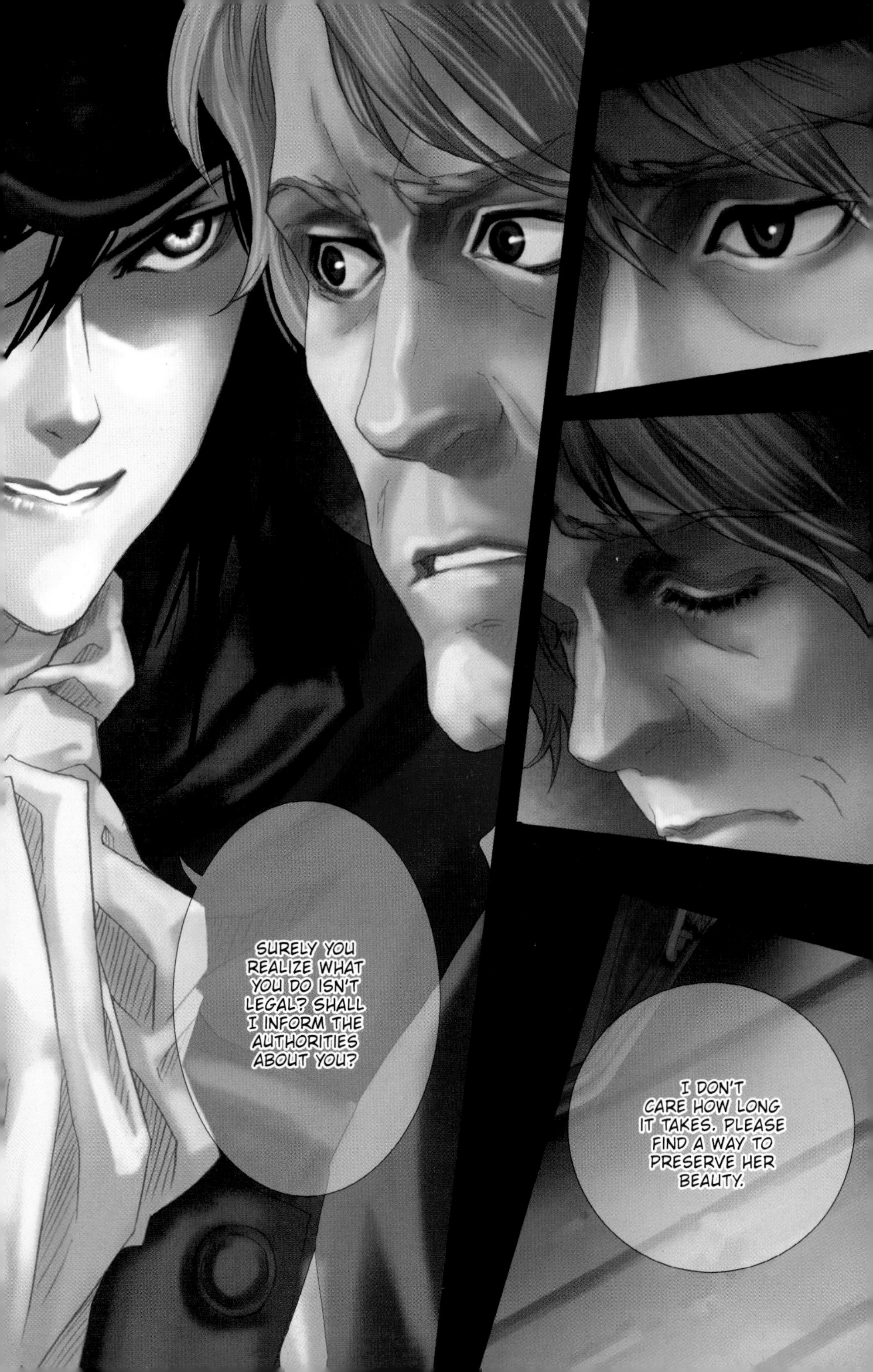
I DON'T CARE HOW LONG IT TAKES. PLEASE FIND A WAY TO PRESERVE HER BEAUTY.
SURELY YOU REALIZE WHAT YOU DO ISN'T LEGAL? SHALL I INFORM THE AUTHORITIES ABOUT YOU?

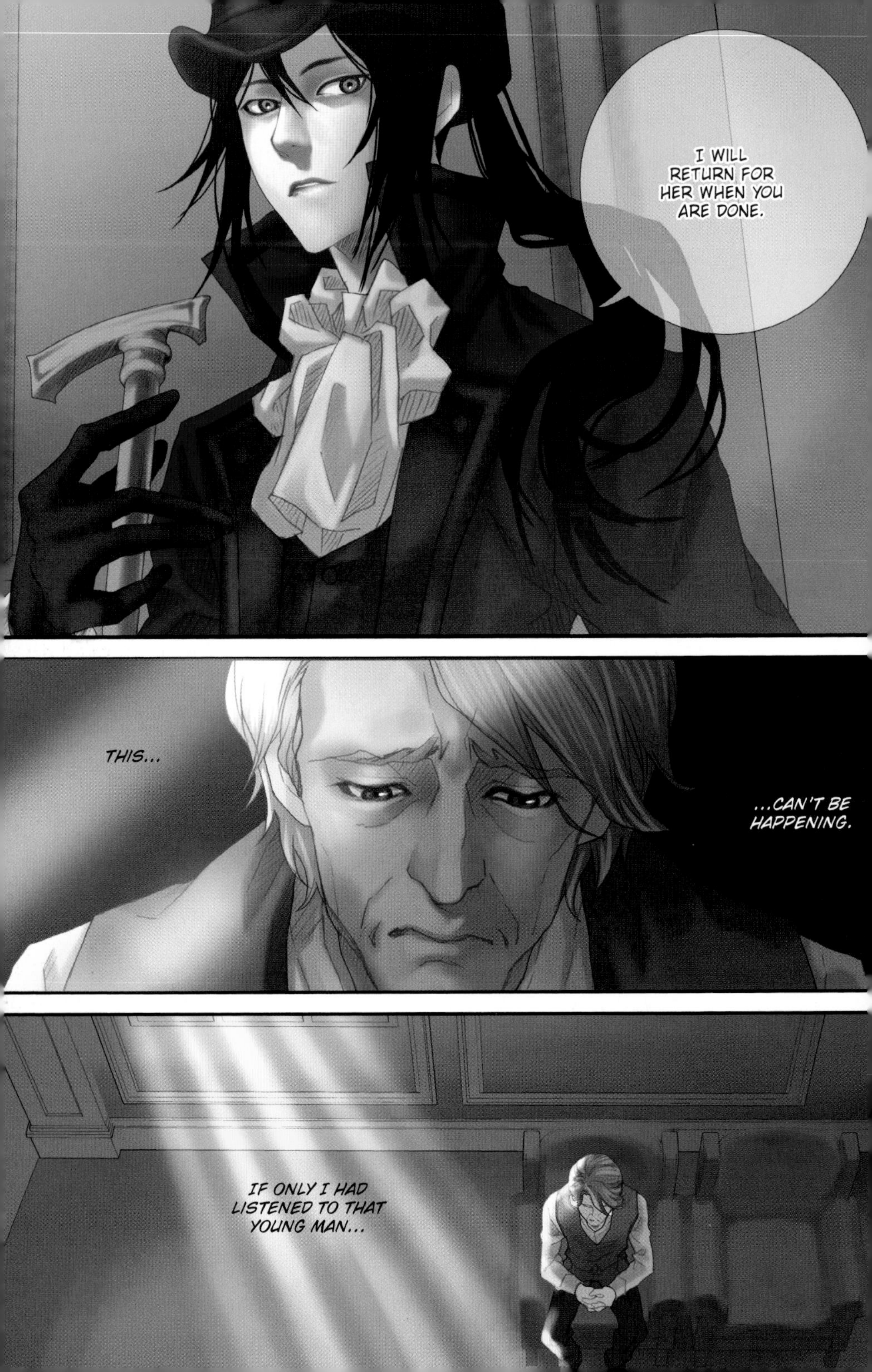
I WILL RETURN FOR HER WHEN YOU ARE DONE.
THIS...
...CAN'T BE HAPPENING.
IF ONLY I HAD LISTENED TO THAT YOUNG MAN...

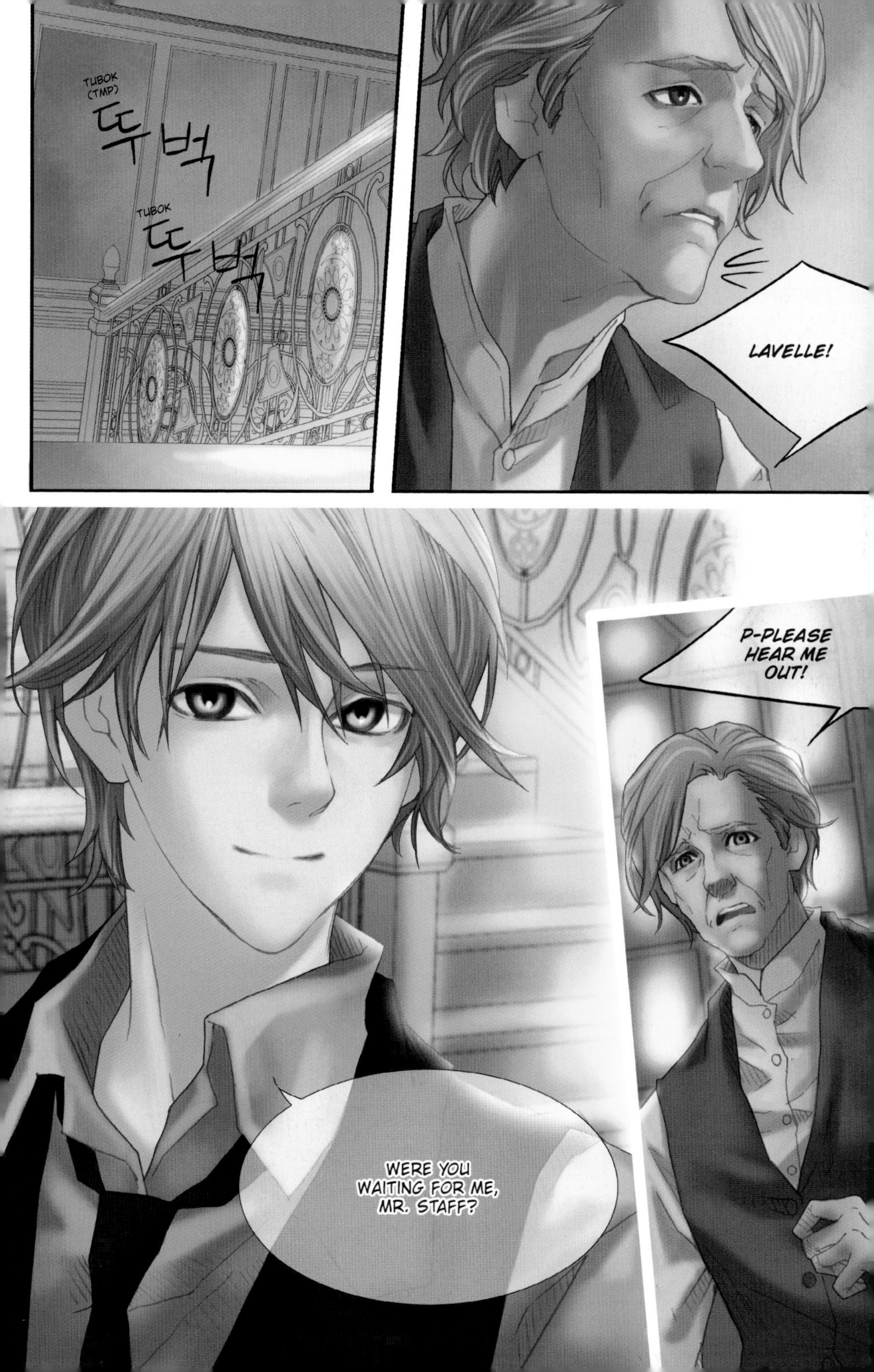
TUBOK (TMP)
뚜벅
TUBOK
뚜벅
LAVELLE!
WERE YOU WAITING FOR ME, MR. STAFF?
P-PLEASE HEAR ME OUT!

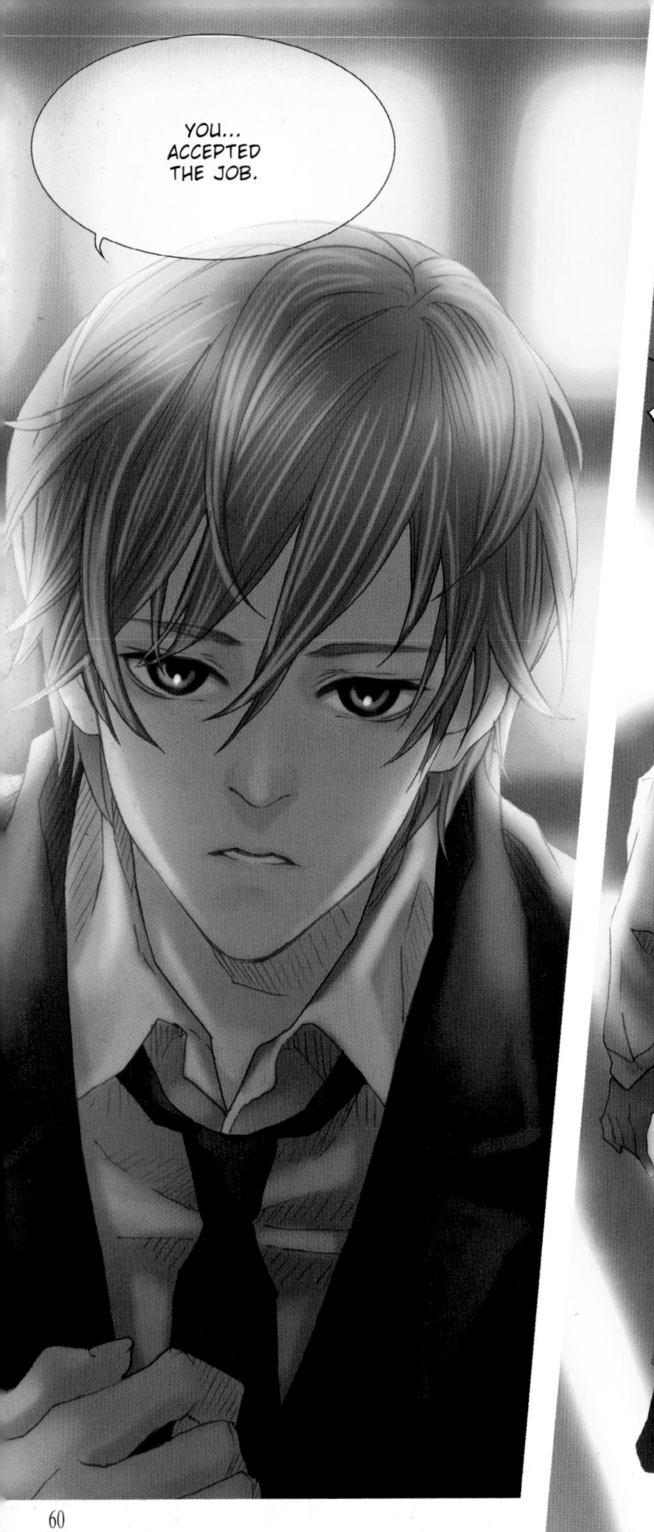
YOU... ACCEPTED THE JOB.

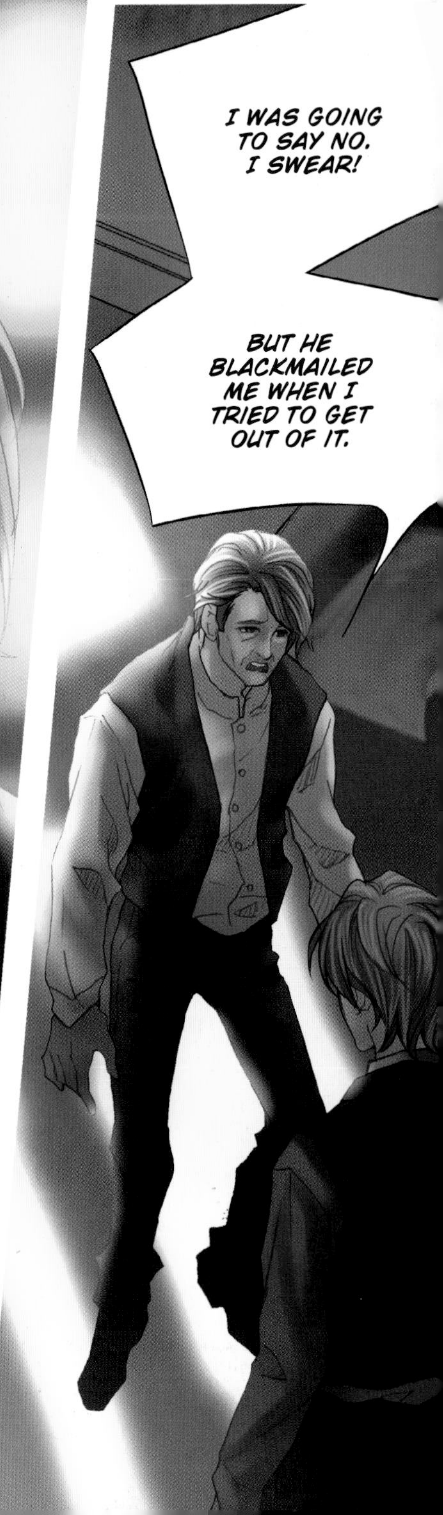
I WAS GOING TO SAY NO. I SWEAR!
BUT HE BLACKMAILED ME WHEN I TRIED TO GET OUT OF IT.

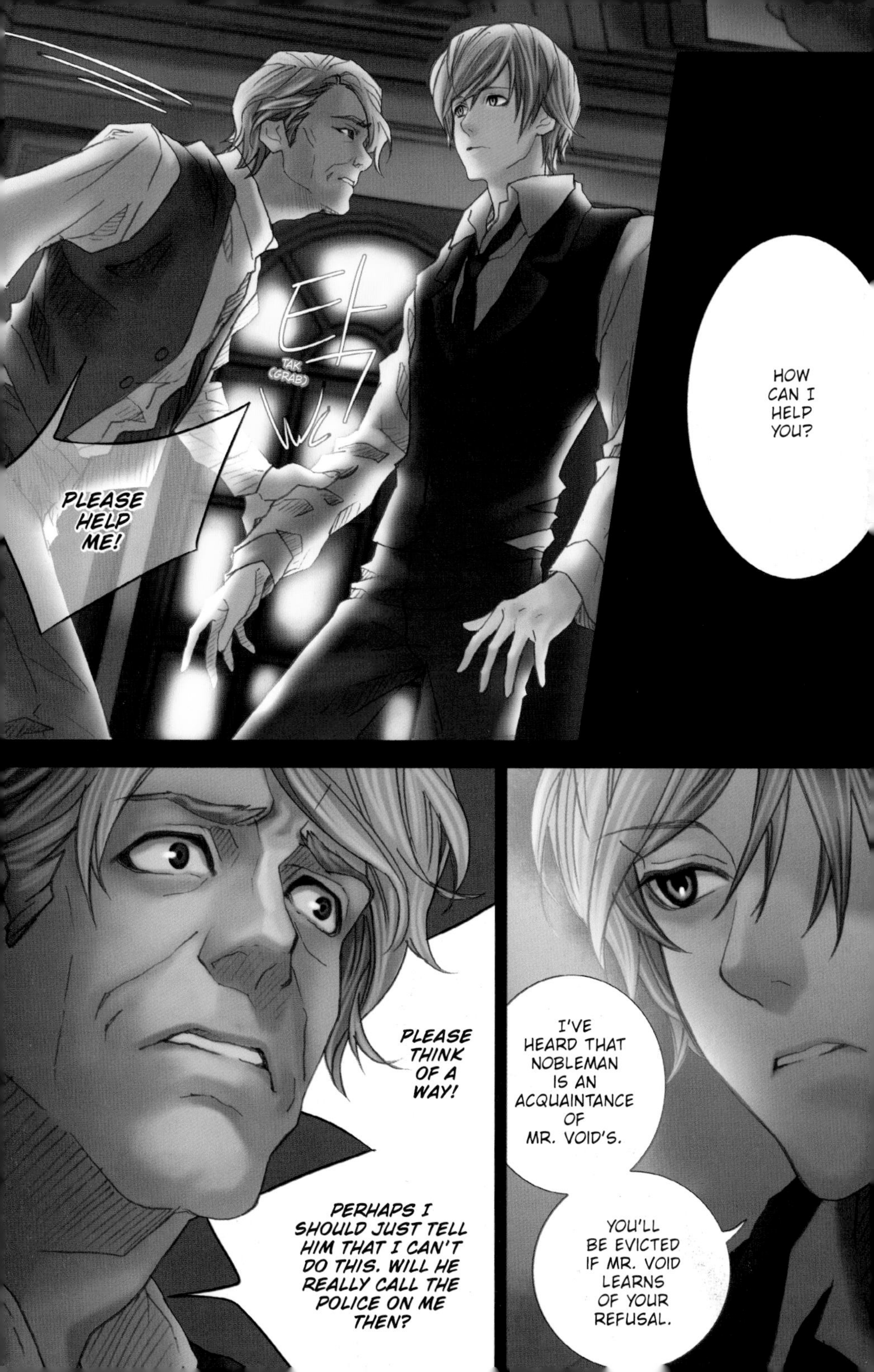
HOW CAN I HELP YOU?
TAK (GRAB)
PLEASE HELP ME!
I'VE HEARD THAT NOBLEMAN IS AN ACQUAINTANCE OF MR. VOID'S.
YOU'LL BE EVICTED IF MR. VOID LEARNS OF YOUR REFUSAL.
PLEASE THINK OF A WAY!
PERHAPS I SHOULD JUST TELL HIM THAT I CAN'T DO THIS. WILL HE REALLY CALL THE POLICE ON ME THEN?

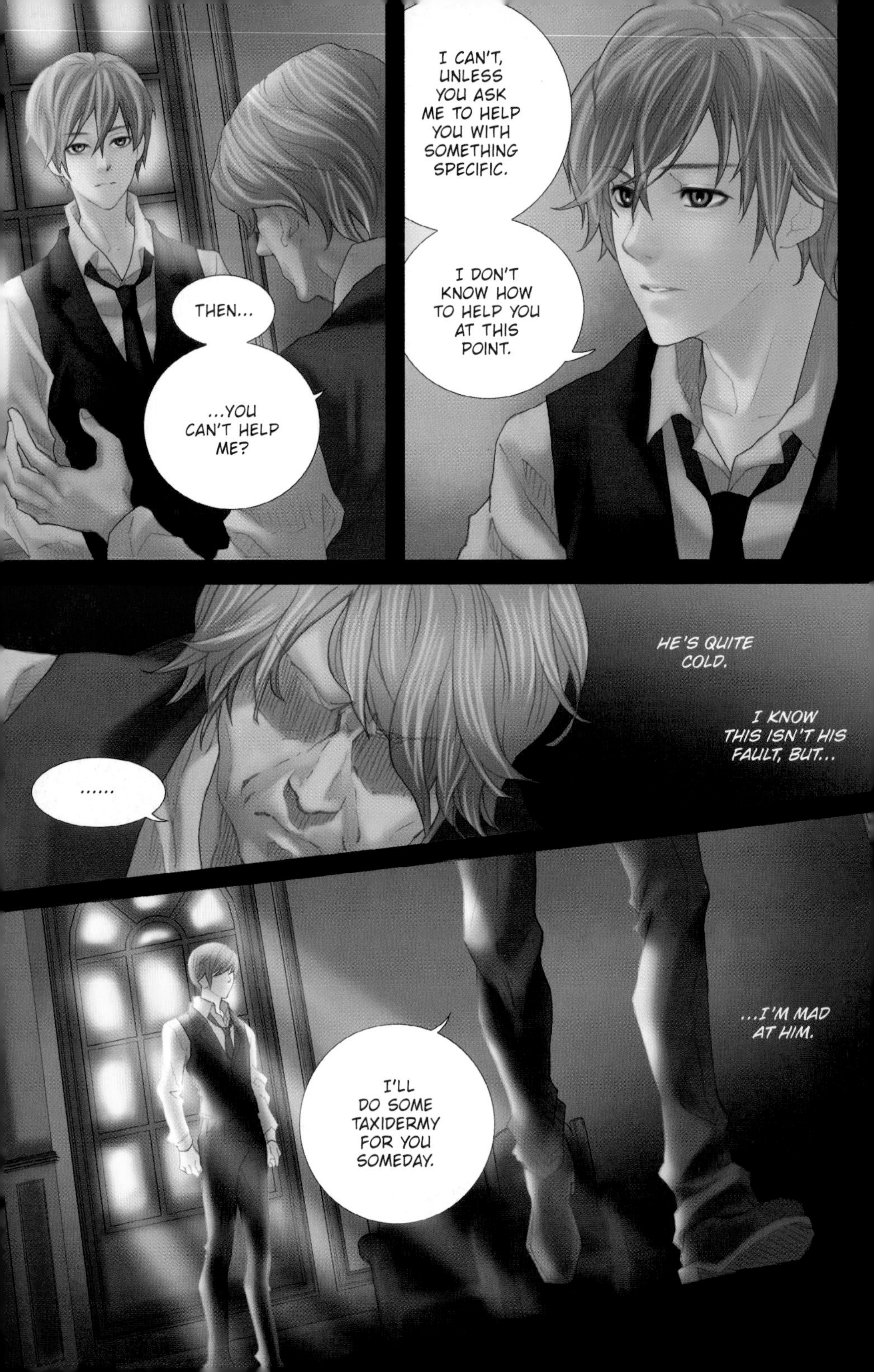
THEN...
...YOU CAN'T HELP ME?
I CAN'T, UNLESS YOU ASK ME TO HELP YOU WITH SOMETHING SPECIFIC.
I DON'T KNOW HOW TO HELP YOU AT THIS POINT.
......
HE'S QUITE COLD.
I KNOW THIS ISN'T HIS FAULT, BUT...
...I'M MAD AT HIM.
I'LL DO SOME TAXIDERMY FOR YOU SOMEDAY.

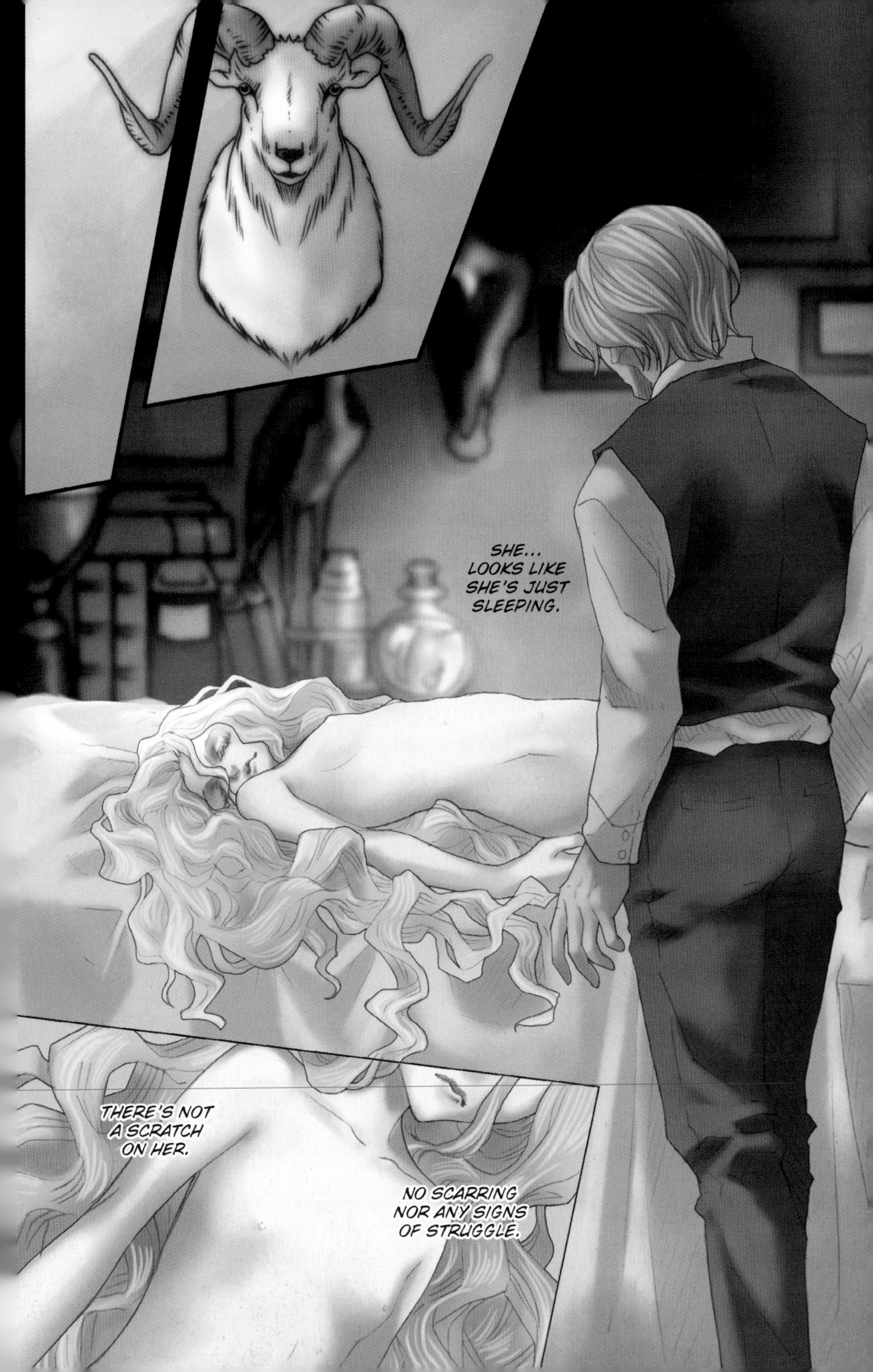
SHE... LOOKS LIKE SHE'S JUST SLEEPING.
THERE'S NOT A SCRATCH ON HER.
NO SCARRING NOR ANY SIGNS OF STRUGGLE.

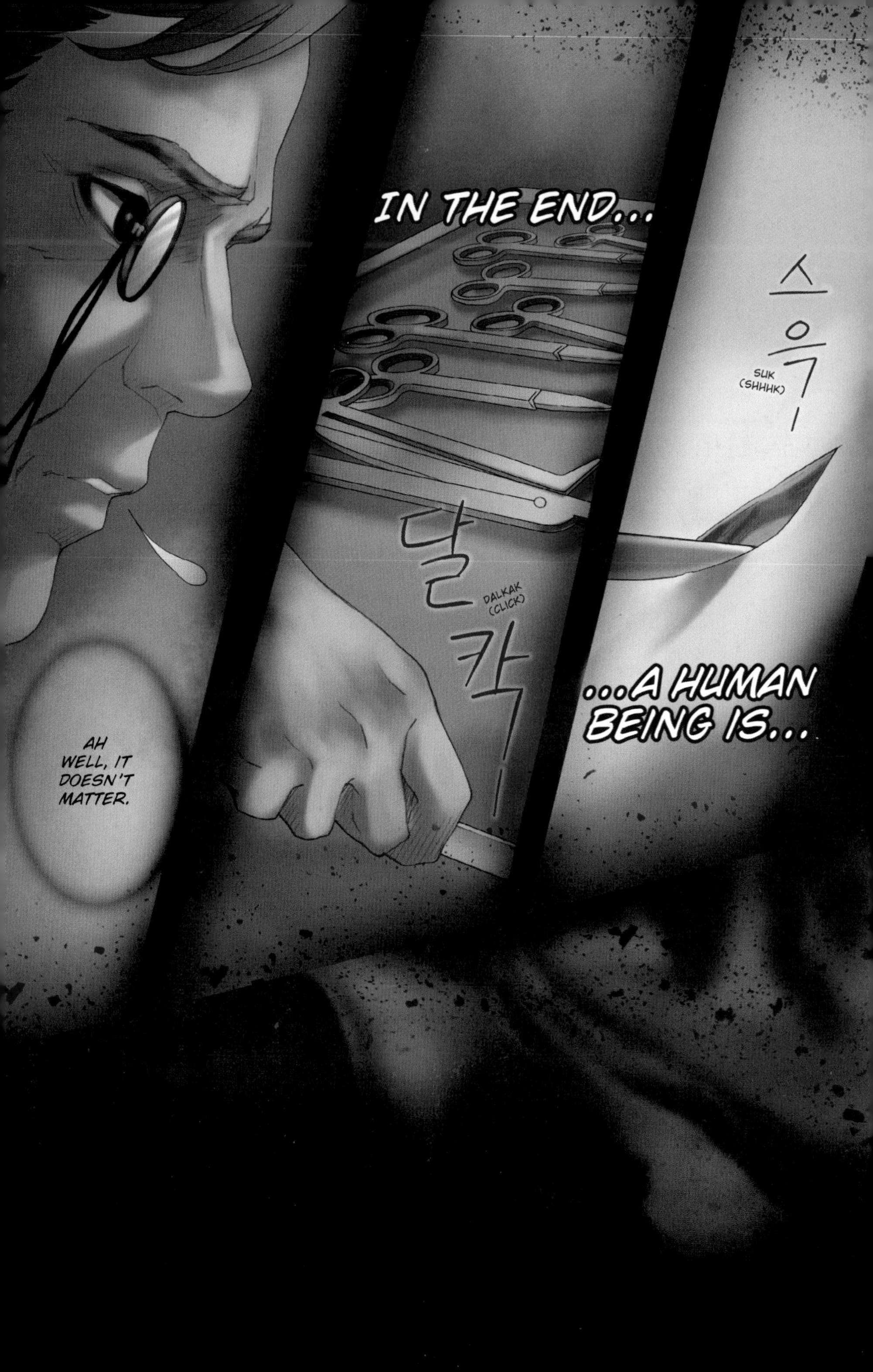
AH WELL, IT DOESN'T MATTER.
IN THE END...
달칵
DALKAK (CLICK)
스윽
SUK (SHHHK)
...A HUMAN BEING IS...

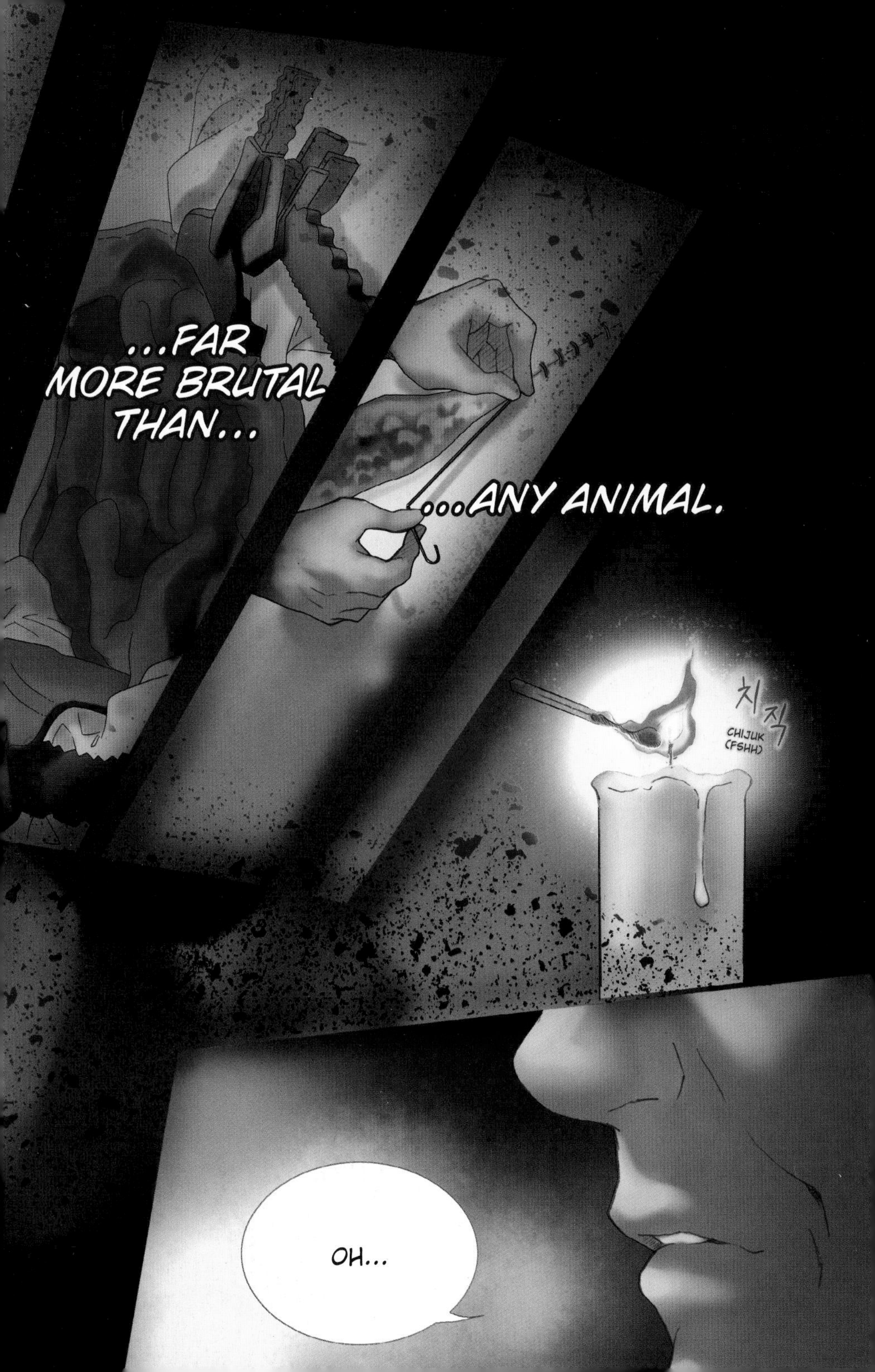
...FAR MORE BRUTAL THAN...
...ANY ANIMAL.
치직
CHIJUK (FSHH)
OH...

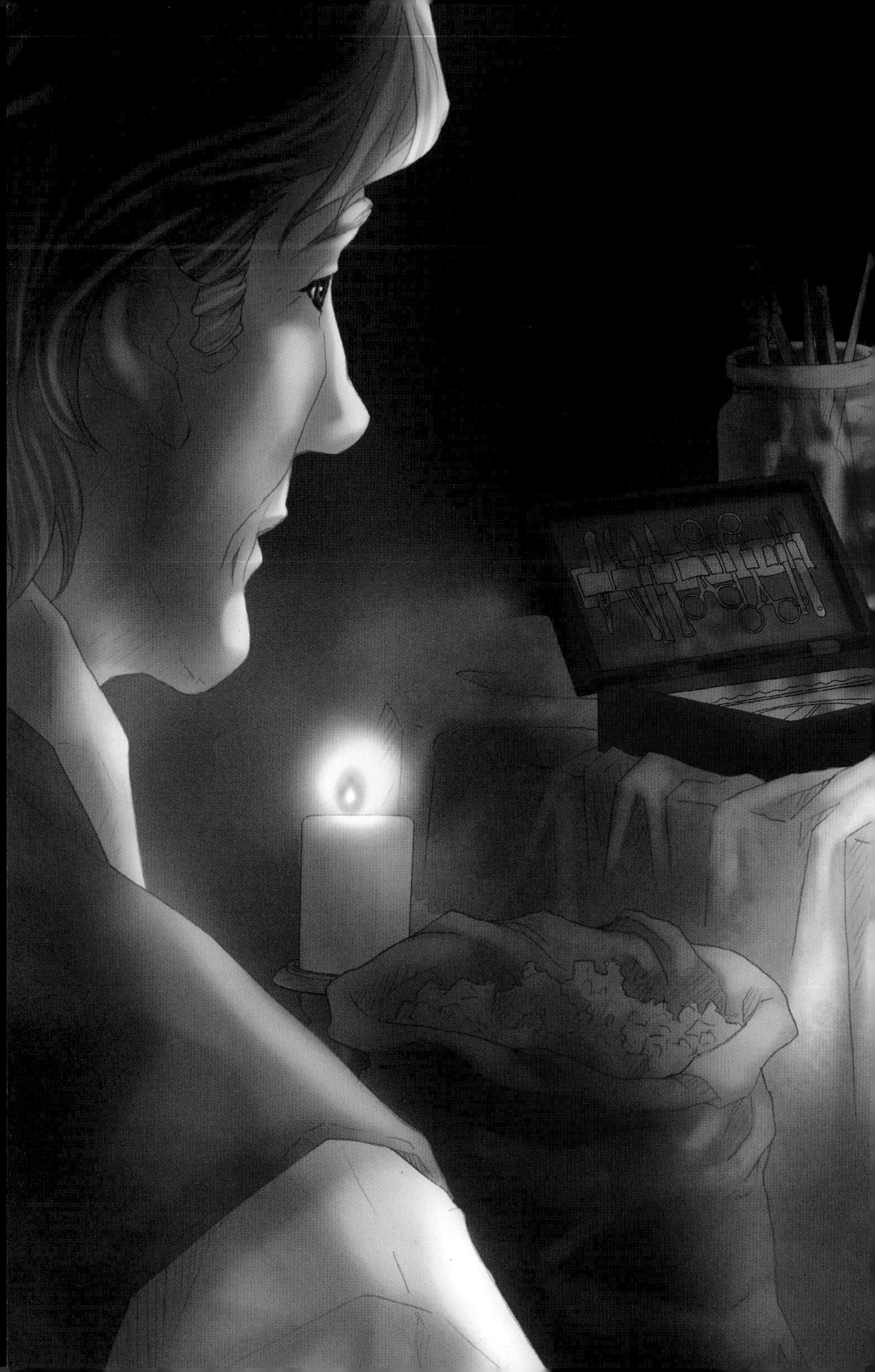

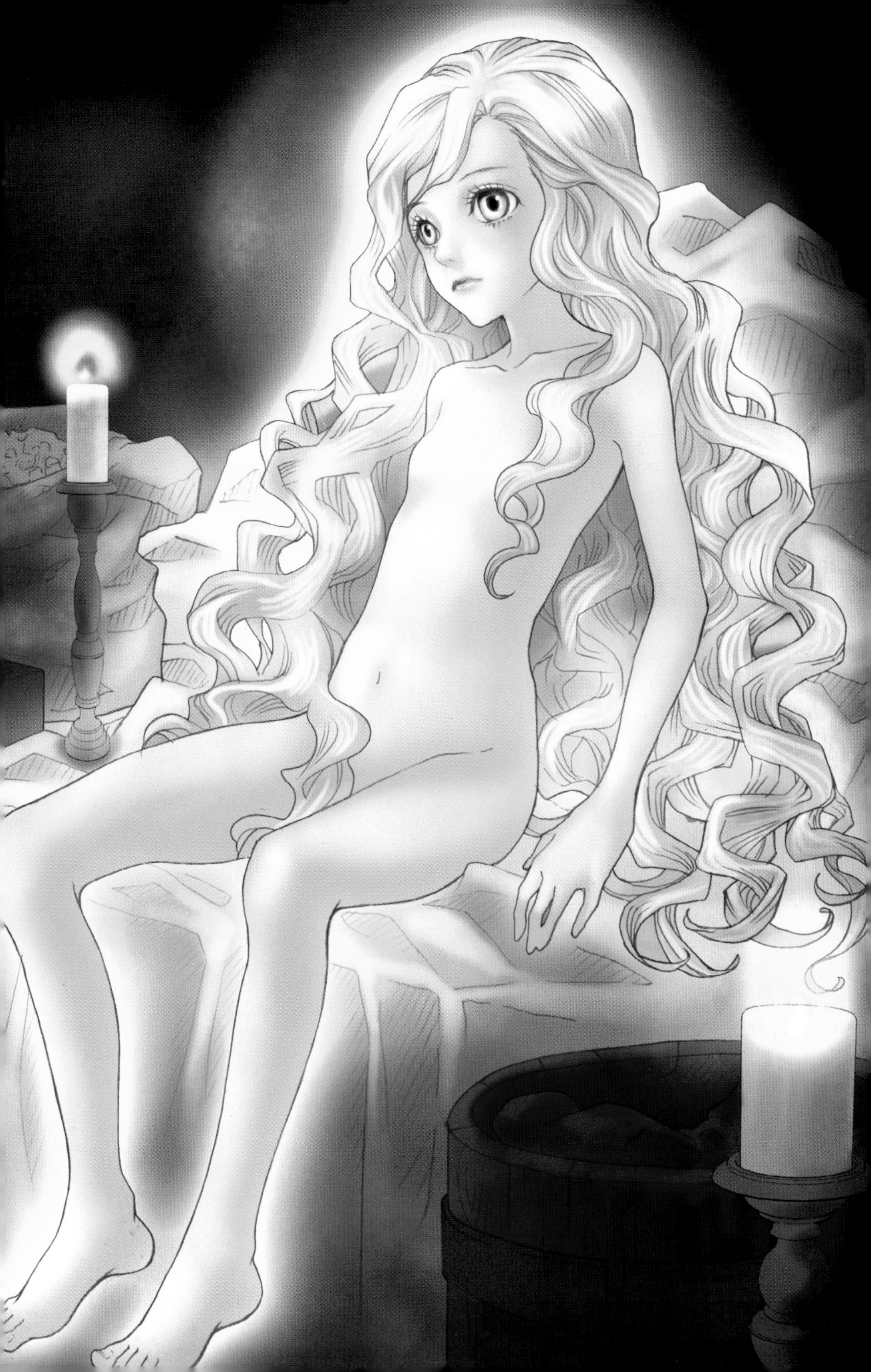

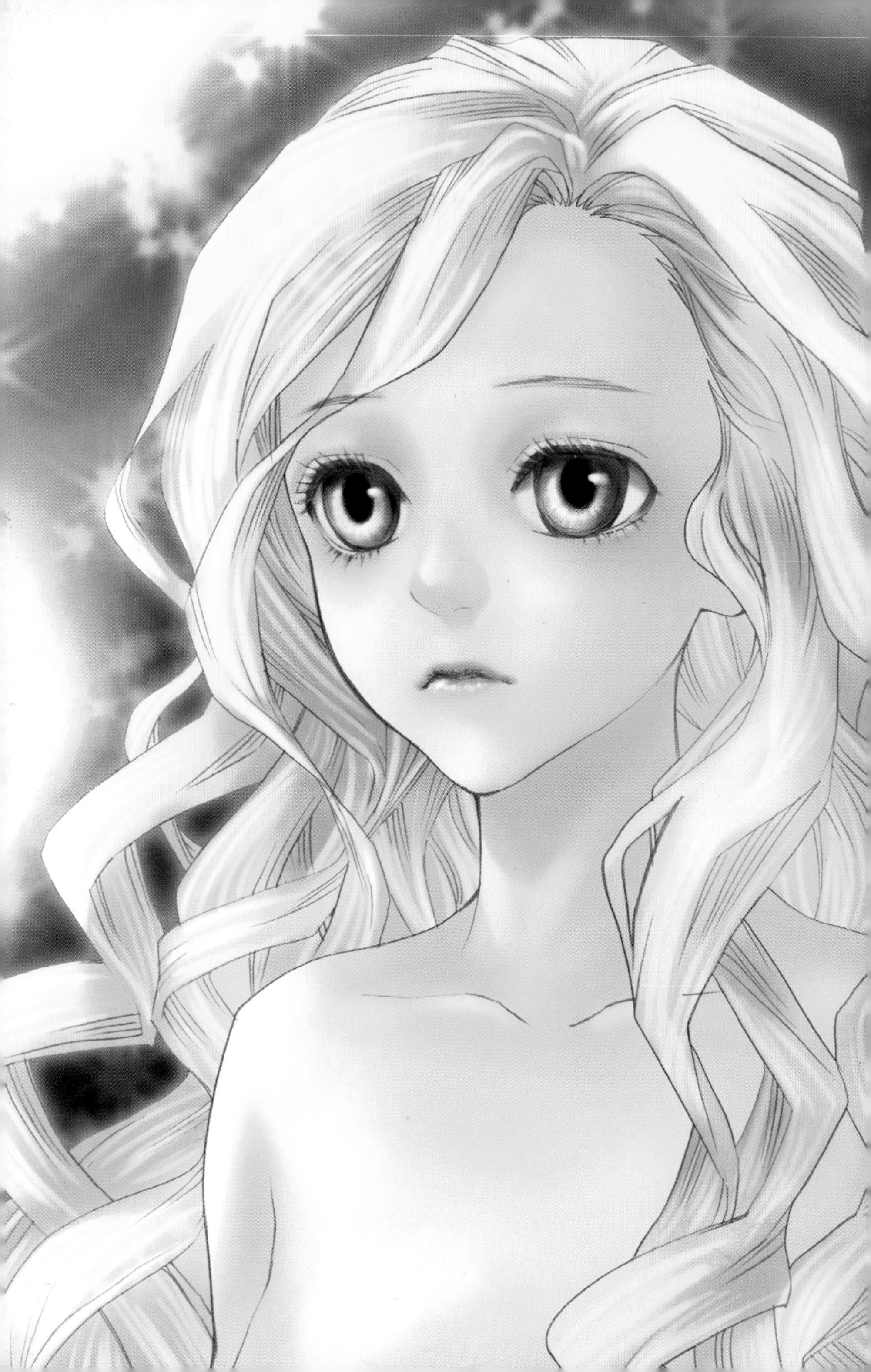

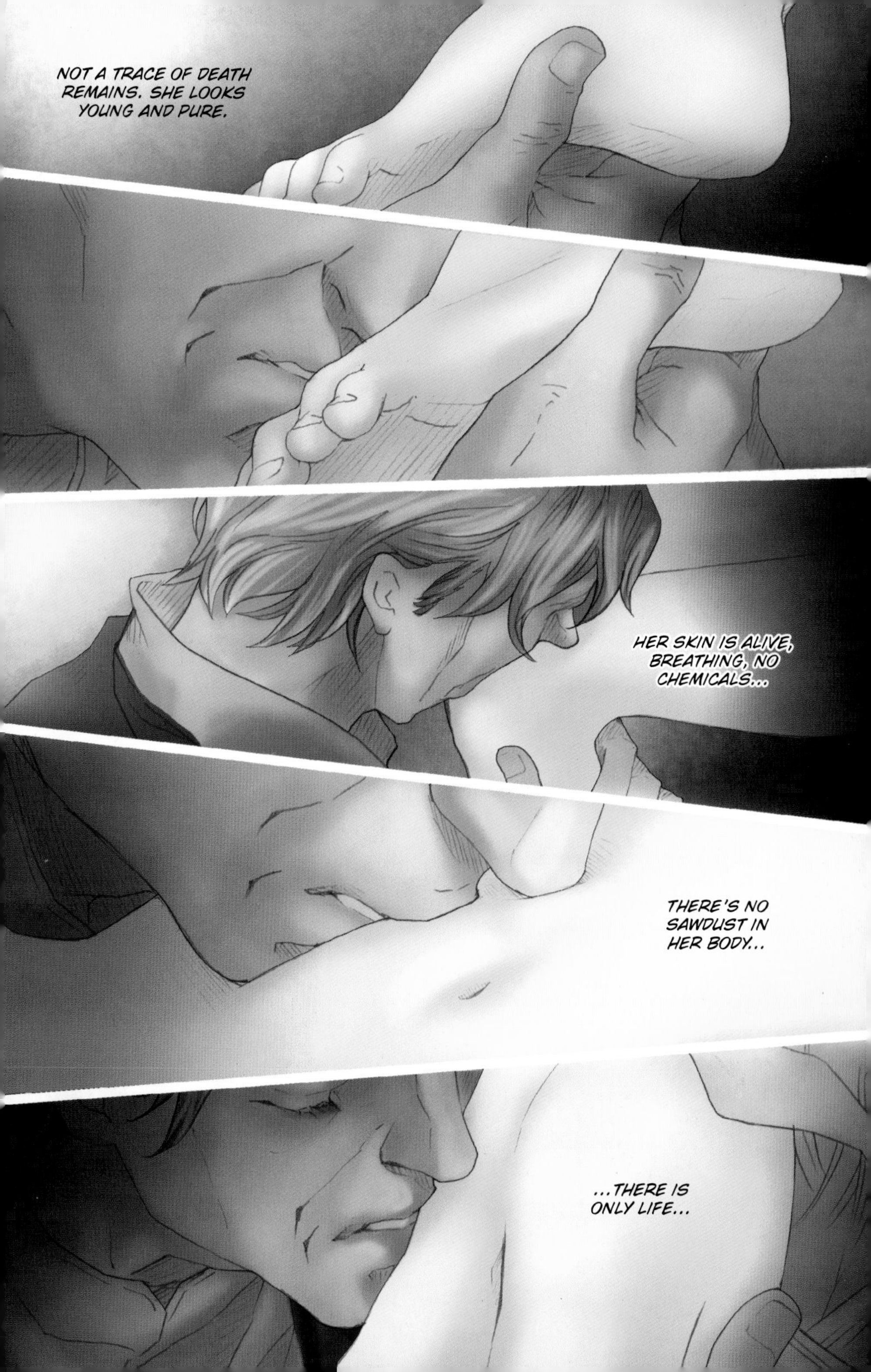
NOT A TRACE OF DEATH REMAINS. SHE LOOKS YOUNG AND PURE.
HER SKIN IS ALIVE, BREATHING, NO CHEMICALS...
THERE'S NO SAWDUST IN HER BODY...
...THERE IS ONLY LIFE...

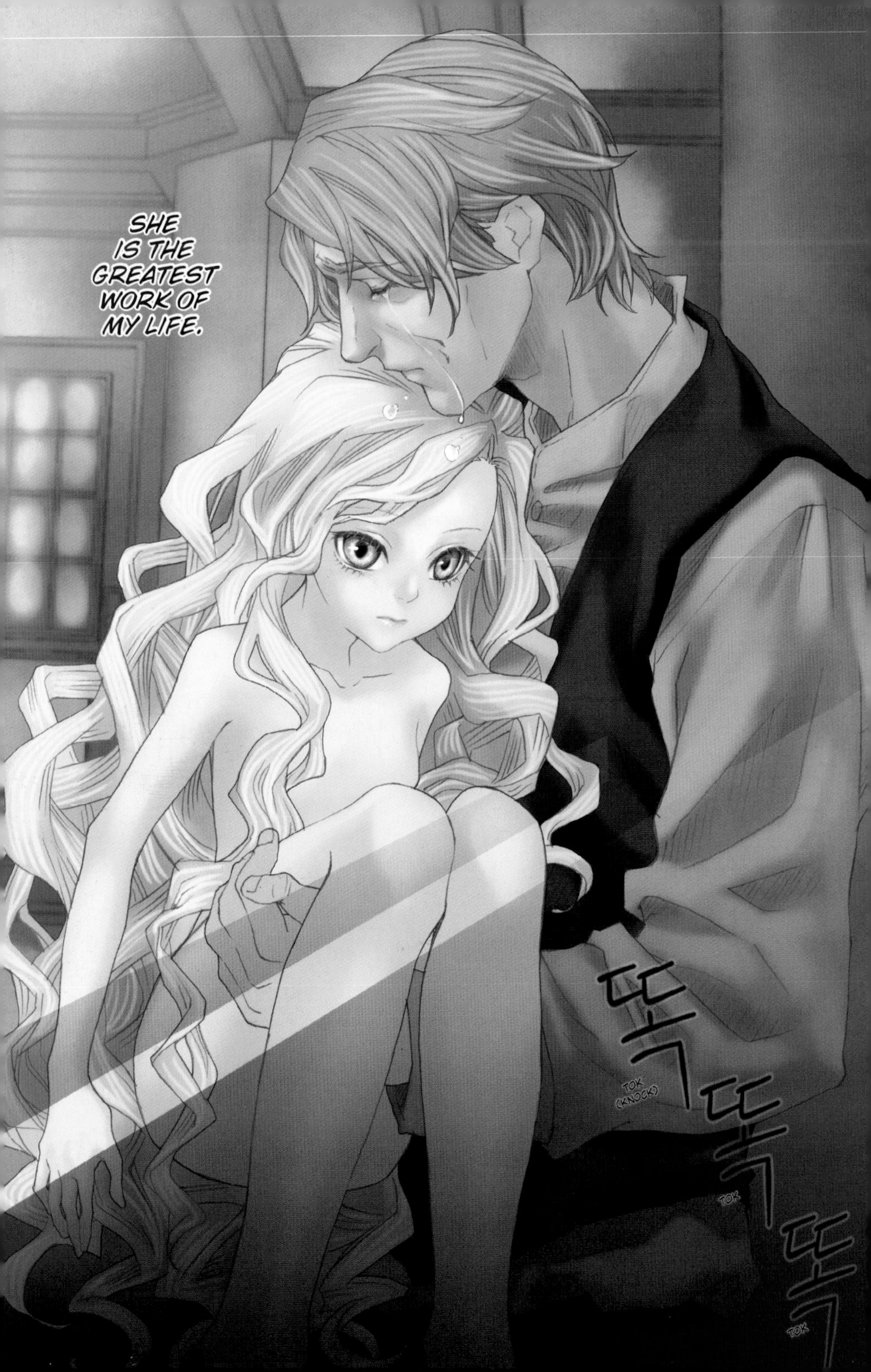
SHE IS THE GREATEST WORK OF MY LIFE.
또
TOK (KNOCK)
또
TOK
또
TOK

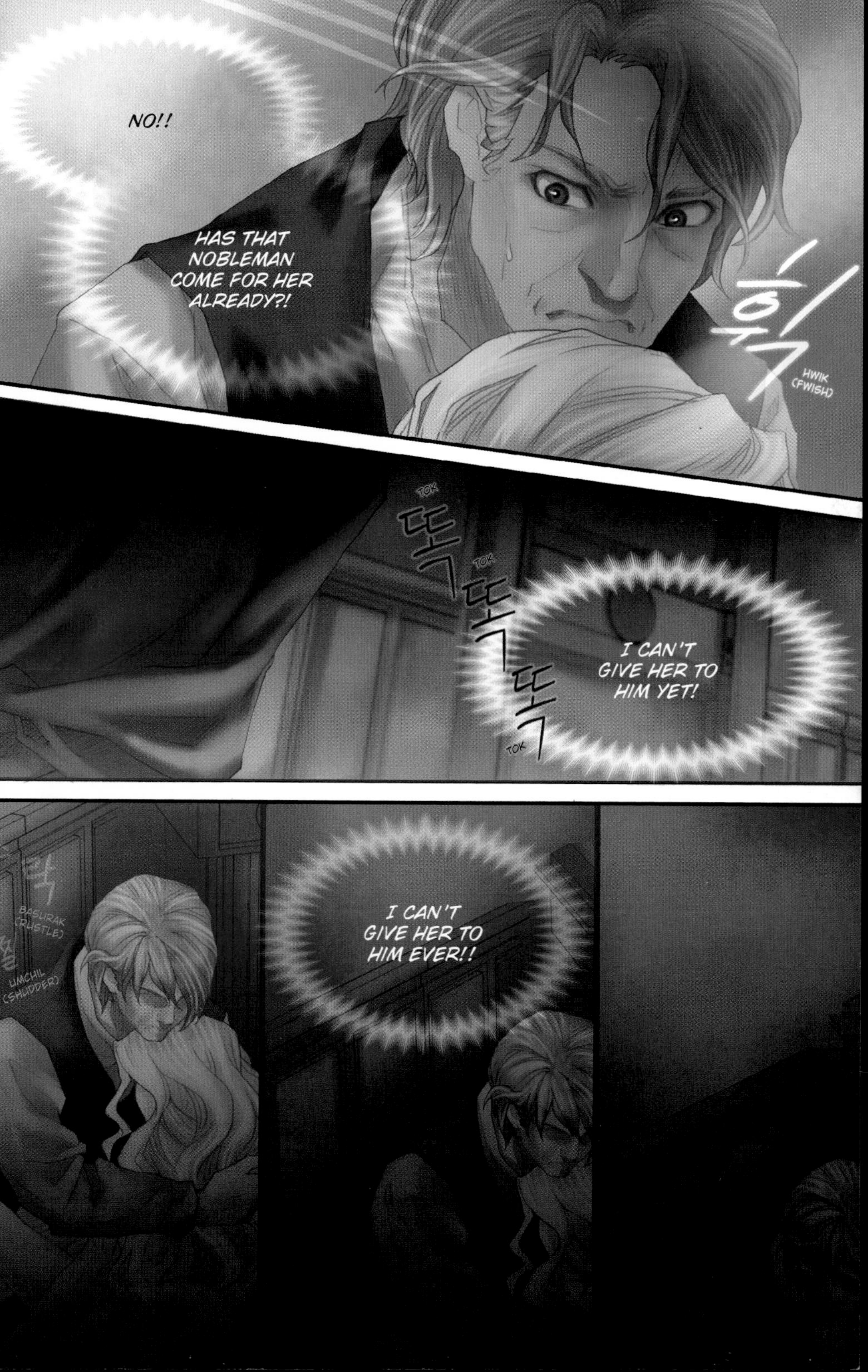
NO!!
HAS THAT NOBLEMAN COME FOR HER ALREADY?!
휙
HWIK (FWISH)
TOK
똑
TOK
똑
TOK
똑
I CAN'T GIVE HER TO HIM YET!
BASURAK (RUSTLE)
UMCHIL (SHUDDER)
I CAN'T GIVE HER TO HIM EVER!!

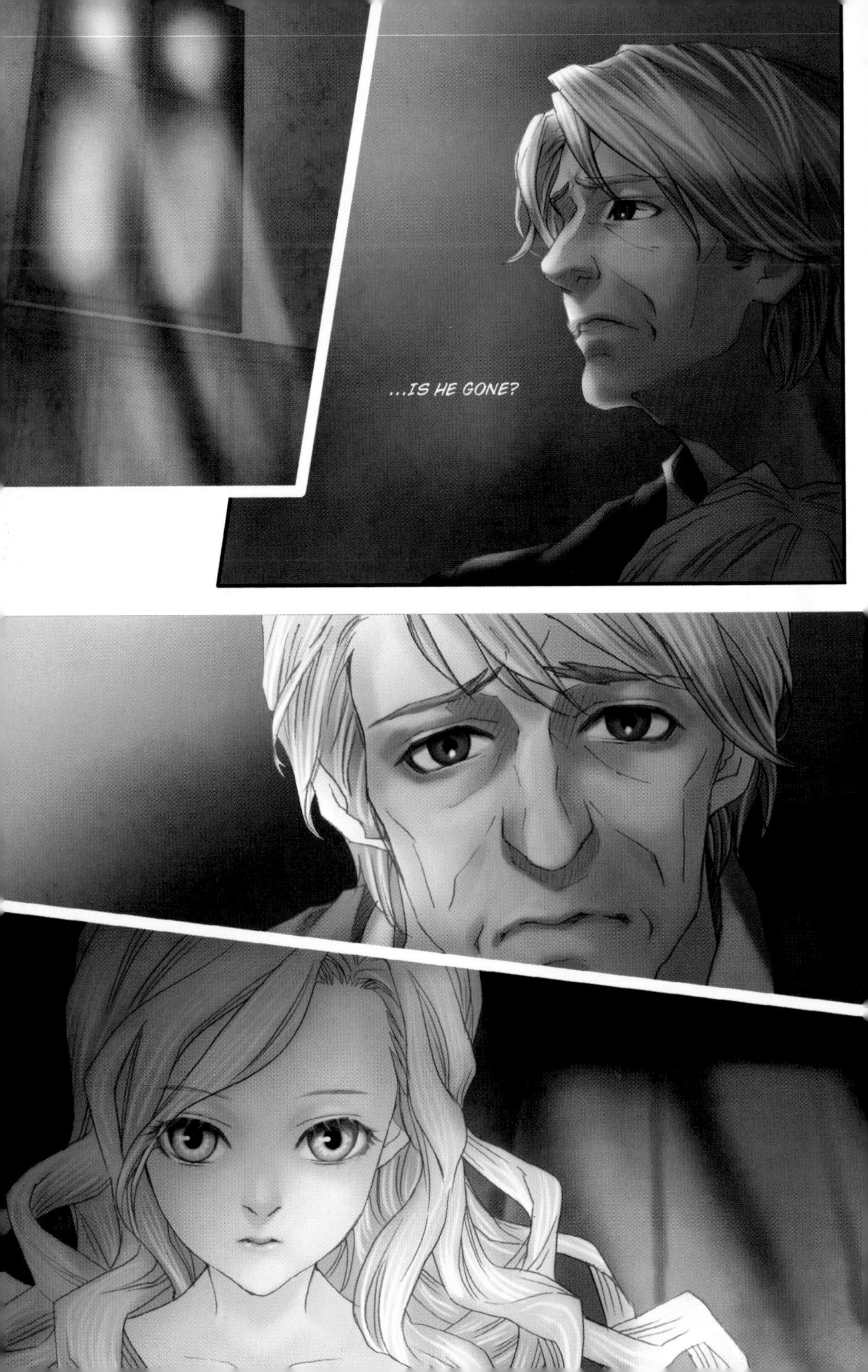
...IS HE GONE?

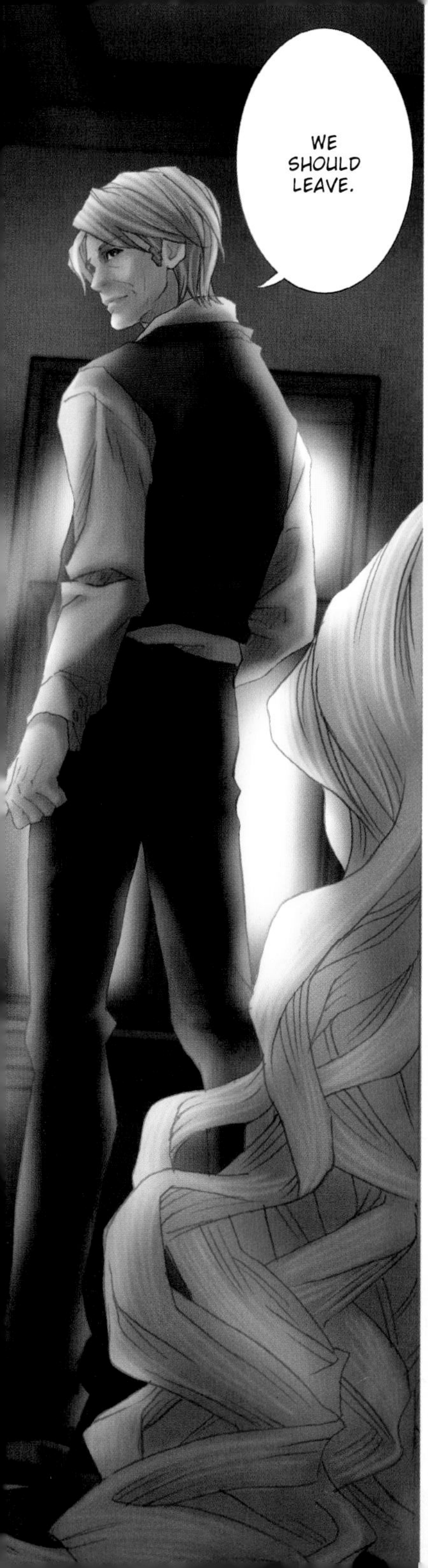
WE SHOULD LEAVE.

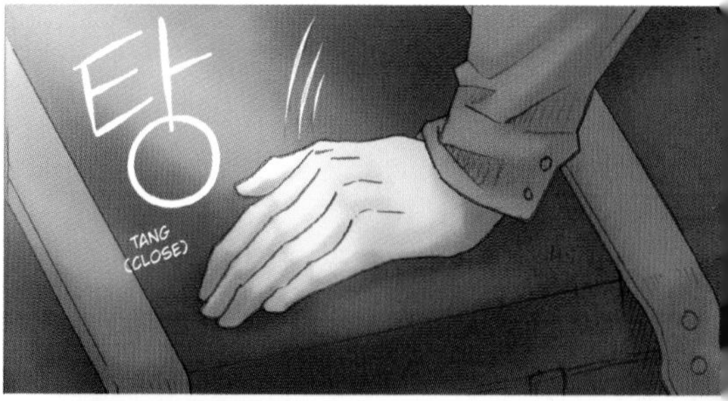
탕
TANG (CLOSE)

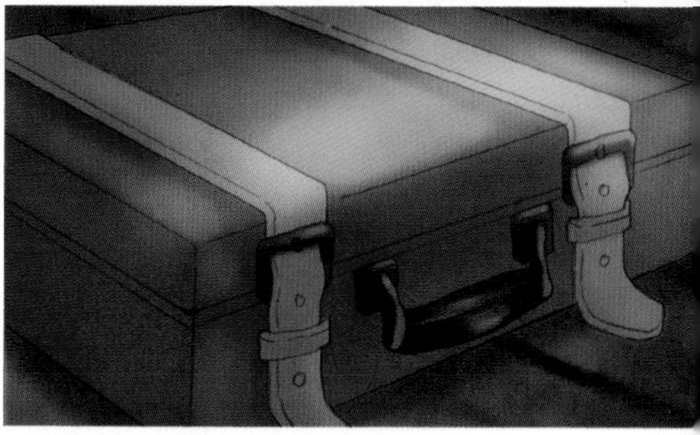

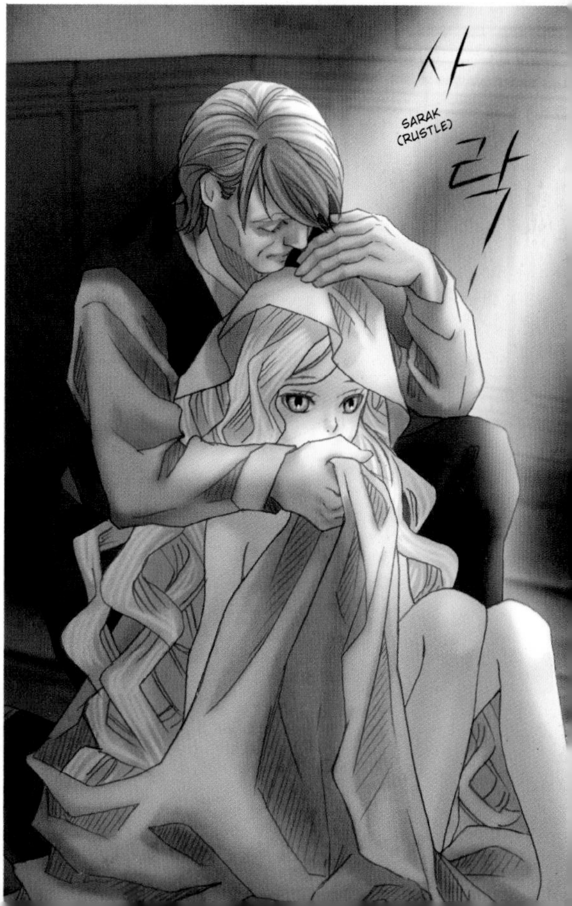
사락
SARAK (RUSTLE)

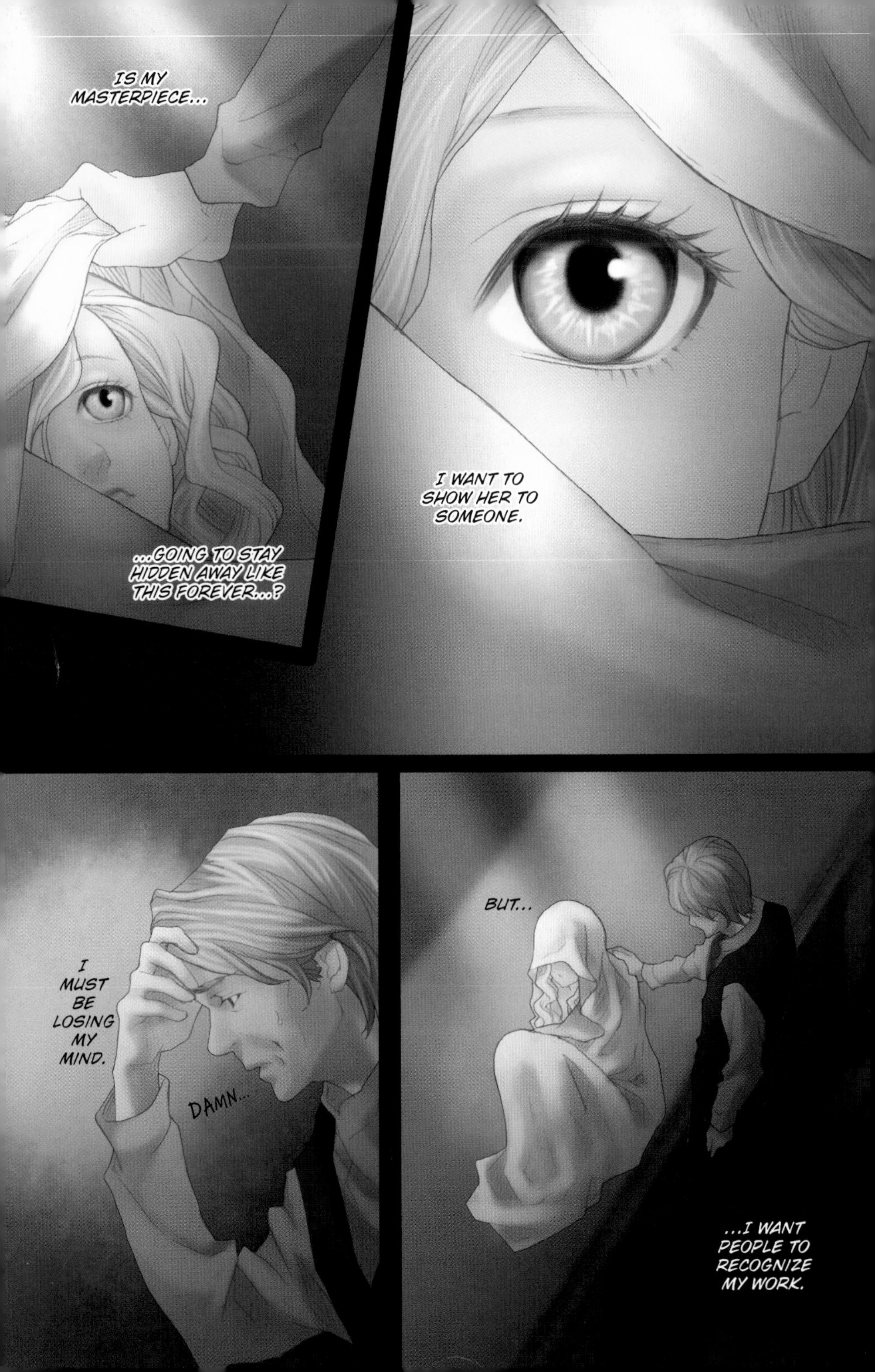
I WANT TO SHOW HER TO SOMEONE.
IS MY MASTERPIECE...
...GOING TO STAY HIDDEN AWAY LIKE THIS FOREVER...?
BUT...
...I WANT PEOPLE TO RECOGNIZE MY WORK.
I MUST BE LOSING MY MIND.
DAMN...

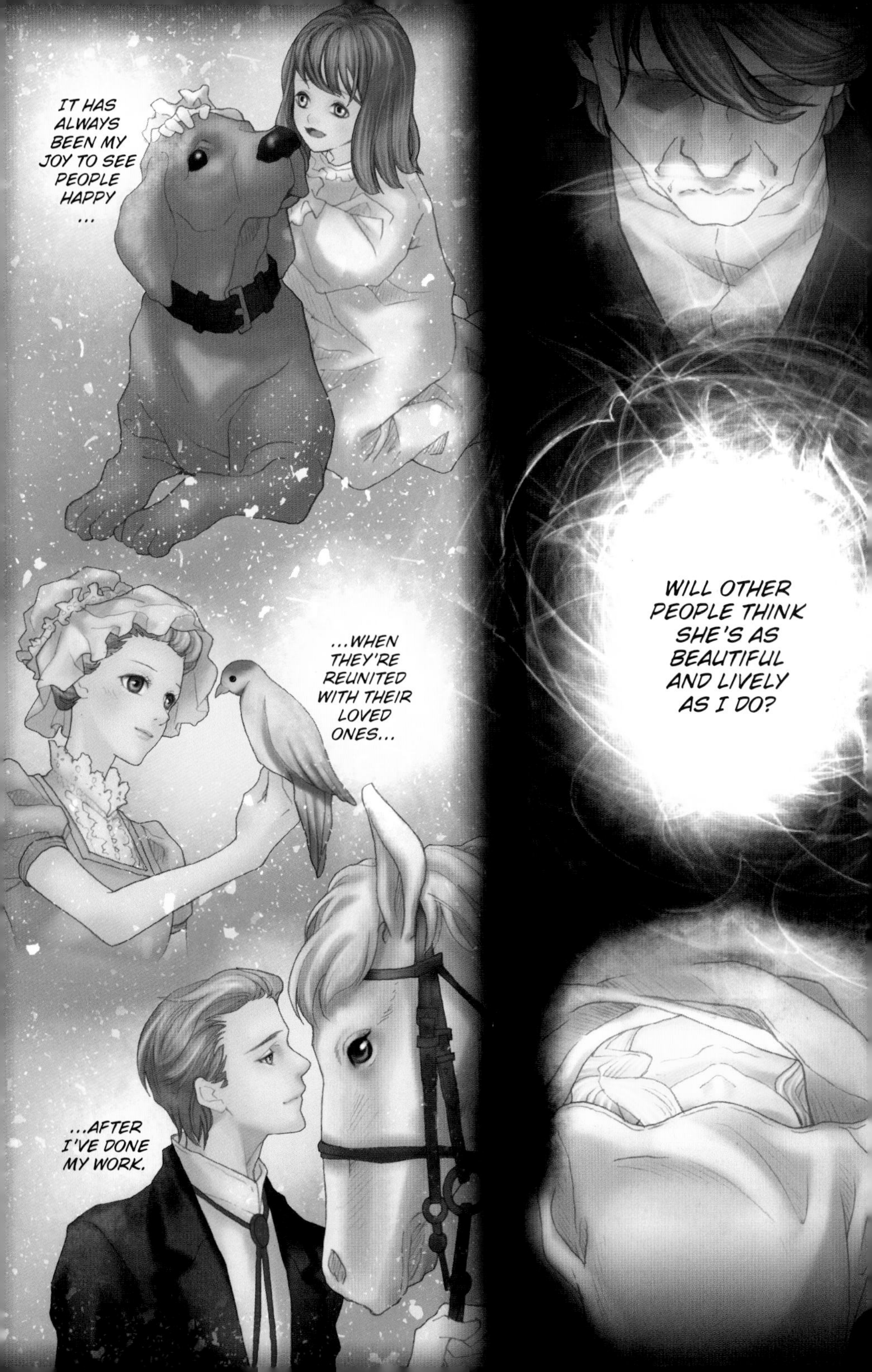
WILL OTHER PEOPLE THINK SHE'S AS BEAUTIFUL AND LIVELY AS I DO?
IT HAS ALWAYS BEEN MY JOY TO SEE PEOPLE HAPPY ...
...WHEN THEY'RE REUNITED WITH THEIR LOVED ONES...
...AFTER I'VE DONE MY WORK.

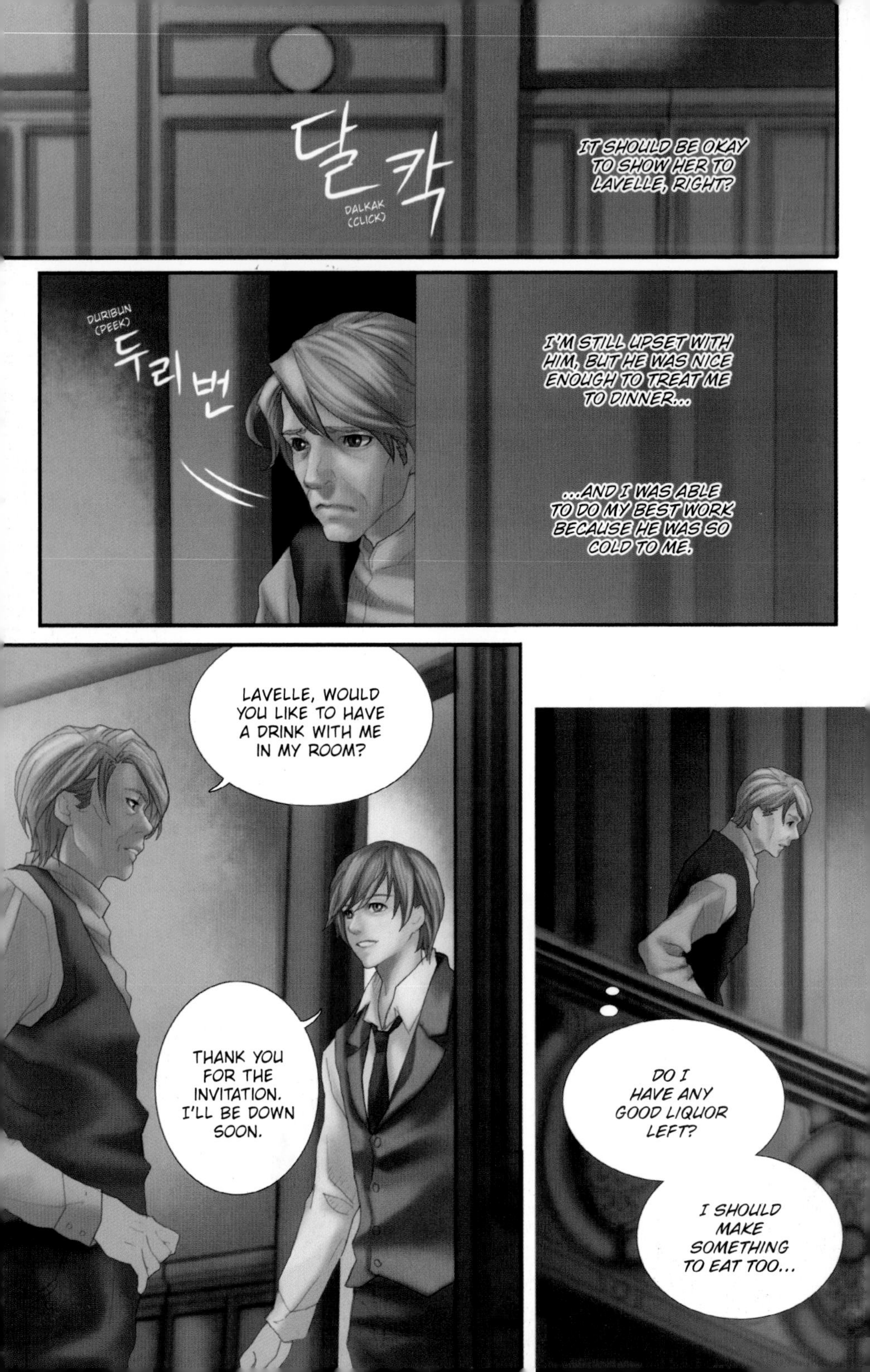
달칵
DALKAK (CLICK)
IT SHOULD BE OKAY TO SHOW HER TO LAVELLE, RIGHT?
DURIBUN (PEEK)
두리번
I'M STILL UPSET WITH HIM, BUT HE WAS NICE ENOUGH TO TREAT ME TO DINNER...
...AND I WAS ABLE TO DO MY BEST WORK BECAUSE HE WAS SO COLD TO ME.
LAVELLE, WOULD YOU LIKE TO HAVE A DRINK WITH ME IN MY ROOM?
THANK YOU FOR THE INVITATION. I'LL BE DOWN SOON.
DO I HAVE ANY GOOD LIQUOR LEFT?
I SHOULD MAKE SOMETHING TO EAT TOO...

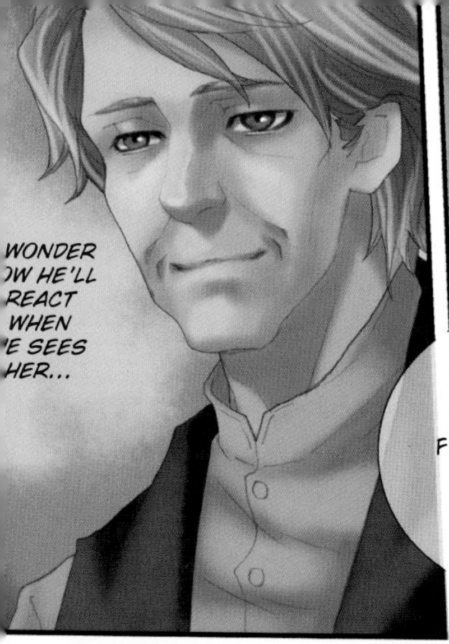
WONDER OW HE'LL REACT WHEN E SEES HER...

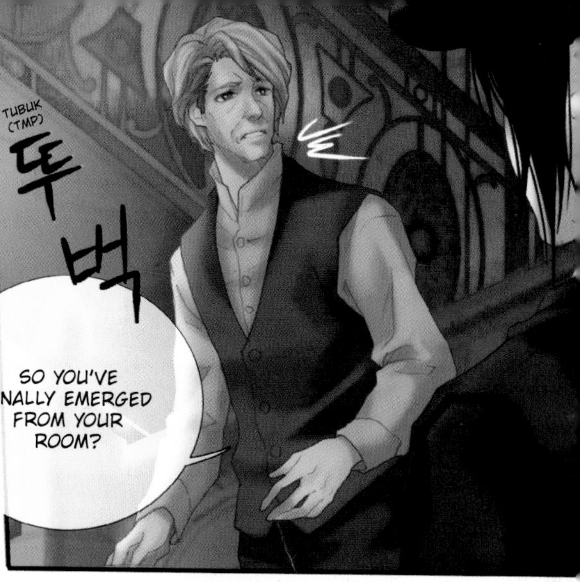
TUBUK (TMP)
뚜벅
SO YOU'VE FINALLY EMERGED FROM YOUR ROOM?

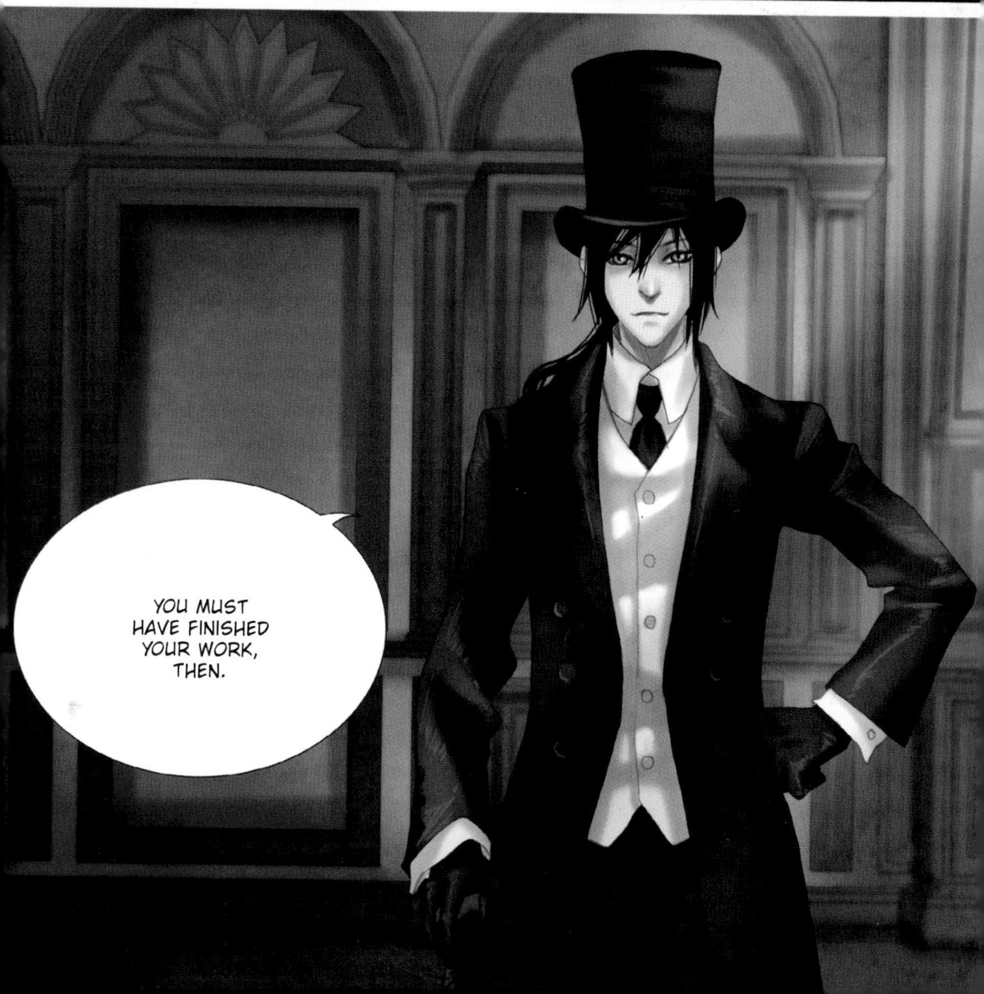
YOU MUST HAVE FINISHED YOUR WORK, THEN.

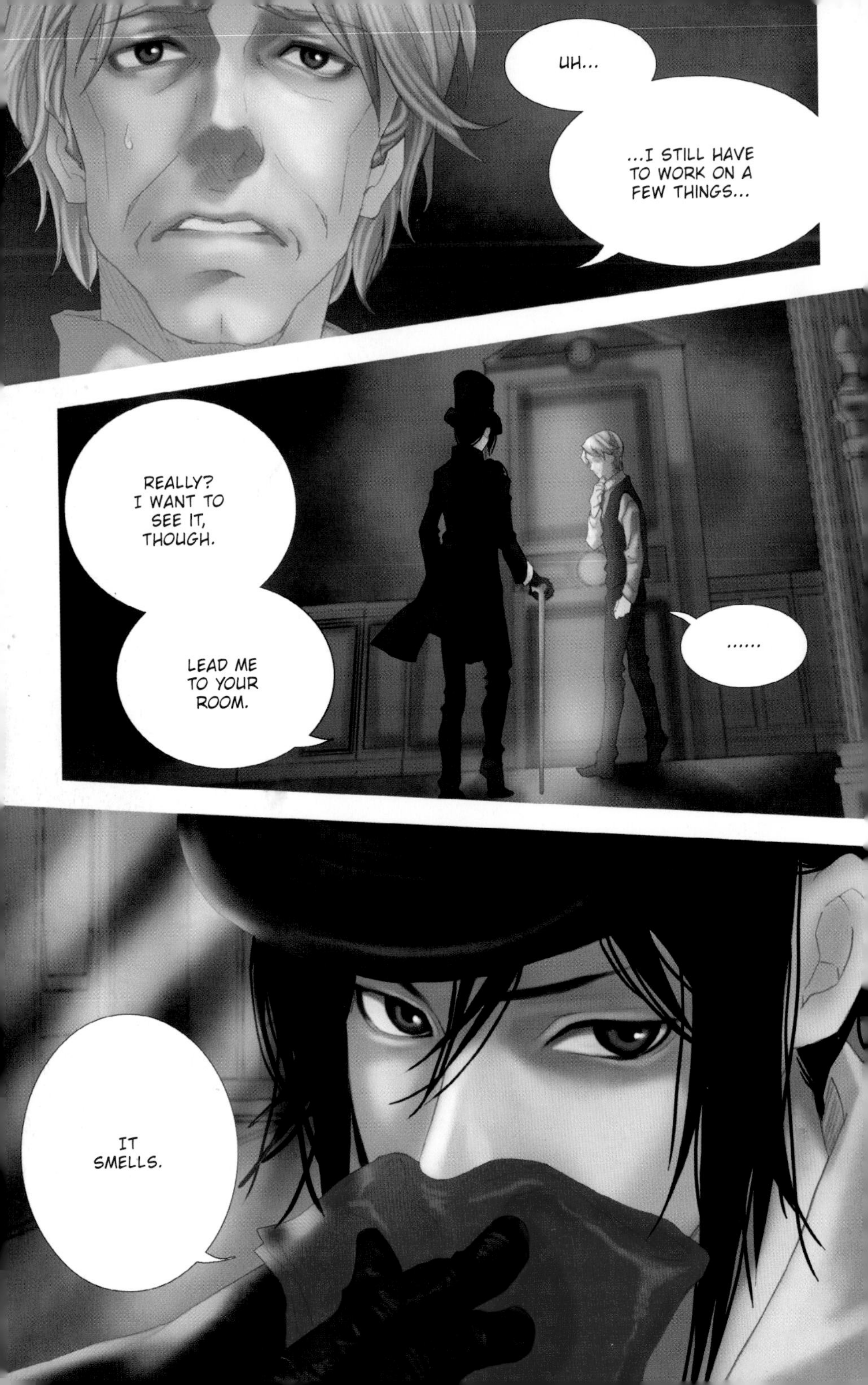
UH...
...I STILL HAVE TO WORK ON A FEW THINGS...
REALLY? I WANT TO SEE IT, THOUGH.
LEAD ME TO YOUR ROOM.
......
IT SMELLS.

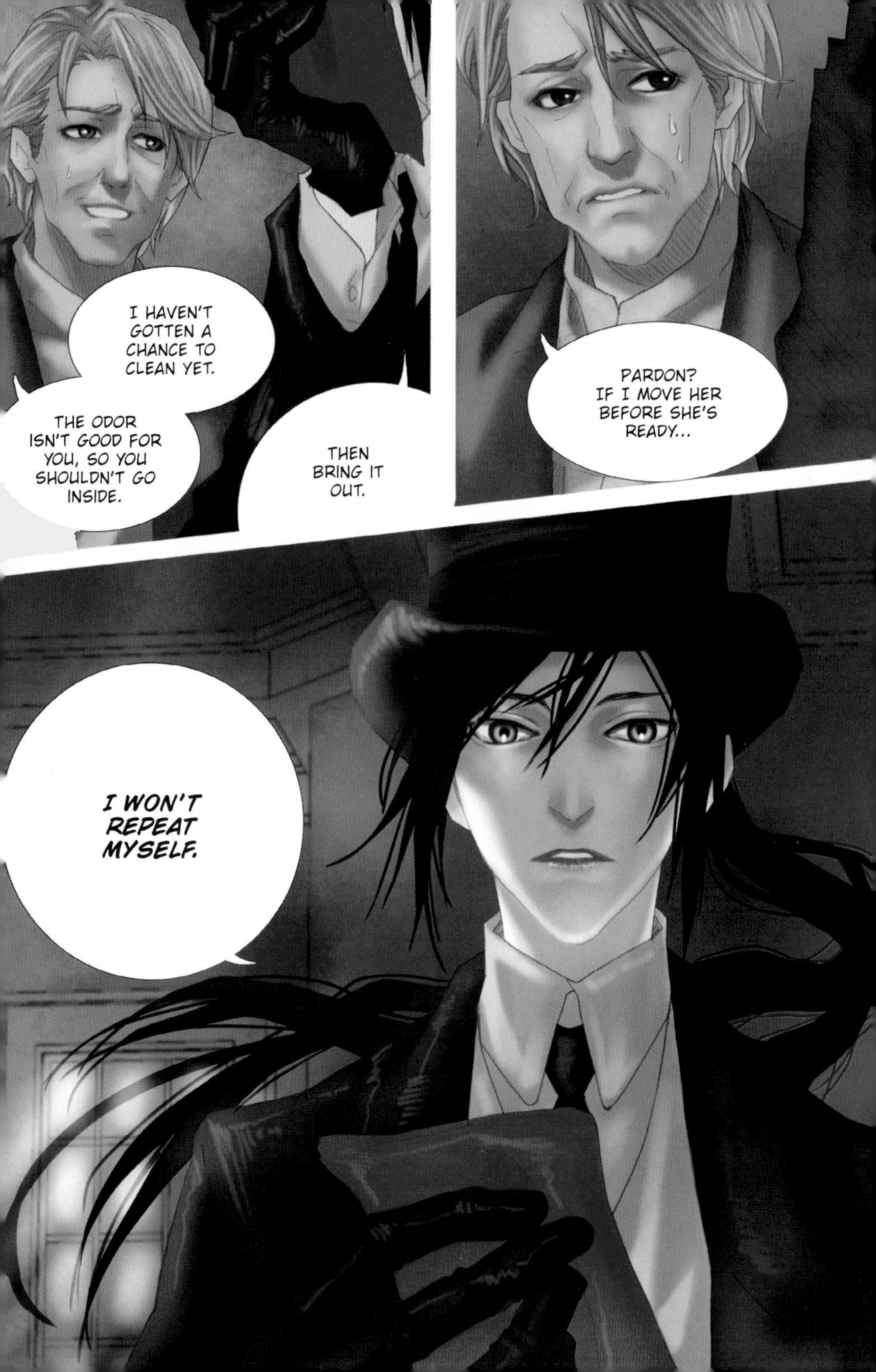
I HAVEN'T GOTTEN A CHANCE TO CLEAN YET.
THE ODOR ISN'T GOOD FOR YOU, SO YOU SHOULDN'T GO INSIDE.
THEN BRING IT OUT.
PARDON? IF I MOVE HER BEFORE SHE'S READY...
I WON'T REPEAT MYSELF.

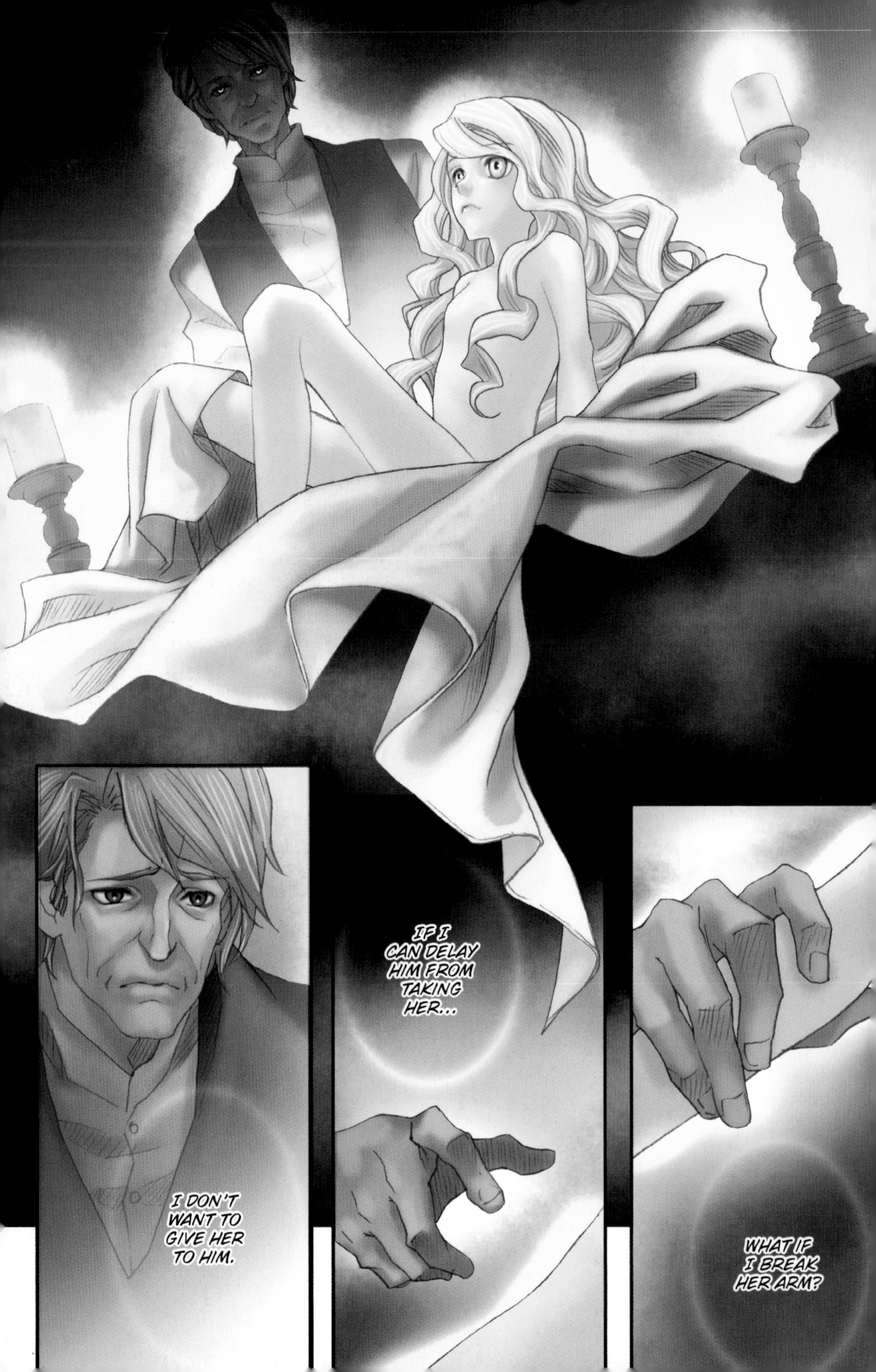
I DON'T WANT TO GIVE HER TO HIM.
IF I CAN DELAY HIM FROM TAKING HER...
WHAT IF I BREAK HER ARM?

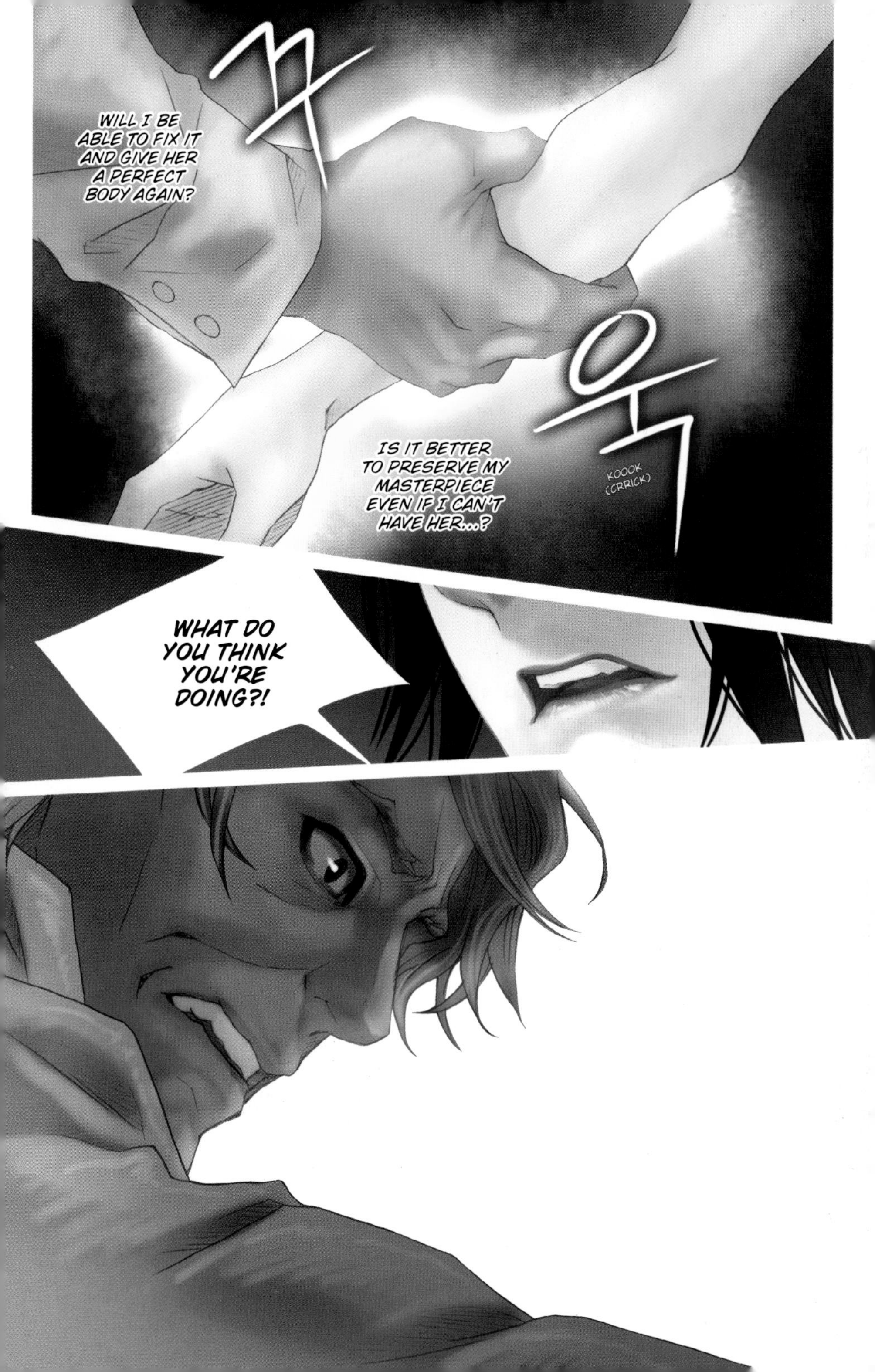
WILL I BE ABLE TO FIX IT AND GIVE HER A PERFECT BODY AGAIN?
IS IT BETTER TO PRESERVE MY MASTERPIECE EVEN IF I CAN'T HAVE HER...?
KOOOK (CRRICK)
WHAT DO YOU THINK YOU'RE DOING?!

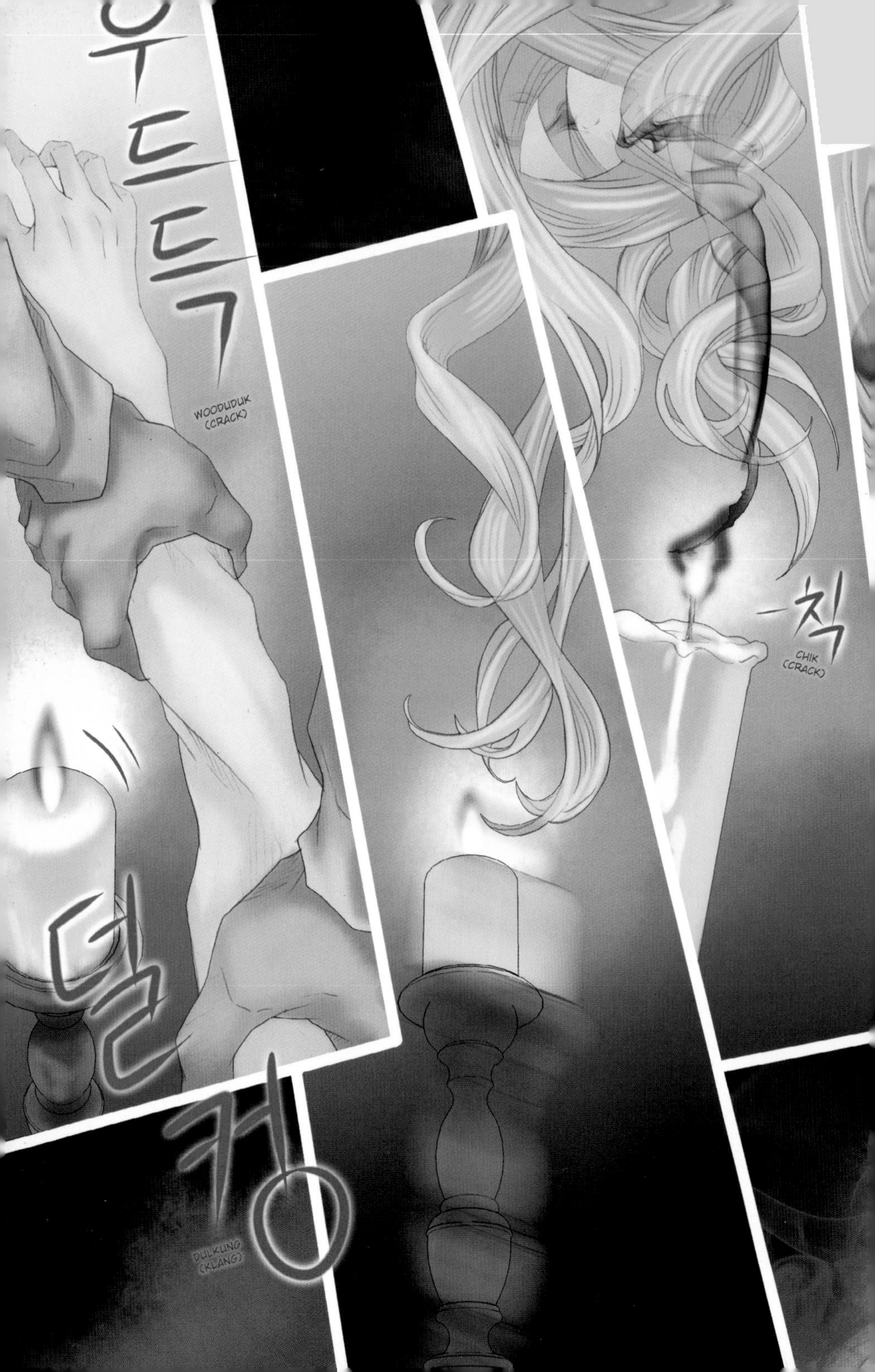
우드드득
WOODUDUK (CRACK)
덜컹
DULKUNG (KLANG)
칙
CHIK (CRACK)

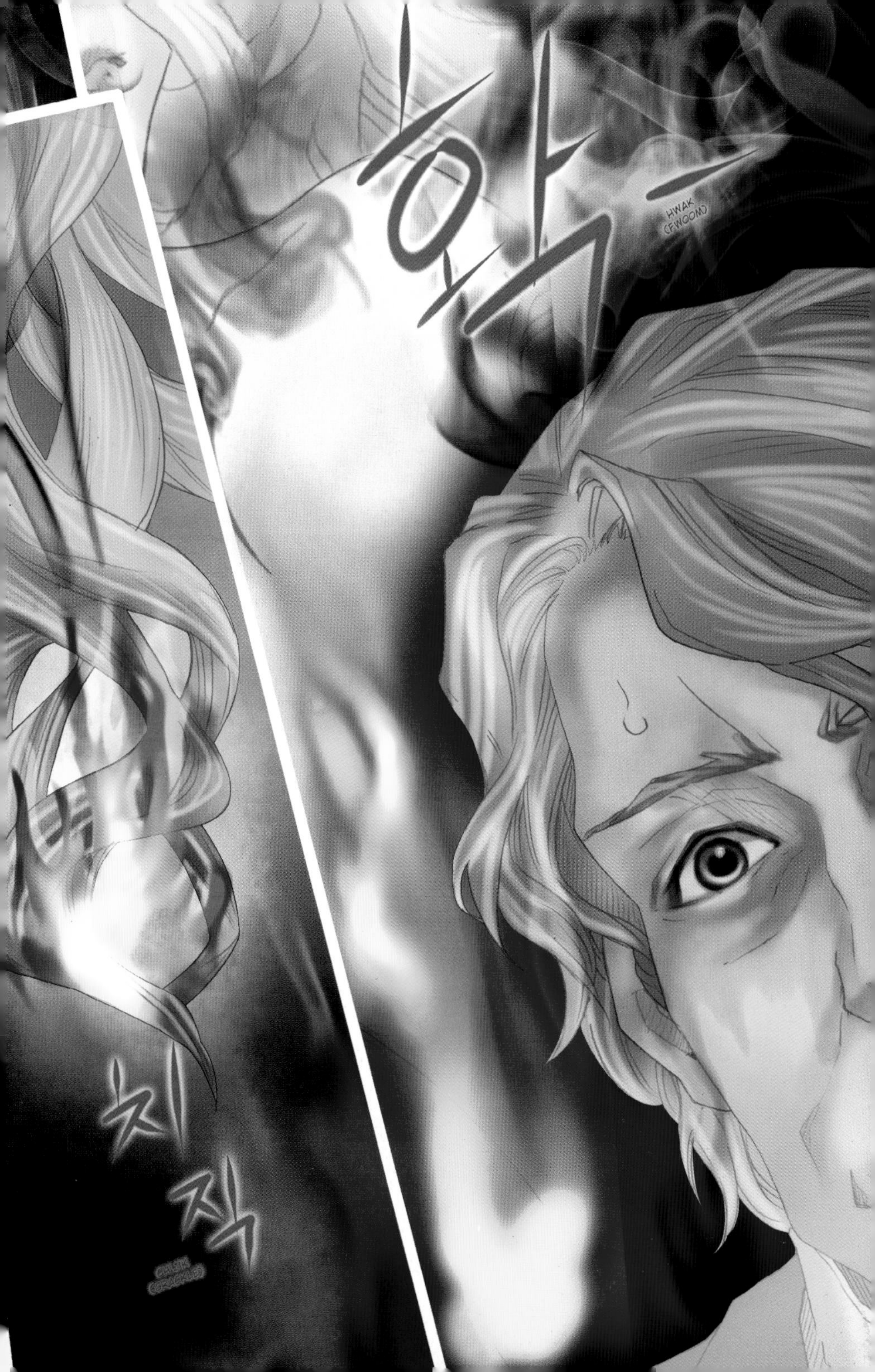
화악
HWAK (FWOOM)
치직
CHIJIK (CRACKLE)

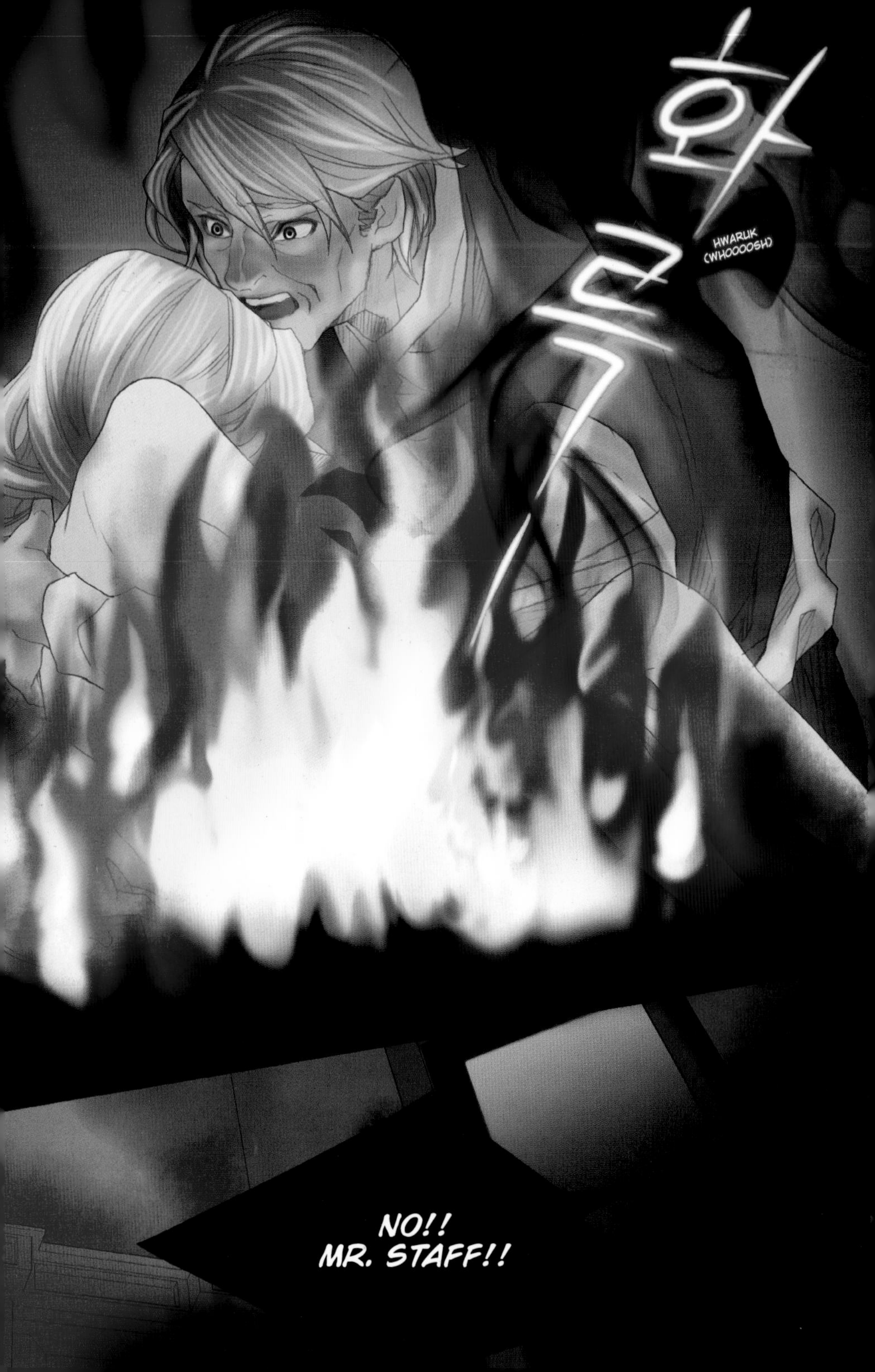
화르륵
HWARUK
(WHOOOOSH)
NO!!
MR. STAFF!!

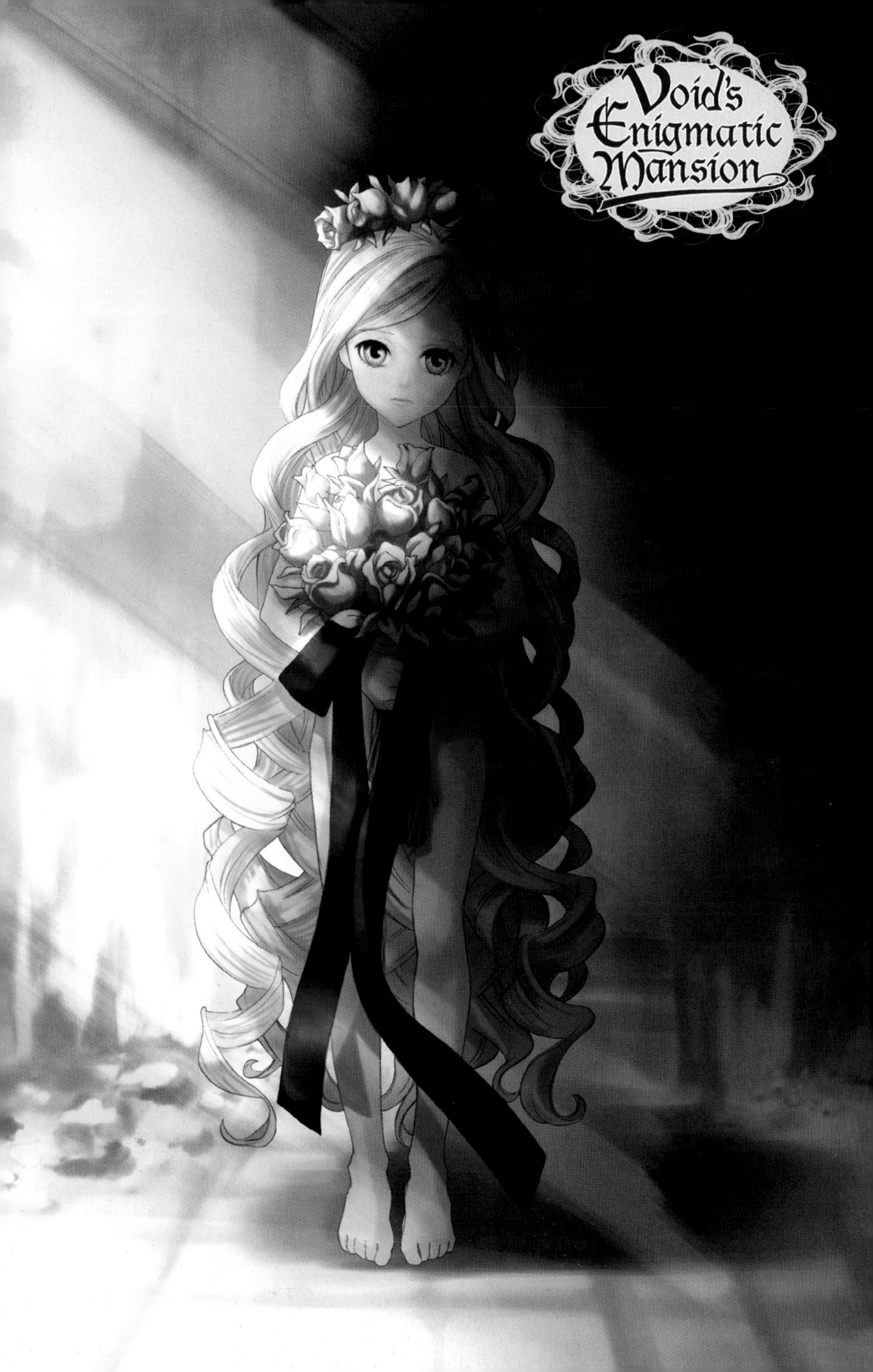
Void's Enigmatic Mansion

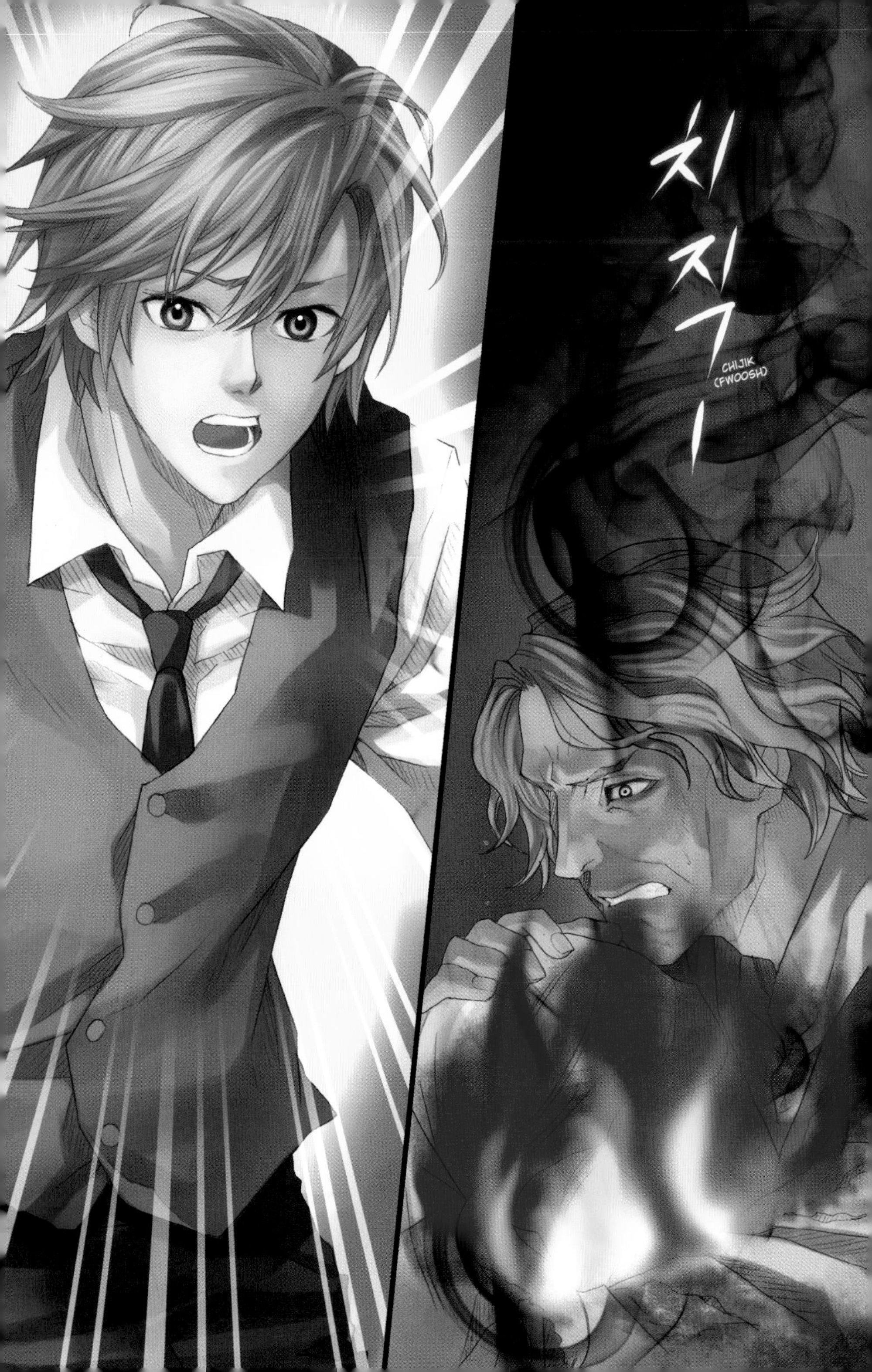
치지직ー
CHIJIK
(FWOOSH)

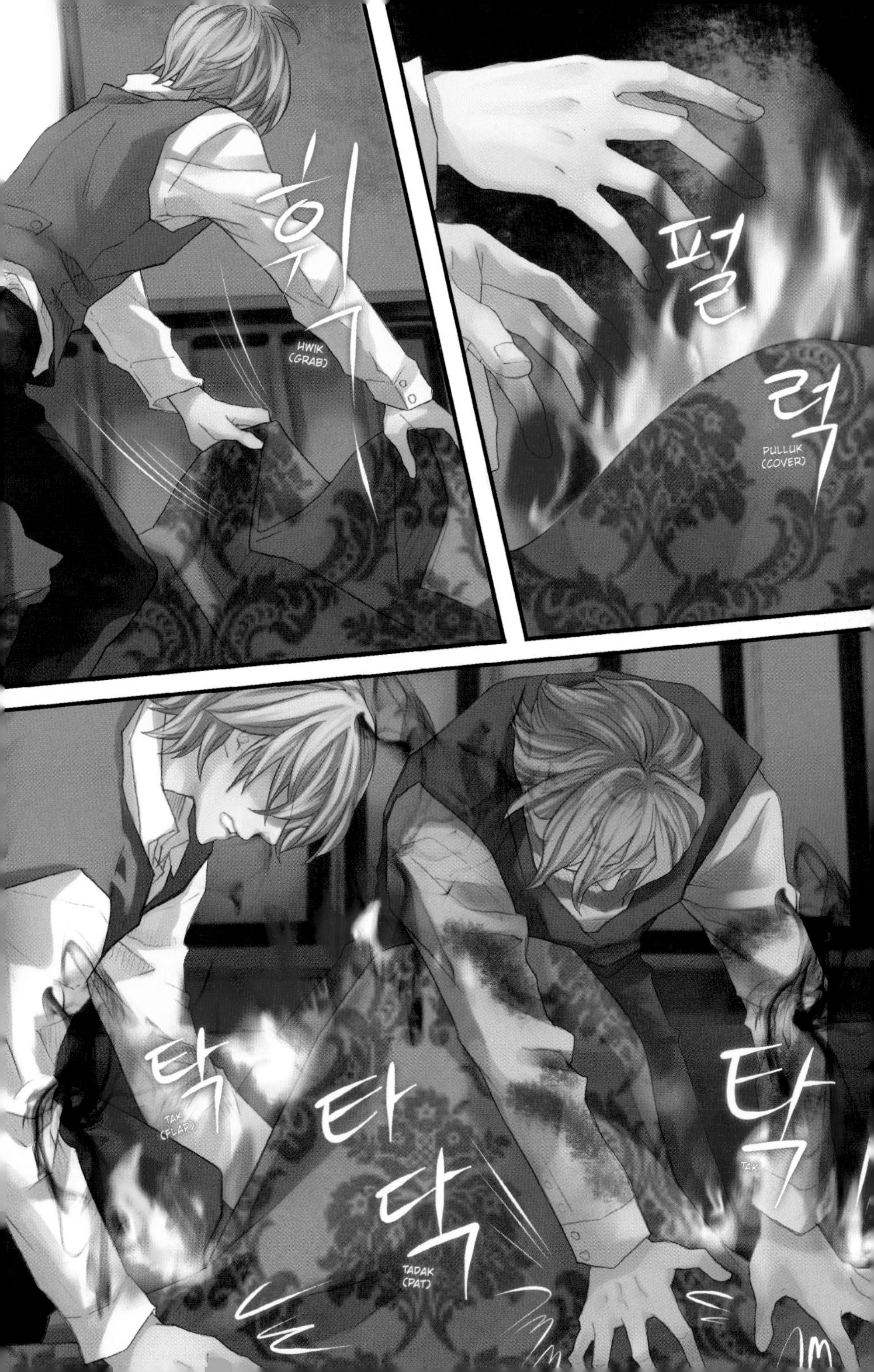
휙
HWIK (GRAB)
펄럭
PULLUK (COVER)
탁
TAK (FLAP)
타닥
TADAK (PAT)
탁
TAK

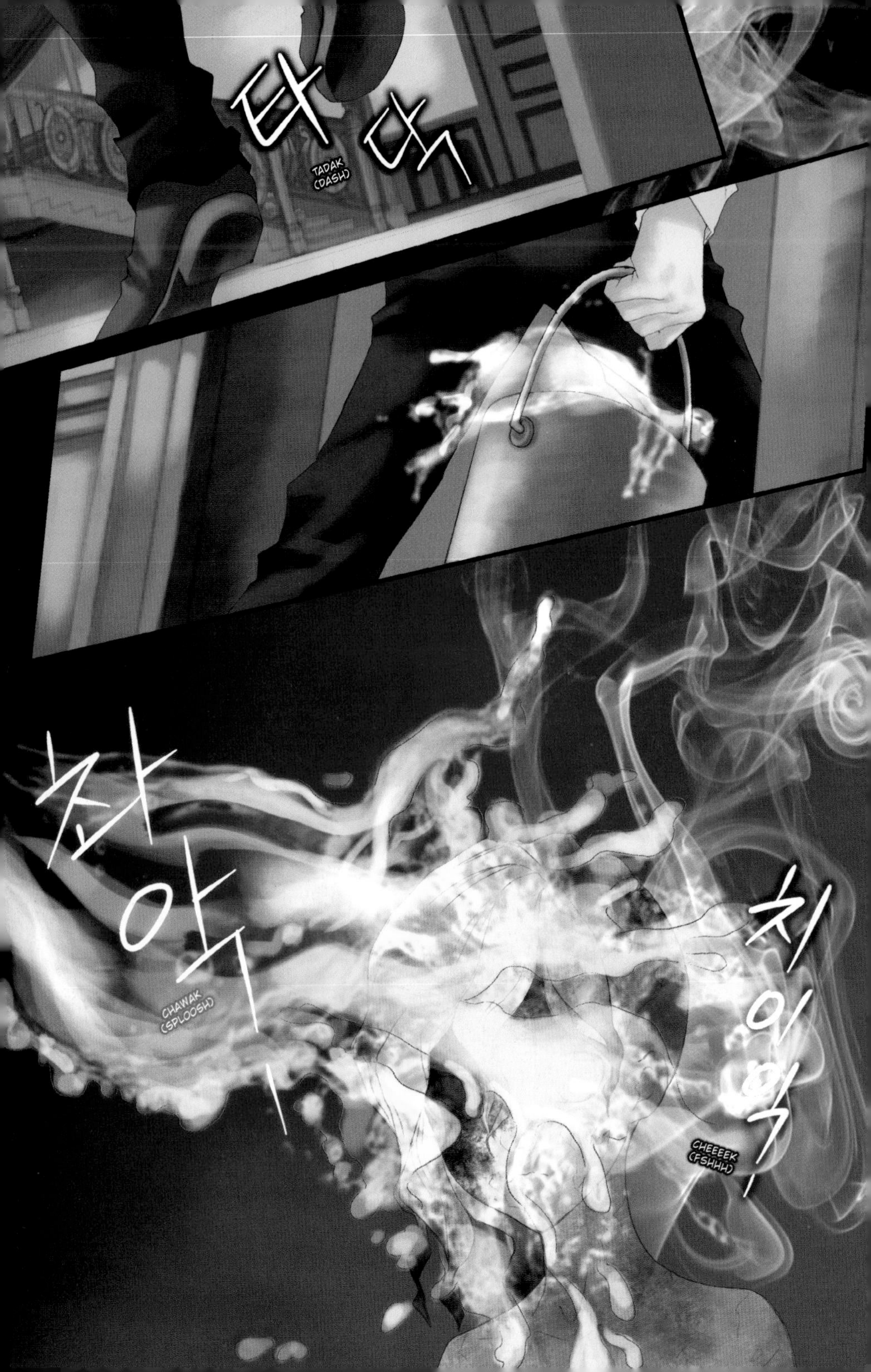

타닥
TADAK (DASH)
촤악
CHAWAK (SPLOOSH)
치이익
CHEEEEK (FSHHH)

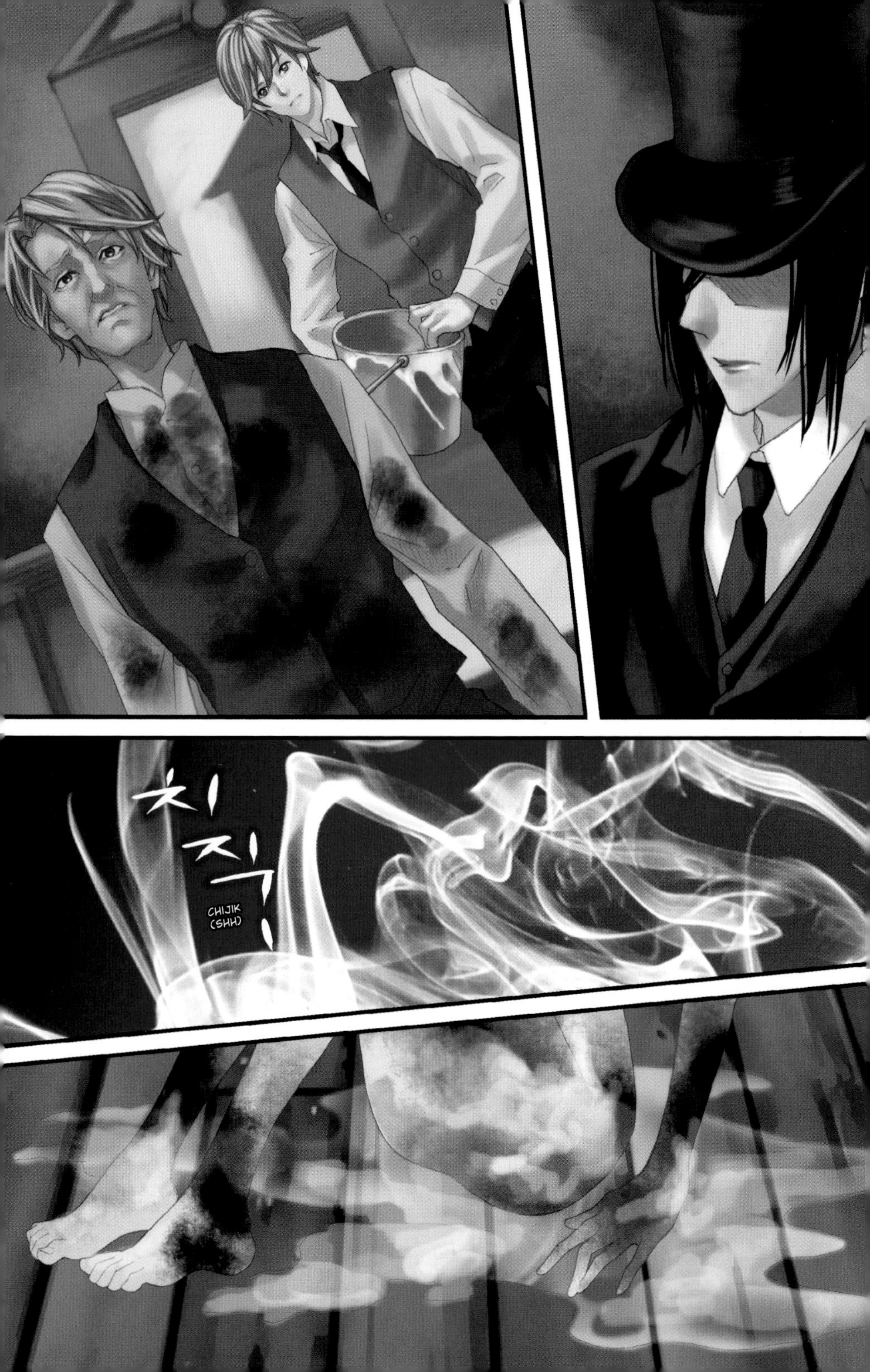
CHIJIK
(SHH)

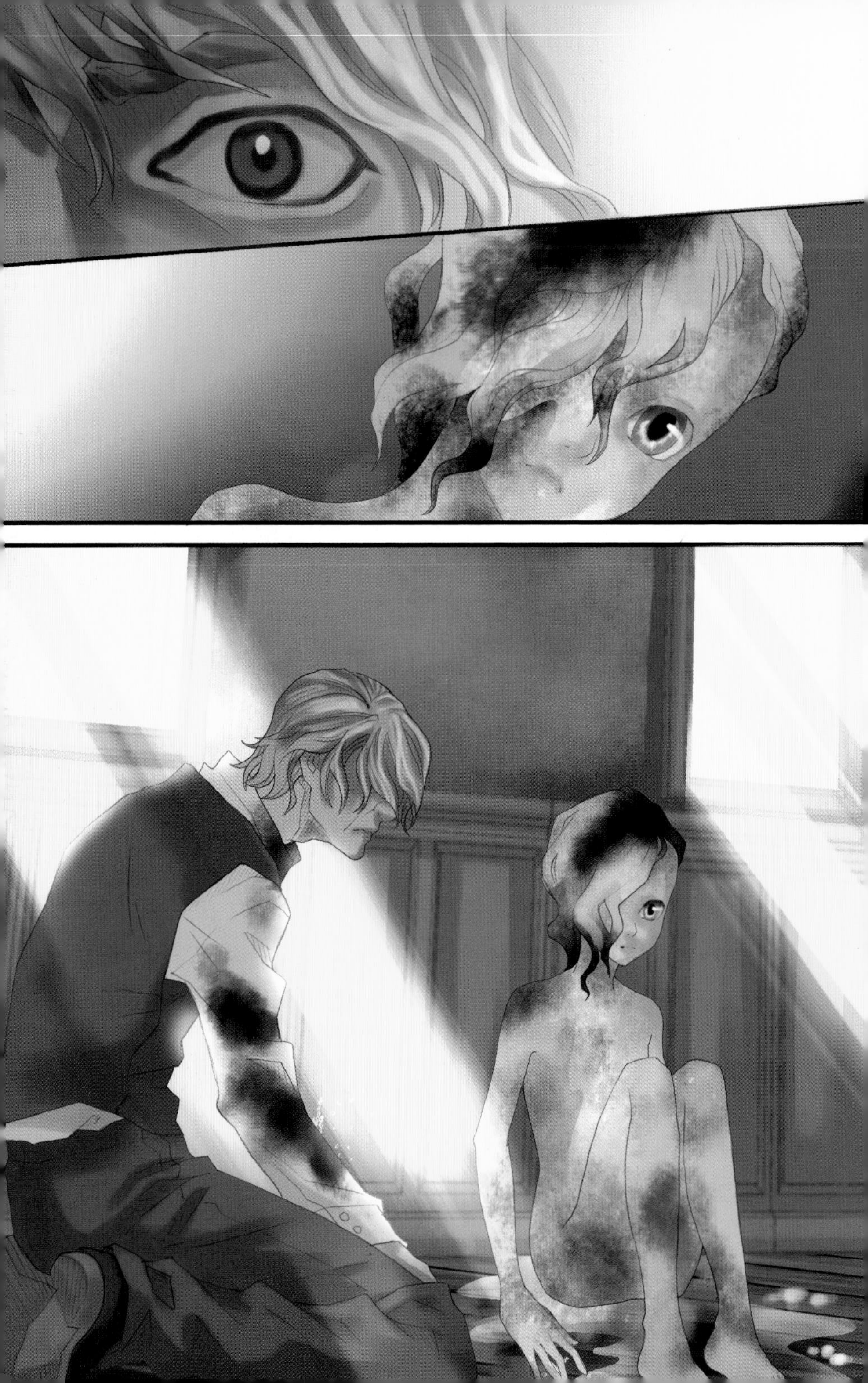

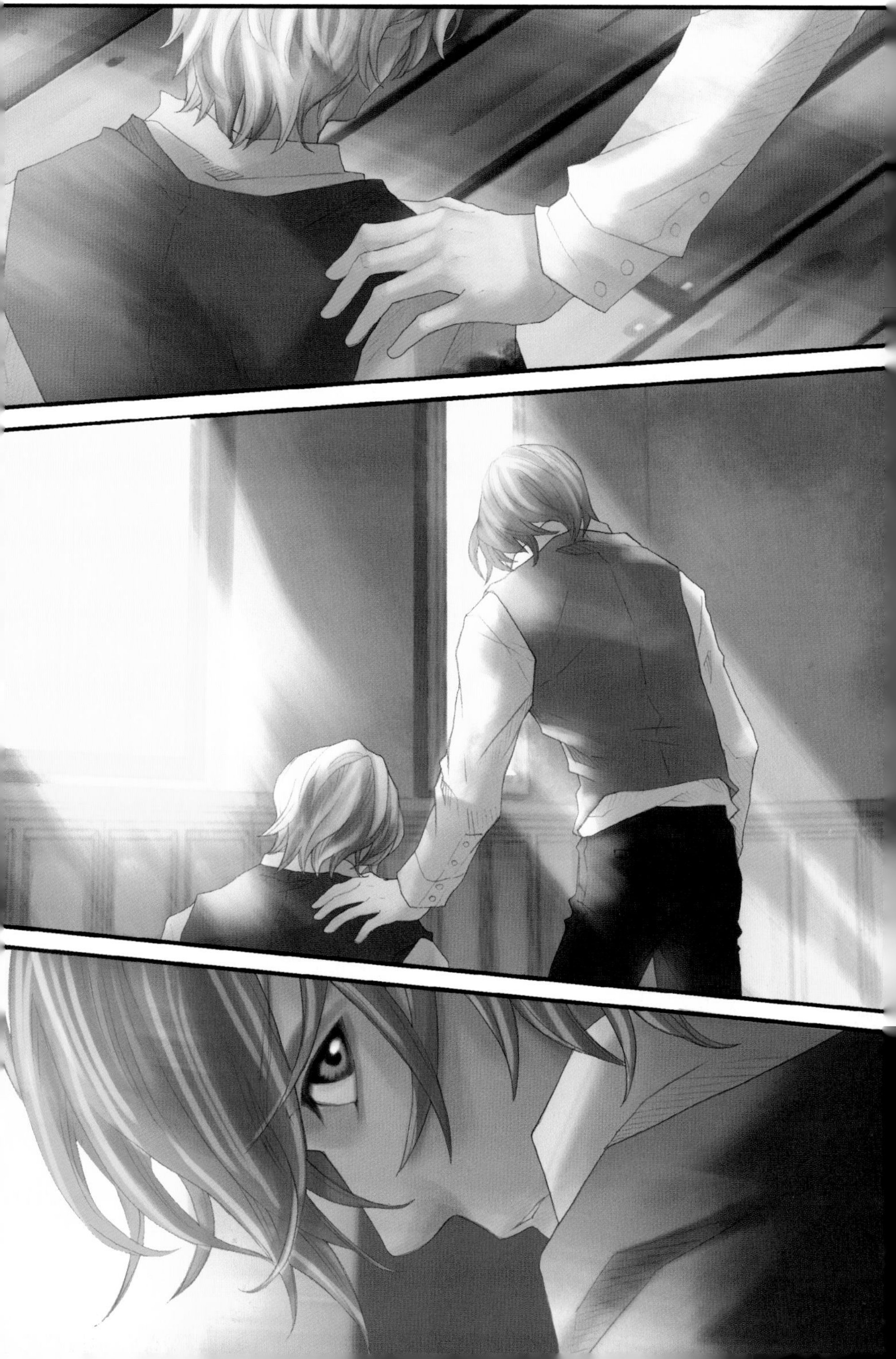

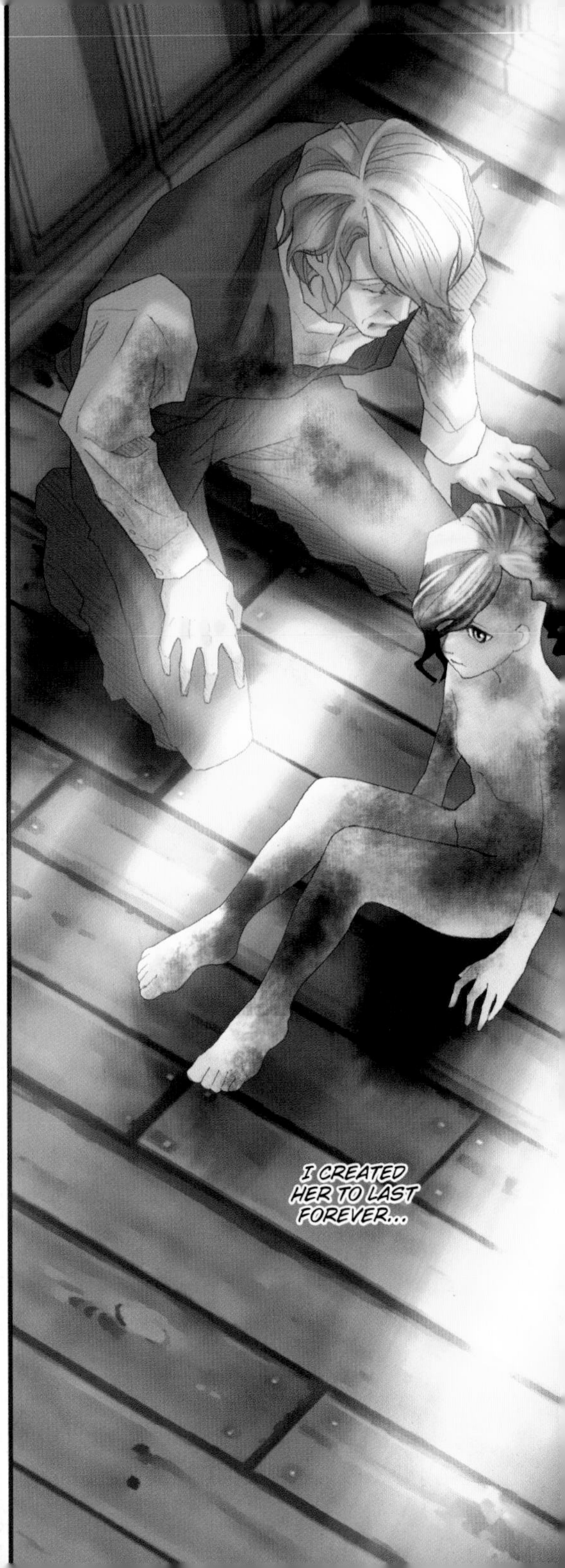
I CREATED HER TO LAST FOREVER...

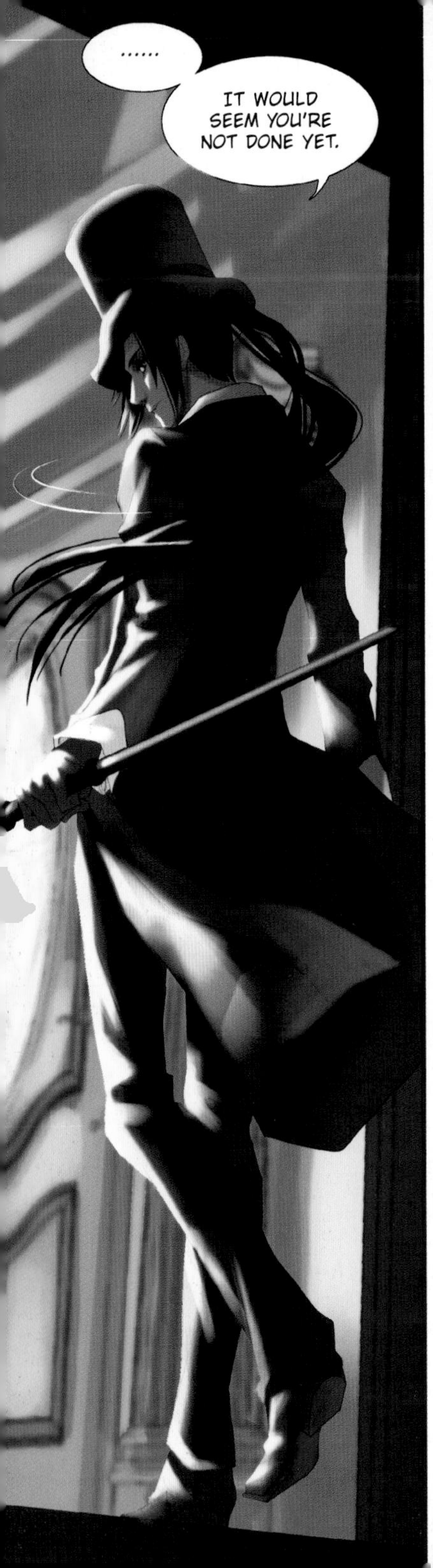
......
IT WOULD SEEM YOU'RE NOT DONE YET.

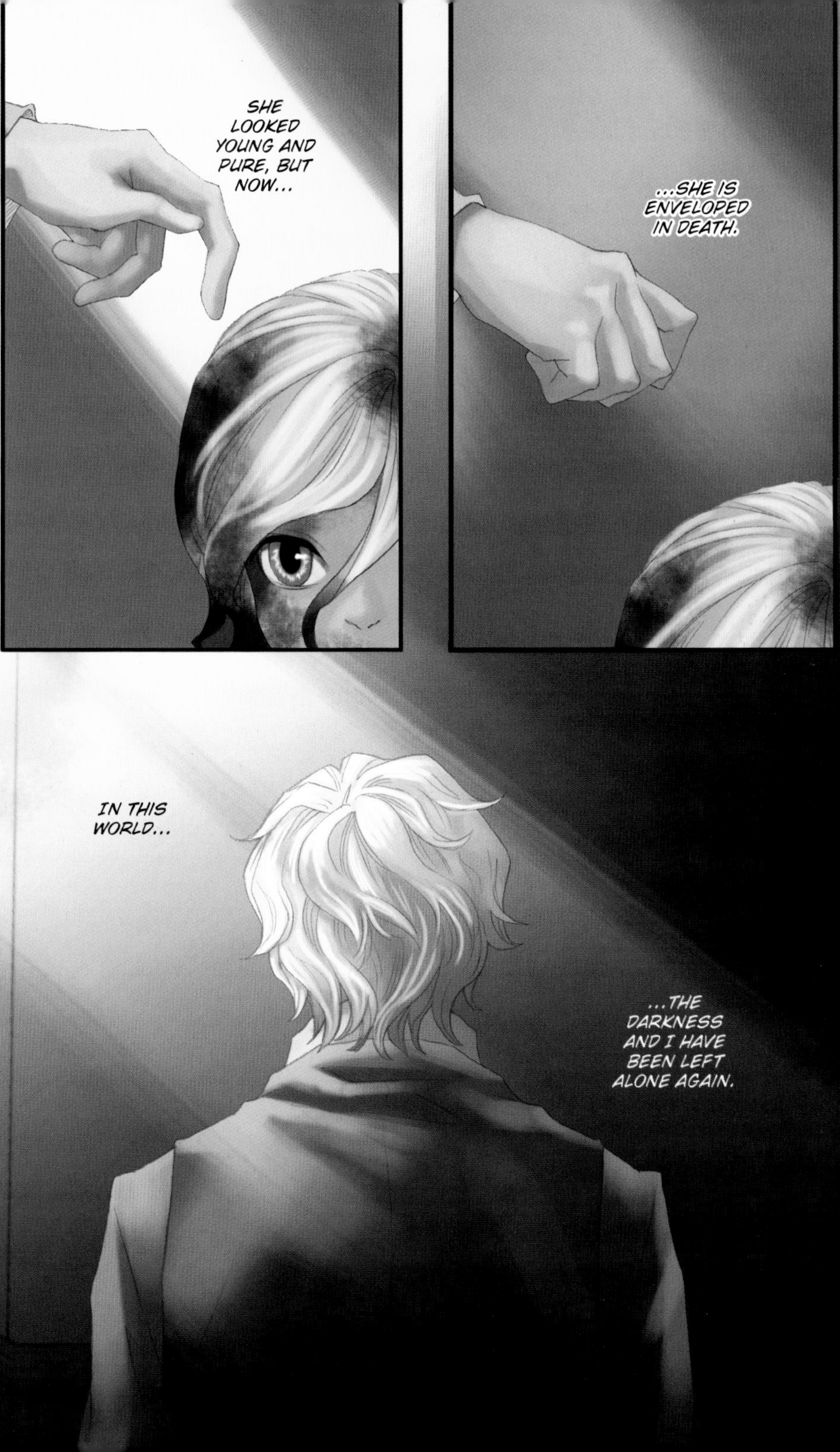
SHE LOOKED YOUNG AND PURE, BUT NOW...
...SHE IS ENVELOPED IN DEATH.
IN THIS WORLD...
...THE DARKNESS AND I HAVE BEEN LEFT ALONE AGAIN.

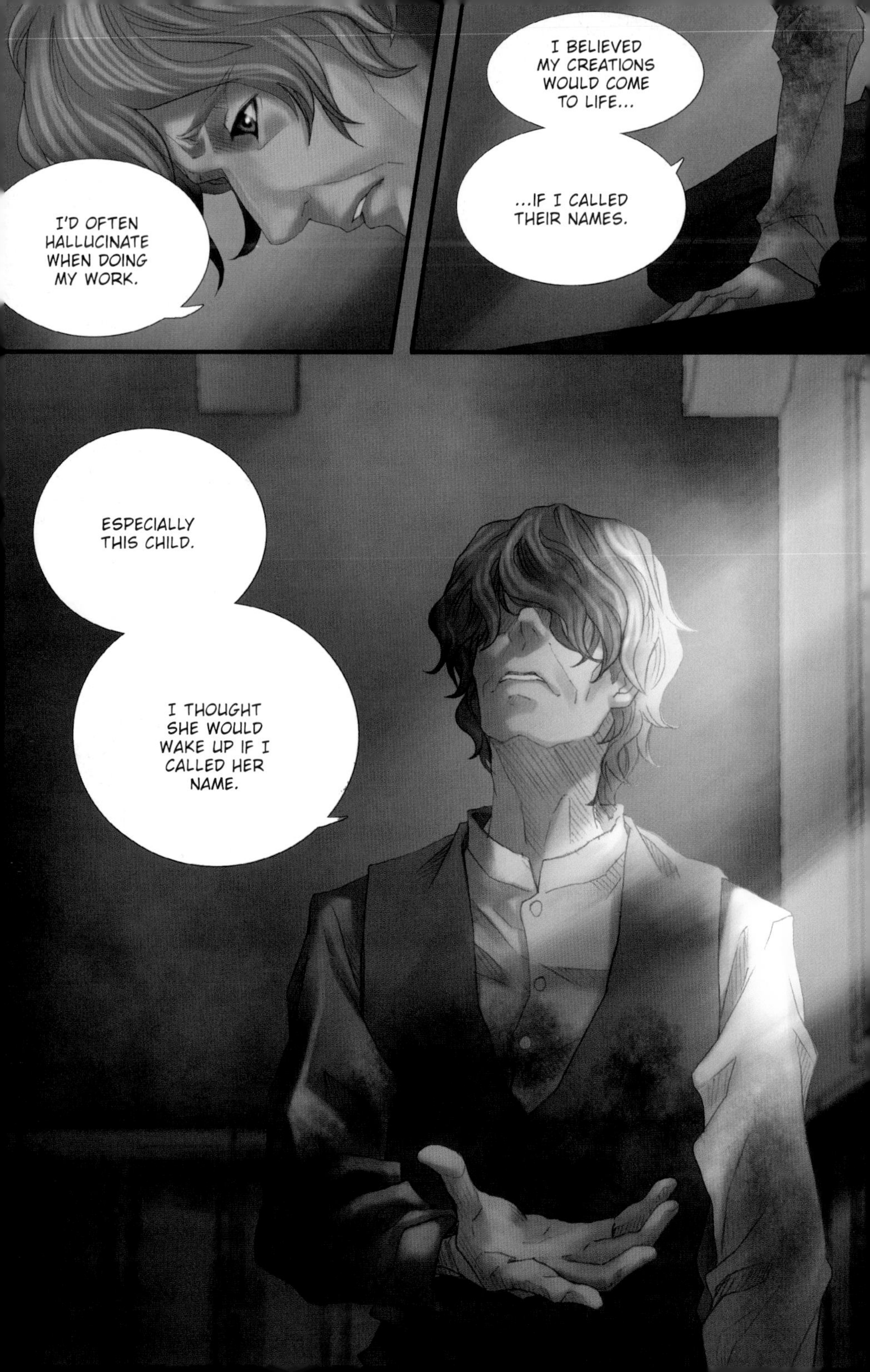
I BELIEVED MY CREATIONS WOULD COME TO LIFE...
...IF I CALLED THEIR NAMES.
I'D OFTEN HALLUCINATE WHEN DOING MY WORK.
ESPECIALLY THIS CHILD.
I THOUGHT SHE WOULD WAKE UP IF I CALLED HER NAME.

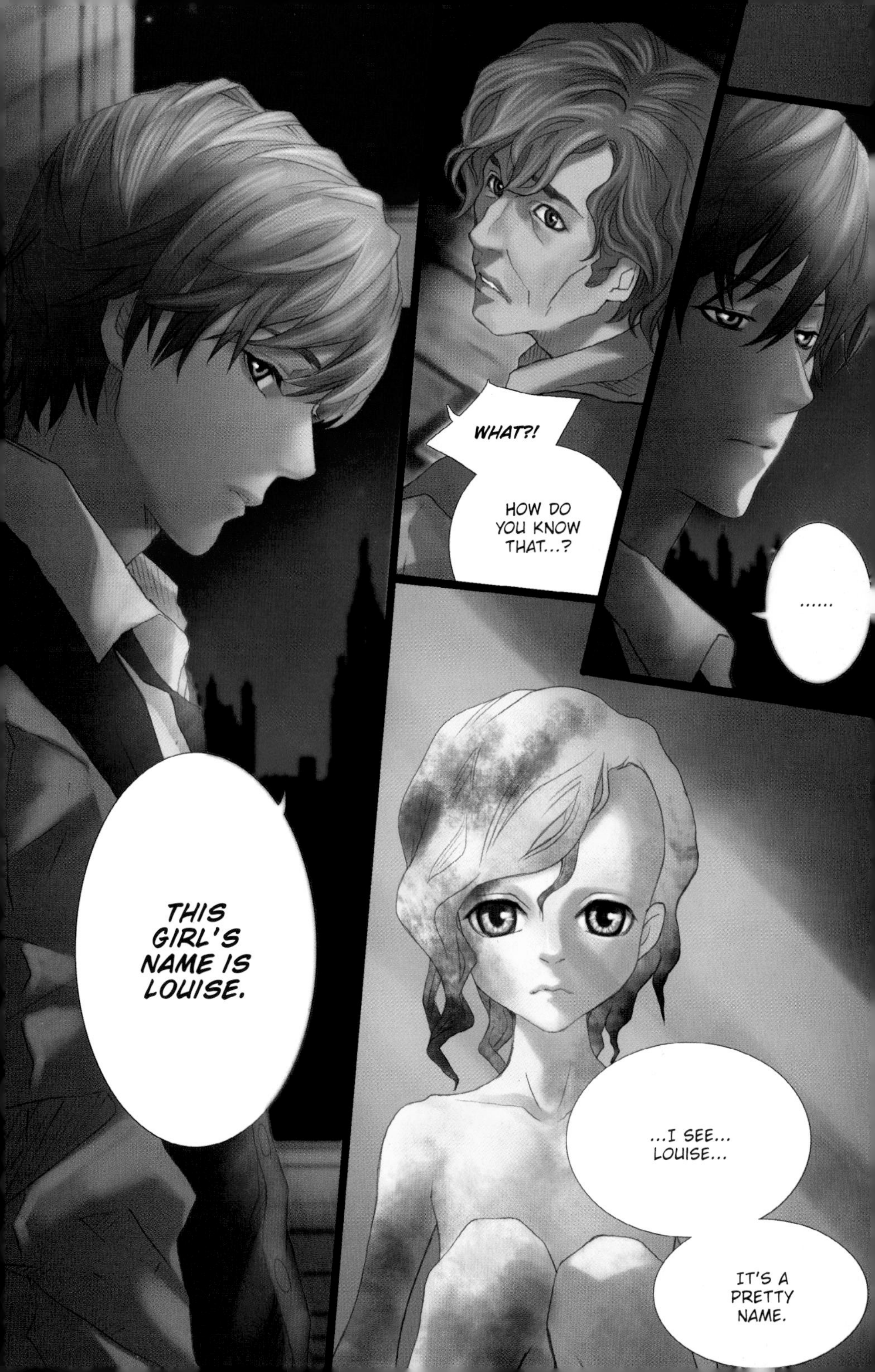
THIS GIRL'S NAME IS LOUISE.
WHAT?!
HOW DO YOU KNOW THAT...?
......
...I SEE... LOUISE...
IT'S A PRETTY NAME.

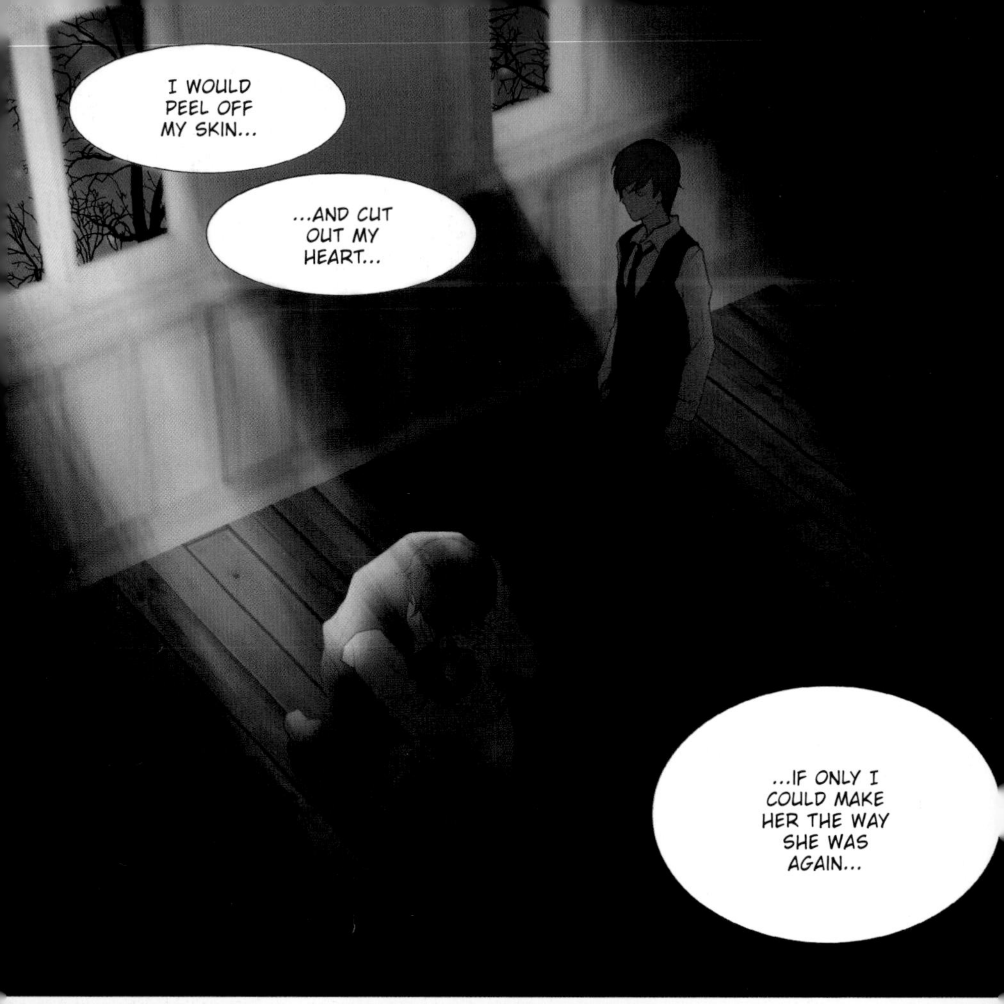
I WOULD PEEL OFF MY SKIN...
...AND CUT OUT MY HEART...
...IF ONLY I COULD MAKE HER THE WAY SHE WAS AGAIN...
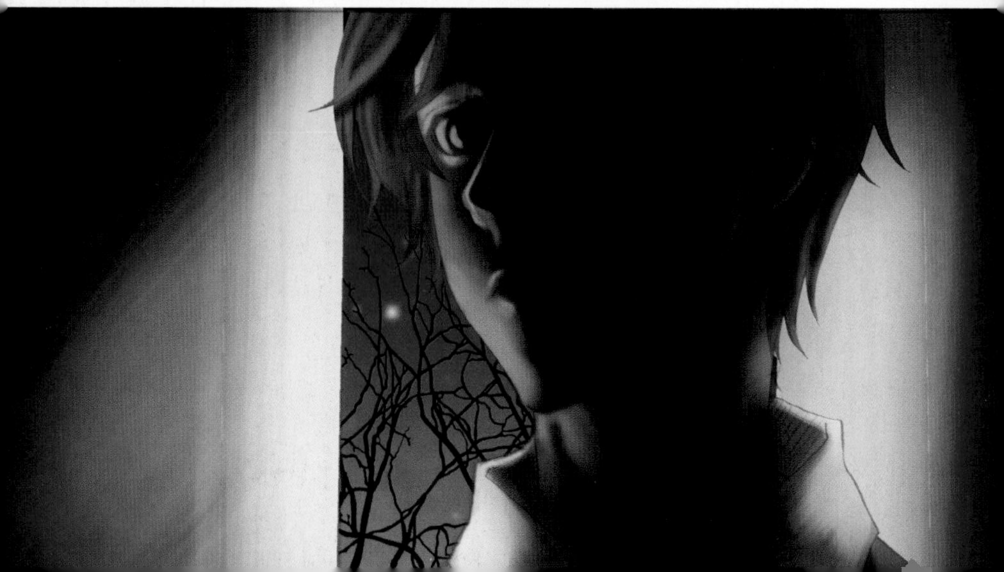

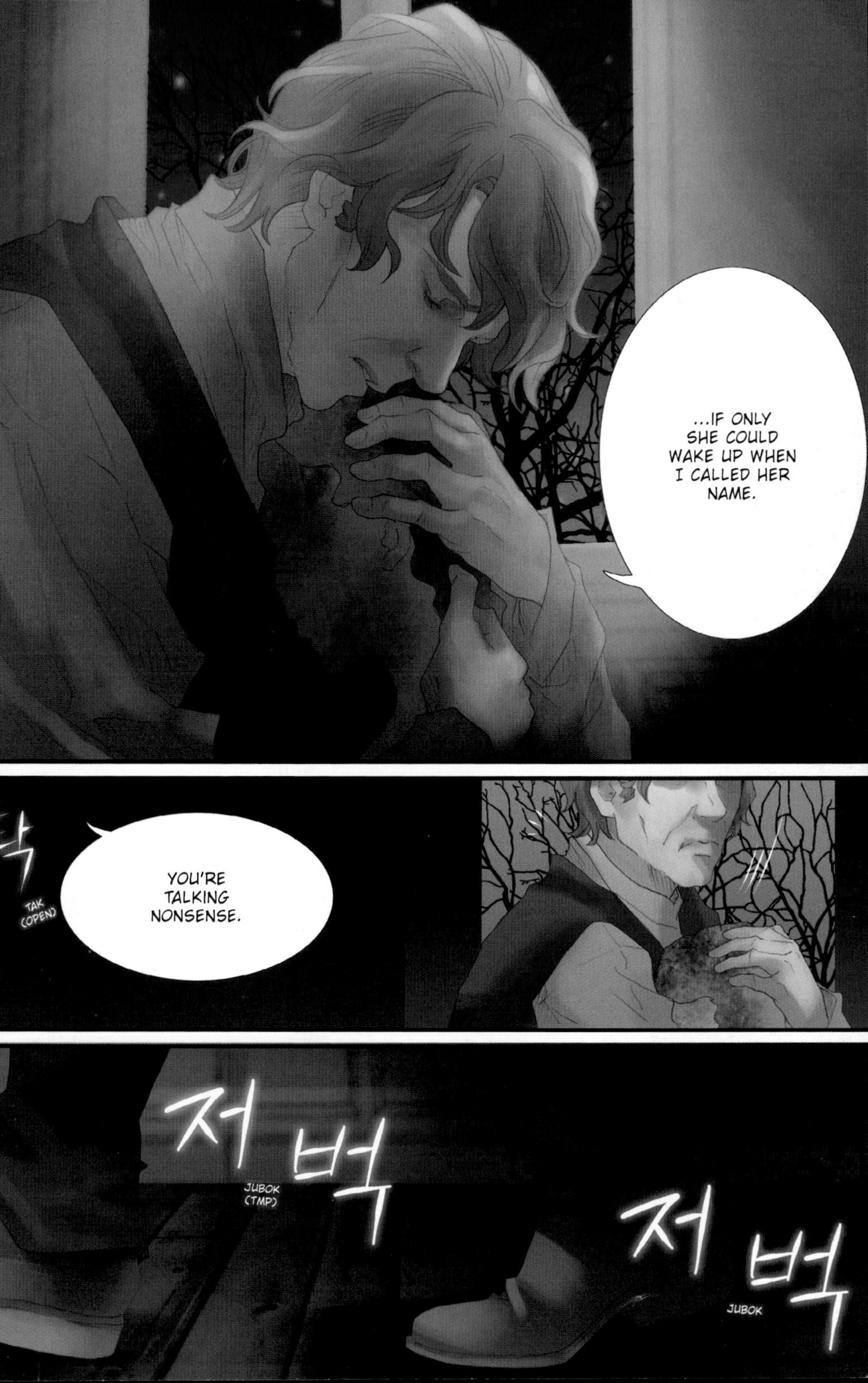
...IF ONLY SHE COULD WAKE UP WHEN I CALLED HER NAME.
탁
TAK (OPEN)
YOU'RE TALKING NONSENSE.
저벅
JUBOK (TMP)
저벅
JUBOK

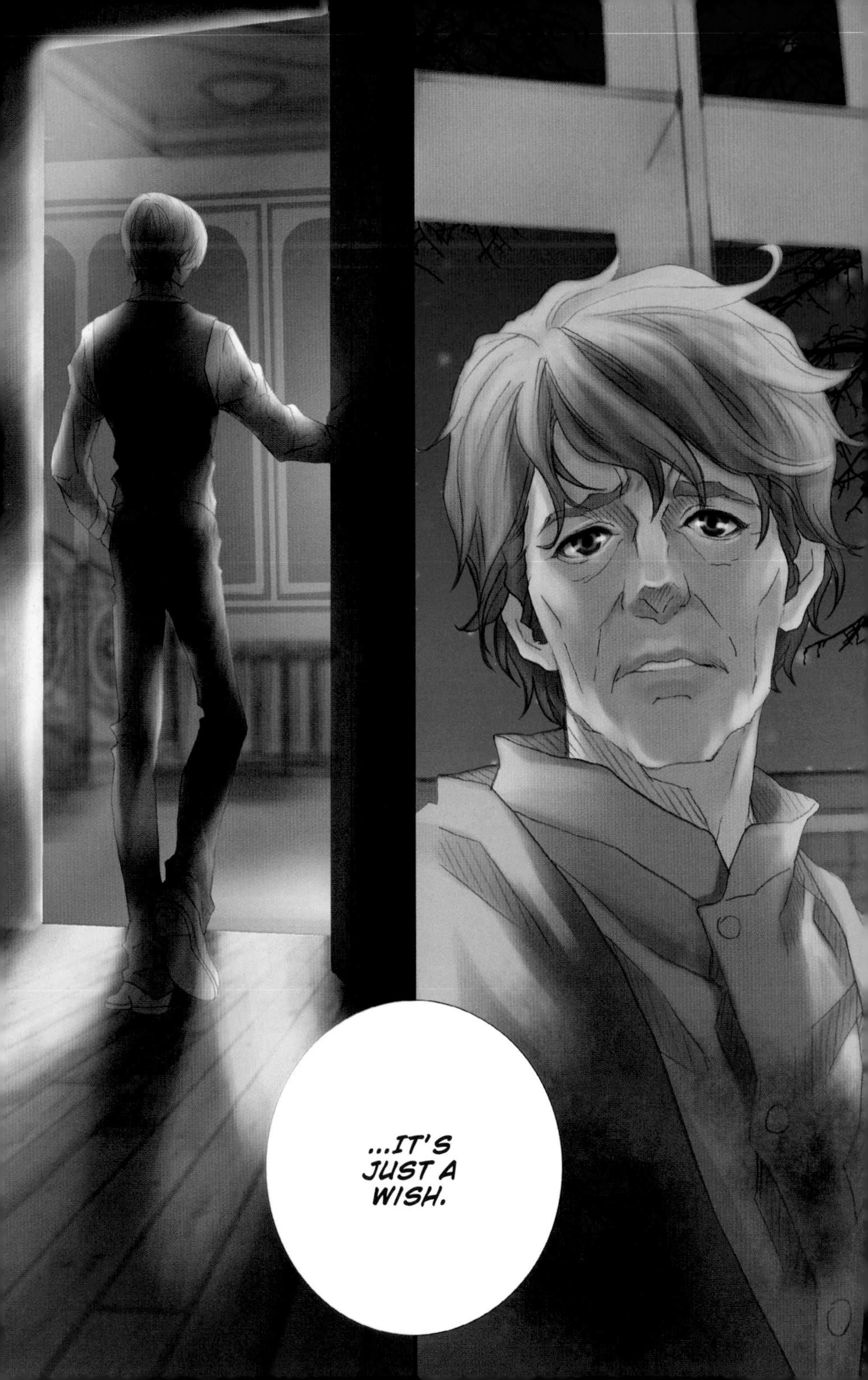
...IT'S JUST A WISH.

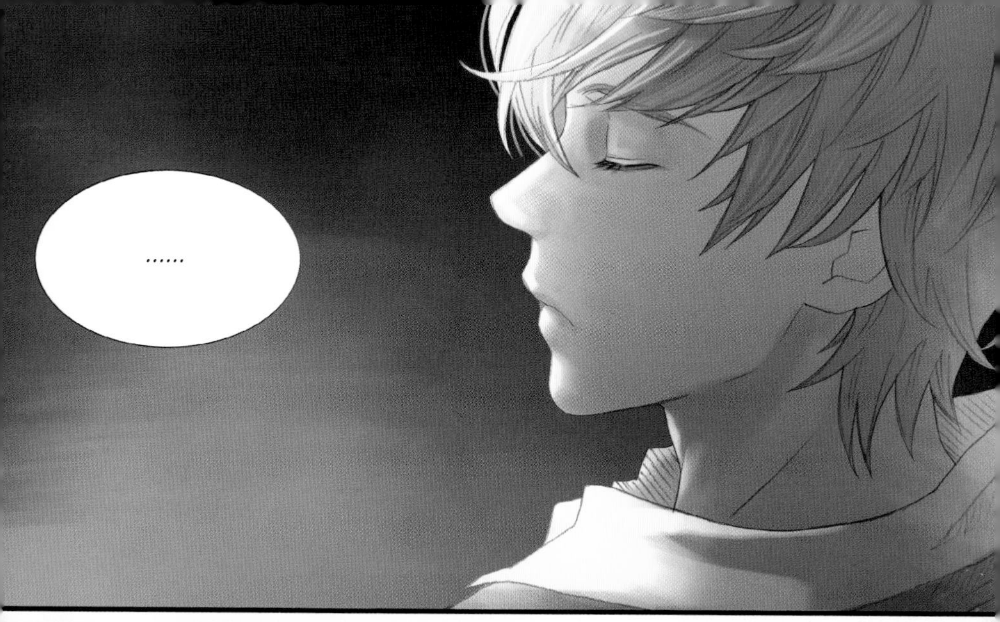
......
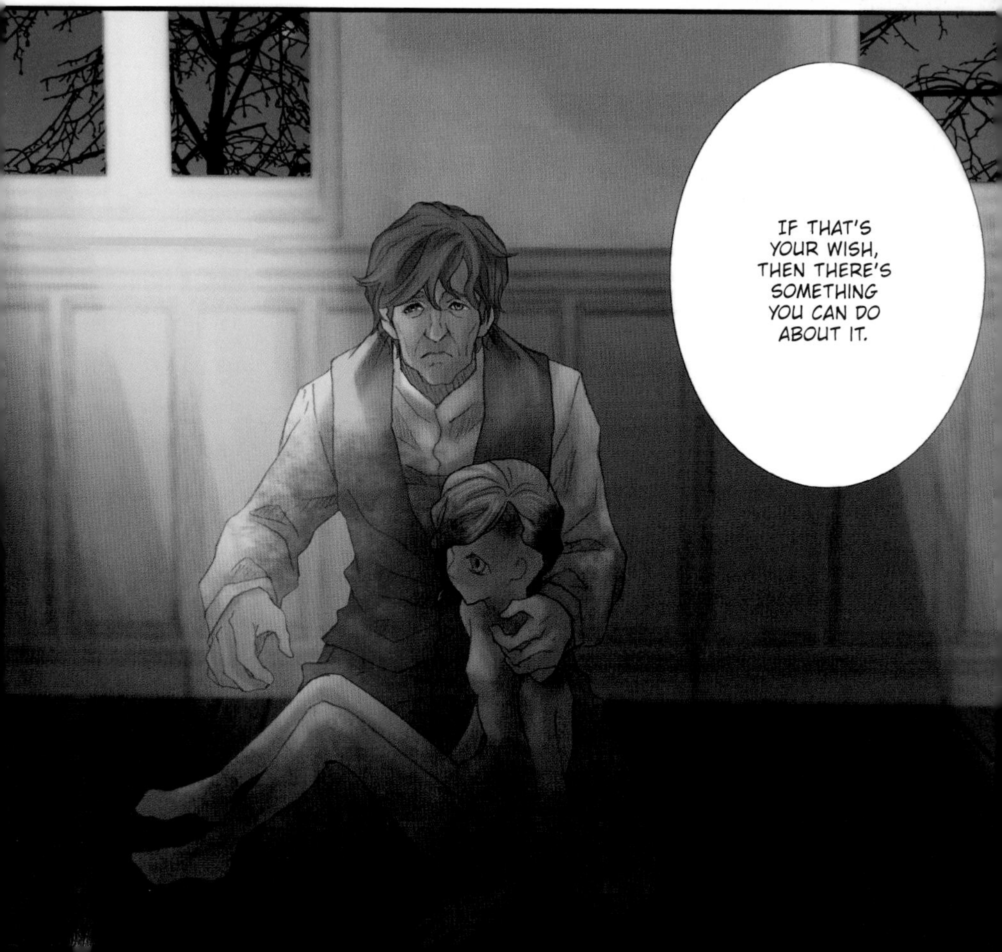
IF THAT'S YOUR WISH, THEN THERE'S SOMETHING YOU CAN DO ABOUT IT.

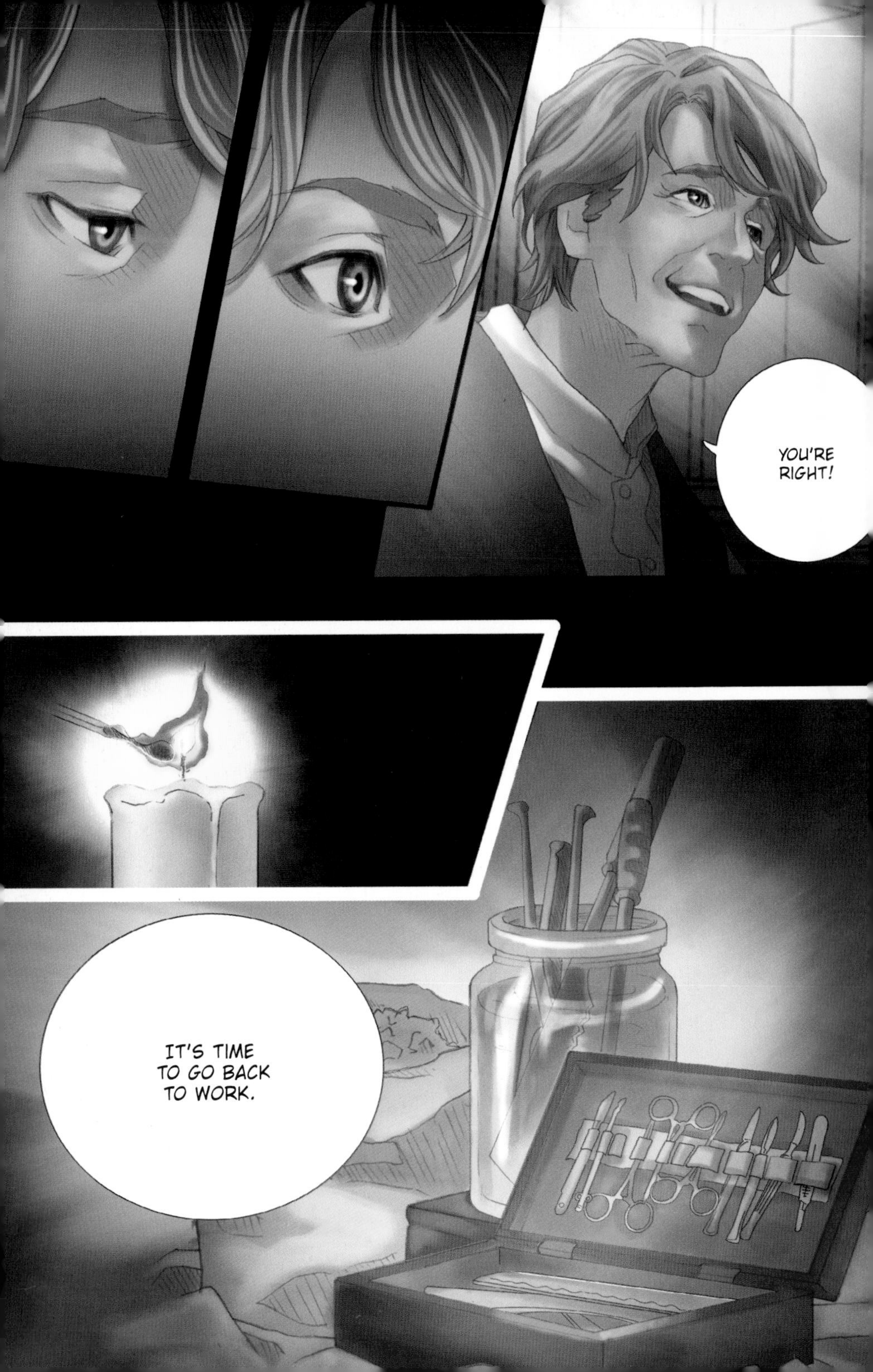
YOU'RE RIGHT!
IT'S TIME TO GO BACK TO WORK.

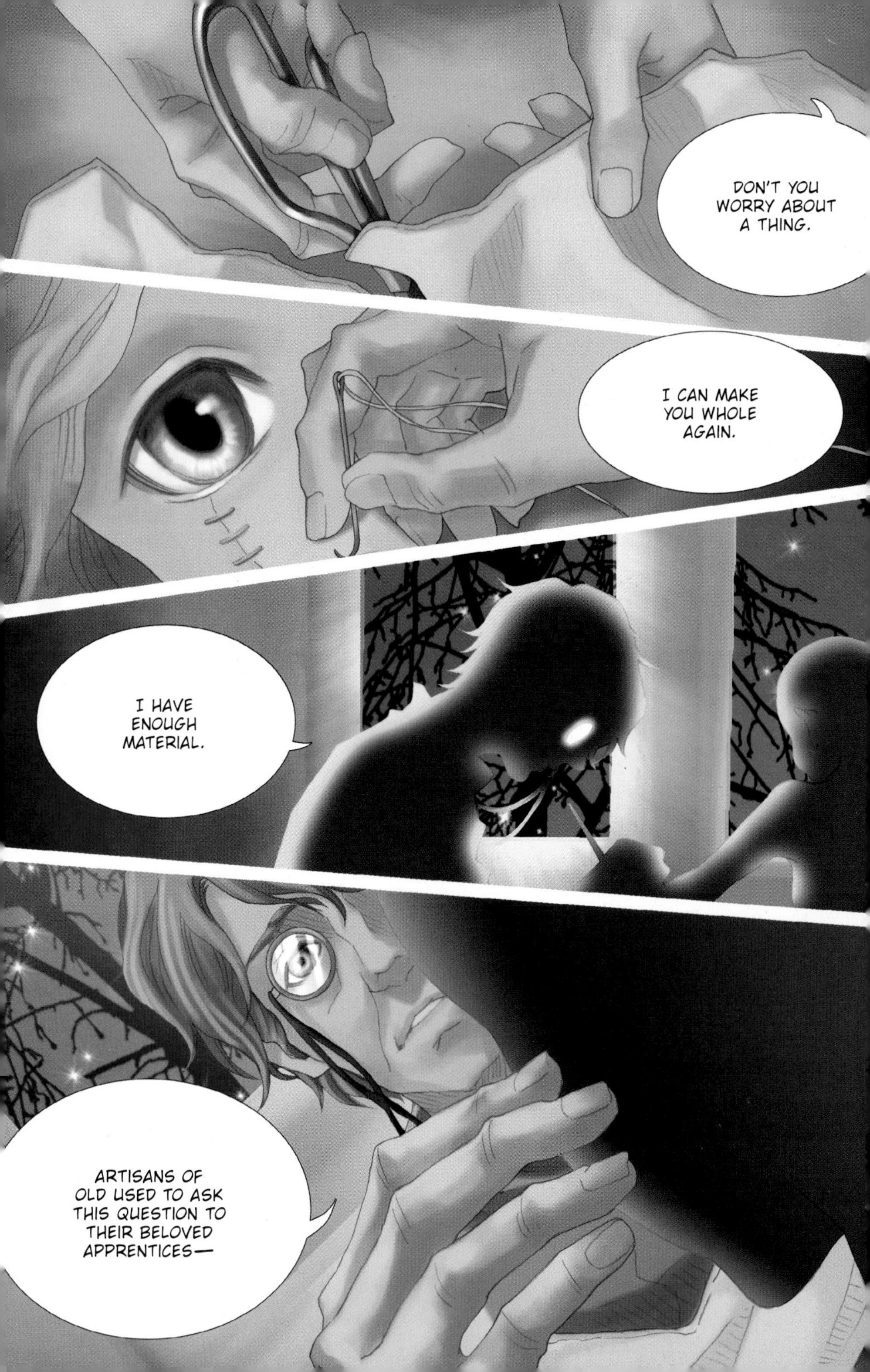
DON'T YOU WORRY ABOUT A THING.
I CAN MAKE YOU WHOLE AGAIN.
I HAVE ENOUGH MATERIAL.
ARTISANS OF OLD USED TO ASK THIS QUESTION TO THEIR BELOVED APPRENTICES—

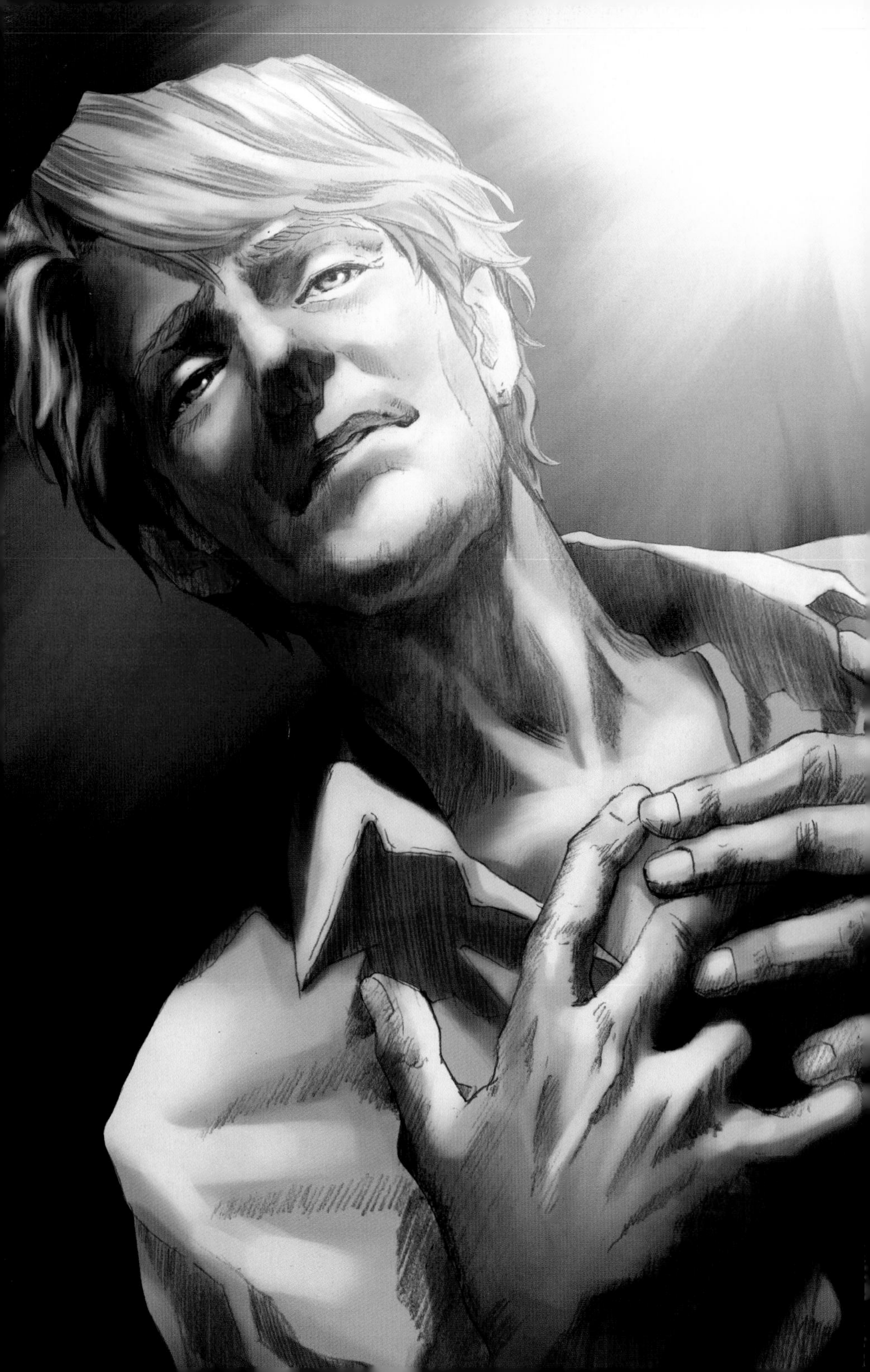

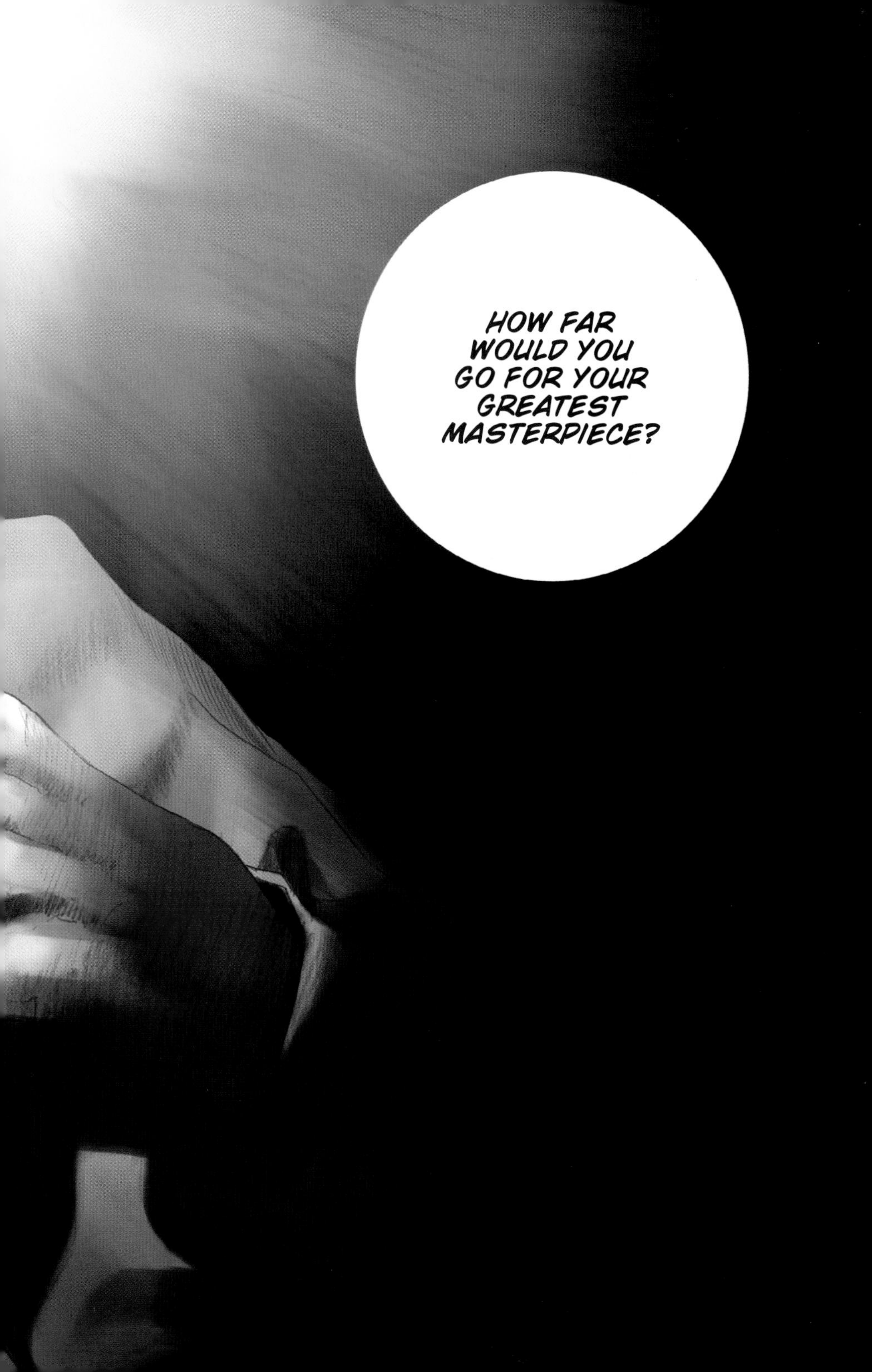
HOW FAR WOULD YOU GO FOR YOUR GREATEST MASTERPIECE?

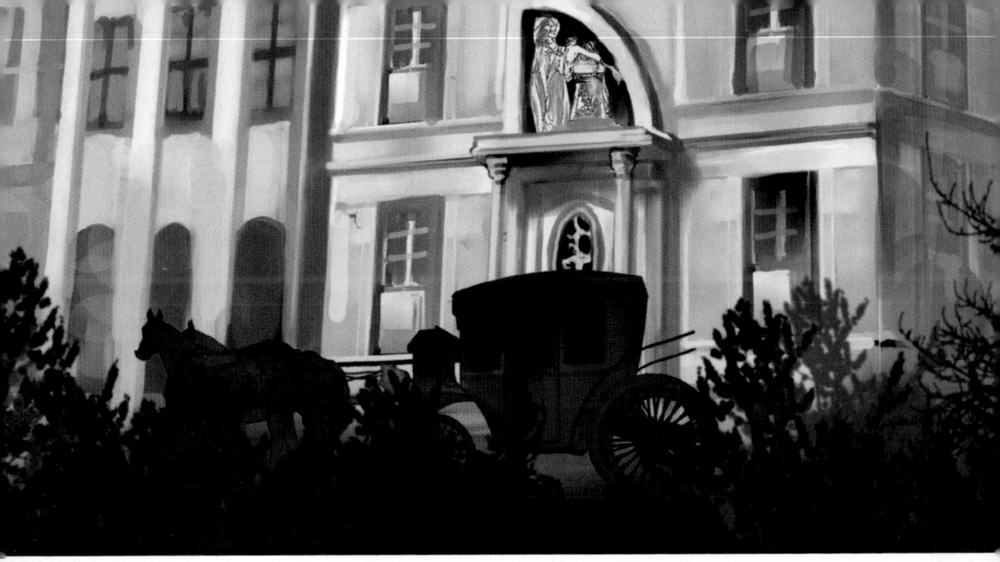
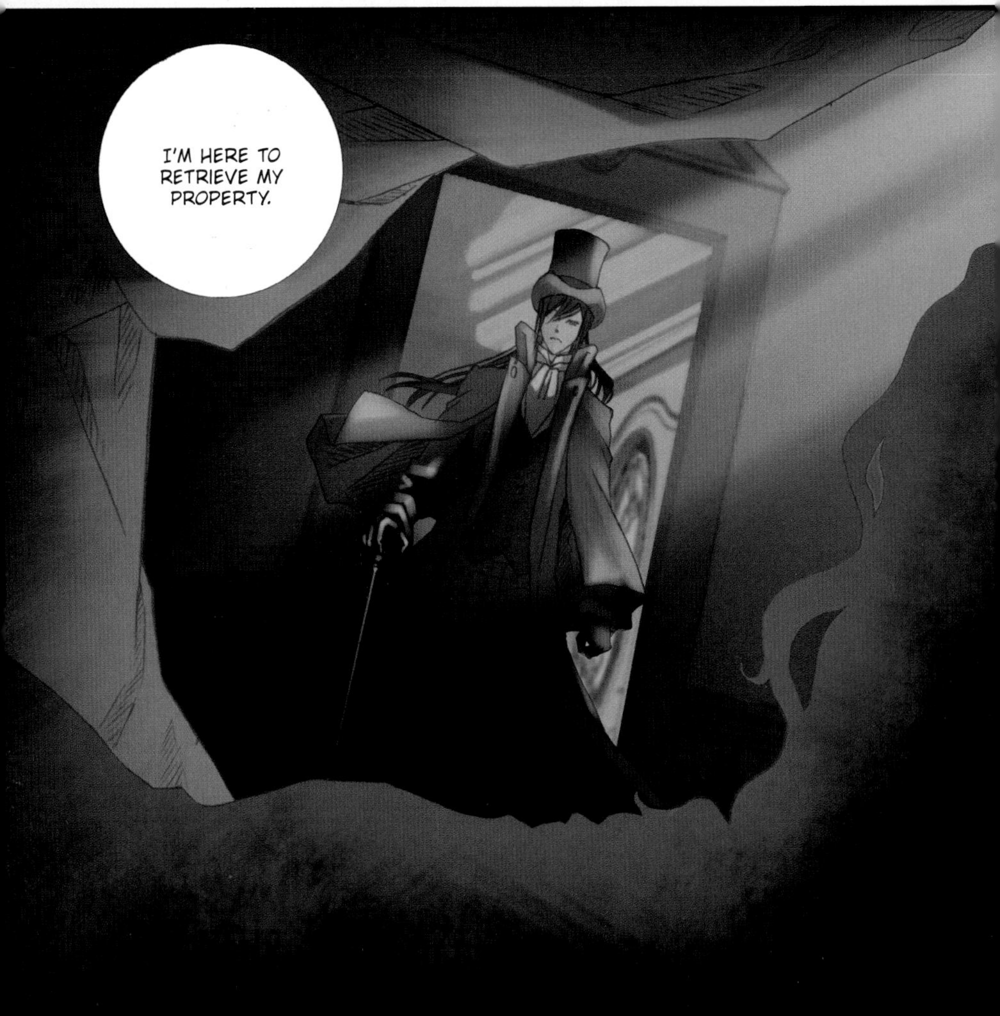
I'M HERE TO RETRIEVE MY PROPERTY.

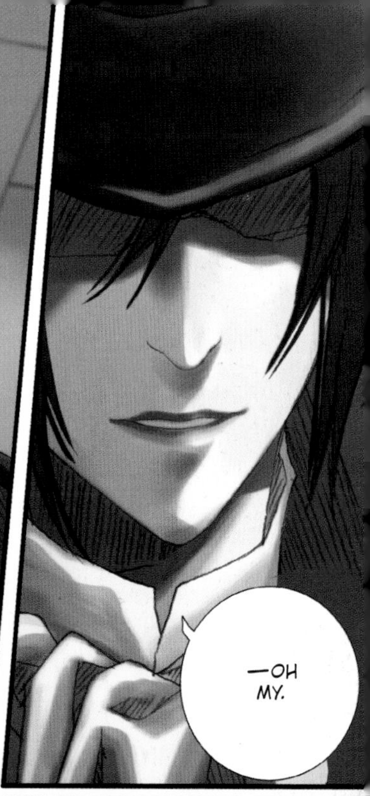
—OH MY.
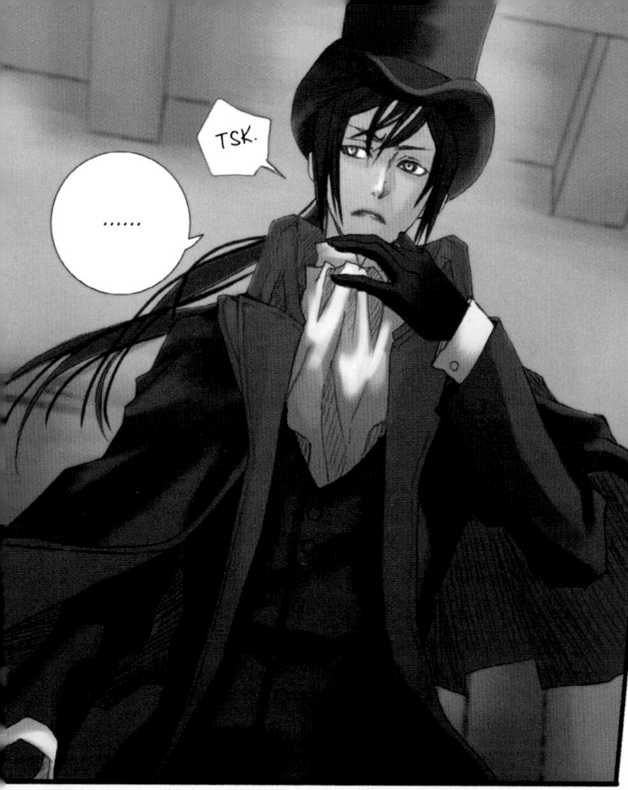
TSK.
......
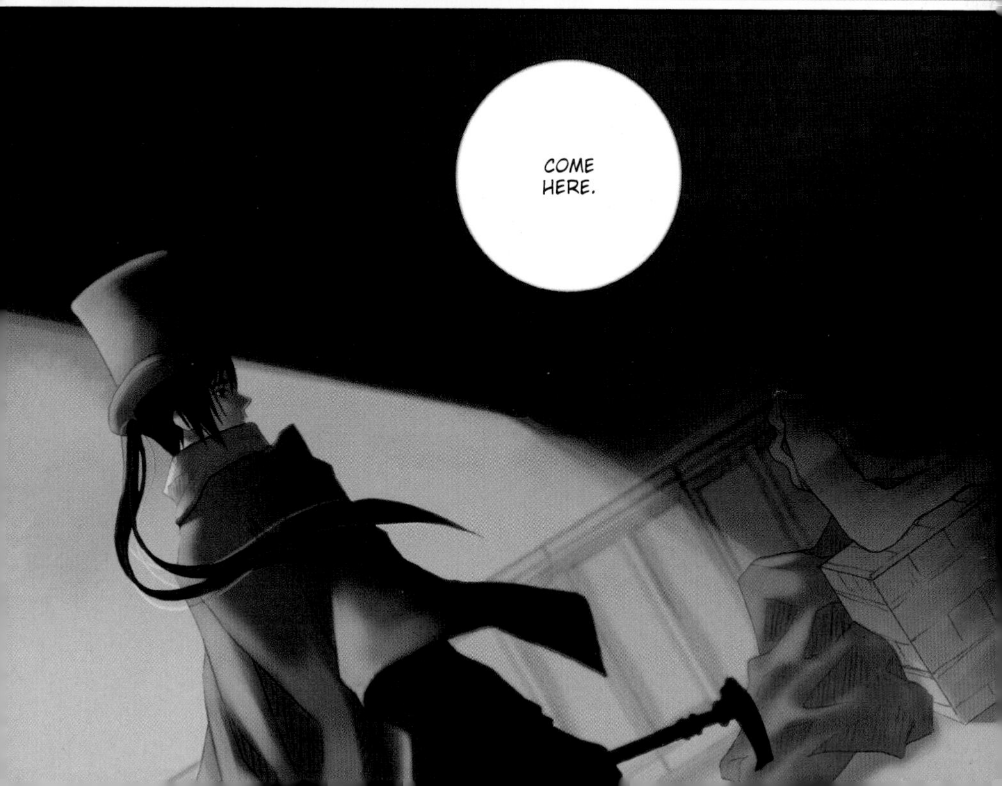
COME HERE.

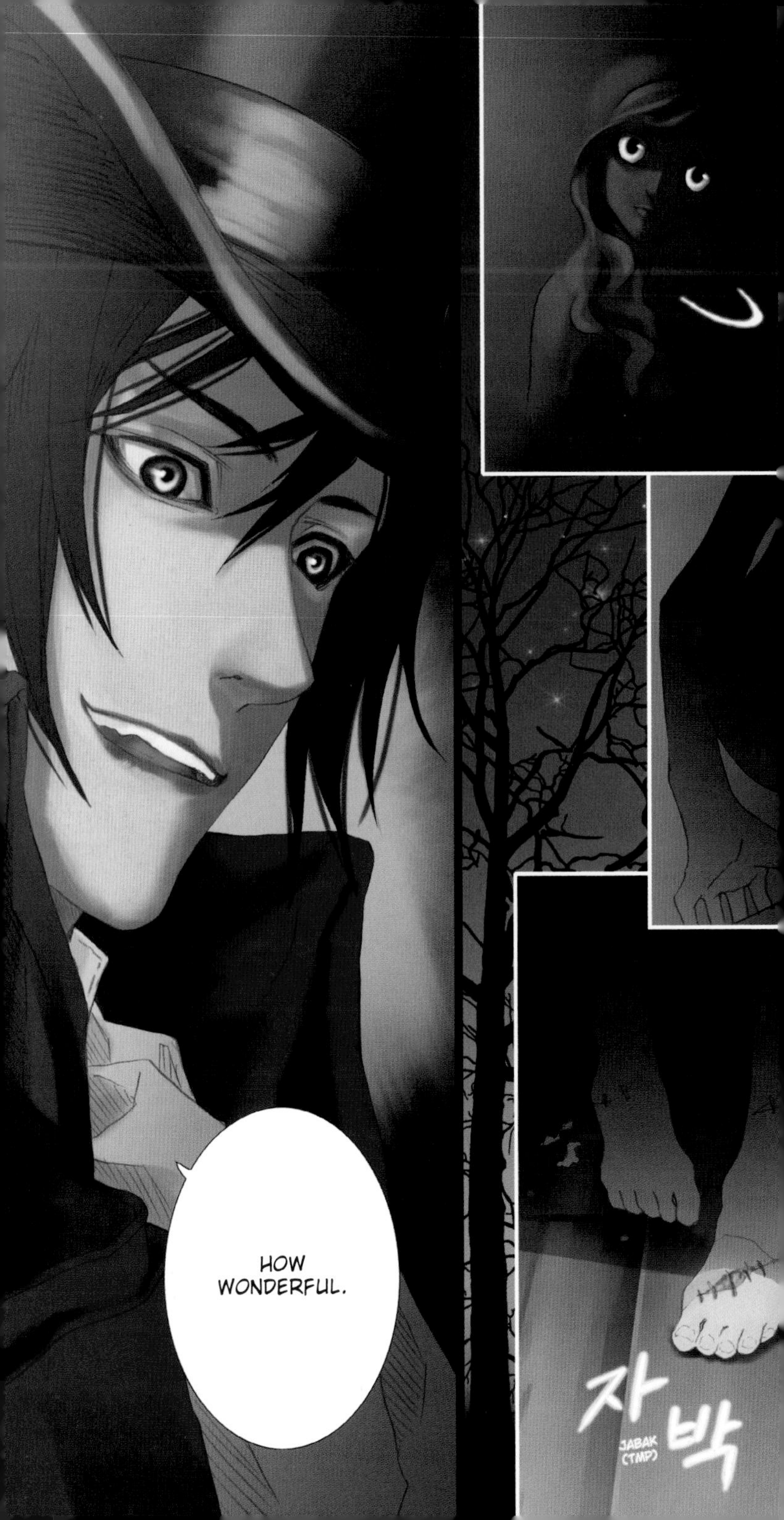
HOW WONDERFUL.
자박
JABAK (TMP)

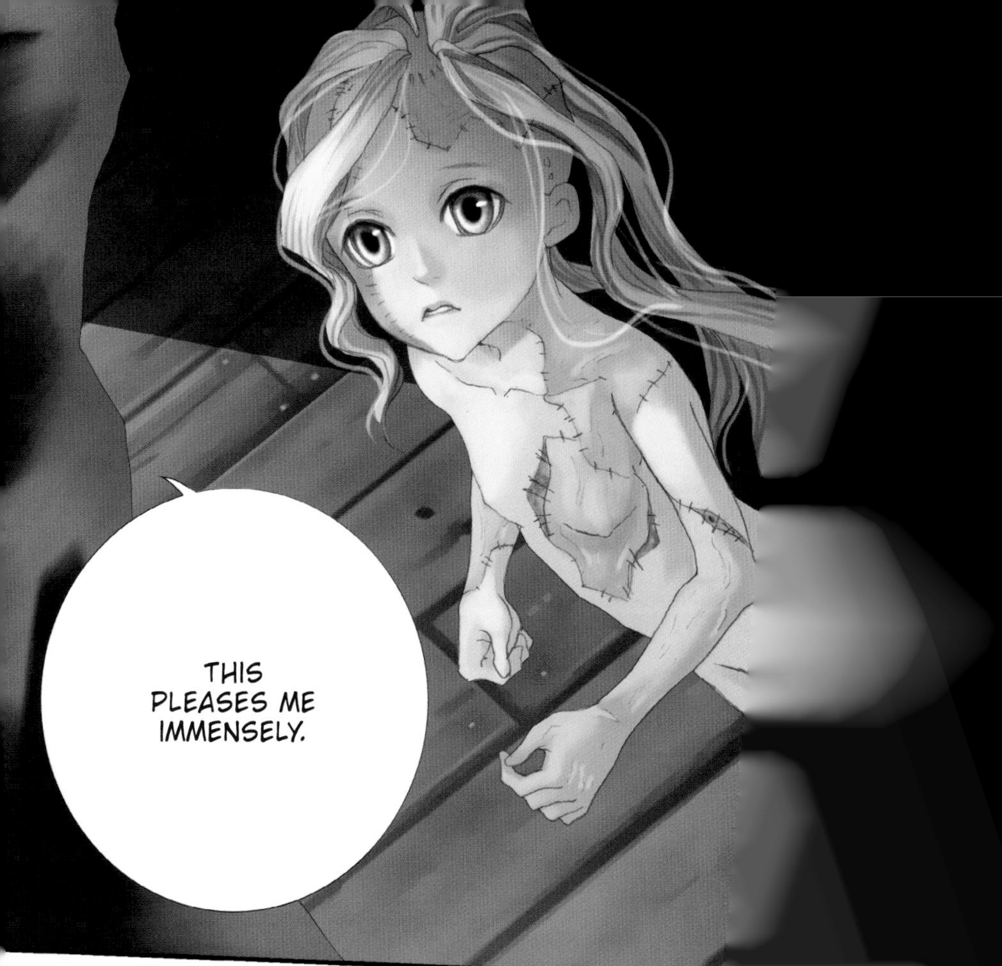
THIS PLEASES ME IMMENSELY.

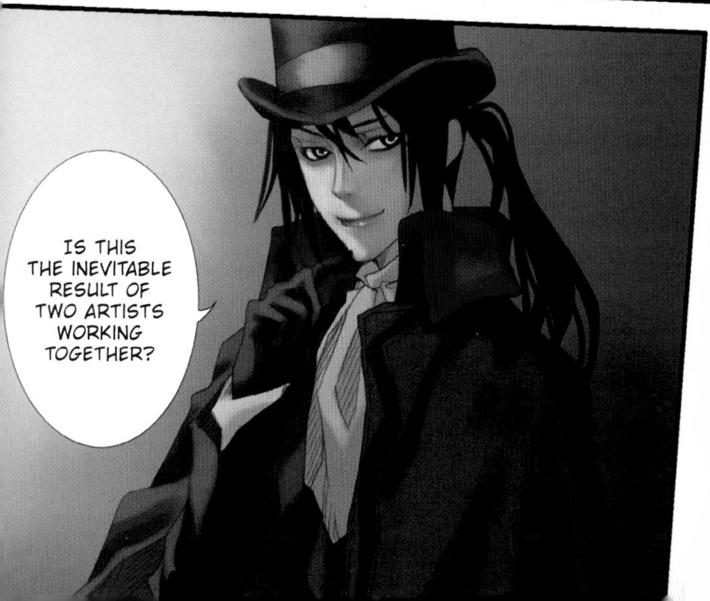
IS THIS THE INEVITABLE RESULT OF TWO ARTISTS WORKING TOGETHER?

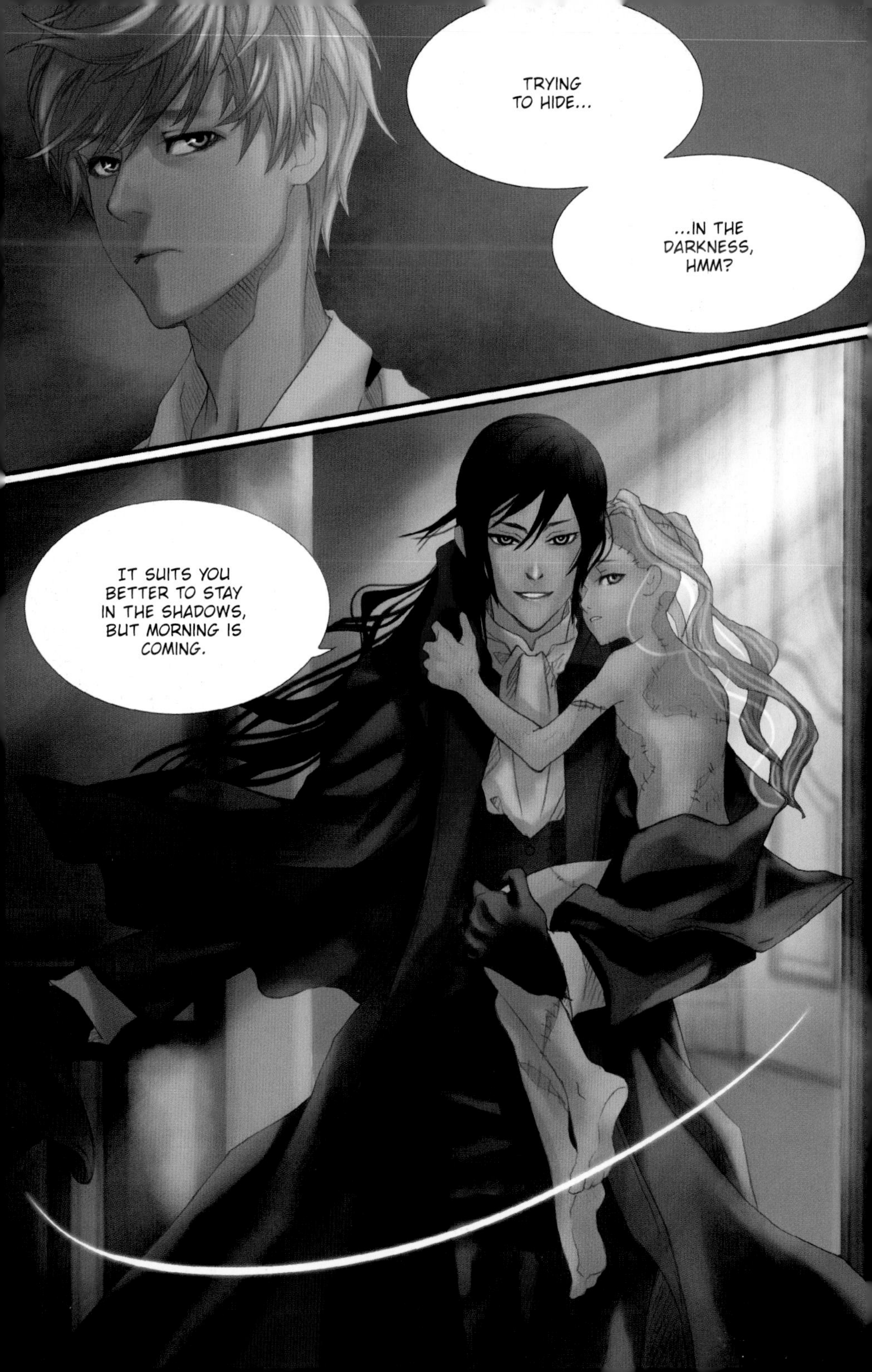
TRYING TO HIDE...
...IN THE DARKNESS, HMM?
IT SUITS YOU BETTER TO STAY IN THE SHADOWS, BUT MORNING IS COMING.

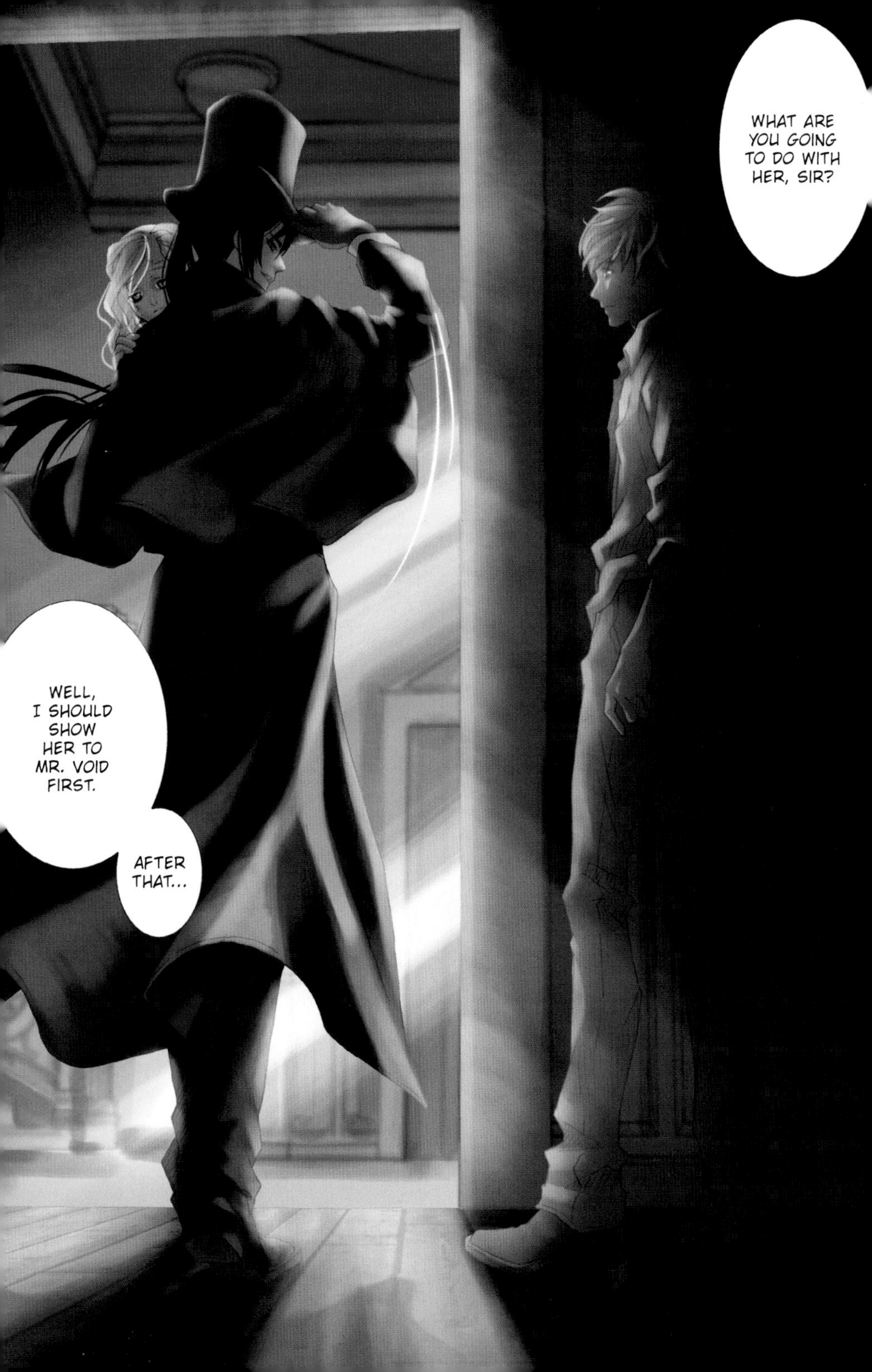
WHAT ARE YOU GOING TO DO WITH HER, SIR?
WELL, I SHOULD SHOW HER TO MR. VOID FIRST.
AFTER THAT...

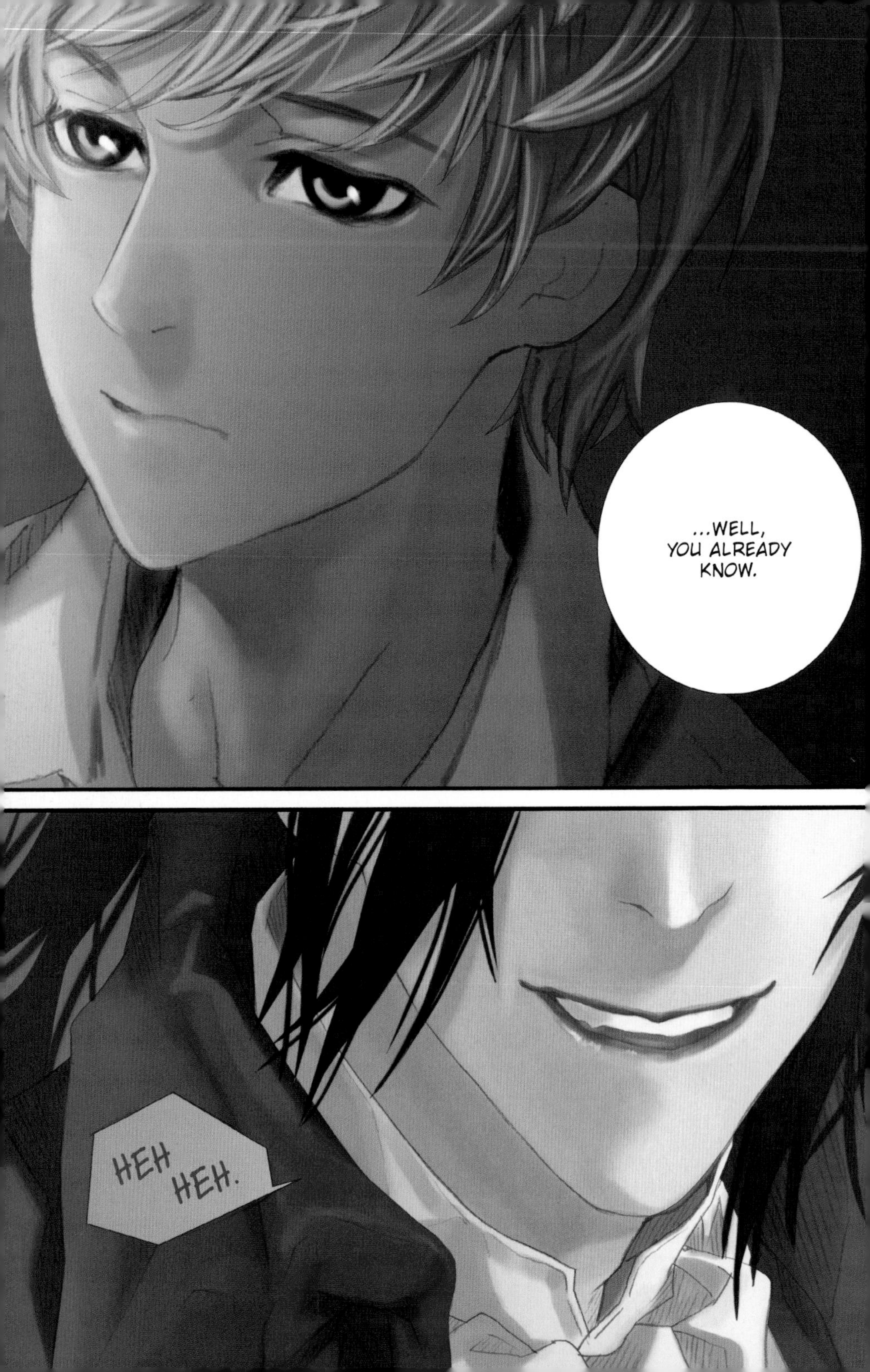
...WELL, YOU ALREADY KNOW.
HEH HEH.

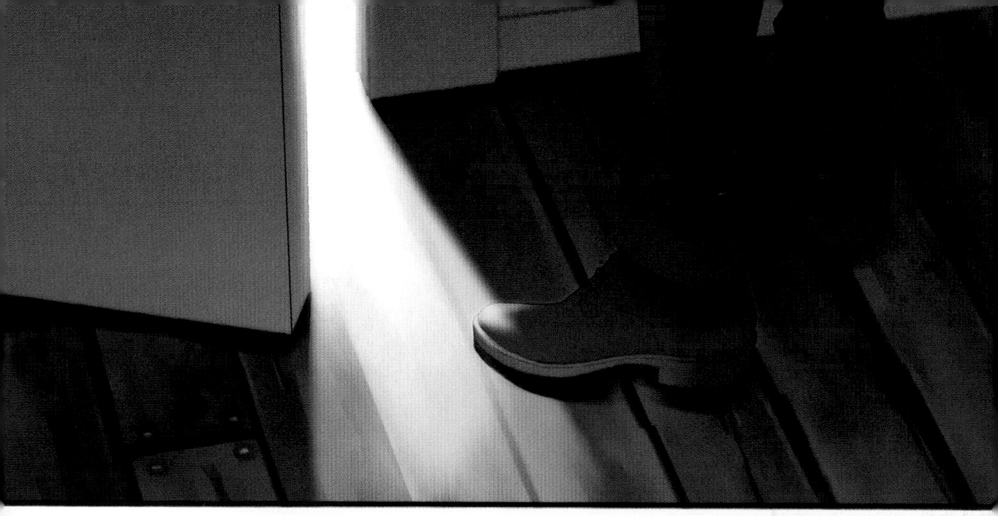
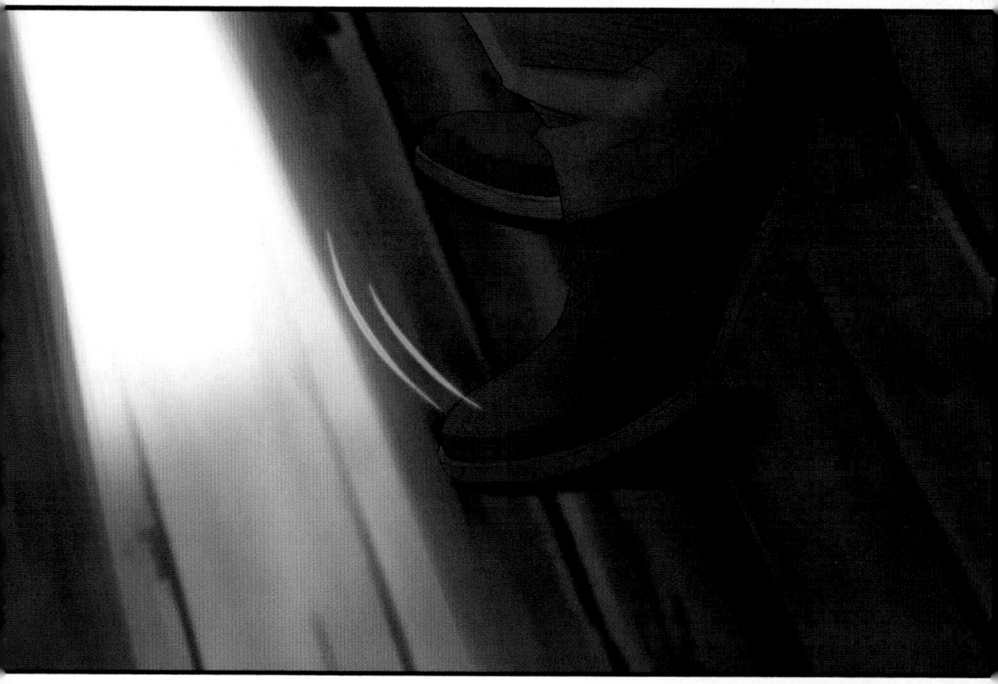
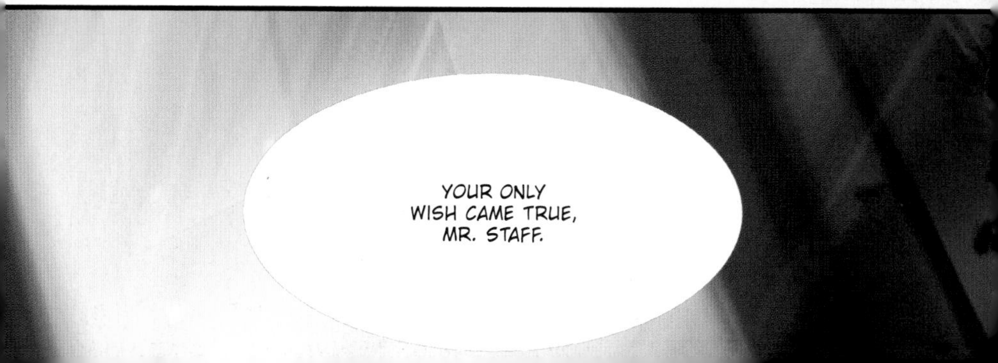
YOUR ONLY WISH CAME TRUE, MR. STAFF.

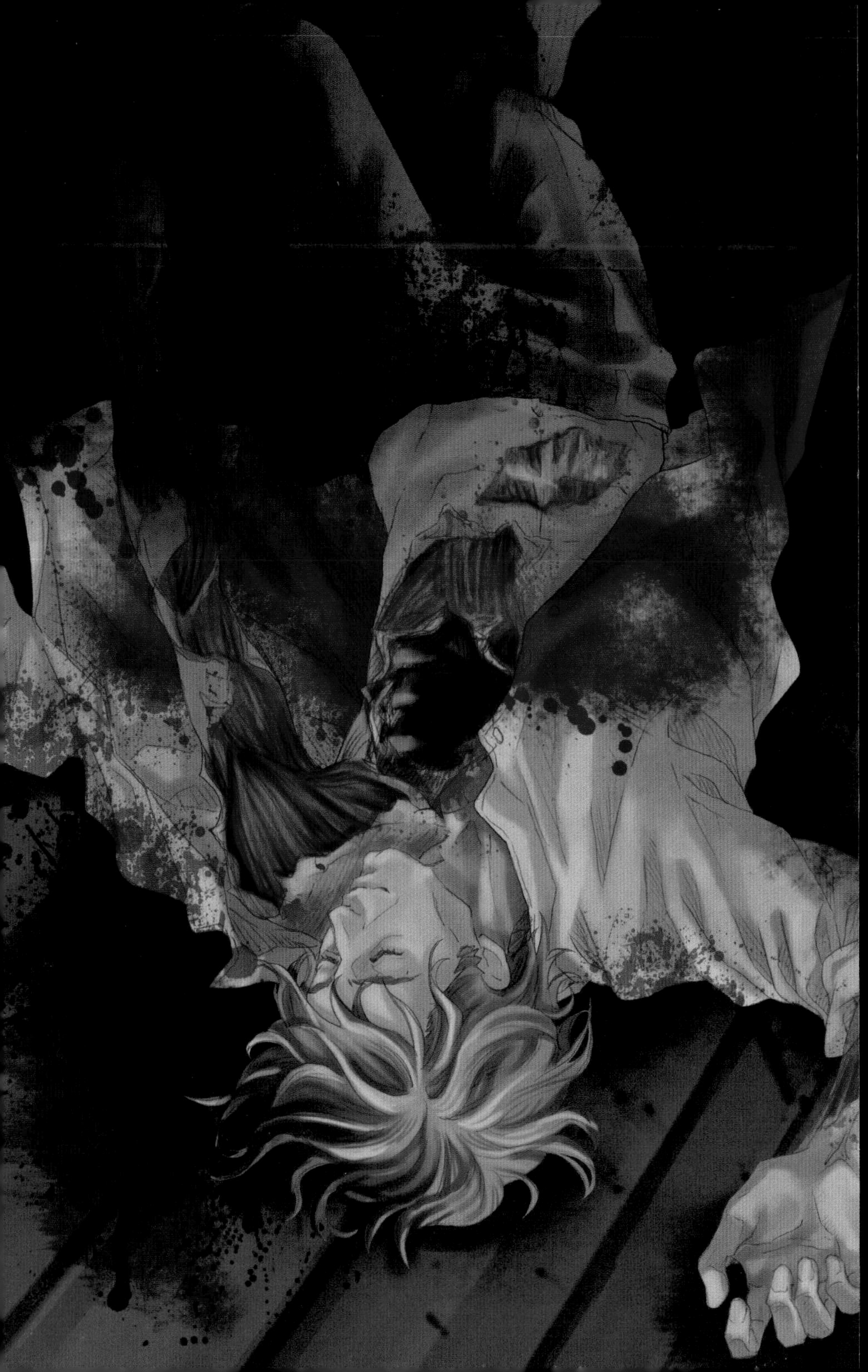

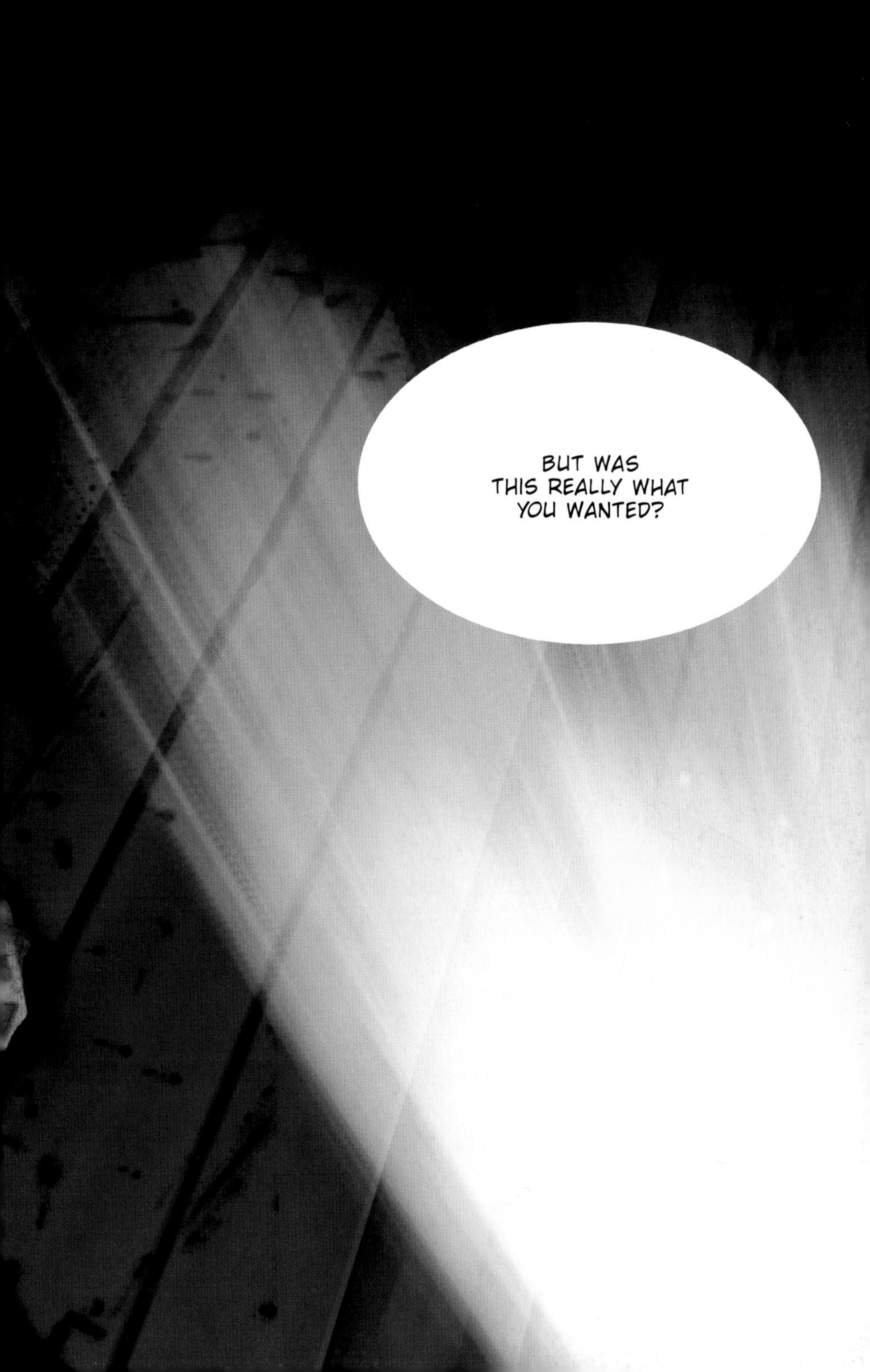
BUT WAS THIS REALLY WHAT YOU WANTED?

Void's Enigmatic Mansion

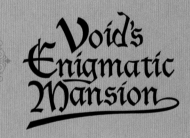

"

How long must
he grant the
wishes of others?

"

"

Until his own
comes true.

"

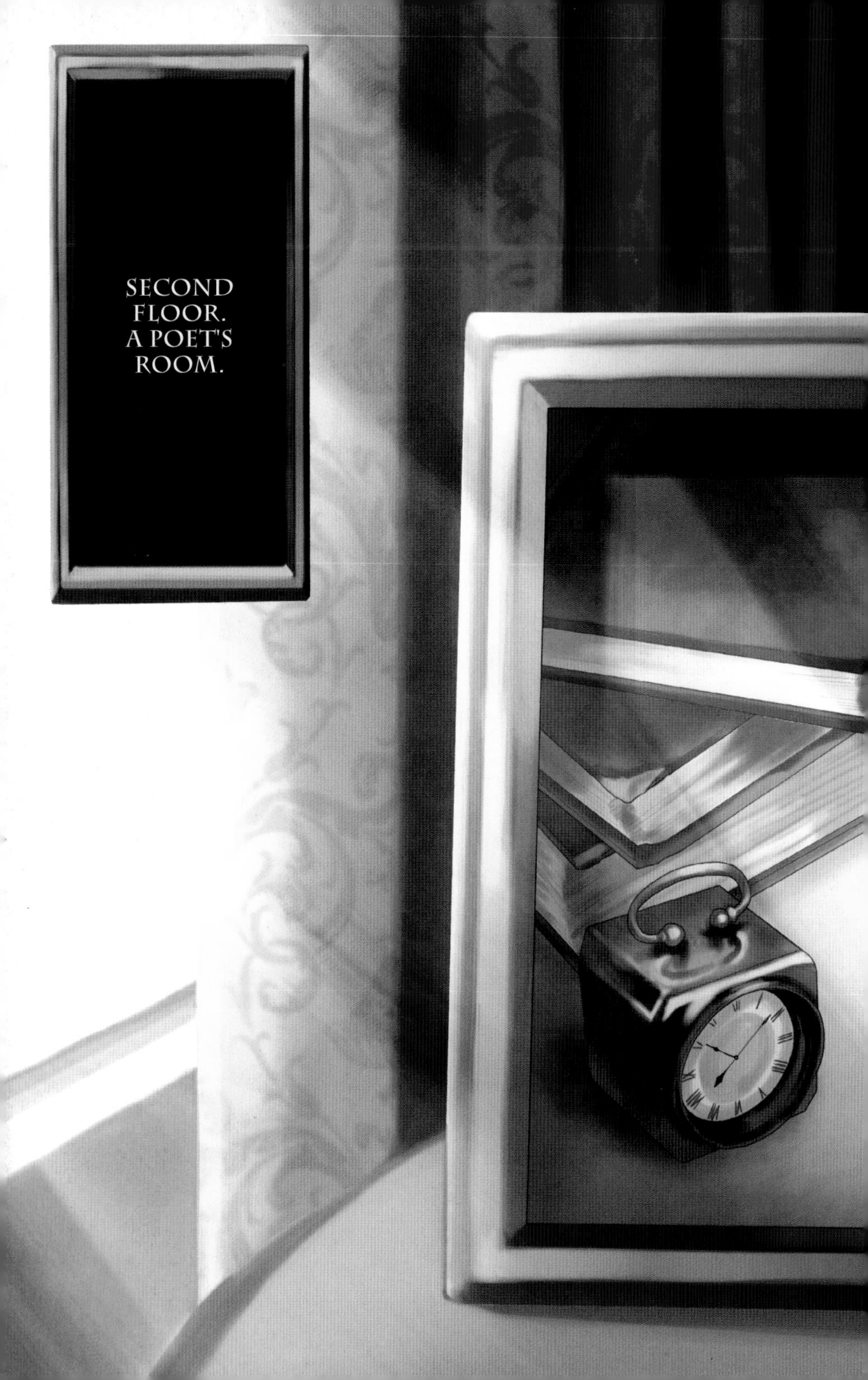
SECOND FLOOR. A POET'S ROOM.

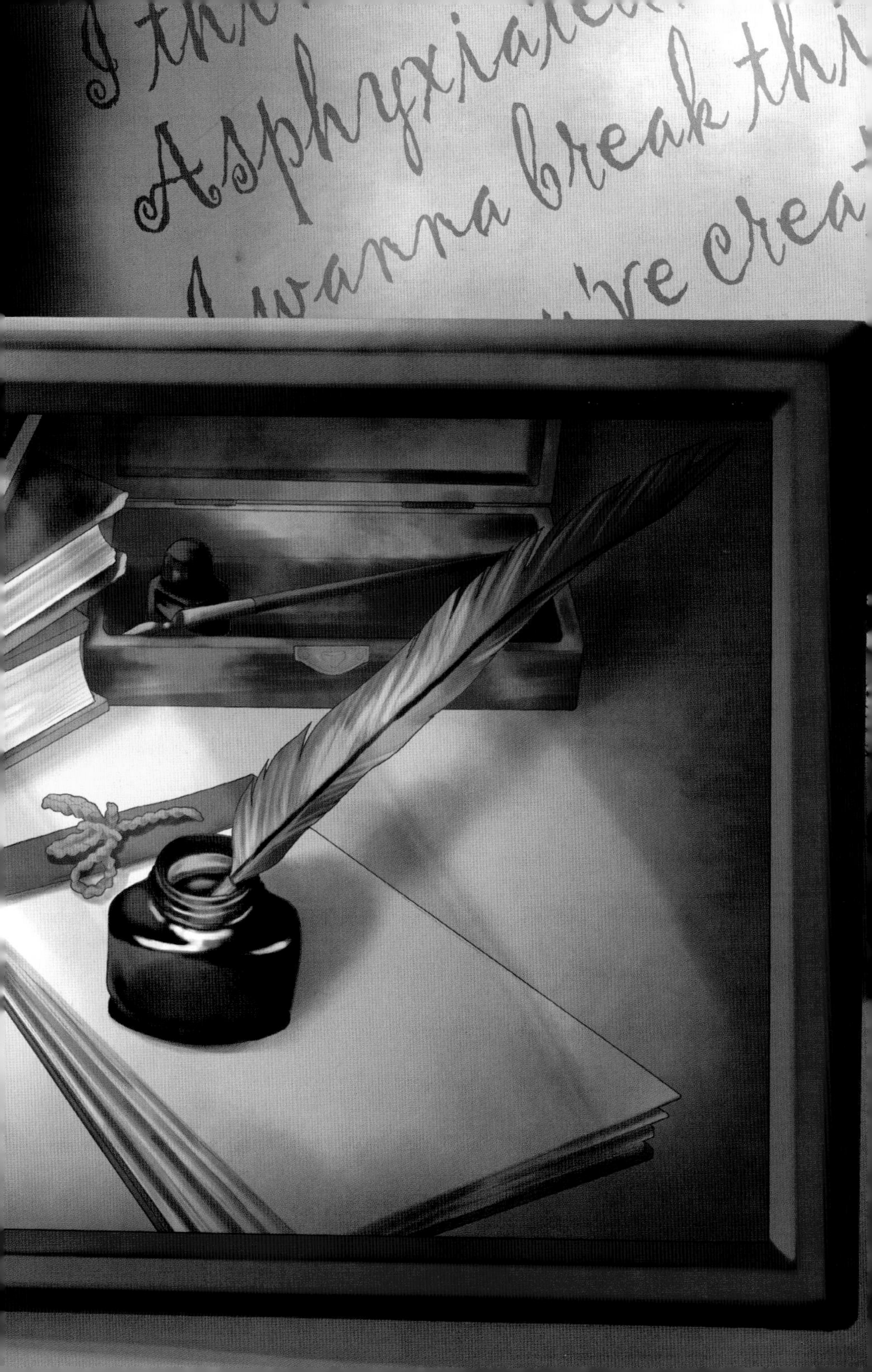
wanna break

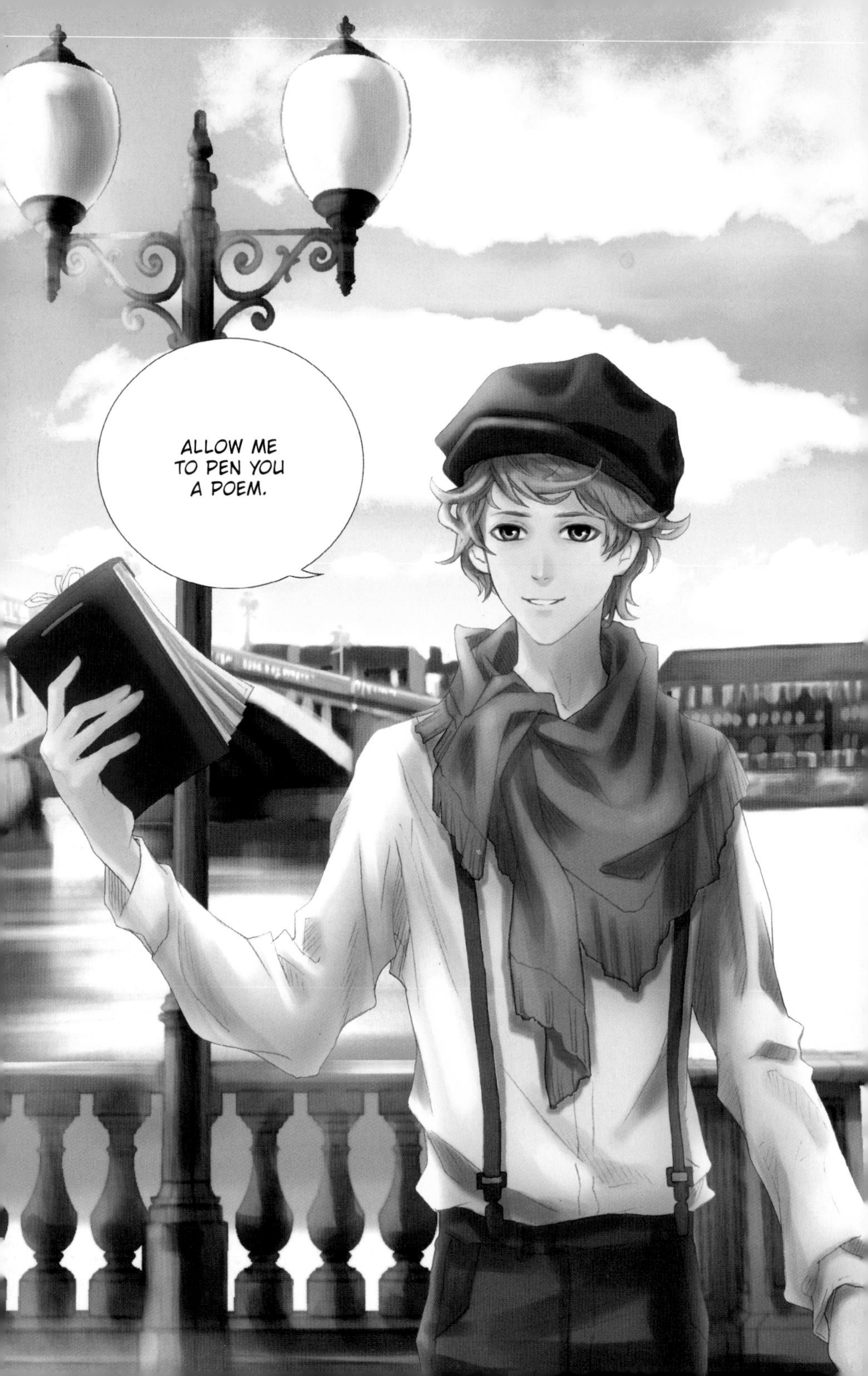
ALLOW ME TO PEN YOU A POEM.

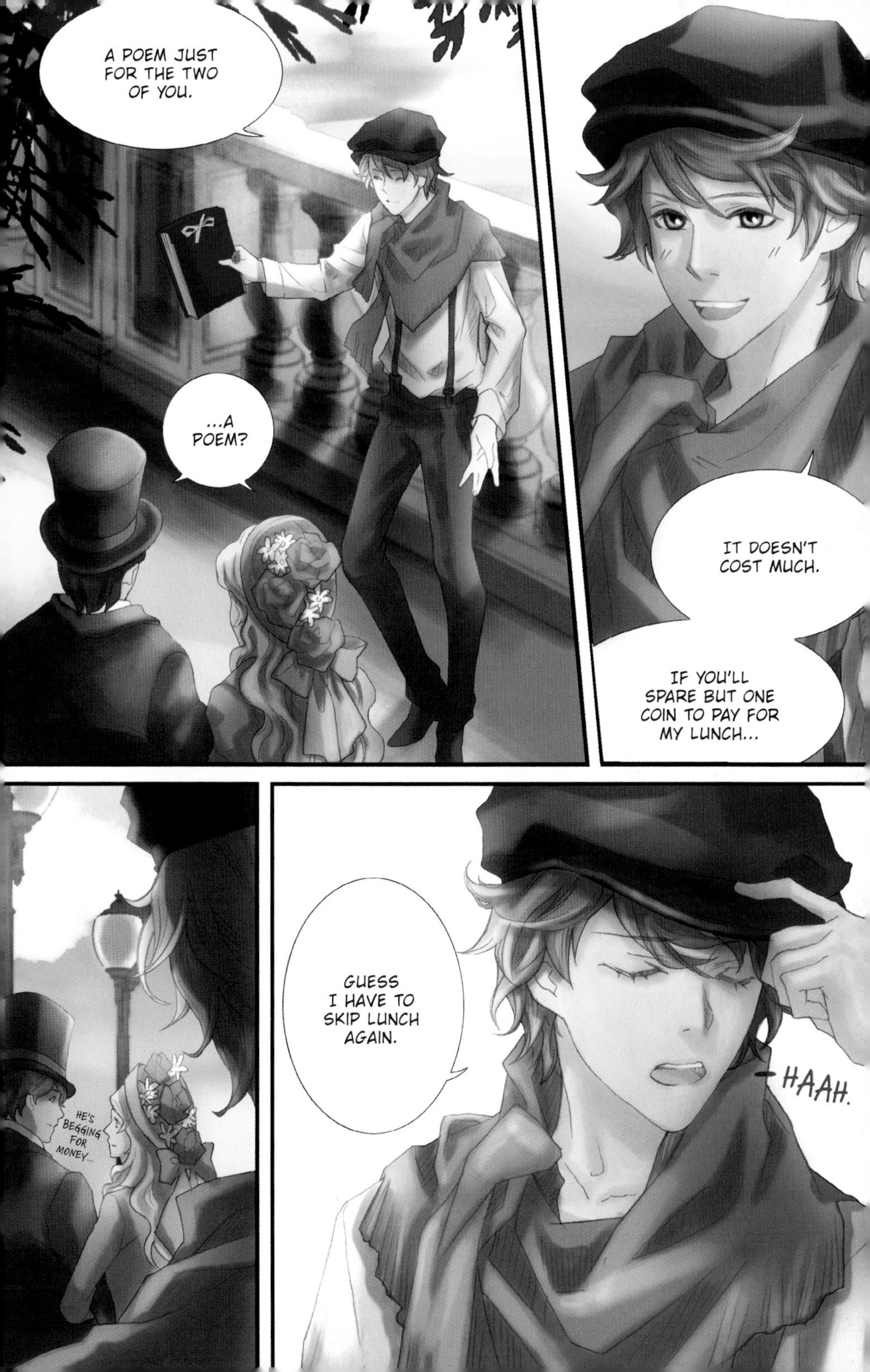
A POEM JUST FOR THE TWO OF YOU.
...A POEM?
IT DOESN'T COST MUCH.
IF YOU'LL SPARE BUT ONE COIN TO PAY FOR MY LUNCH...
HE'S BEGGING FOR MONEY...
GUESS I HAVE TO SKIP LUNCH AGAIN.
-HAAH.

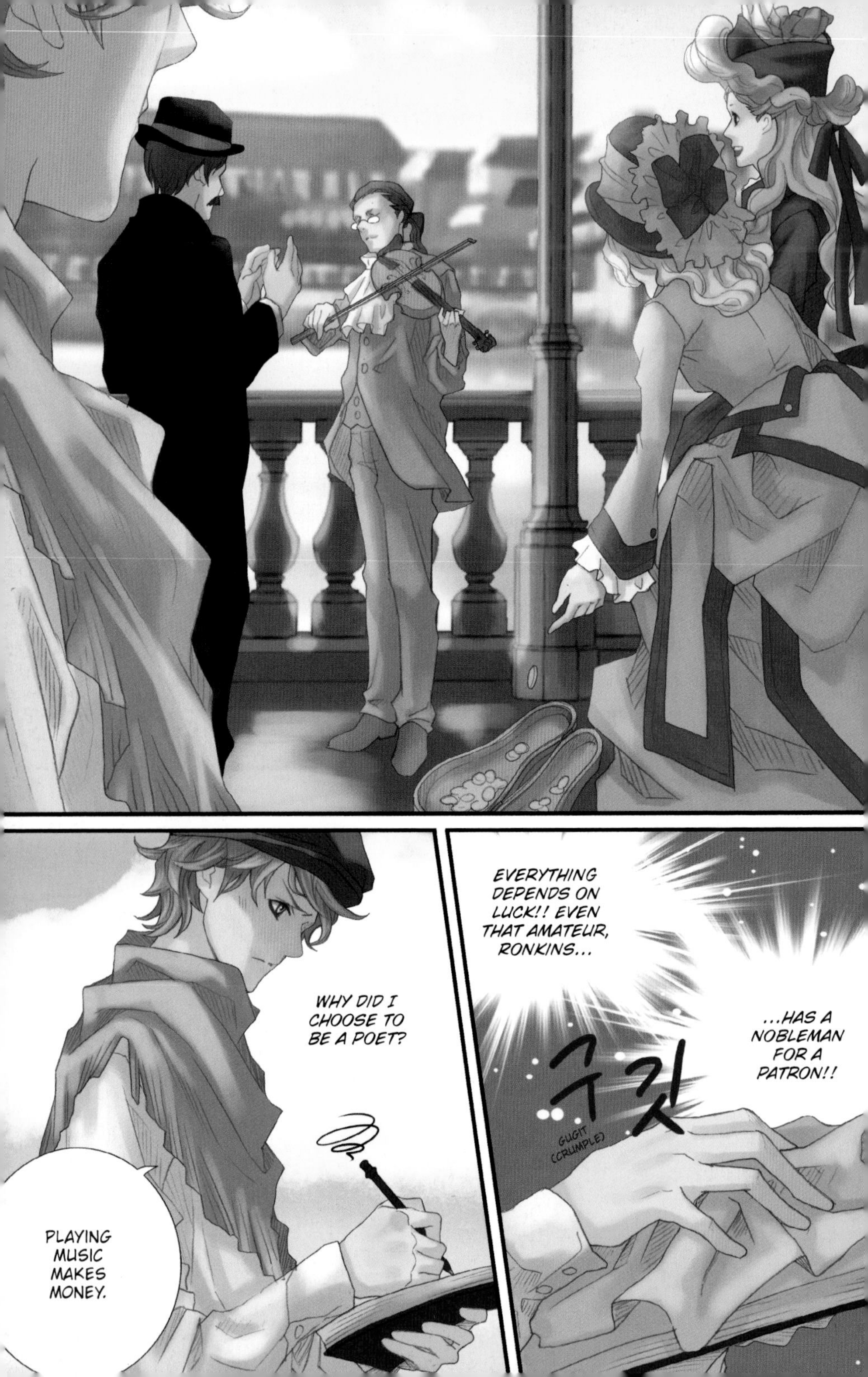
WHY DID I CHOOSE TO BE A POET?
PLAYING MUSIC MAKES MONEY.
EVERYTHING DEPENDS ON LUCK!! EVEN THAT AMATEUR, RONKINS...
...HAS A NOBLEMAN FOR A PATRON!!
구깃
GUGIT (CRUMPLE)

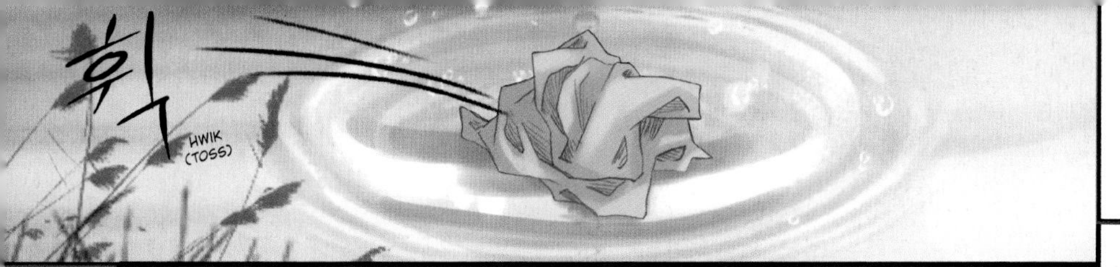
휙
HWIK
(TOSS)

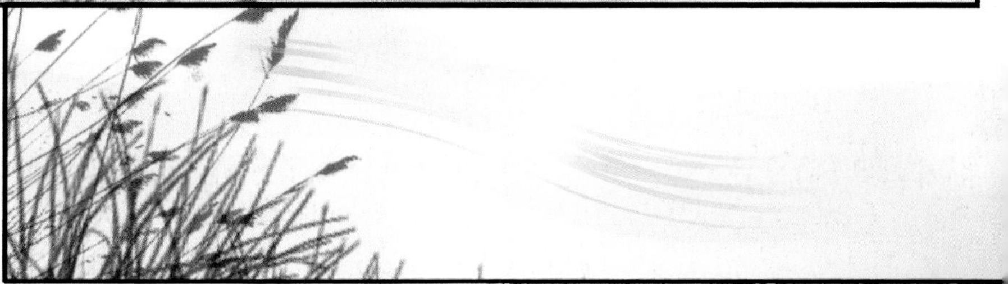

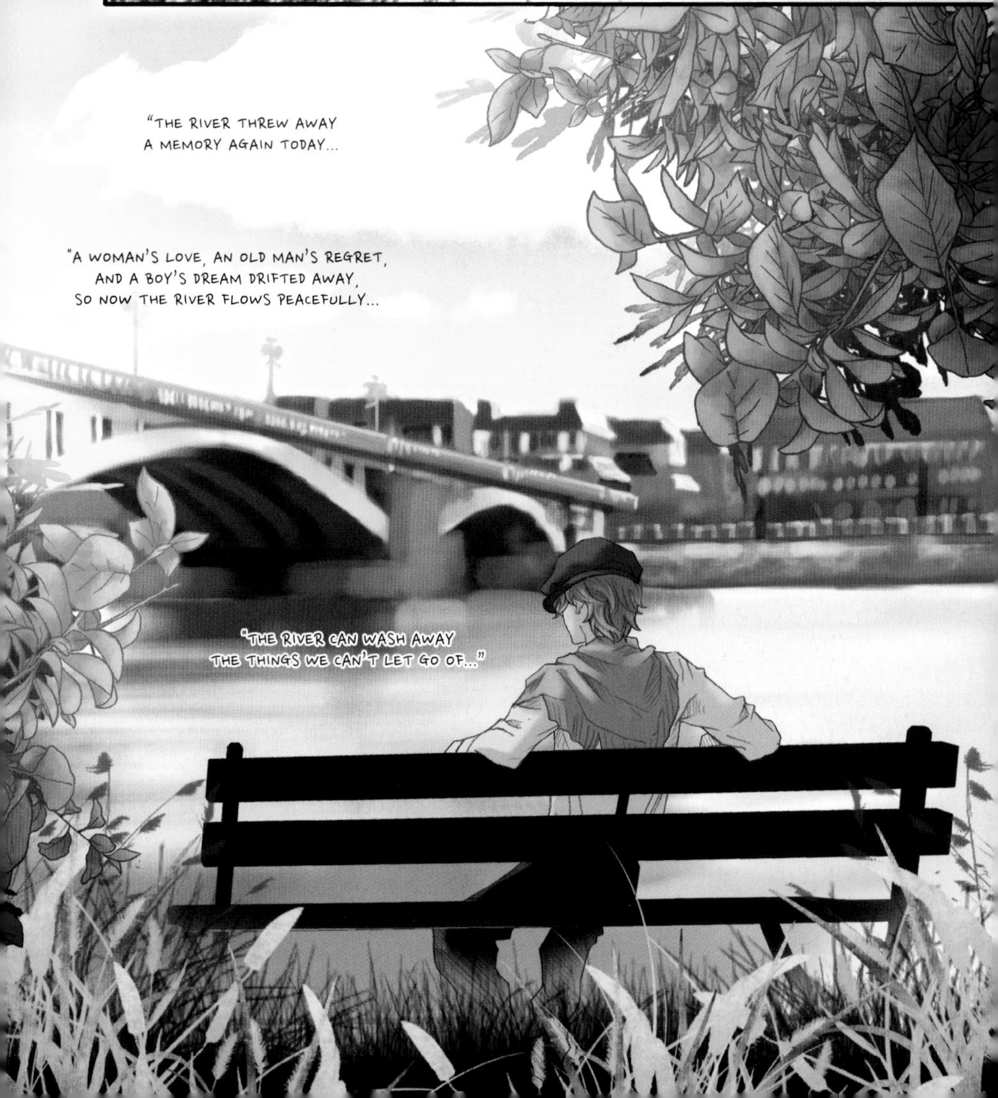
"THE RIVER THREW AWAY
A MEMORY AGAIN TODAY...
"A WOMAN'S LOVE, AN OLD MAN'S REGRET,
AND A BOY'S DREAM DRIFTED AWAY,
SO NOW THE RIVER FLOWS PEACEFULLY...
"THE RIVER CAN WASH AWAY
THE THINGS WE CAN'T LET GO OF..."

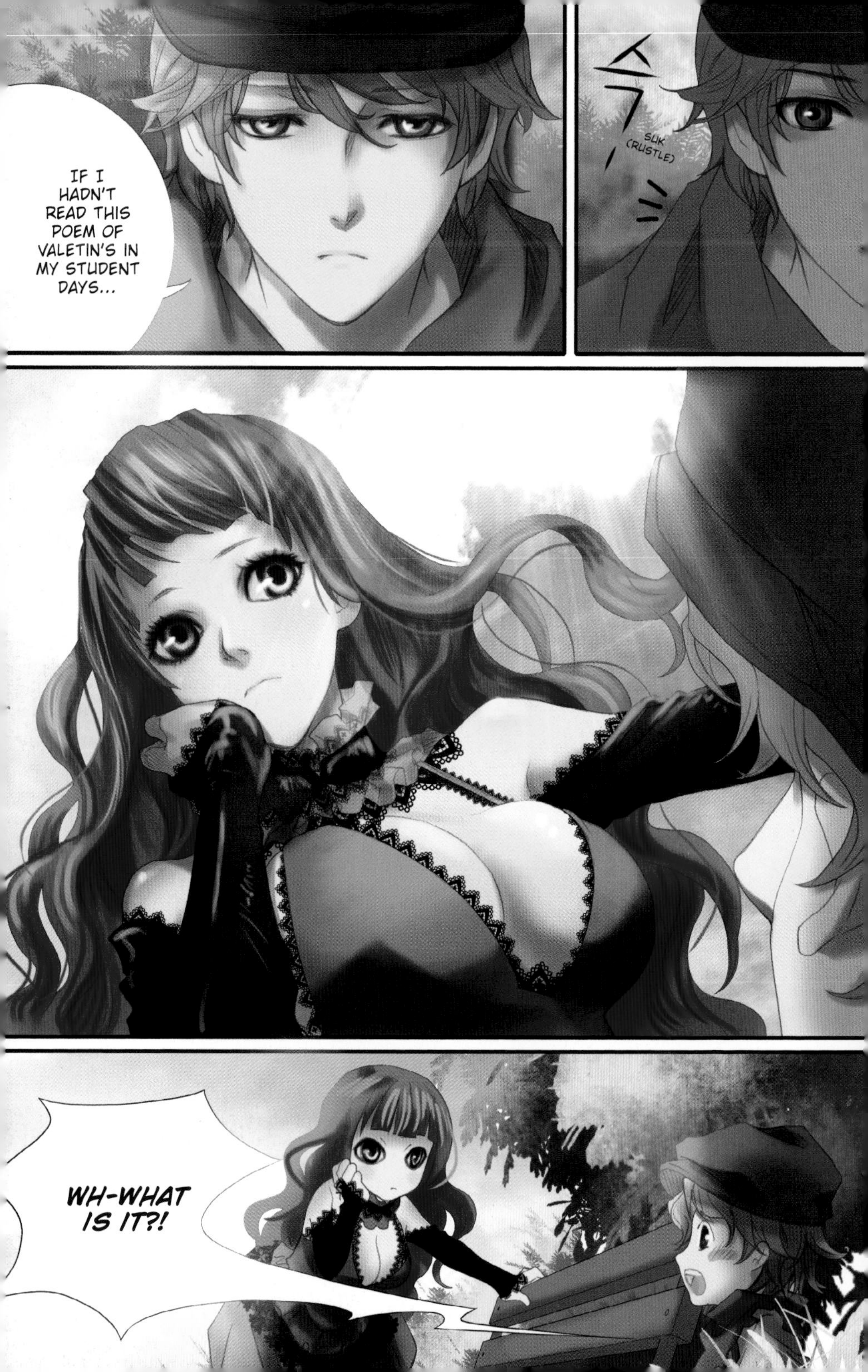
SUK (RUSTLE)
IF I HADN'T READ THIS POEM OF VALETIN'S IN MY STUDENT DAYS...
WH-WHAT IS IT?!

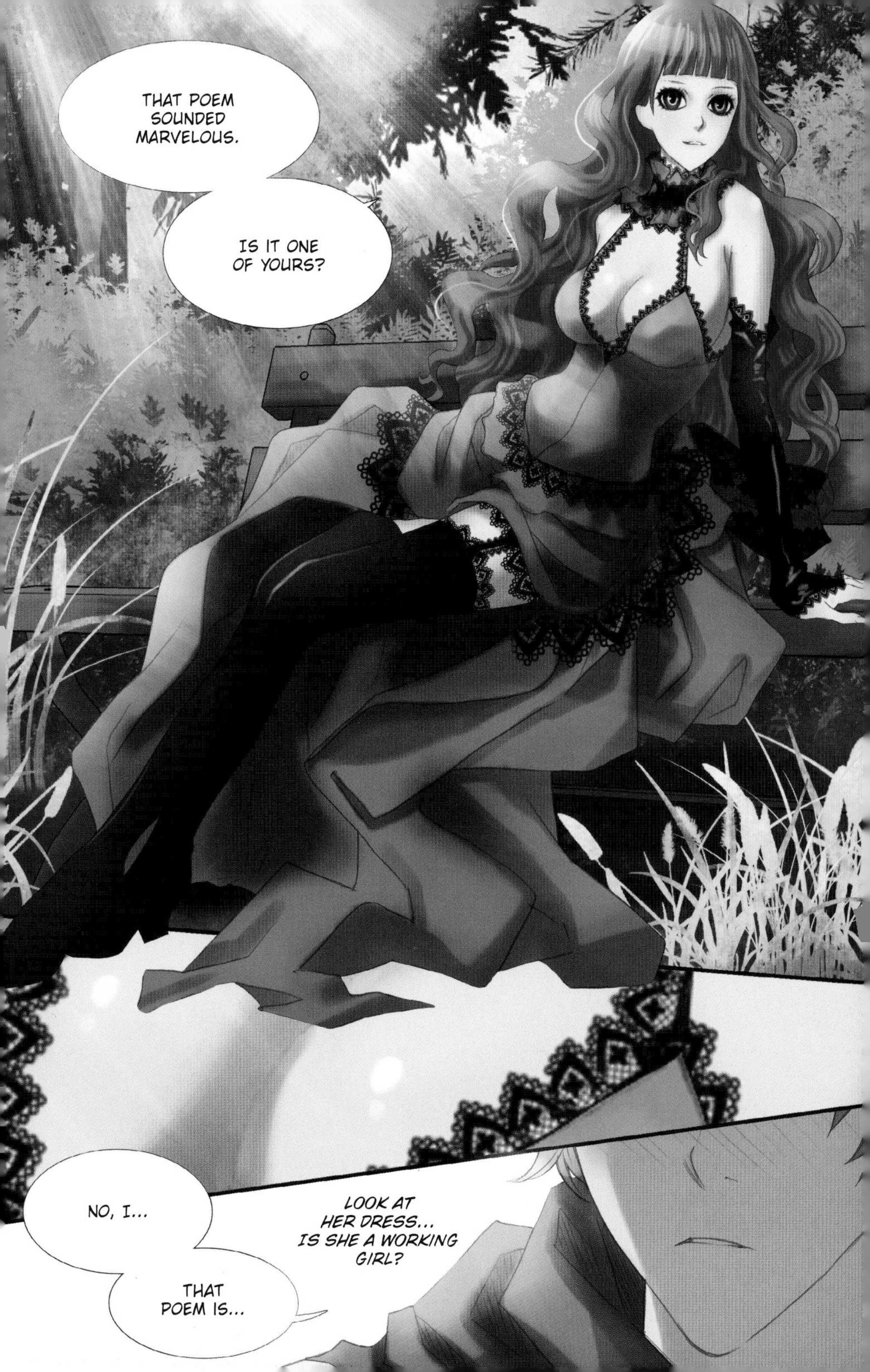
THAT POEM SOUNDED MARVELOUS.
IS IT ONE OF YOURS?
NO, I...
THAT POEM IS...
LOOK AT HER DRESS... IS SHE A WORKING GIRL?

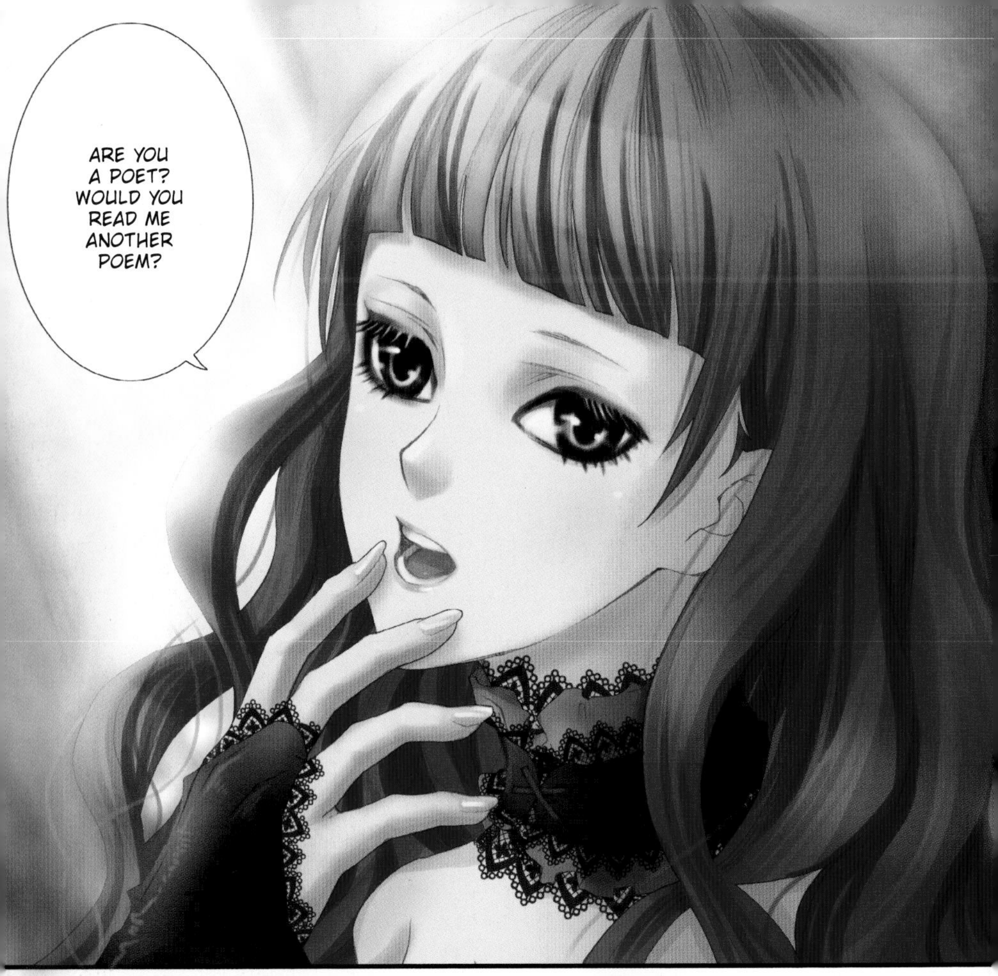
ARE YOU A POET? WOULD YOU READ ME ANOTHER POEM?
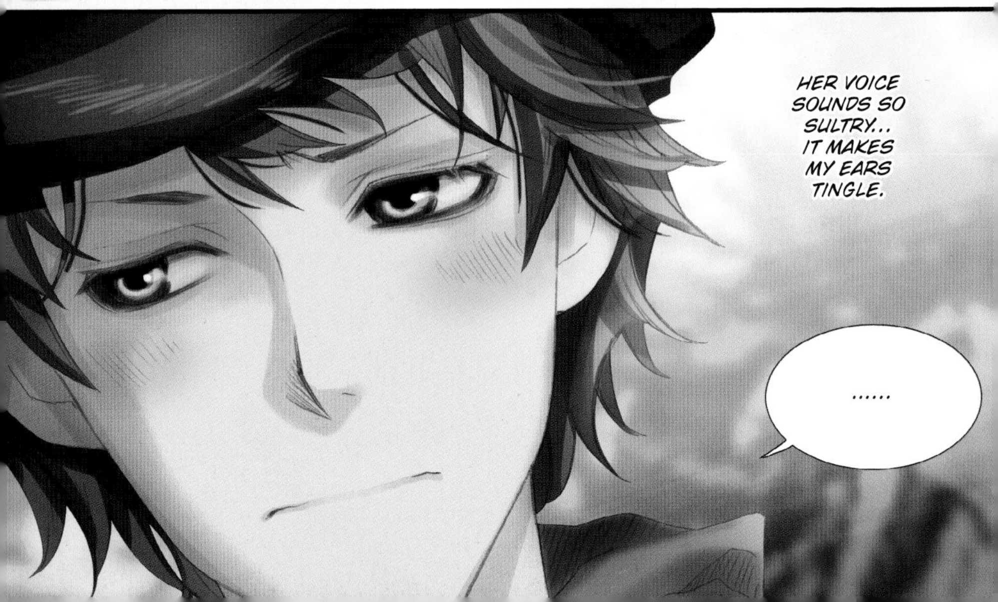
HER VOICE SOUNDS SO SULTRY... IT MAKES MY EARS TINGLE.
......

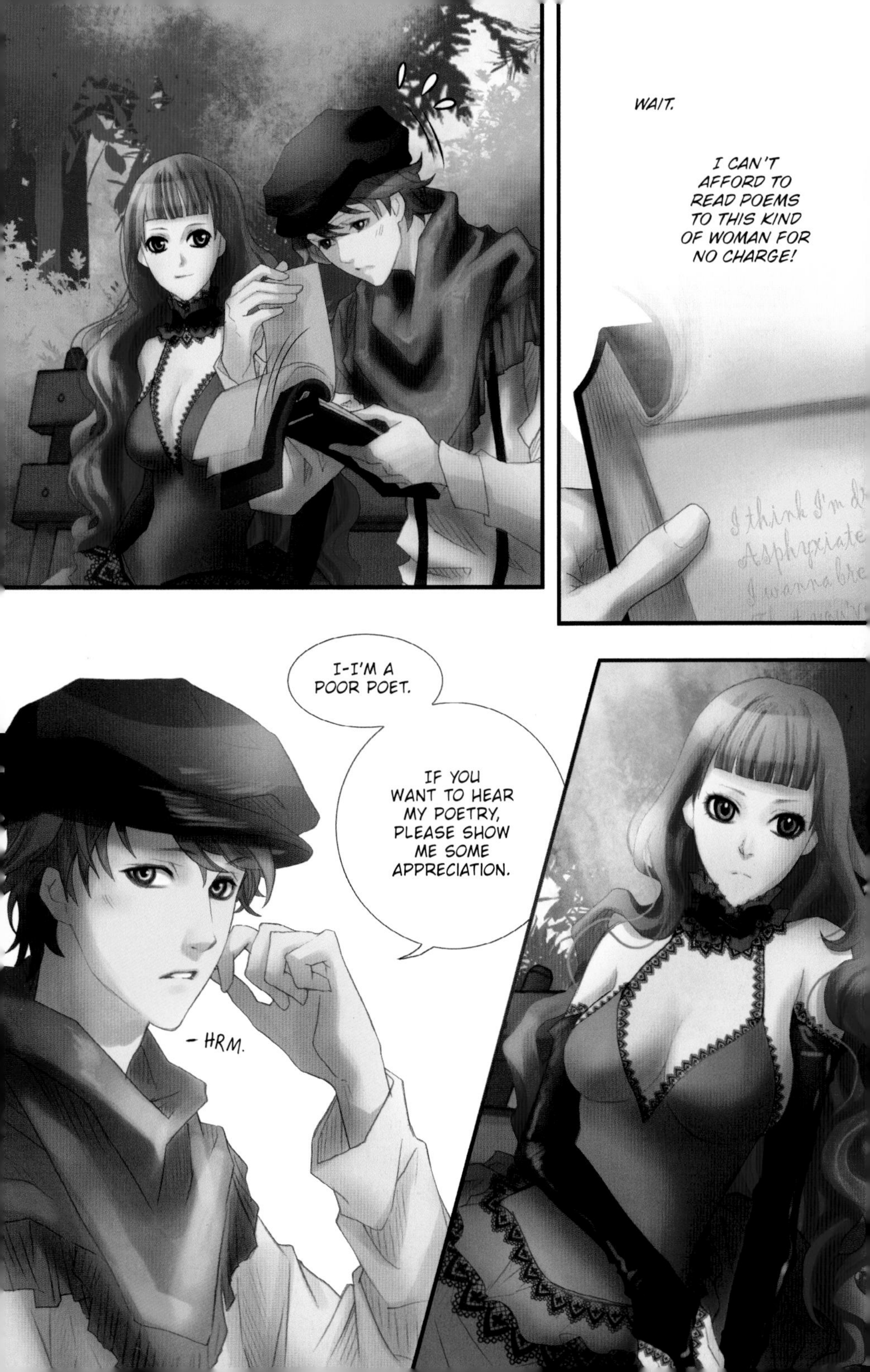
WAIT.
I CAN'T AFFORD TO READ POEMS TO THIS KIND OF WOMAN FOR NO CHARGE!
I-I'M A POOR POET.
IF YOU WANT TO HEAR MY POETRY, PLEASE SHOW ME SOME APPRECIATION.
- HRM.

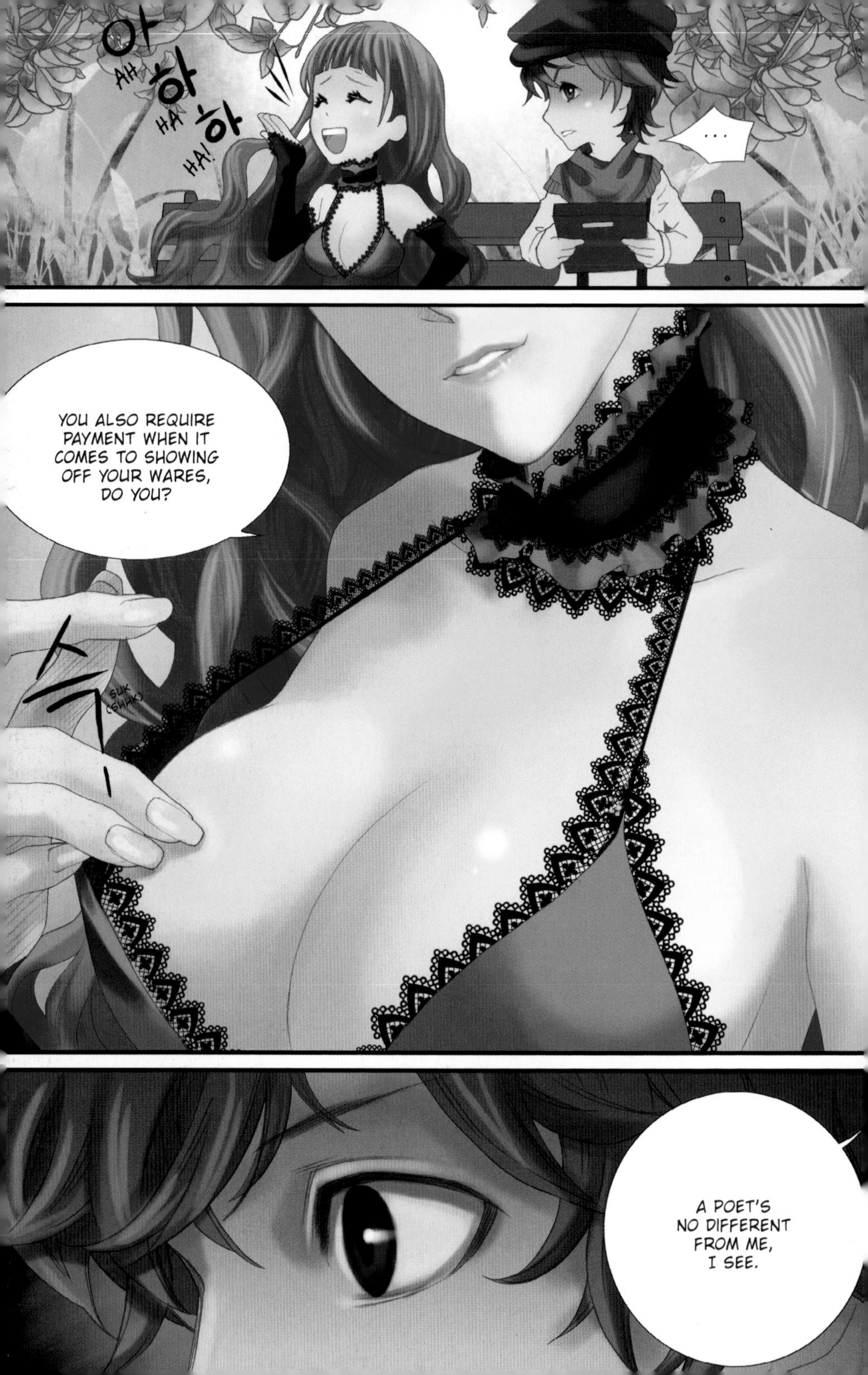
아 AH 하 HA 하 HA!
...
YOU ALSO REQUIRE PAYMENT WHEN IT COMES TO SHOWING OFF YOUR WARES, DO YOU?
스 SUK (SHHK)
A POET'S NO DIFFERENT FROM ME, I SEE.

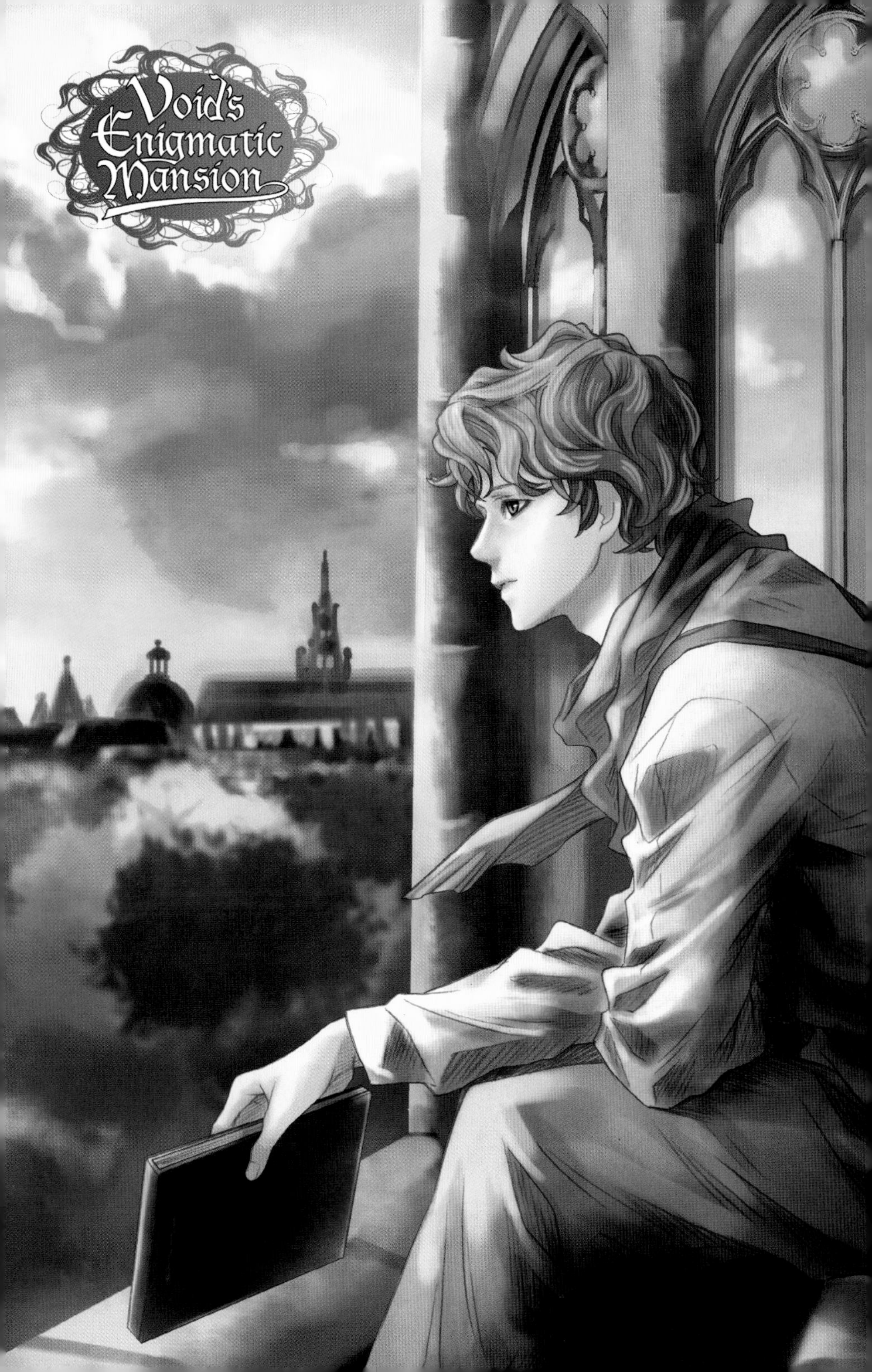
Void's Enigmatic Mansion

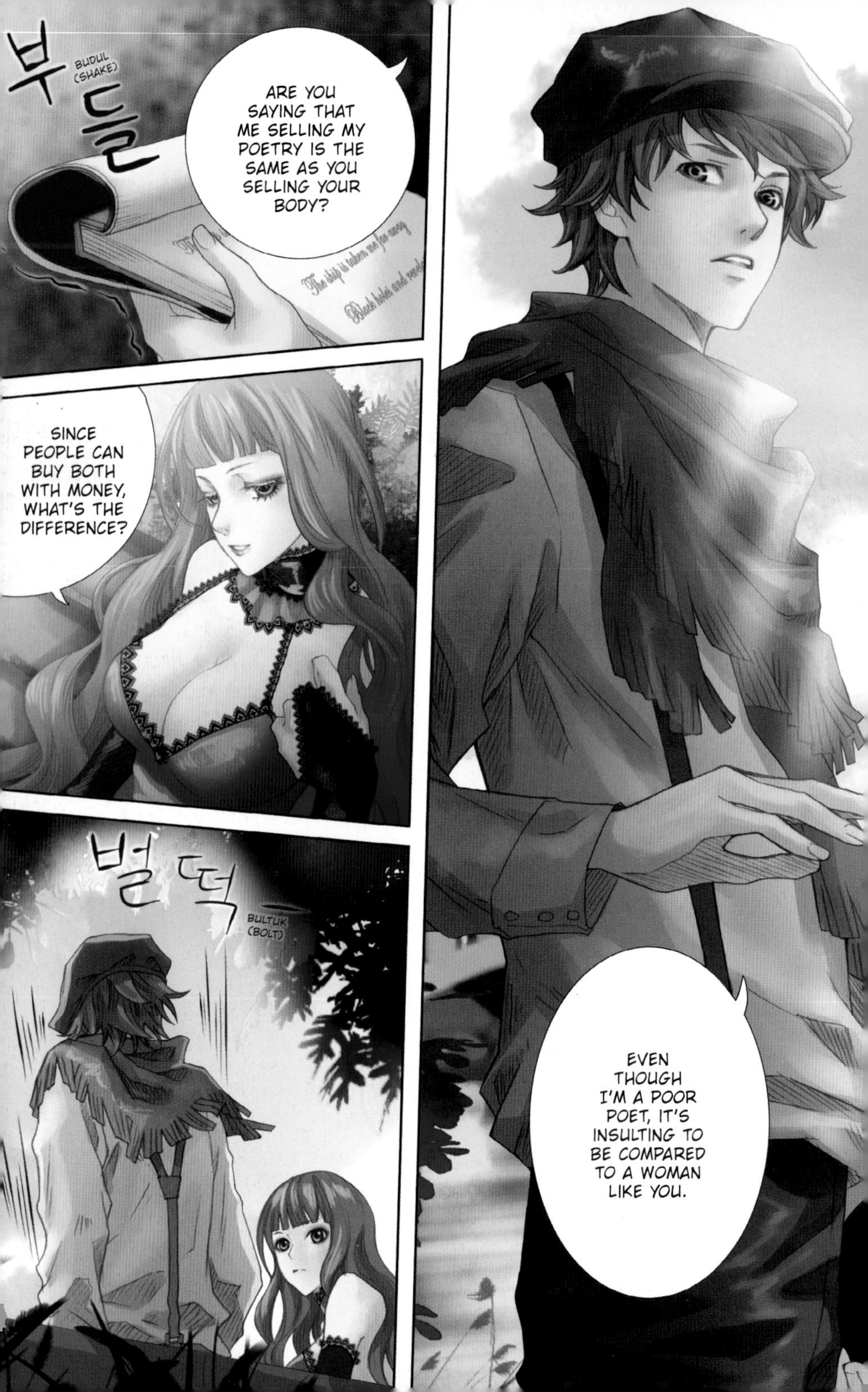
부들
BUDUL (SHAKE)
ARE YOU SAYING THAT ME SELLING MY POETRY IS THE SAME AS YOU SELLING YOUR BODY?
SINCE PEOPLE CAN BUY BOTH WITH MONEY, WHAT'S THE DIFFERENCE?
벌떡
BULTUK (BOLT)
EVEN THOUGH I'M A POOR POET, IT'S INSULTING TO BE COMPARED TO A WOMAN LIKE YOU.

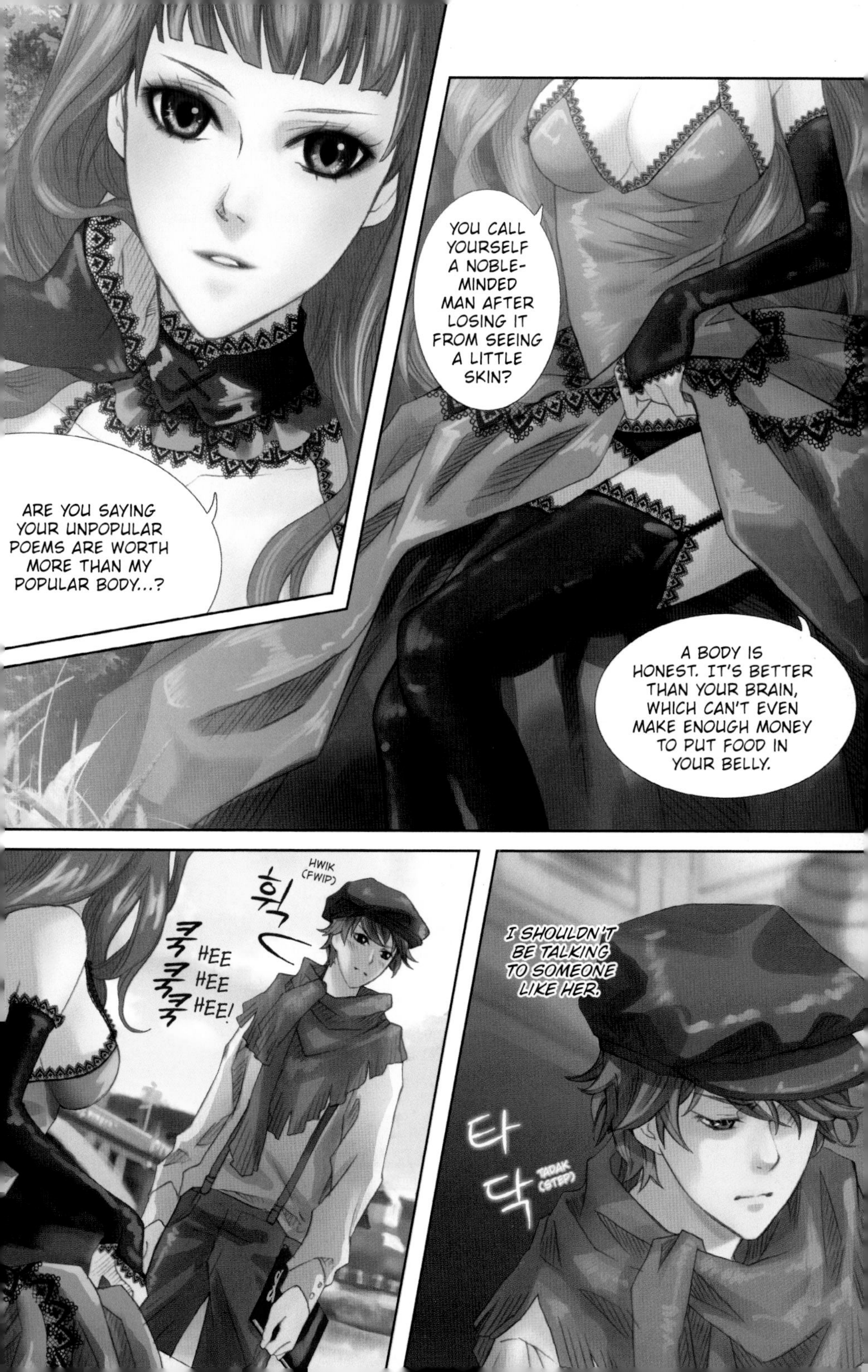

ARE YOU SAYING YOUR UNPOPULAR POEMS ARE WORTH MORE THAN MY POPULAR BODY...?
YOU CALL YOURSELF A NOBLE-MINDED MAN AFTER LOSING IT FROM SEEING A LITTLE SKIN?
A BODY IS HONEST. IT'S BETTER THAN YOUR BRAIN, WHICH CAN'T EVEN MAKE ENOUGH MONEY TO PUT FOOD IN YOUR BELLY.
휙
HWIK (FWIP)
쿡쿡쿡
HEE HEE HEE!
I SHOULDN'T BE TALKING TO SOMEONE LIKE HER.
타닥
TADAK (STEP)

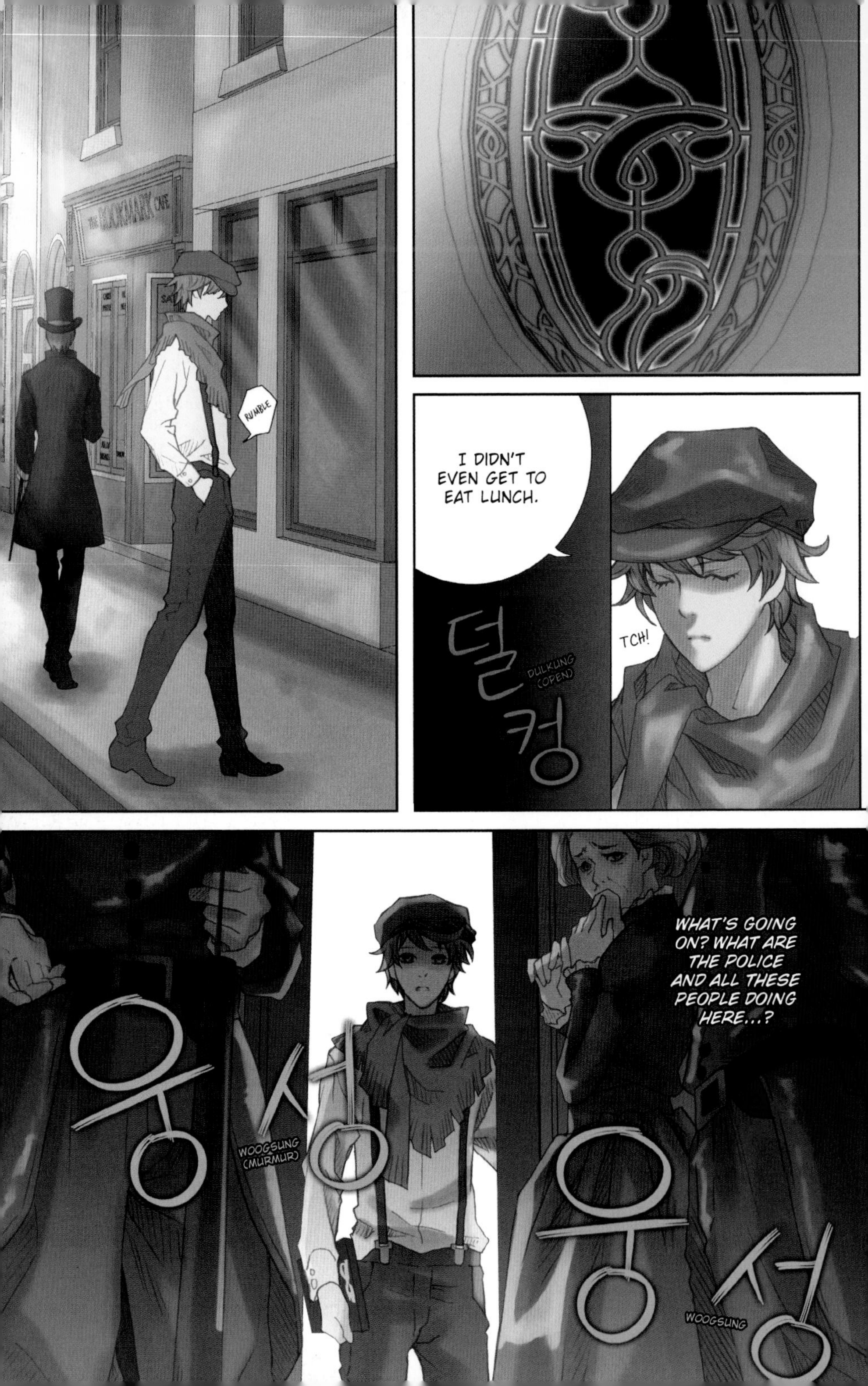
THE BOOKMARK CAFE
RUMBLE
I DIDN'T EVEN GET TO EAT LUNCH.
덜컹
DULKUNG (OPEN)
TCH!
웅성
WOOGSUNG (MURMUR)
WHAT'S GOING ON? WHAT ARE THE POLICE AND ALL THESE PEOPLE DOING HERE...?
웅성
WOOGSUNG

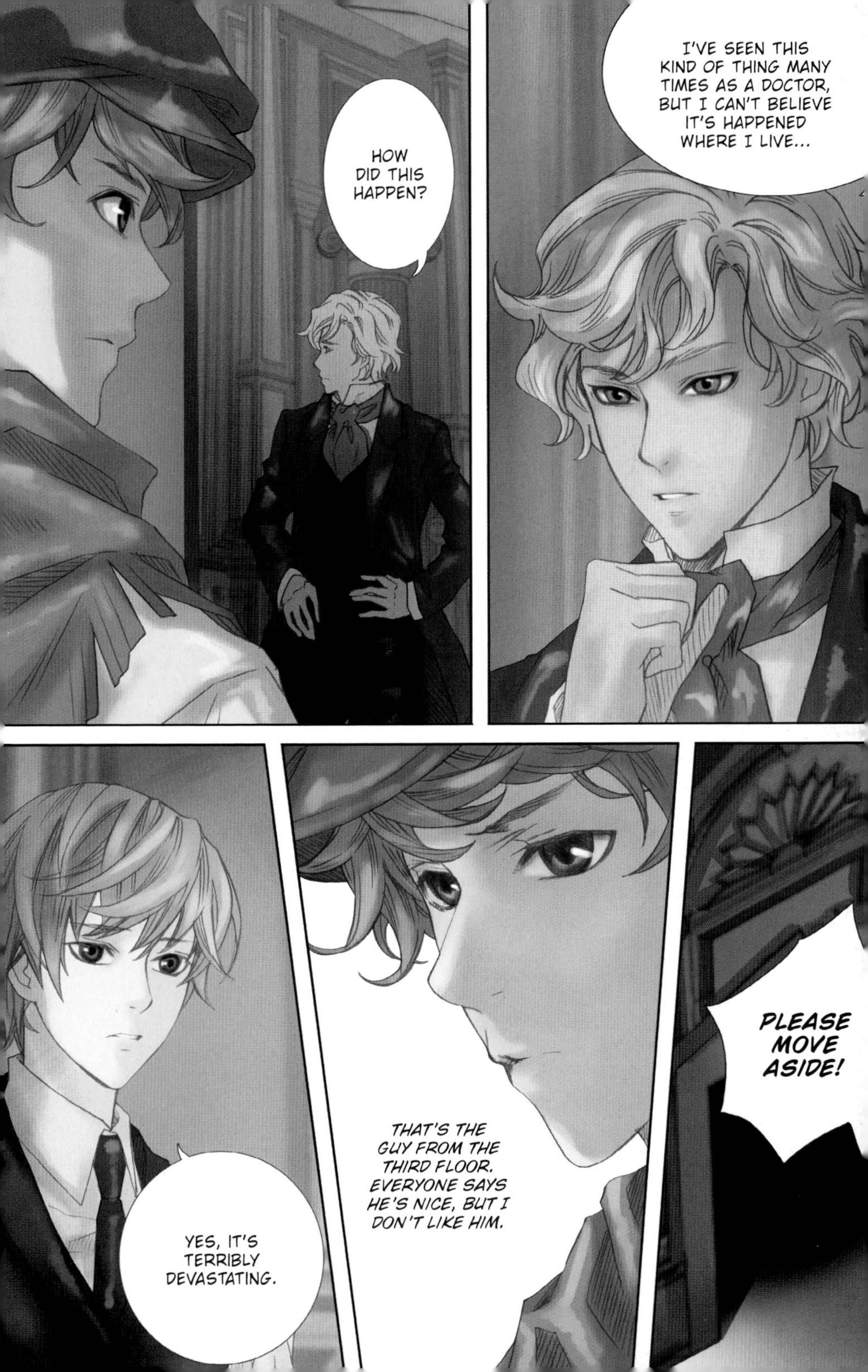
HOW DID THIS HAPPEN?
I'VE SEEN THIS KIND OF THING MANY TIMES AS A DOCTOR, BUT I CAN'T BELIEVE IT'S HAPPENED WHERE I LIVE...
YES, IT'S TERRIBLY DEVASTATING.
THAT'S THE GUY FROM THE THIRD FLOOR. EVERYONE SAYS HE'S NICE, BUT I DON'T LIKE HIM.
PLEASE MOVE ASIDE!

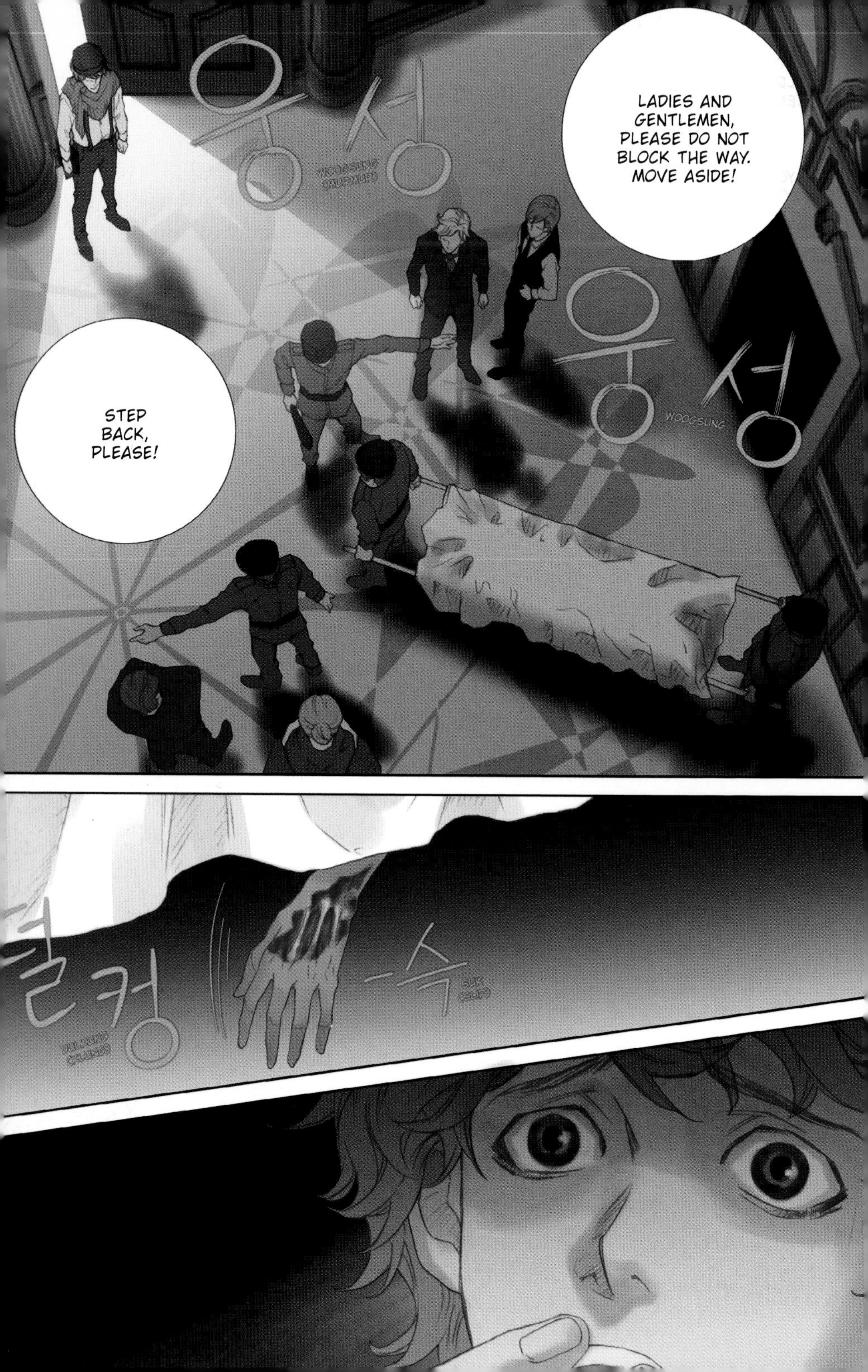
WOOGSUNG (MURMUR)
LADIES AND GENTLEMEN, PLEASE DO NOT BLOCK THE WAY. MOVE ASIDE!
STEP BACK, PLEASE!
WOOGSUNG
DULKUNG (KLUNG)
SUK (SLIP)

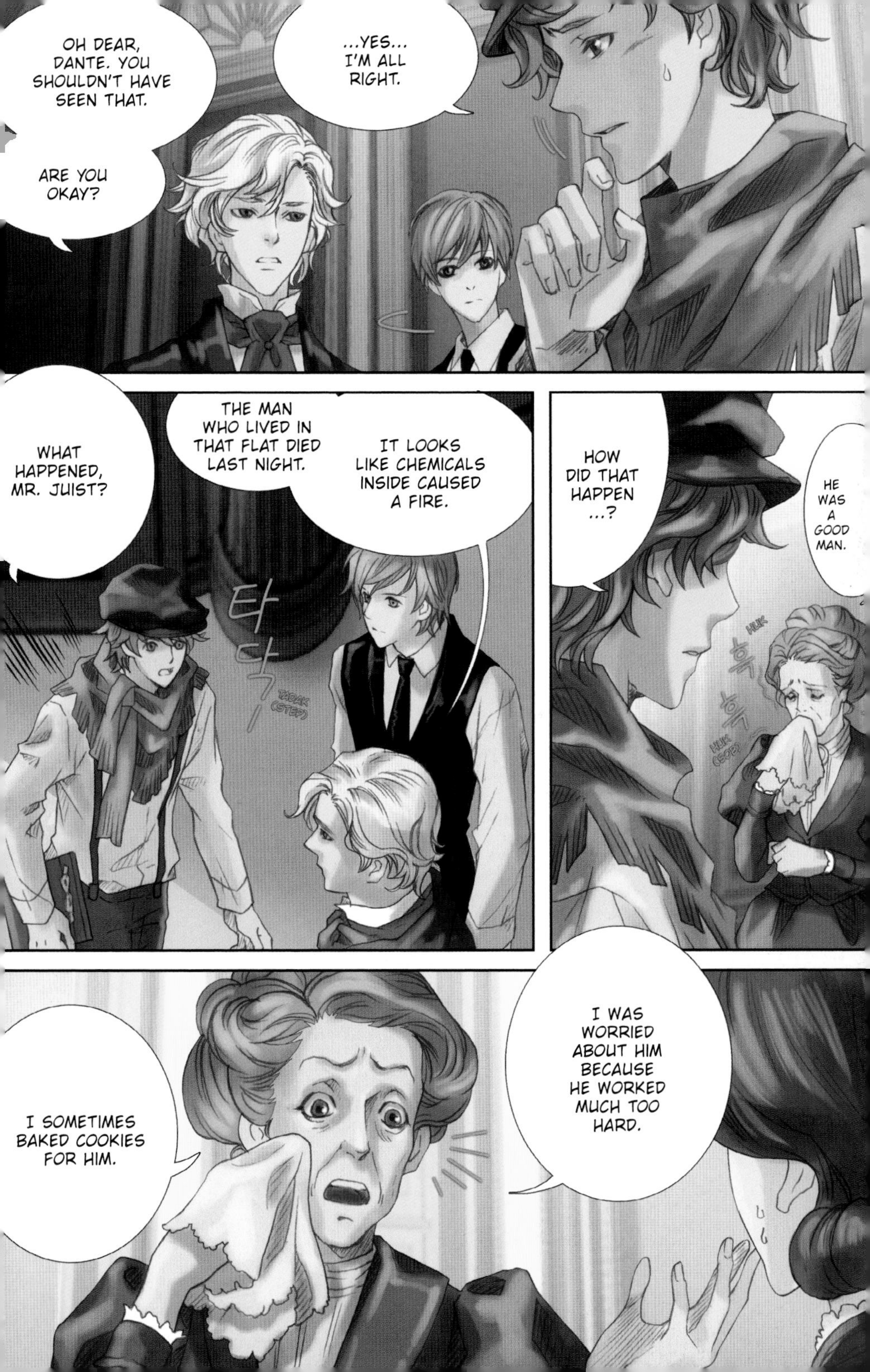
OH DEAR, DANTE. YOU SHOULDN'T HAVE SEEN THAT.
ARE YOU OKAY?
...YES... I'M ALL RIGHT.
WHAT HAPPENED, MR. JUIST?
THE MAN WHO LIVED IN THAT FLAT DIED LAST NIGHT.
IT LOOKS LIKE CHEMICALS INSIDE CAUSED A FIRE.
타닥
TADAK (STEP)
HOW DID THAT HAPPEN ...?
HE WAS A GOOD MAN.
HUK
흑 흑
HUK (SOB)
I SOMETIMES BAKED COOKIES FOR HIM.
I WAS WORRIED ABOUT HIM BECAUSE HE WORKED MUCH TOO HARD.

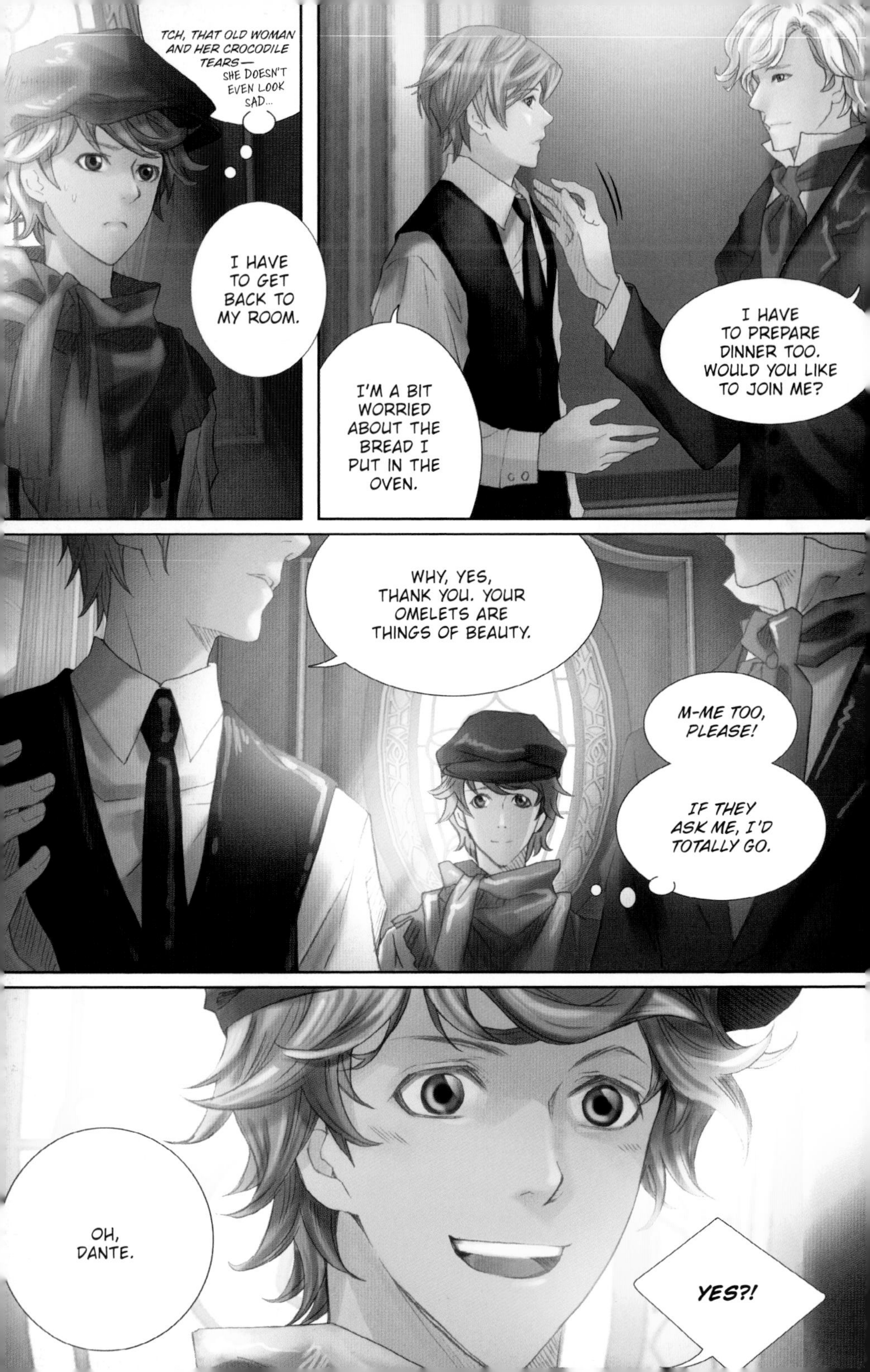
TCH, THAT OLD WOMAN AND HER CROCODILE TEARS— SHE DOESN'T EVEN LOOK SAD...
I HAVE TO GET BACK TO MY ROOM.
I'M A BIT WORRIED ABOUT THE BREAD I PUT IN THE OVEN.
I HAVE TO PREPARE DINNER TOO. WOULD YOU LIKE TO JOIN ME?
WHY, YES, THANK YOU. YOUR OMELETS ARE THINGS OF BEAUTY.
M-ME TOO, PLEASE!
IF THEY ASK ME, I'D TOTALLY GO.
OH, DANTE.
YES?!

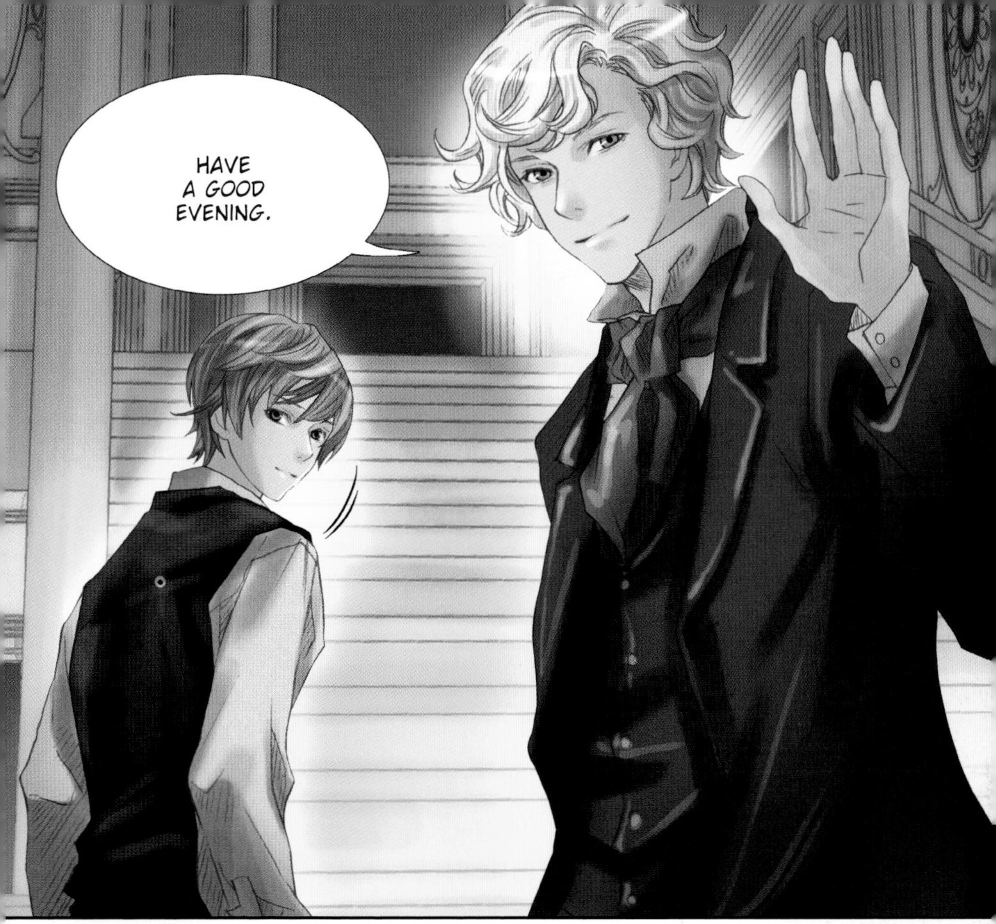
HAVE A GOOD EVENING.
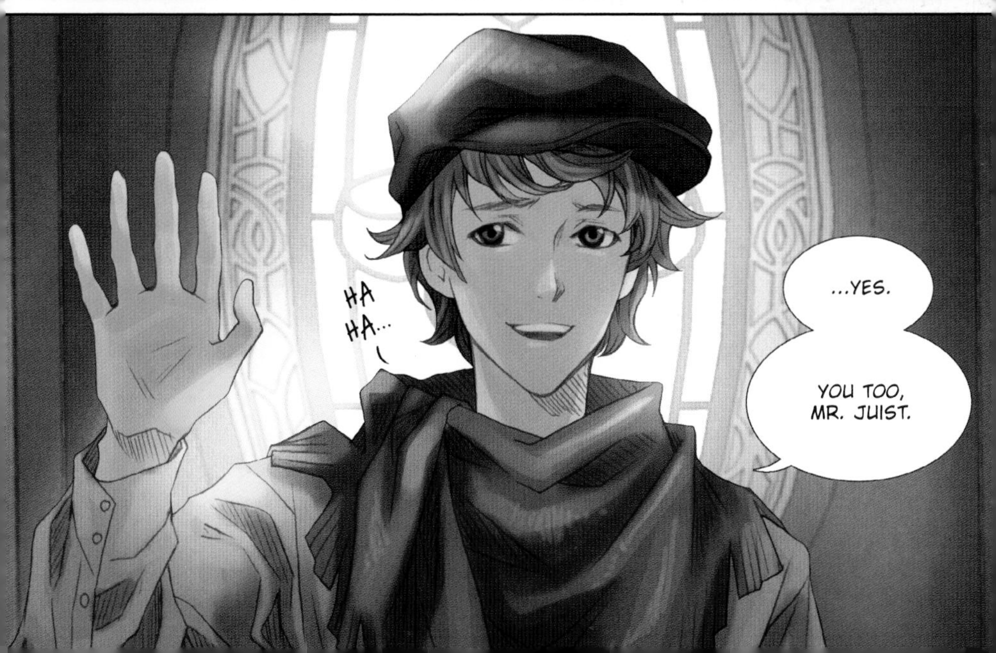
...YES.
YOU TOO, MR. JUIST.
HA HA...

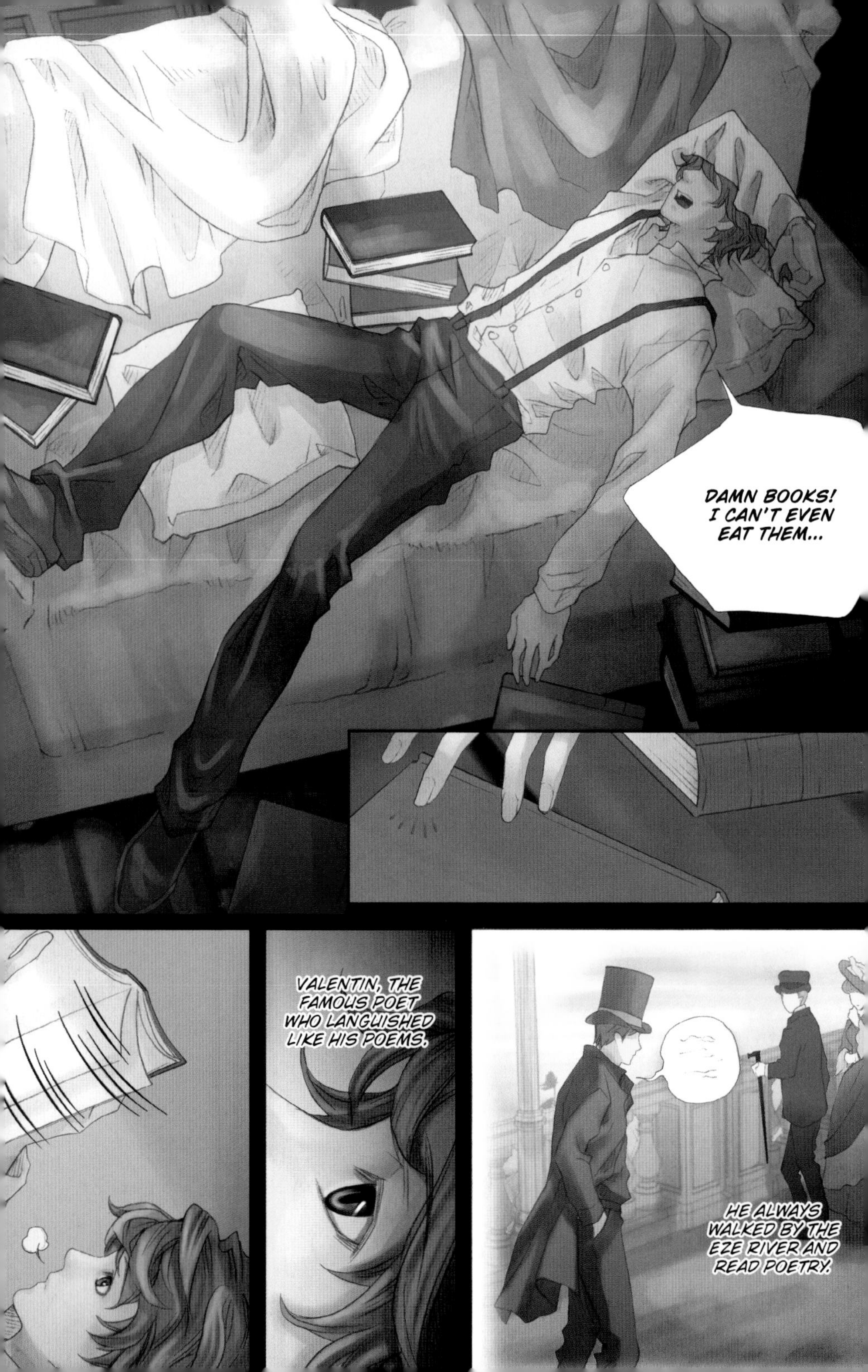
DAMN BOOKS! I CAN'T EVEN EAT THEM...
VALENTIN, THE FAMOUS POET WHO LANGUISHED LIKE HIS POEMS.
HE ALWAYS WALKED BY THE EZE RIVER AND READ POETRY.

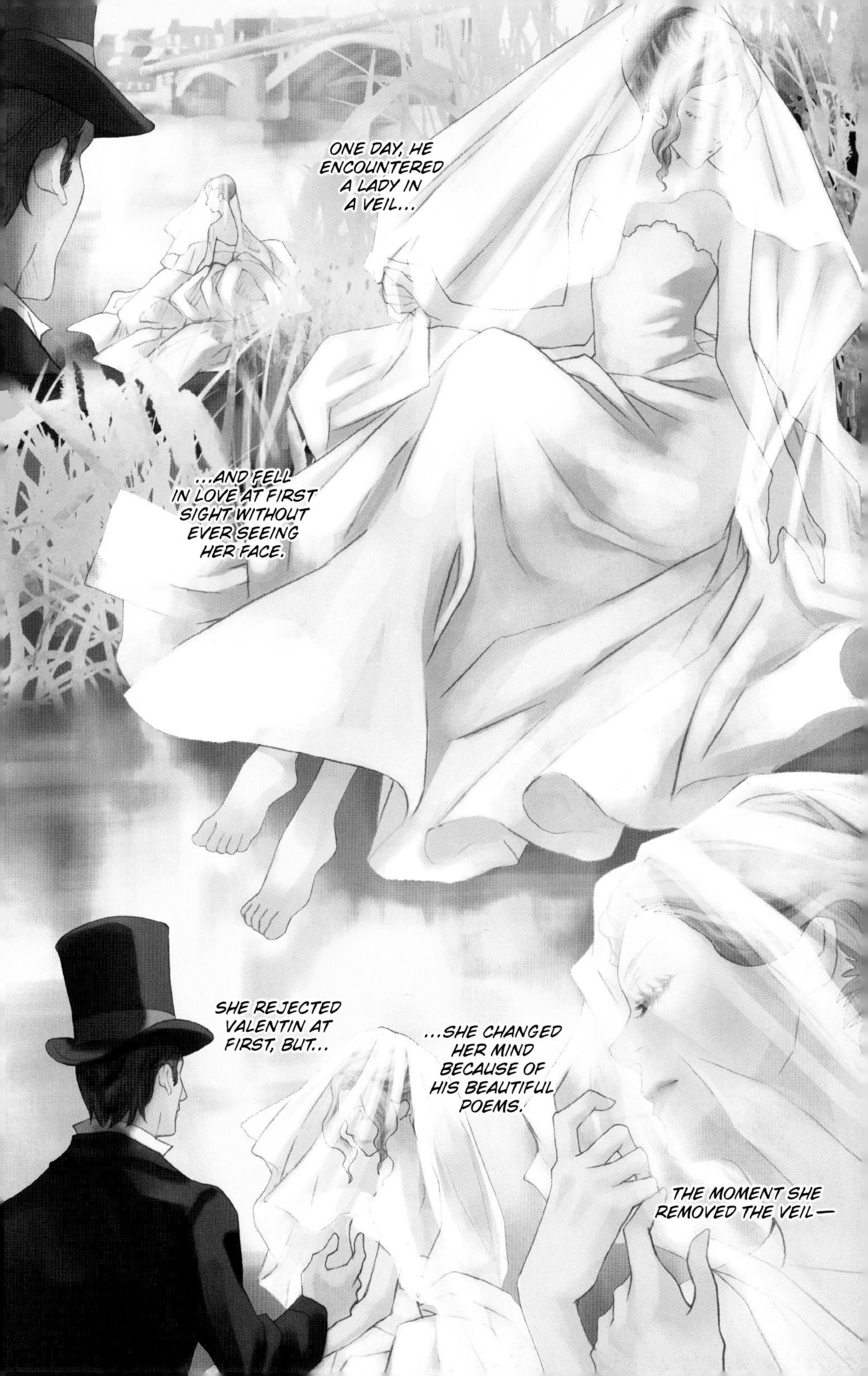
ONE DAY, HE ENCOUNTERED A LADY IN A VEIL...
...AND FELL IN LOVE AT FIRST SIGHT WITHOUT EVER SEEING HER FACE.
SHE REJECTED VALENTIN AT FIRST, BUT...
...SHE CHANGED HER MIND BECAUSE OF HIS BEAUTIFUL POEMS.
THE MOMENT SHE REMOVED THE VEIL—

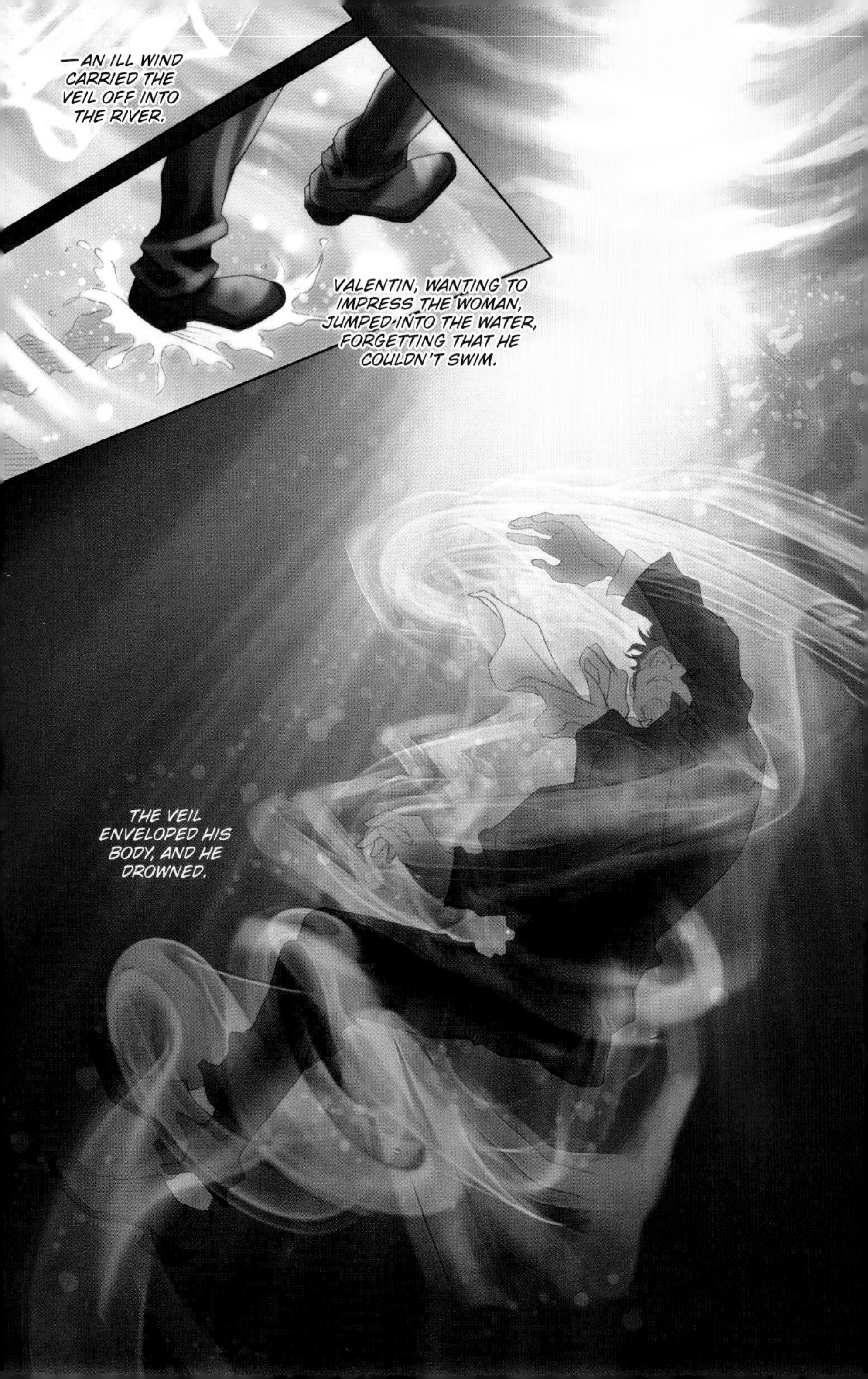
—AN ILL WIND CARRIED THE VEIL OFF INTO THE RIVER.
VALENTIN, WANTING TO IMPRESS THE WOMAN, JUMPED INTO THE WATER, FORGETTING THAT HE COULDN'T SWIM.
THE VEIL ENVELOPED HIS BODY, AND HE DROWNED.

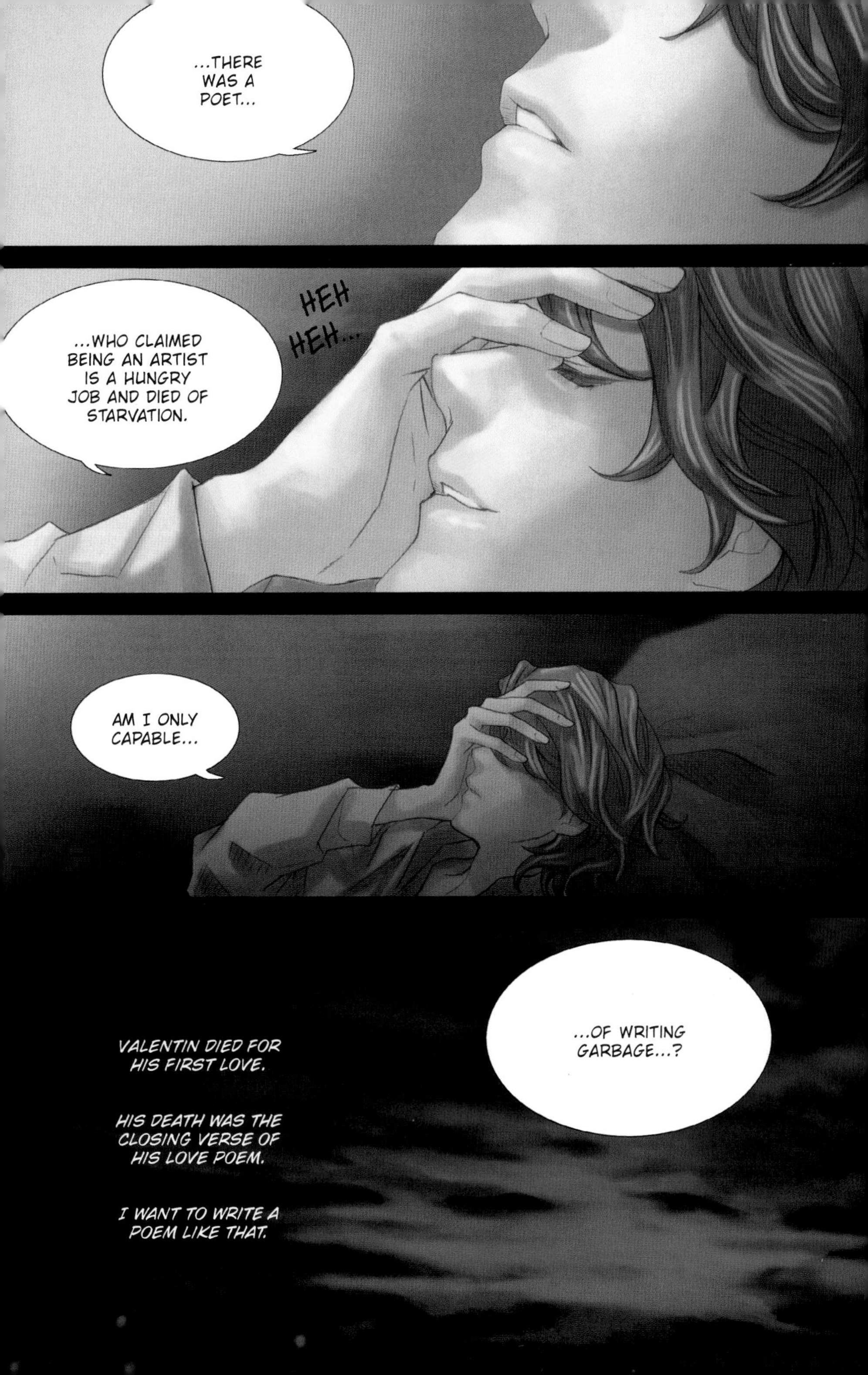
...THERE WAS A POET...
...WHO CLAIMED BEING AN ARTIST IS A HUNGRY JOB AND DIED OF STARVATION.
HEH HEH...
AM I ONLY CAPABLE...
...OF WRITING GARBAGE...?
VALENTIN DIED FOR HIS FIRST LOVE.
HIS DEATH WAS THE CLOSING VERSE OF HIS LOVE POEM.
I WANT TO WRITE A POEM LIKE THAT.

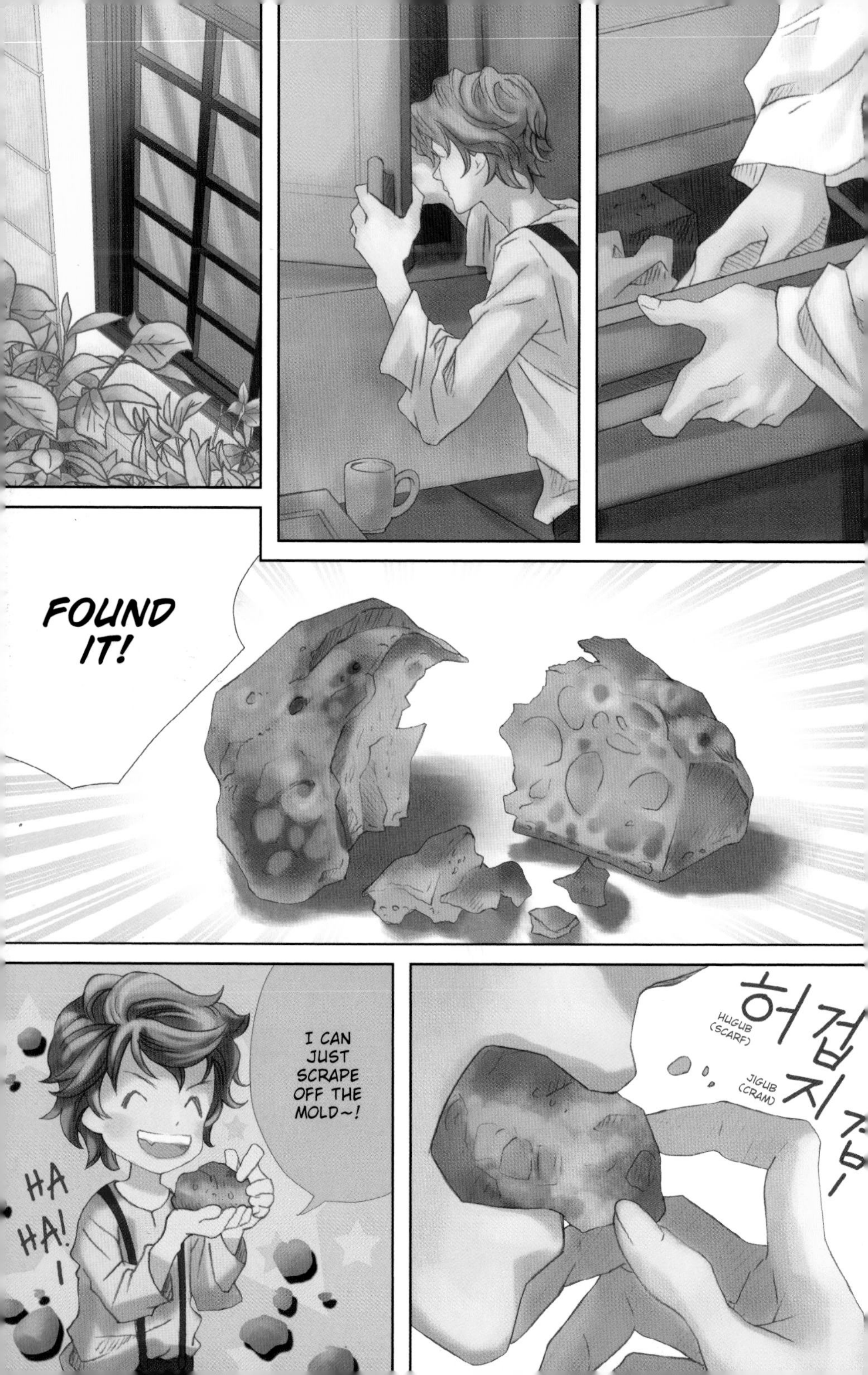
FOUND IT!
I CAN JUST SCRAPE OFF THE MOLD~!
HA HA!
허겁
HUGUB (SCARF)
지겁
JIGUB (CRAM)

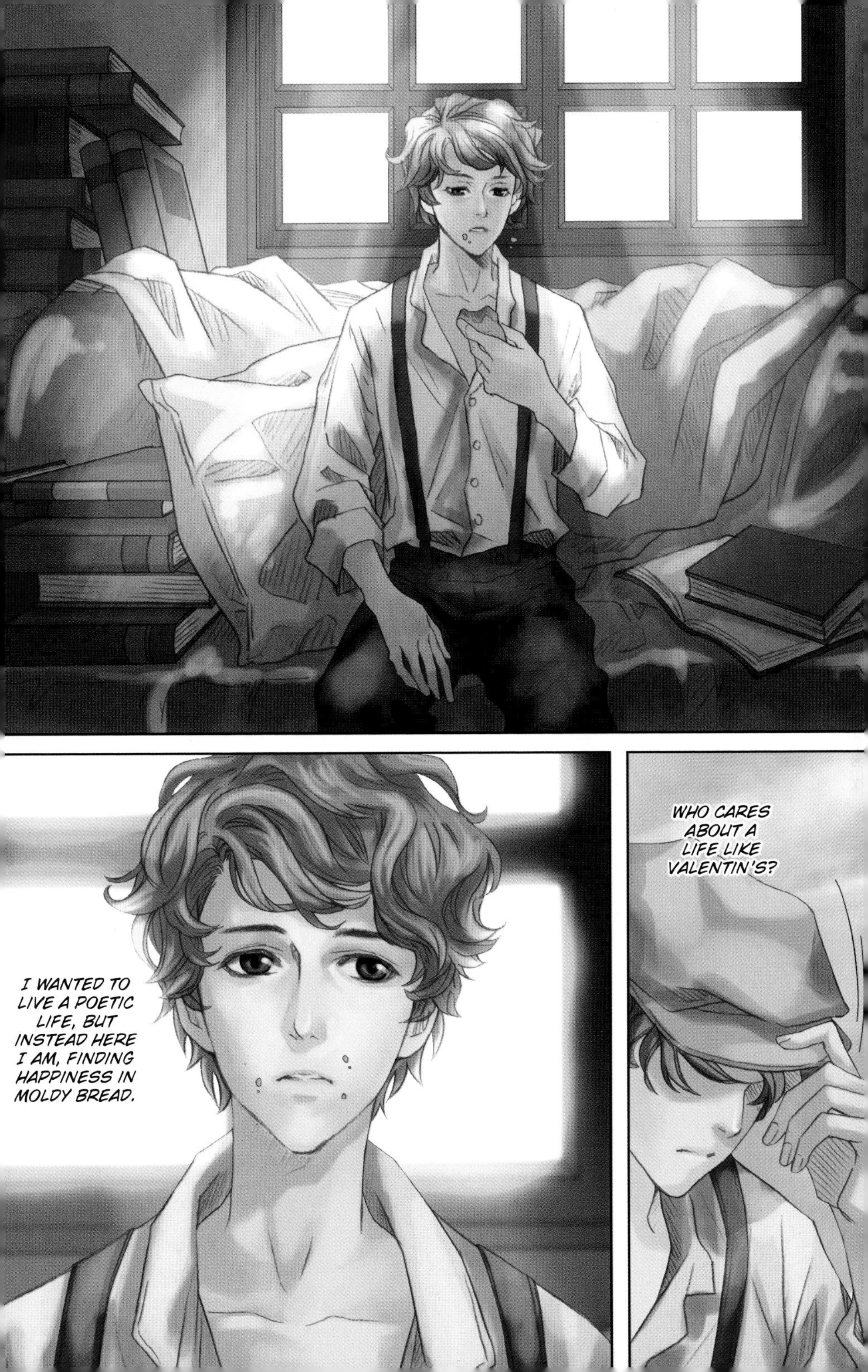
WHO CARES ABOUT A LIFE LIKE VALENTIN'S?
I WANTED TO LIVE A POETIC LIFE, BUT INSTEAD HERE I AM, FINDING HAPPINESS IN MOLDY BREAD.

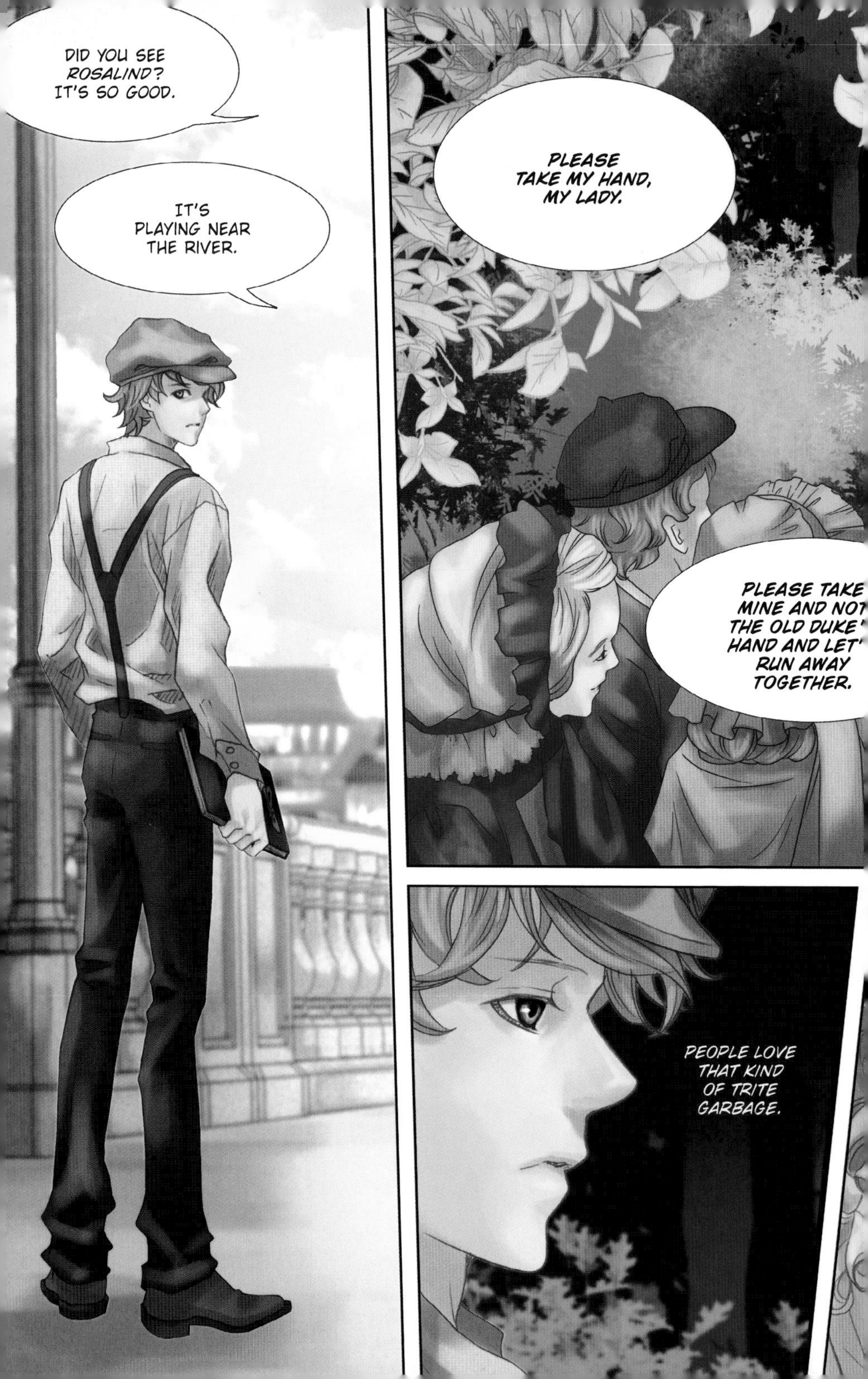
DID YOU SEE ROSALIND? IT'S SO GOOD.
IT'S PLAYING NEAR THE RIVER.
PLEASE TAKE MY HAND, MY LADY.
PLEASE TAKE MINE AND NOT THE OLD DUKE' HAND AND LET' RUN AWAY TOGETHER.
PEOPLE LOVE THAT KIND OF TRITE GARBAGE.

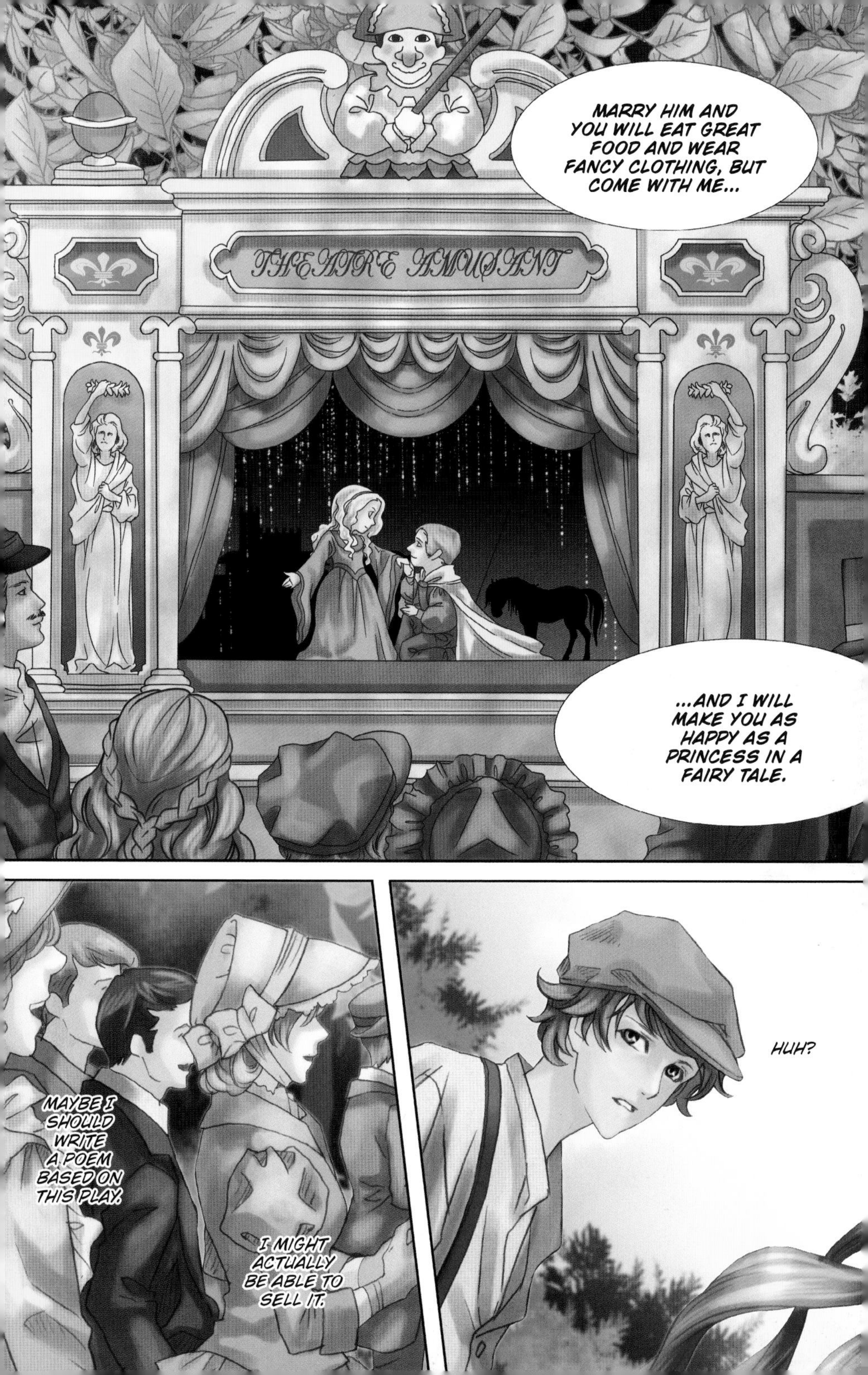
MARRY HIM AND YOU WILL EAT GREAT FOOD AND WEAR FANCY CLOTHING, BUT COME WITH ME...
THEATRE AMUSANT
...AND I WILL MAKE YOU AS HAPPY AS A PRINCESS IN A FAIRY TALE.
MAYBE I SHOULD WRITE A POEM BASED ON THIS PLAY.
I MIGHT ACTUALLY BE ABLE TO SELL IT.
HUH?

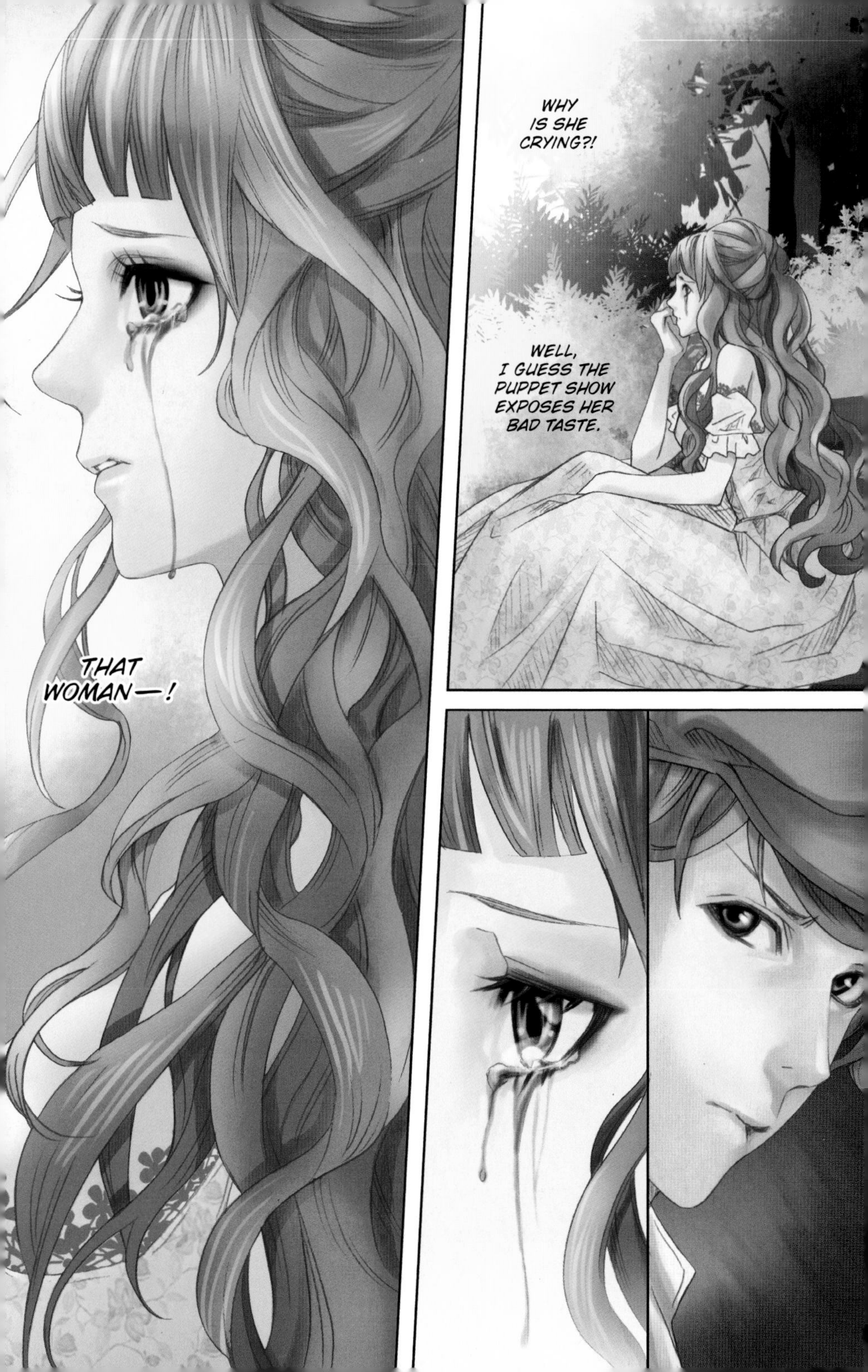
WHY IS SHE CRYING?!
WELL, I GUESS THE PUPPET SHOW EXPOSES HER BAD TASTE.
THAT WOMAN—!

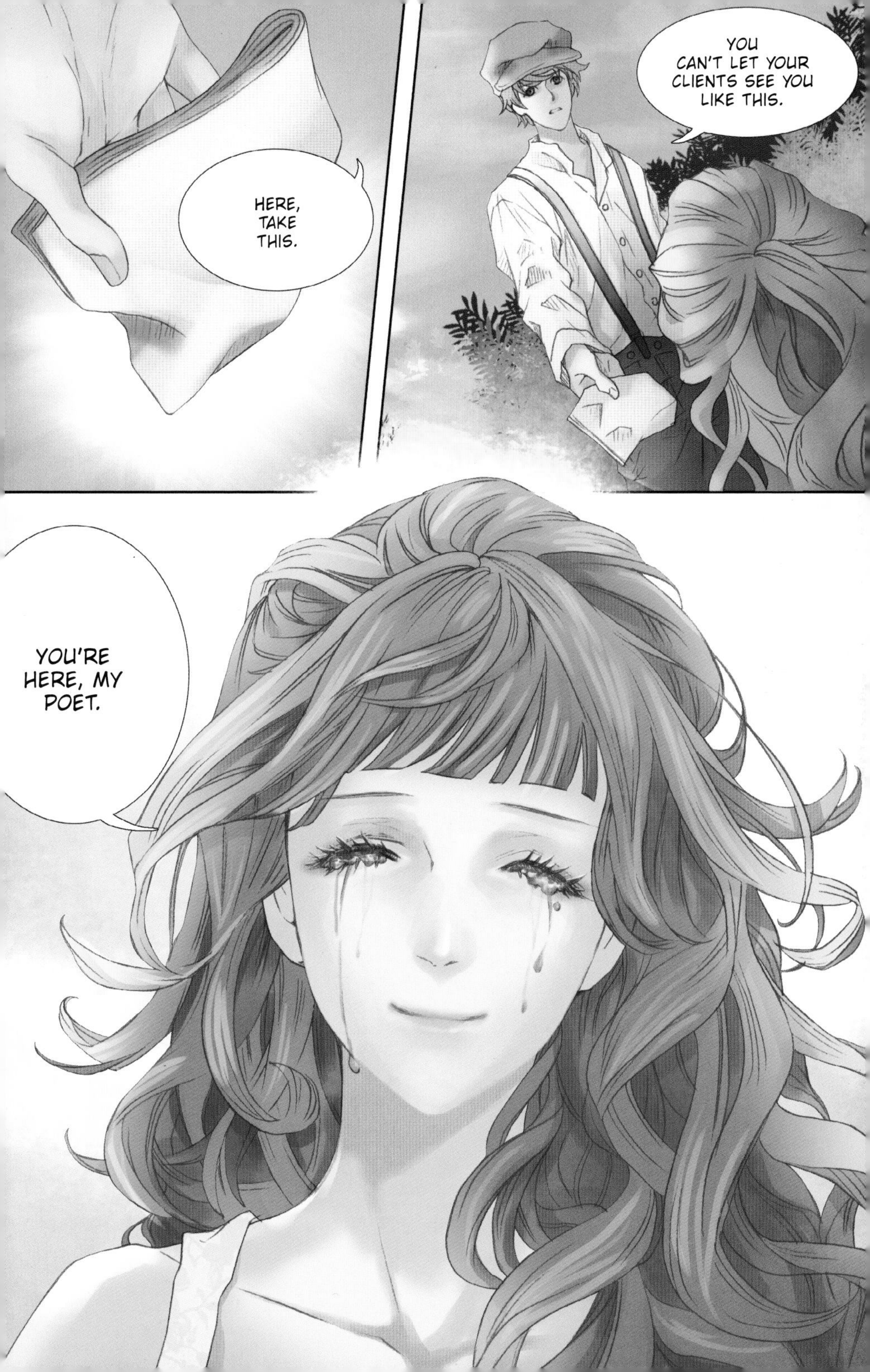
YOU CAN'T LET YOUR CLIENTS SEE YOU LIKE THIS.
HERE, TAKE THIS.
YOU'RE HERE, MY POET.

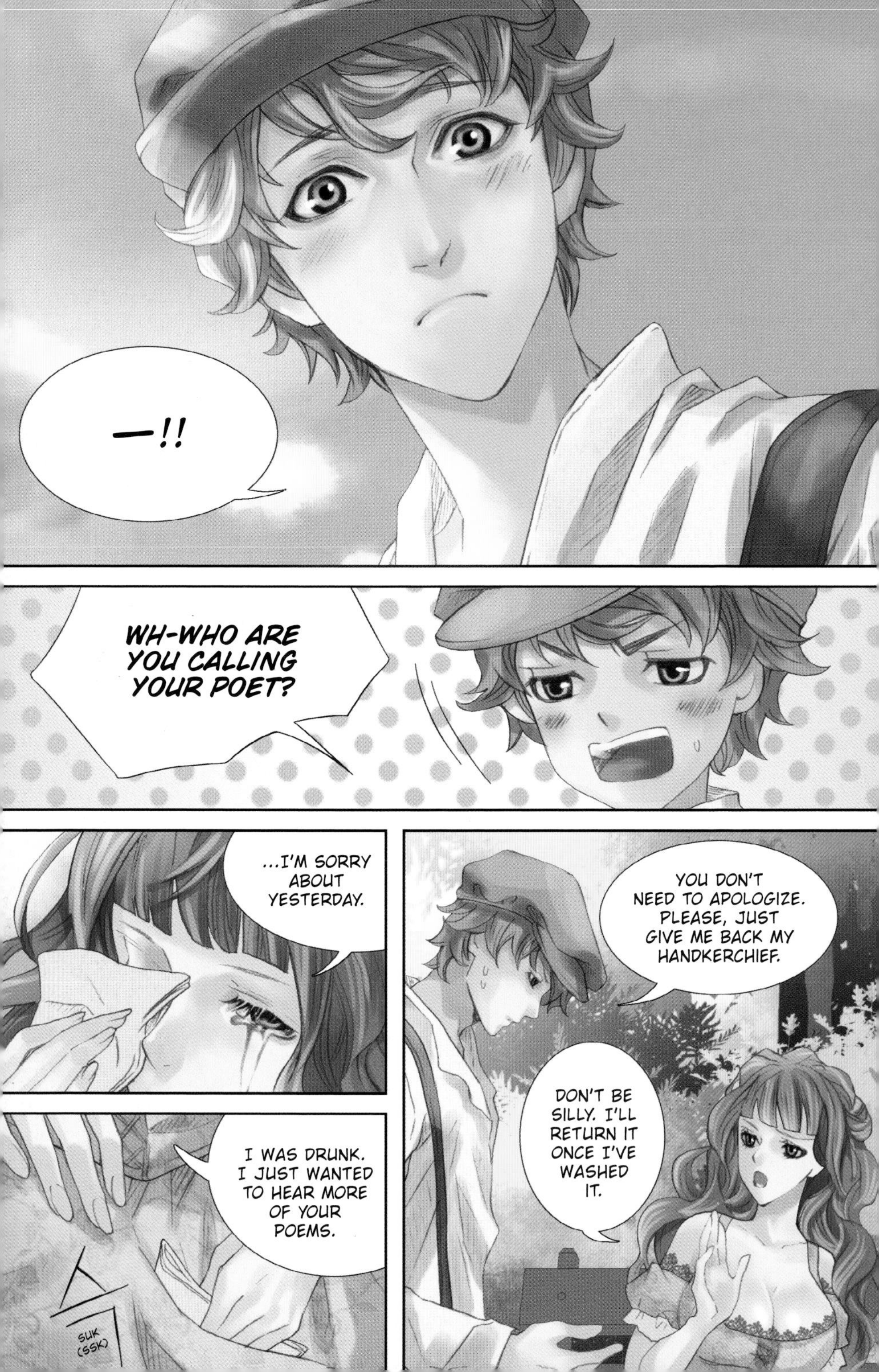
—!!
WH-WHO ARE YOU CALLING YOUR POET?
...I'M SORRY ABOUT YESTERDAY.
I WAS DRUNK. I JUST WANTED TO HEAR MORE OF YOUR POEMS.
SUK (SSK)
YOU DON'T NEED TO APOLOGIZE. PLEASE, JUST GIVE ME BACK MY HANDKERCHIEF.
DON'T BE SILLY. I'LL RETURN IT ONCE I'VE WASHED IT.

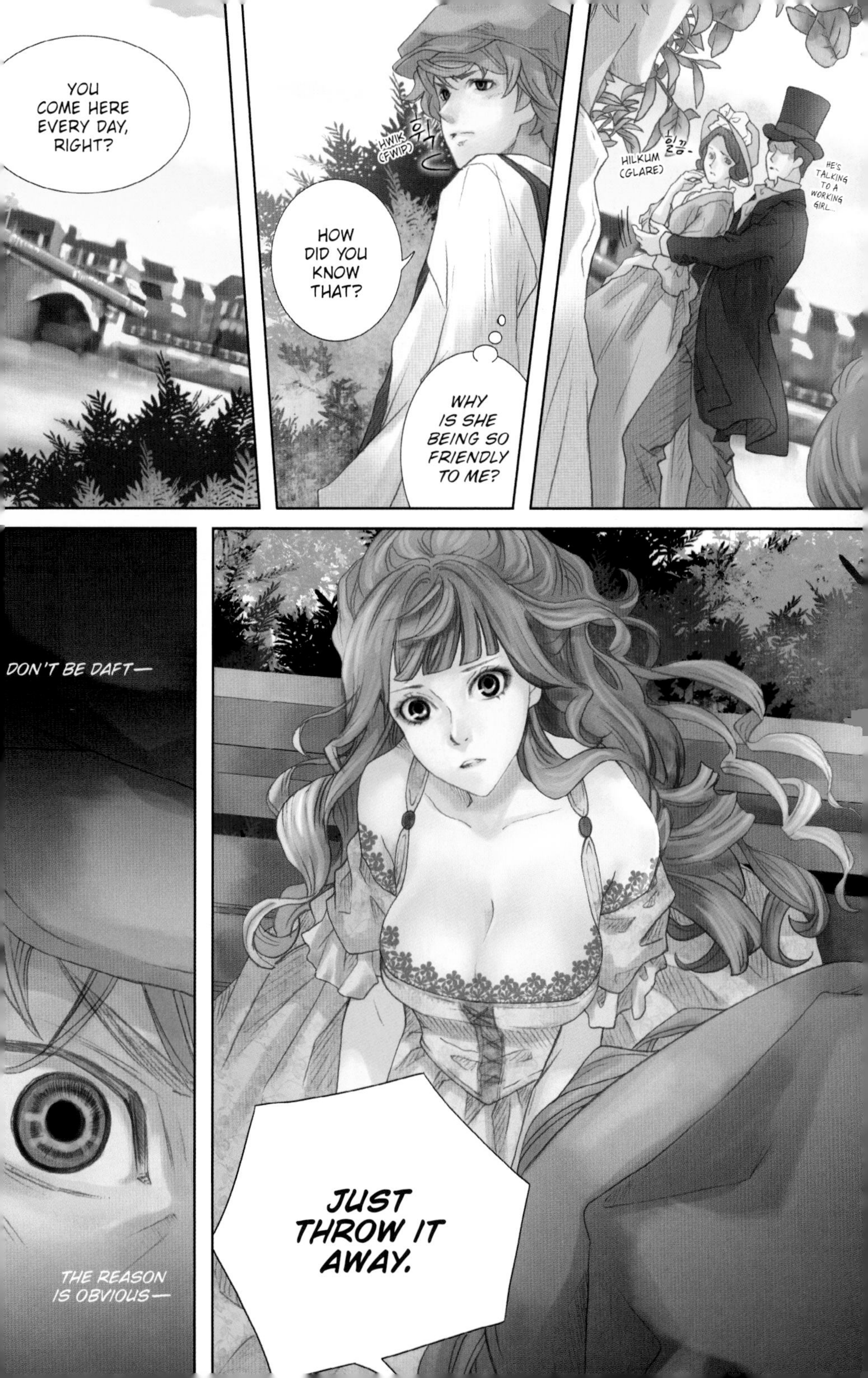
YOU COME HERE EVERY DAY, RIGHT?
HWIK (FWIP)
HOW DID YOU KNOW THAT?
WHY IS SHE BEING SO FRIENDLY TO ME?
HILKUM (GLARE)
HE'S TALKING TO A WORKING GIRL...
DON'T BE DAFT—
THE REASON IS OBVIOUS—
JUST THROW IT AWAY.

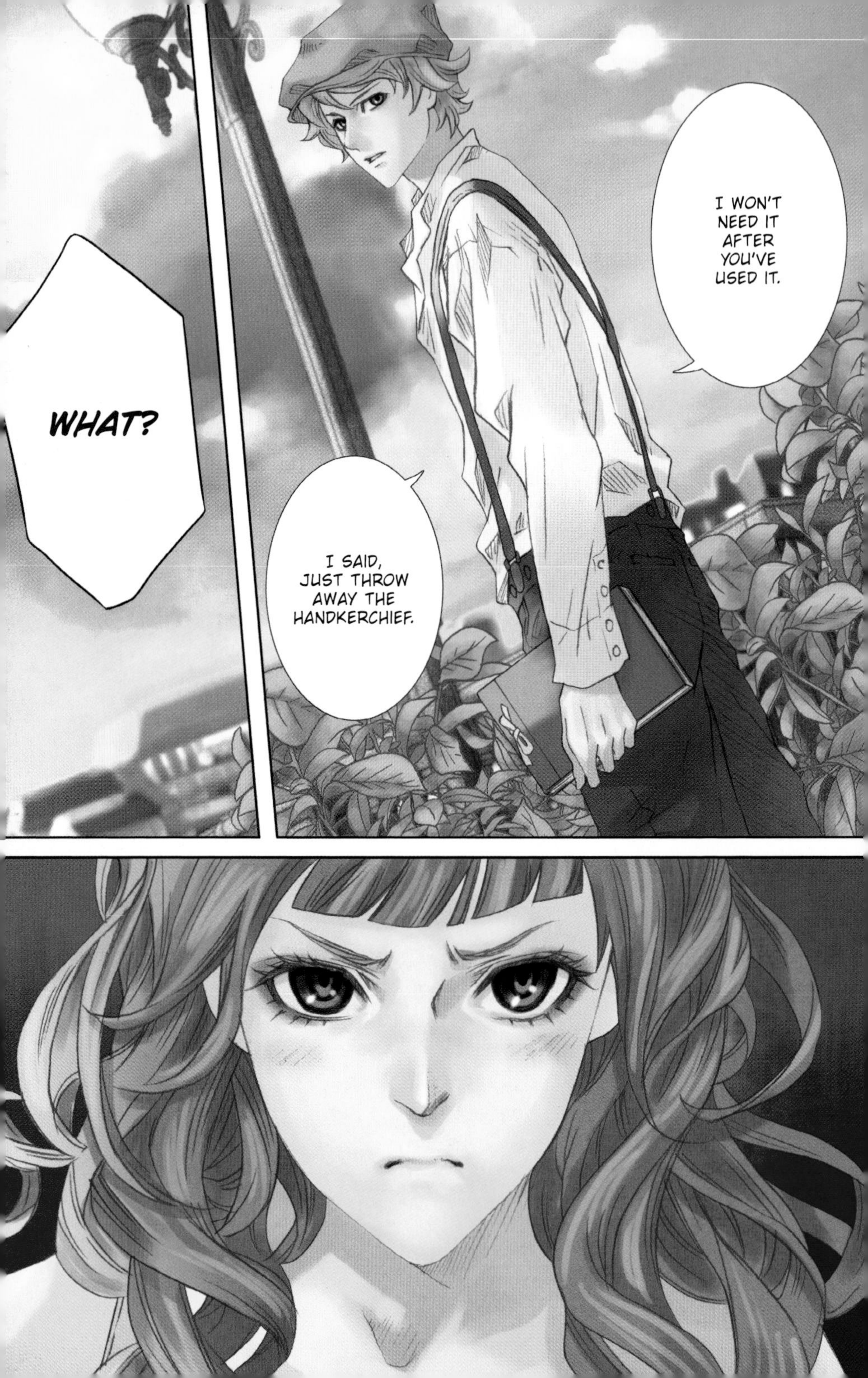
I WON'T NEED IT AFTER YOU'VE USED IT.
I SAID, JUST THROW AWAY THE HANDKERCHIEF.
WHAT?

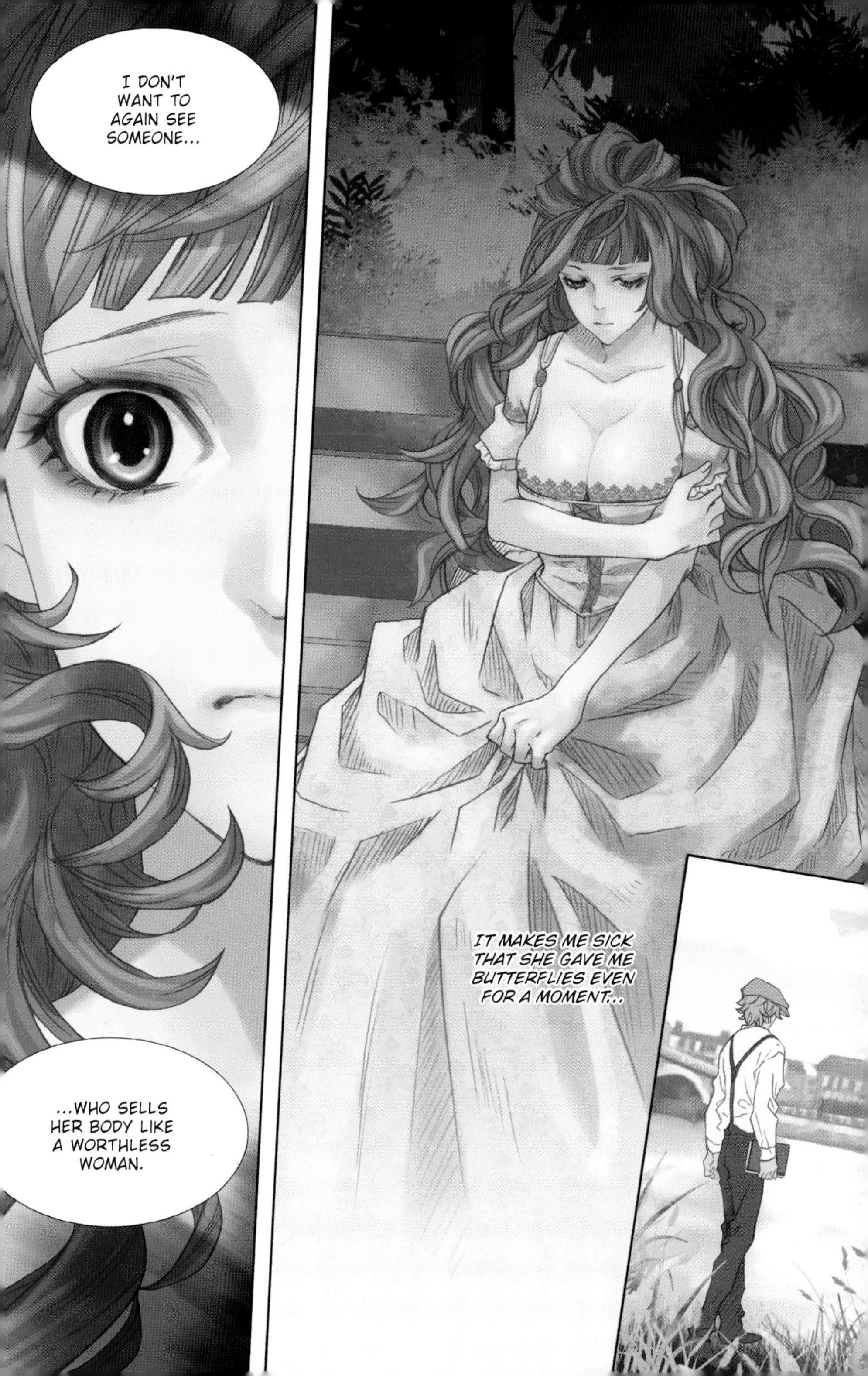
I DON'T WANT TO AGAIN SEE SOMEONE...
...WHO SELLS HER BODY LIKE A WORTHLESS WOMAN.
IT MAKES ME SICK THAT SHE GAVE ME BUTTERFLIES EVEN FOR A MOMENT...

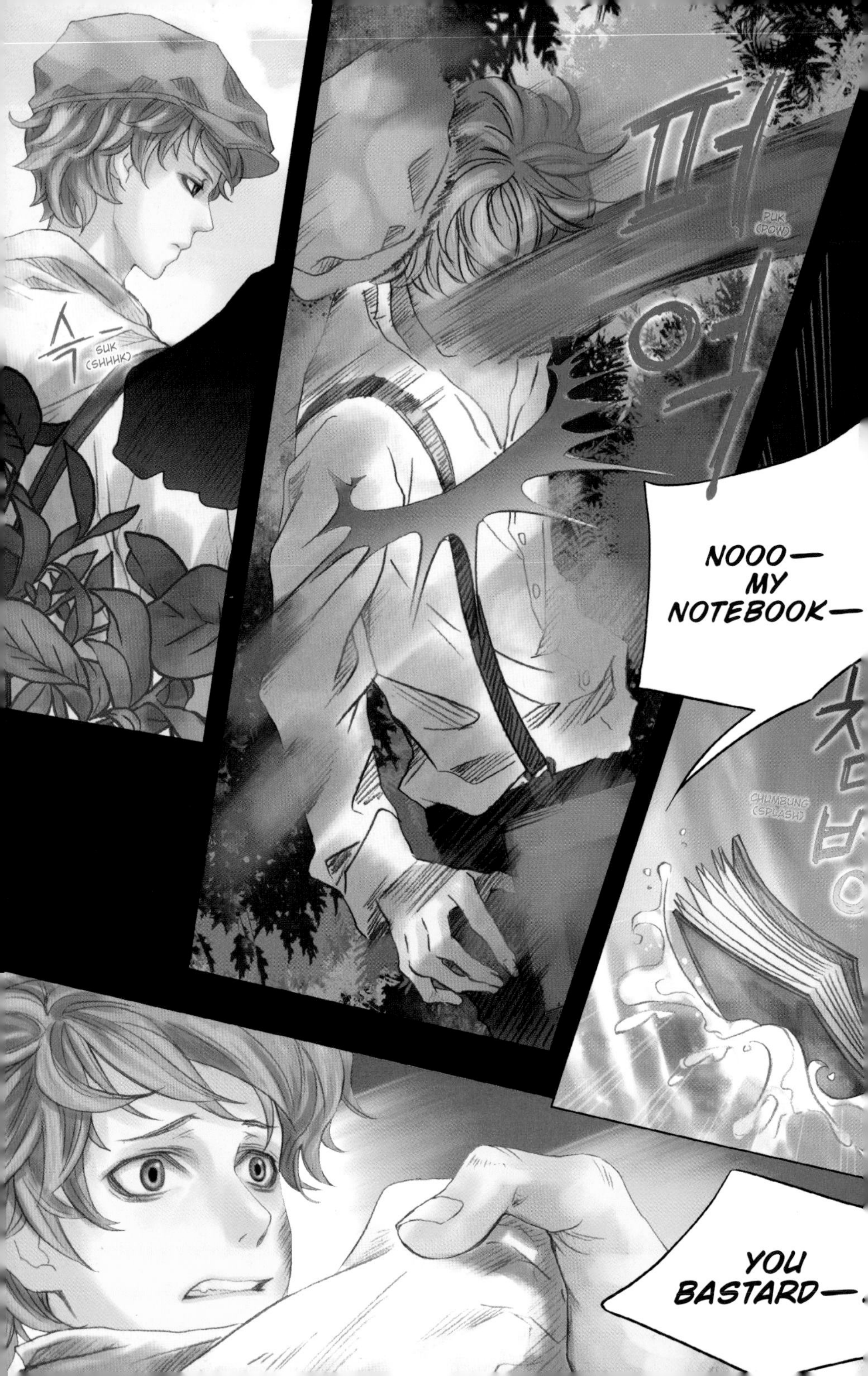
SUK
(SHHHK)
PUK
(POW)
NOOO—
MY
NOTEBOOK—
CHUMBUNG
(SPLASH)
YOU
BASTARD—.

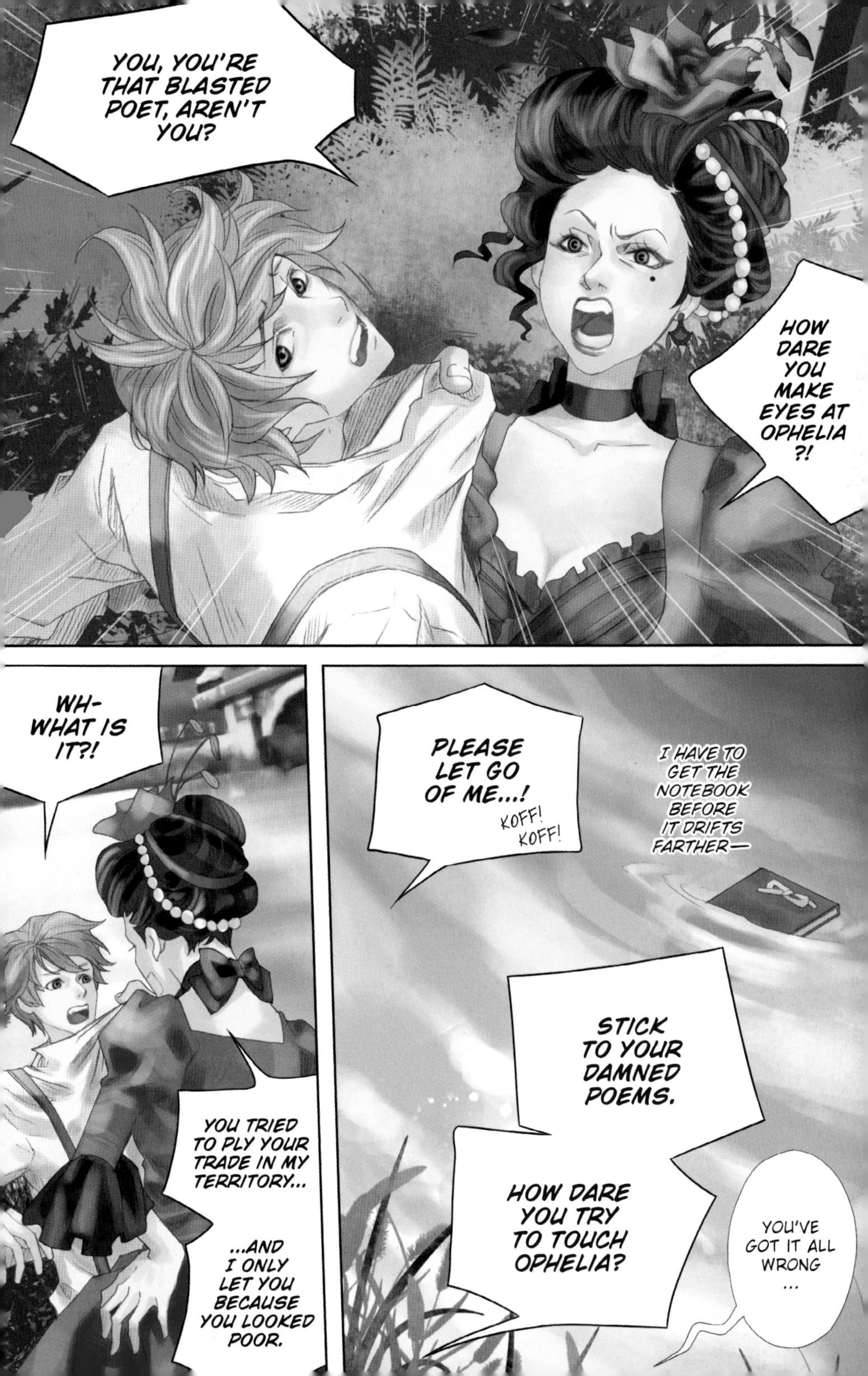
YOU, YOU'RE THAT BLASTED POET, AREN'T YOU?
HOW DARE YOU MAKE EYES AT OPHELIA ?!
WH-WHAT IS IT?!
YOU TRIED TO PLY YOUR TRADE IN MY TERRITORY...
...AND I ONLY LET YOU BECAUSE YOU LOOKED POOR.
PLEASE LET GO OF ME...!
KOFF! KOFF!
I HAVE TO GET THE NOTEBOOK BEFORE IT DRIFTS FARTHER—
STICK TO YOUR DAMNED POEMS.
HOW DARE YOU TRY TO TOUCH OPHELIA?
YOU'VE GOT IT ALL WRONG ...

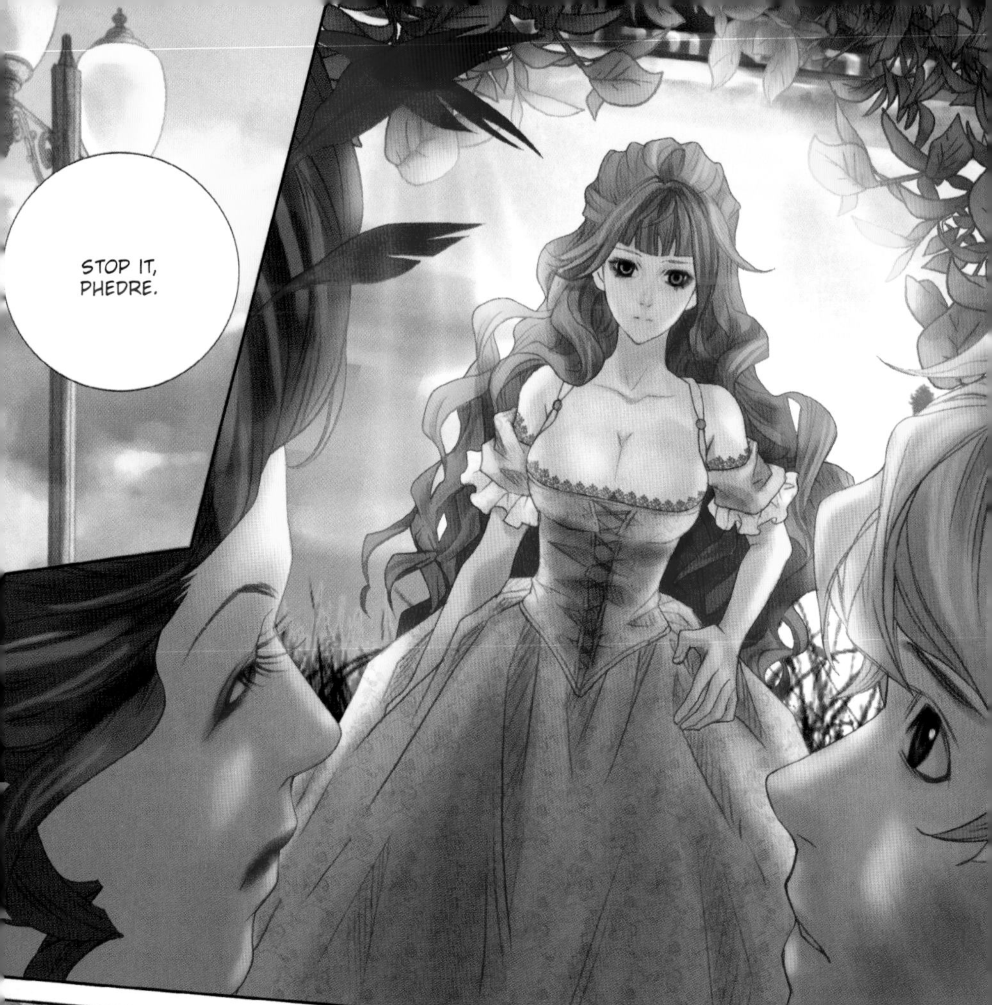
STOP IT, PHEDRE.

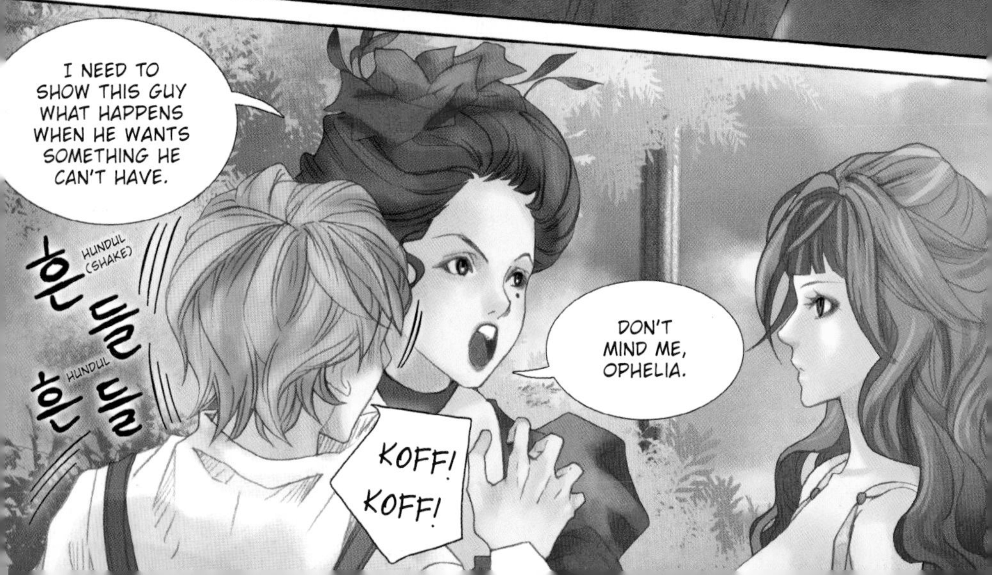
I NEED TO SHOW THIS GUY WHAT HAPPENS WHEN HE WANTS SOMETHING HE CAN'T HAVE.
흔들 HUNDUL (SHAKE)
흔들 HUNDUL
DON'T MIND ME, OPHELIA.
KOFF! KOFF!

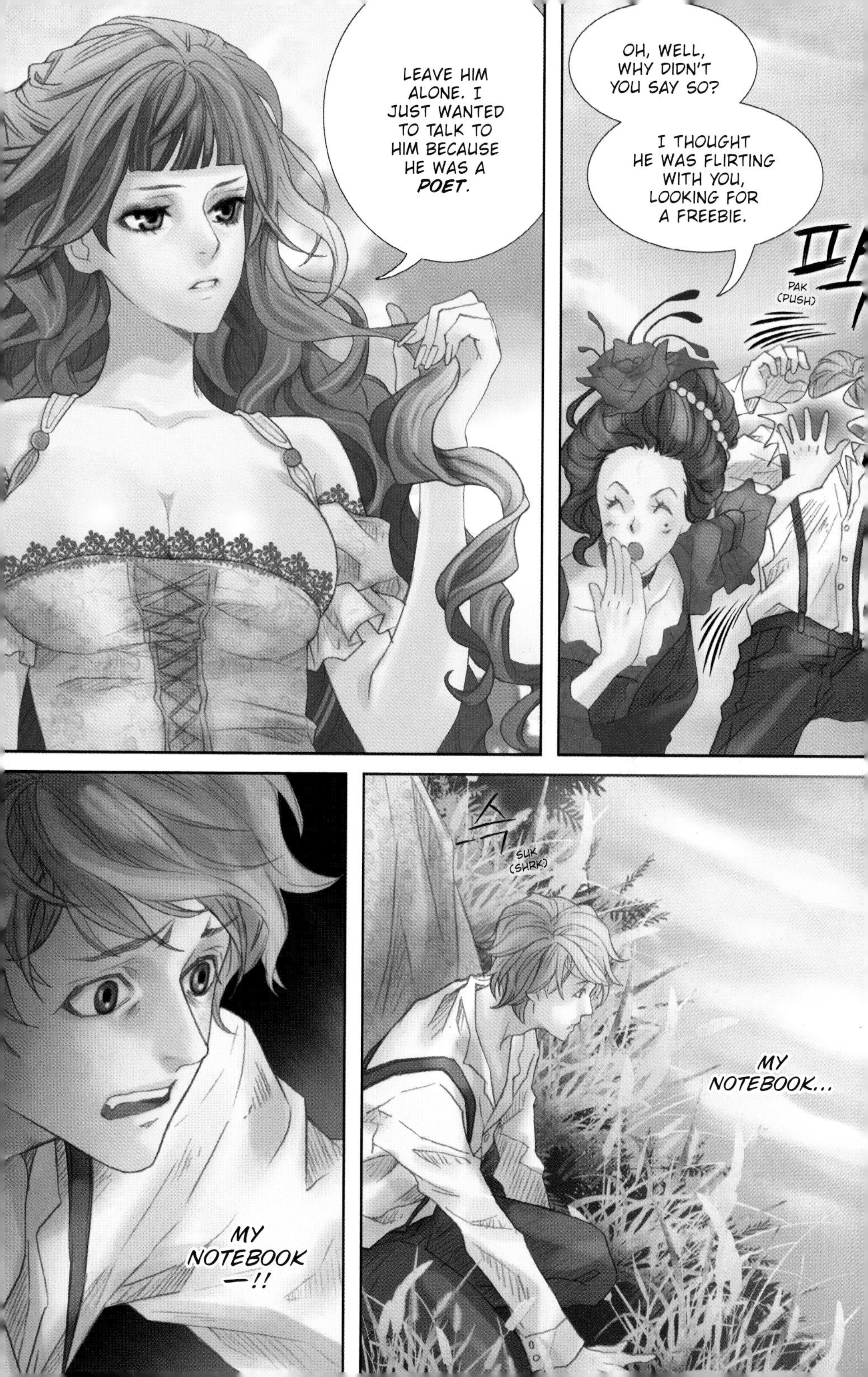
LEAVE HIM ALONE. I JUST WANTED TO TALK TO HIM BECAUSE HE WAS A ***POET***.
OH, WELL, WHY DIDN'T YOU SAY SO?
I THOUGHT HE WAS FLIRTING WITH YOU, LOOKING FOR A FREEBIE.
PAK (PUSH)
MY NOTEBOOK —!!
SUK (SHRK)
MY NOTEBOOK...

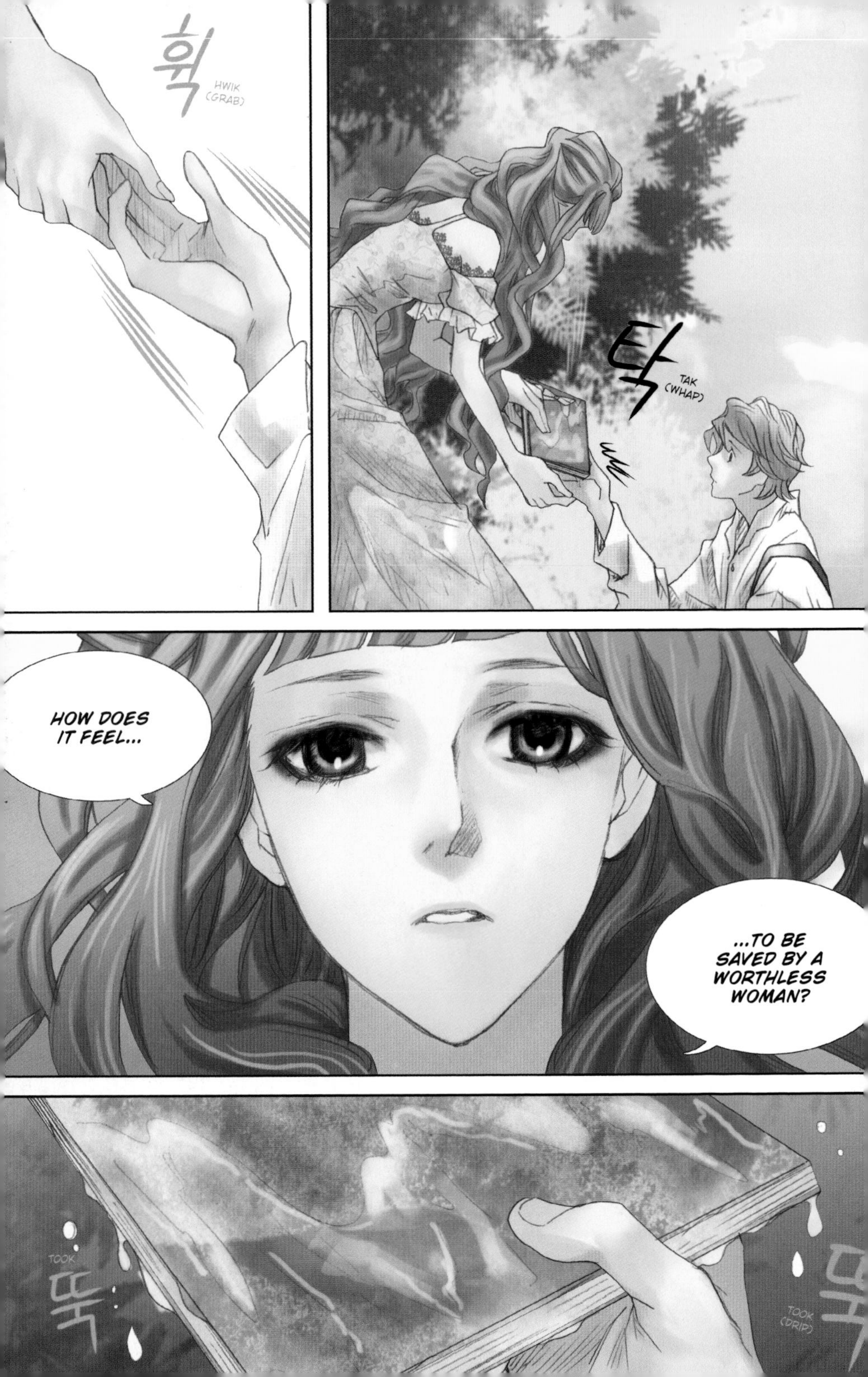

휙
HWIK (GRAB)
탁
TAK (WHAP)
HOW DOES IT FEEL...
...TO BE SAVED BY A WORTHLESS WOMAN?
TOOK
뚝
뚝
TOOK (DRIP)

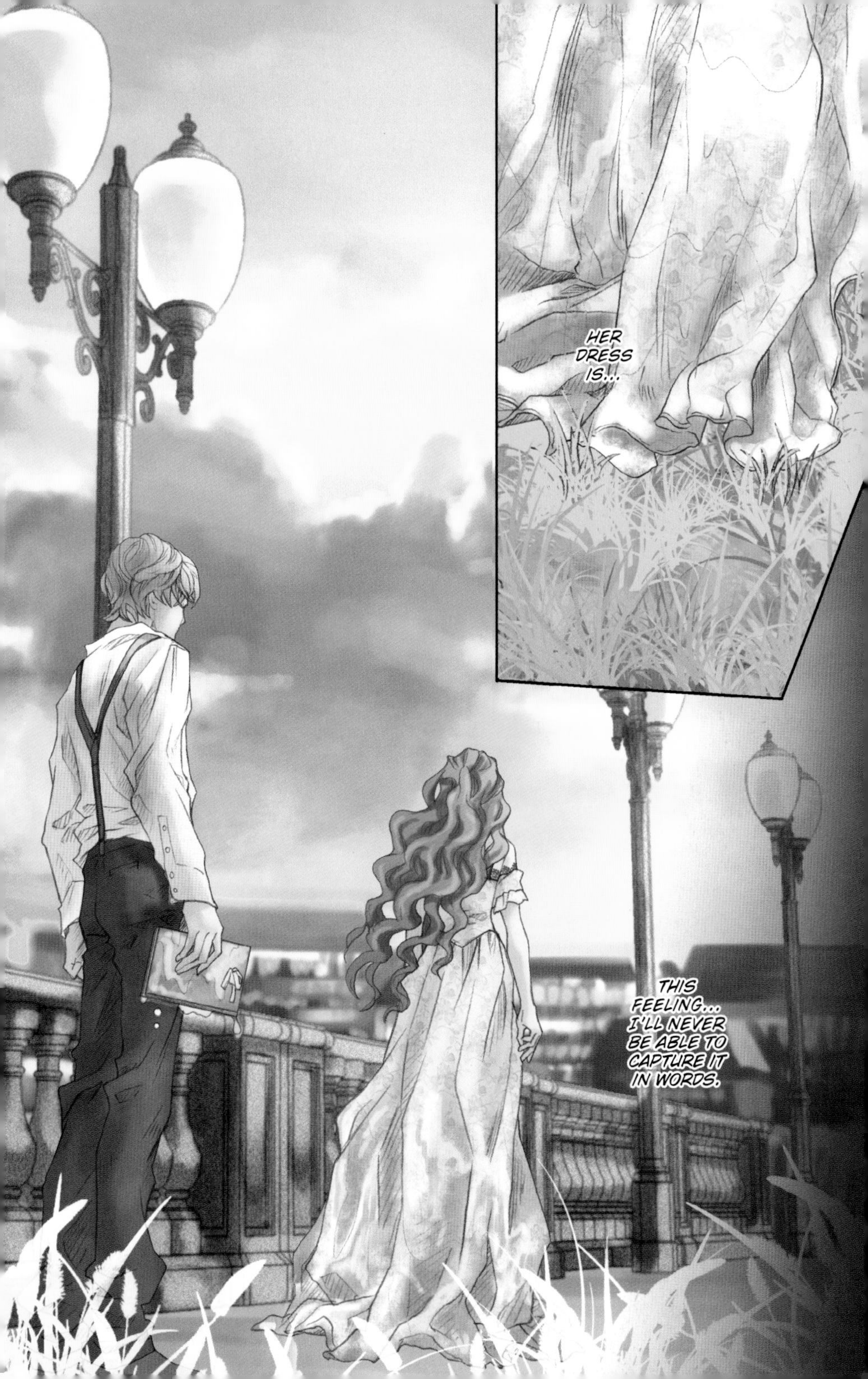
HER DRESS IS...
THIS FEELING... I'LL NEVER BE ABLE TO CAPTURE IT IN WORDS.

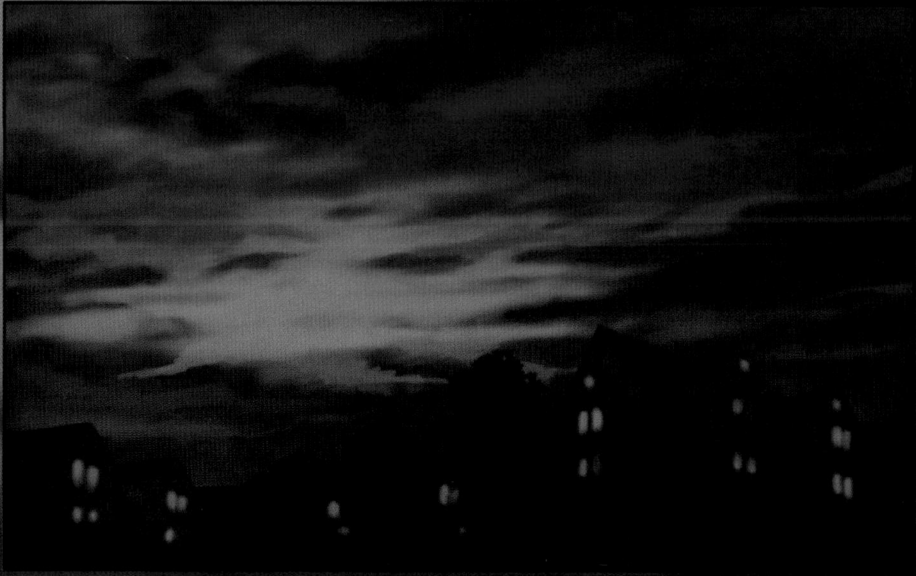

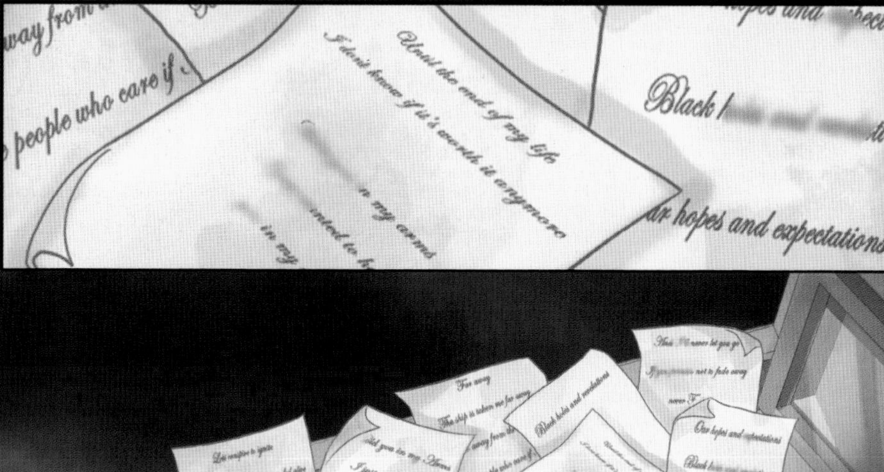
hopes and expectations
Until the end of my life
I don't know if it's worth it anymore
people who care if

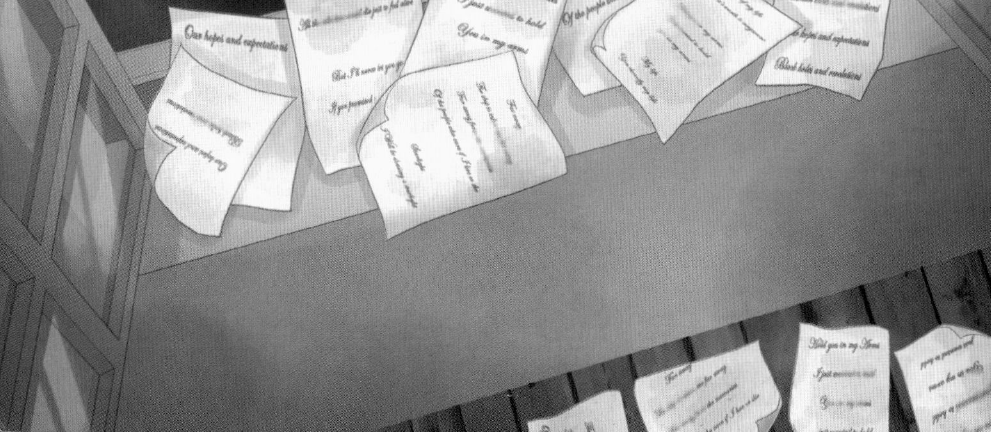
Our hopes and expectations
Black holes and revelations
Hold you in my Arms
You in my arms
Far away

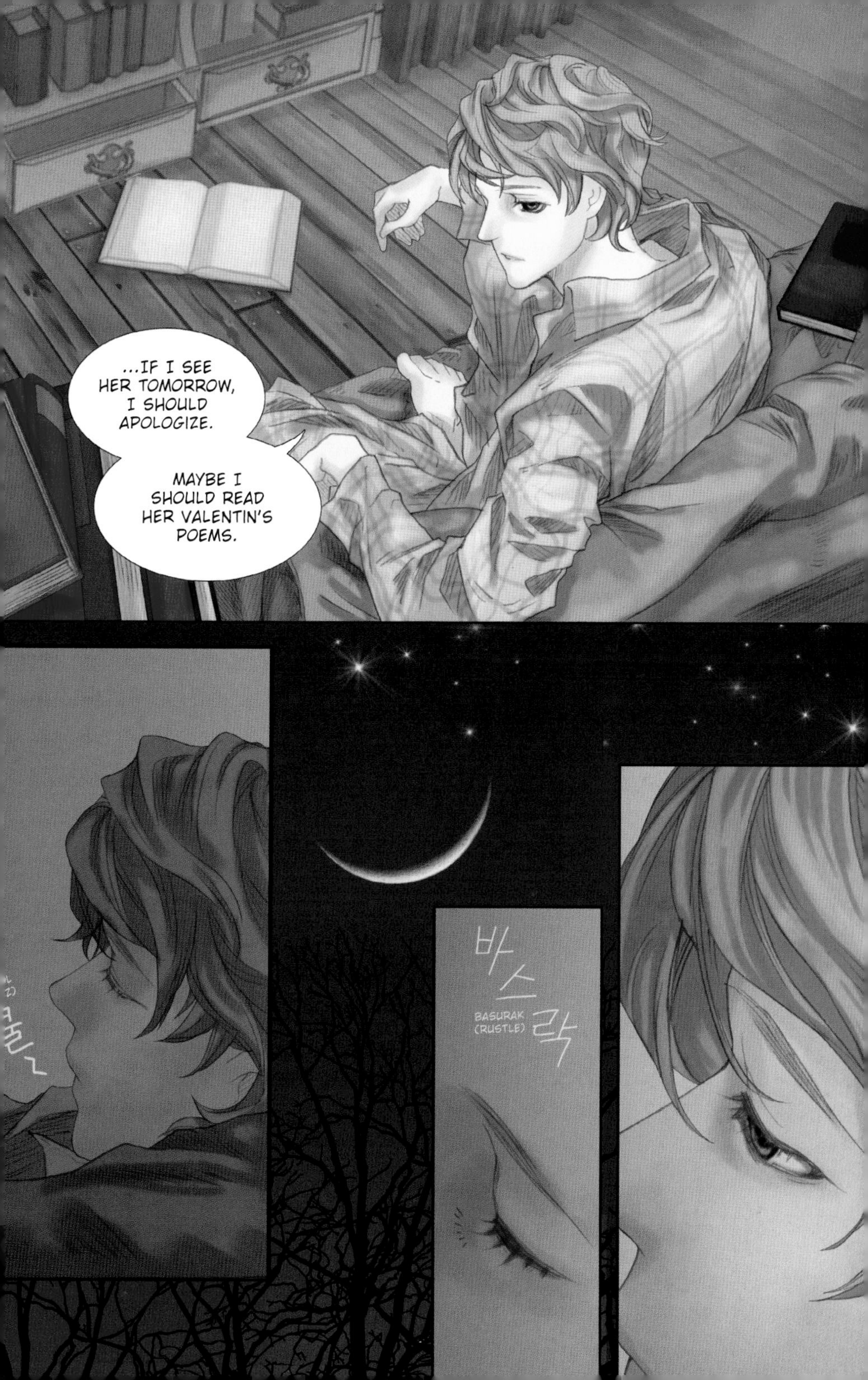
...IF I SEE HER TOMORROW, I SHOULD APOLOGIZE.
MAYBE I SHOULD READ HER VALENTIN'S POEMS.
바스락
BASURAK (RUSTLE)

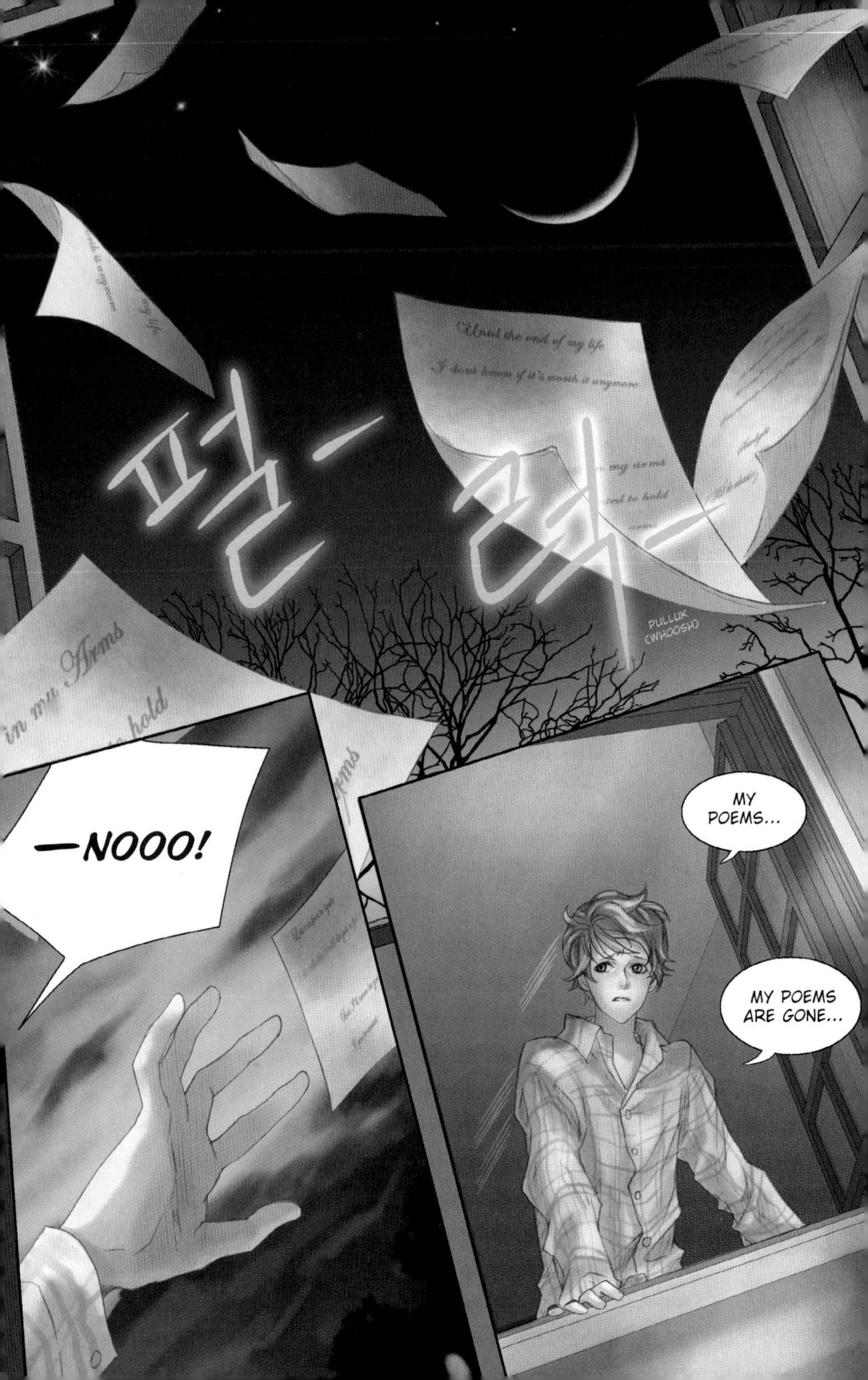
Until the end of my life
I don't know if it's worth it anymore
펄- 럭-
PULLUK (WHOOSH)
in my Arms
—NOOO!
MY POEMS...
MY POEMS ARE GONE...

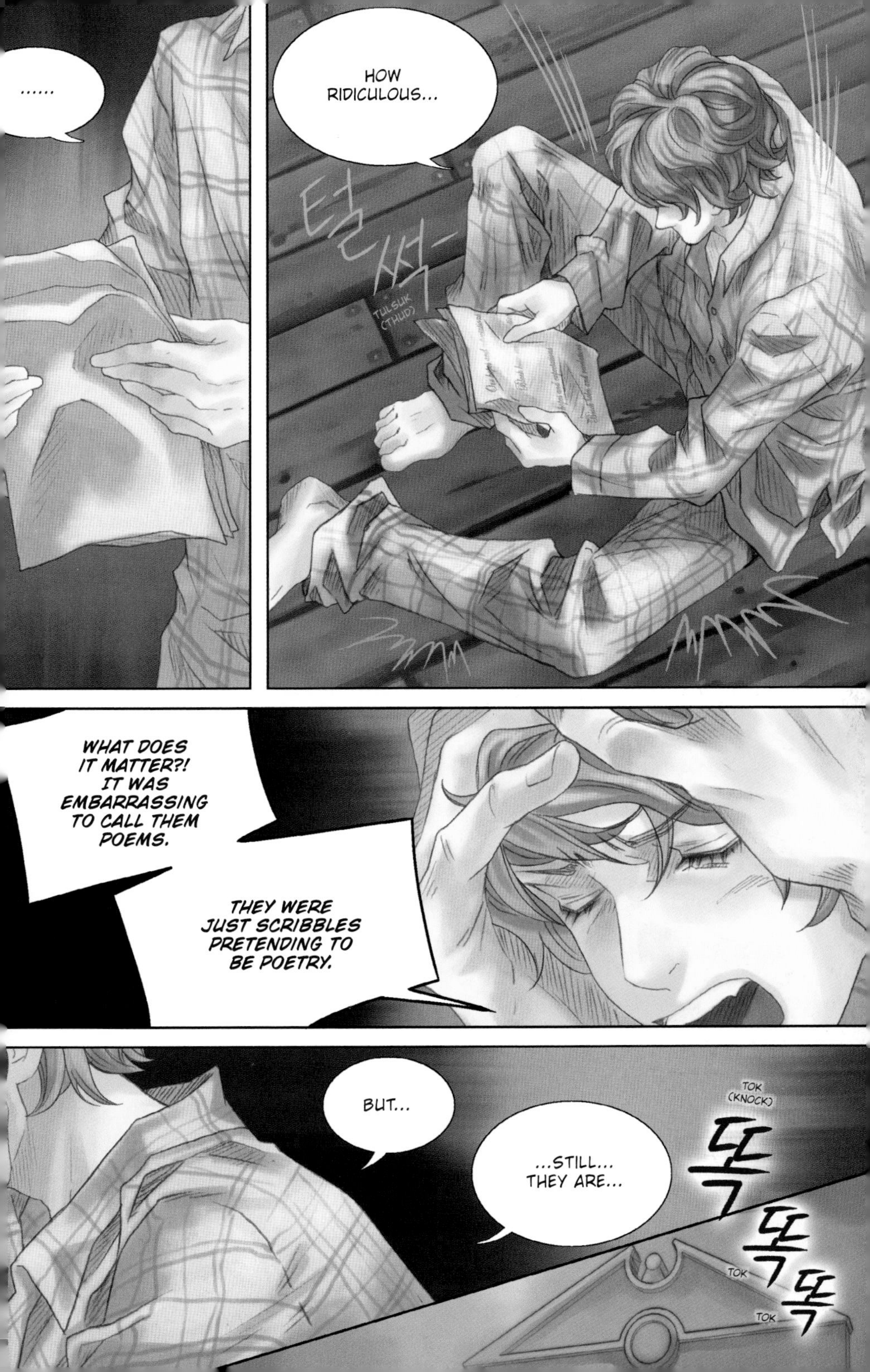
......
HOW RIDICULOUS...
털썩
TULSUK (THUD)
WHAT DOES IT MATTER?! IT WAS EMBARRASSING TO CALL THEM POEMS.
THEY WERE JUST SCRIBBLES PRETENDING TO BE POETRY.
BUT...
...STILL... THEY ARE...
TOK (KNOCK)
똑
똑
TOK
똑
TOK

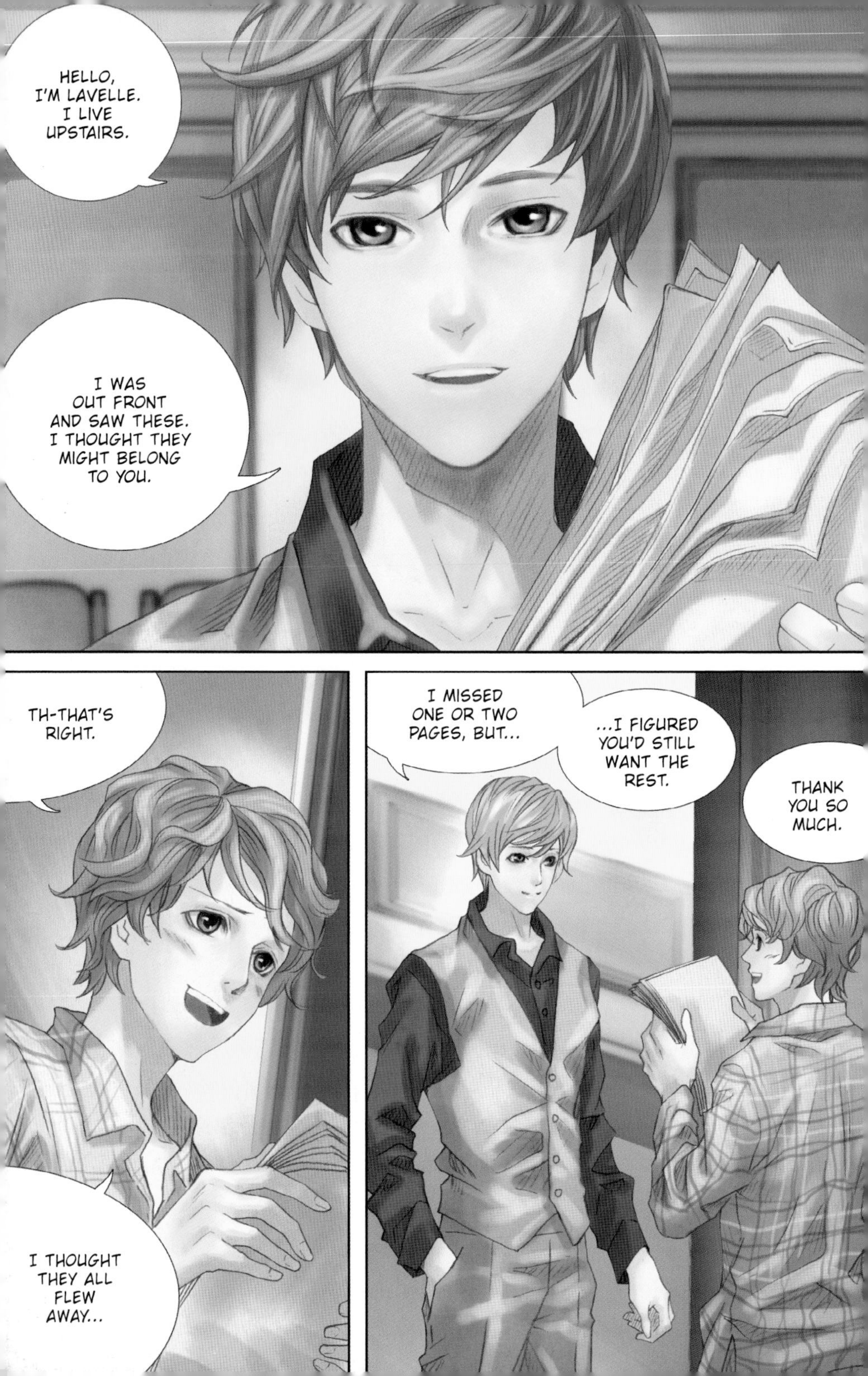
HELLO, I'M LAVELLE. I LIVE UPSTAIRS.
I WAS OUT FRONT AND SAW THESE. I THOUGHT THEY MIGHT BELONG TO YOU.
TH-THAT'S RIGHT.
I THOUGHT THEY ALL FLEW AWAY...
I MISSED ONE OR TWO PAGES, BUT...
...I FIGURED YOU'D STILL WANT THE REST.
THANK YOU SO MUCH.

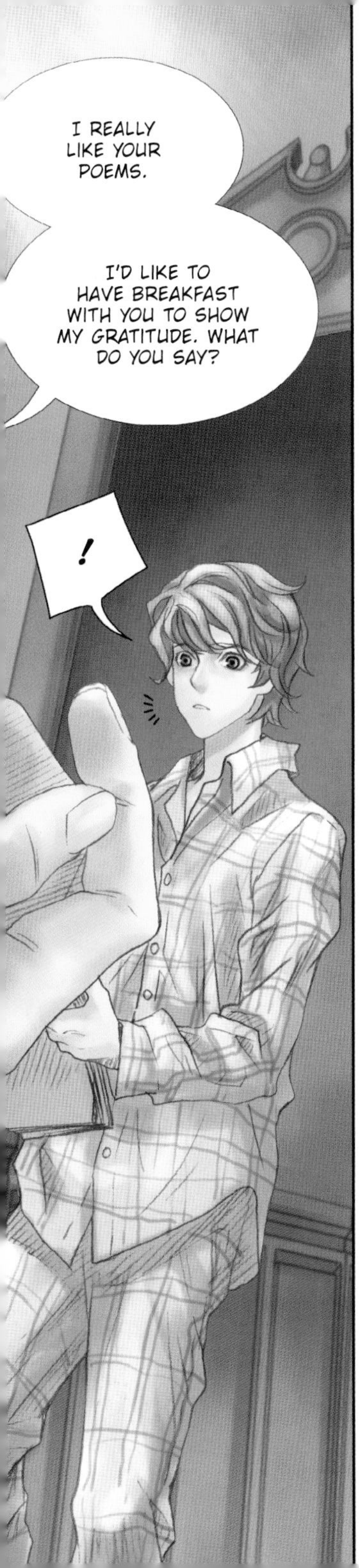
I REALLY LIKE YOUR POEMS.
I'D LIKE TO HAVE BREAKFAST WITH YOU TO SHOW MY GRATITUDE. WHAT DO YOU SAY?
!
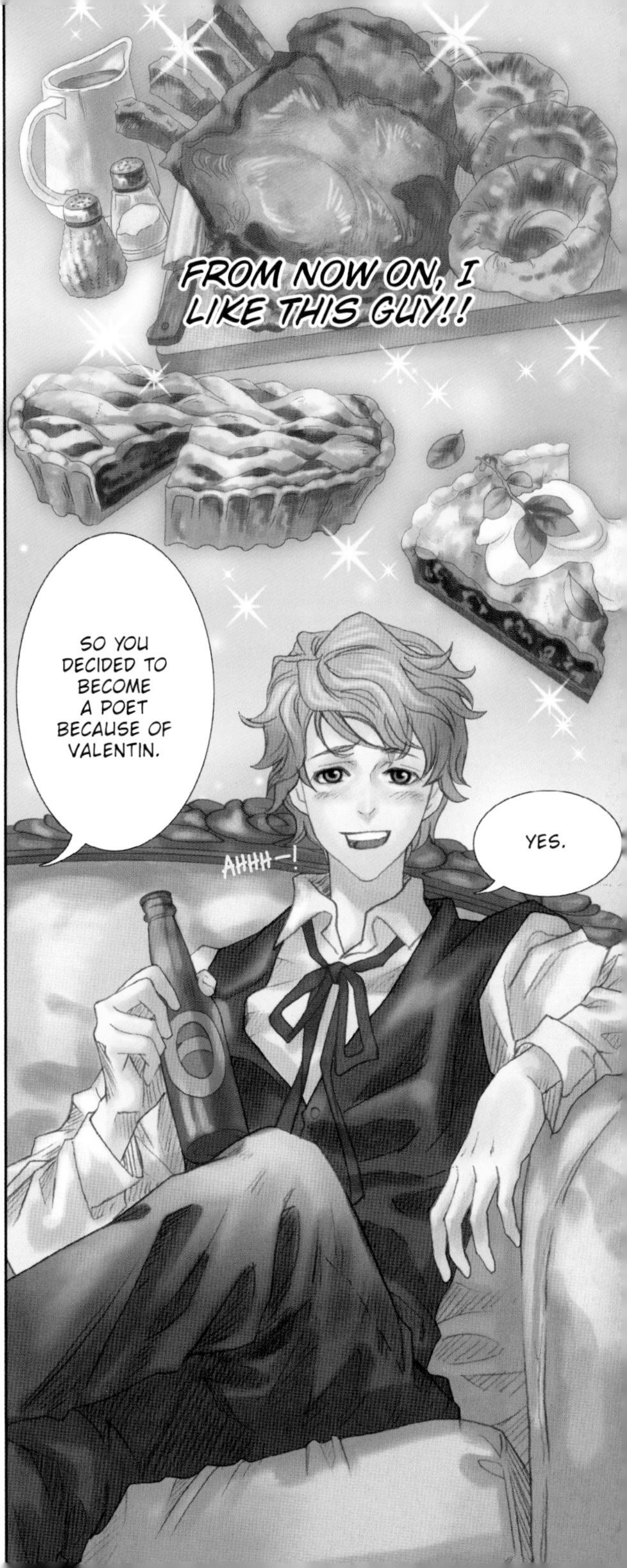
FROM NOW ON, I LIKE THIS GUY!!
SO YOU DECIDED TO BECOME A POET BECAUSE OF VALENTIN.
AHHH—!
YES.

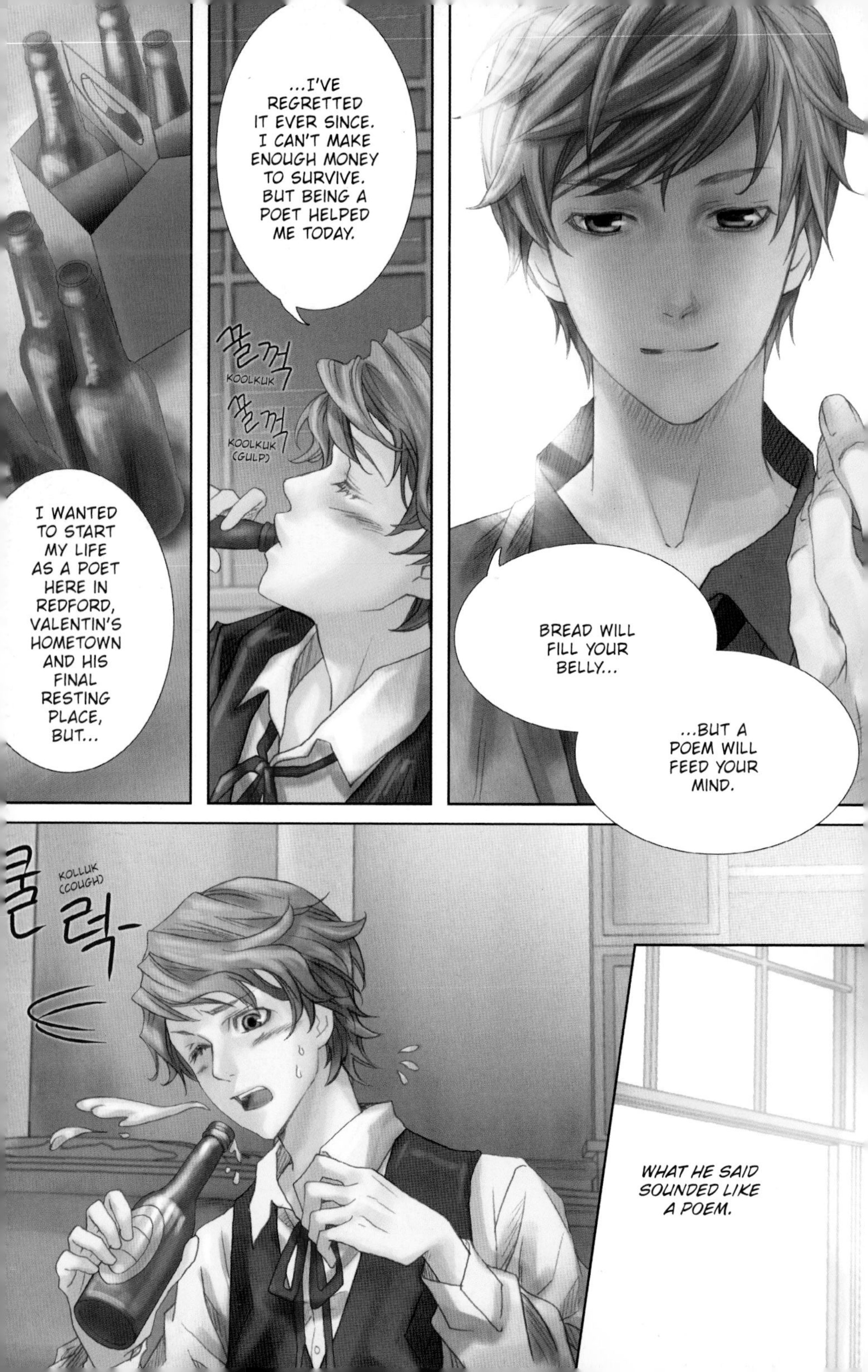
I WANTED TO START MY LIFE AS A POET HERE IN REDFORD, VALENTIN'S HOMETOWN AND HIS FINAL RESTING PLACE, BUT...
...I'VE REGRETTED IT EVER SINCE. I CAN'T MAKE ENOUGH MONEY TO SURVIVE. BUT BEING A POET HELPED ME TODAY.
꿀꺽
KOOLKUK
꿀꺽
KOOLKUK (GULP)
BREAD WILL FILL YOUR BELLY...
...BUT A POEM WILL FEED YOUR MIND.
콜럭-
KOLLUK (COUGH)
WHAT HE SAID SOUNDED LIKE A POEM.

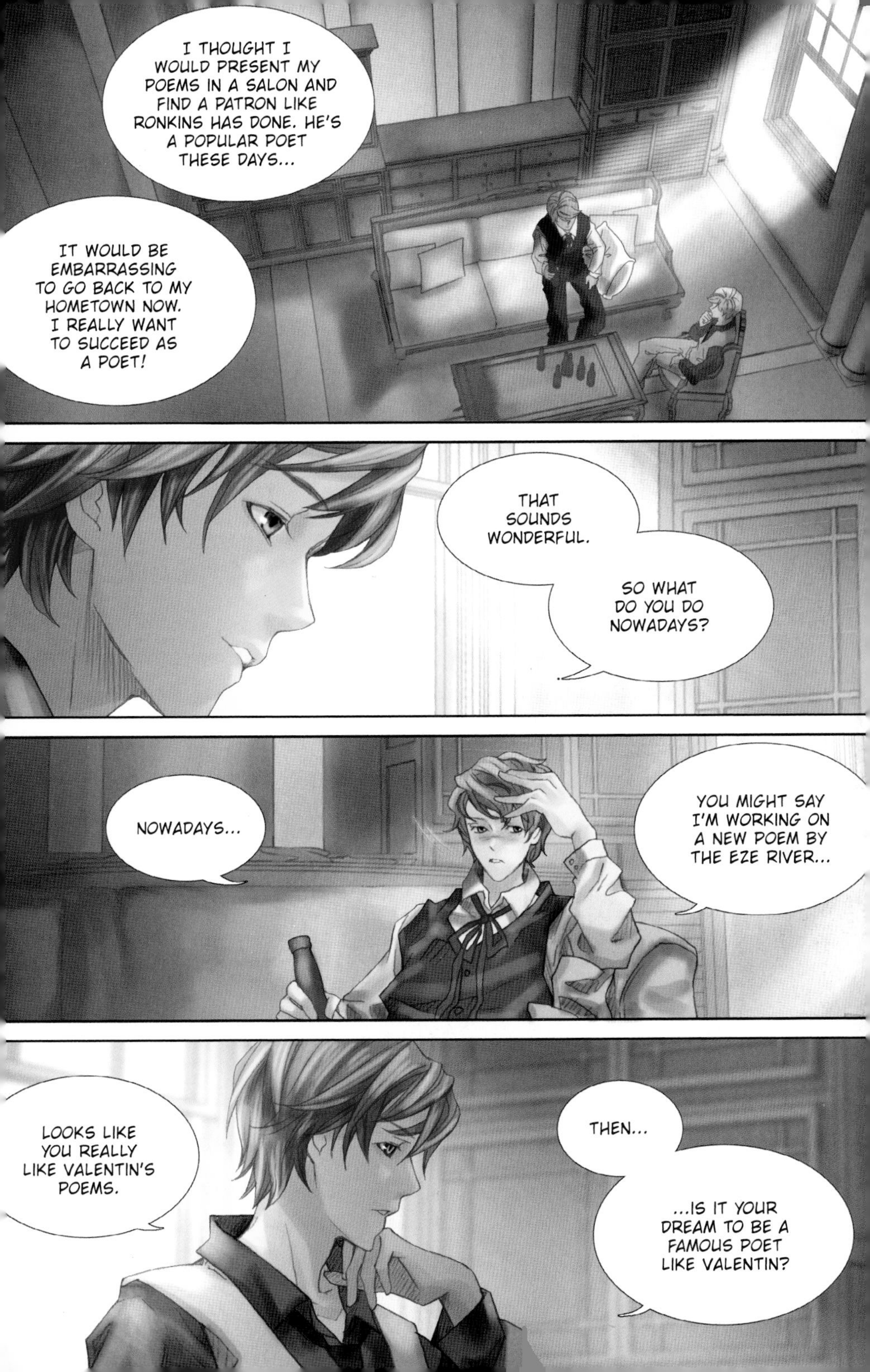
I THOUGHT I WOULD PRESENT MY POEMS IN A SALON AND FIND A PATRON LIKE RONKINS HAS DONE. HE'S A POPULAR POET THESE DAYS...
IT WOULD BE EMBARRASSING TO GO BACK TO MY HOMETOWN NOW. I REALLY WANT TO SUCCEED AS A POET!
THAT SOUNDS WONDERFUL.
SO WHAT DO YOU DO NOWADAYS?
NOWADAYS...
YOU MIGHT SAY I'M WORKING ON A NEW POEM BY THE EZE RIVER...
LOOKS LIKE YOU REALLY LIKE VALENTIN'S POEMS.
THEN...
...IS IT YOUR DREAM TO BE A FAMOUS POET LIKE VALENTIN?

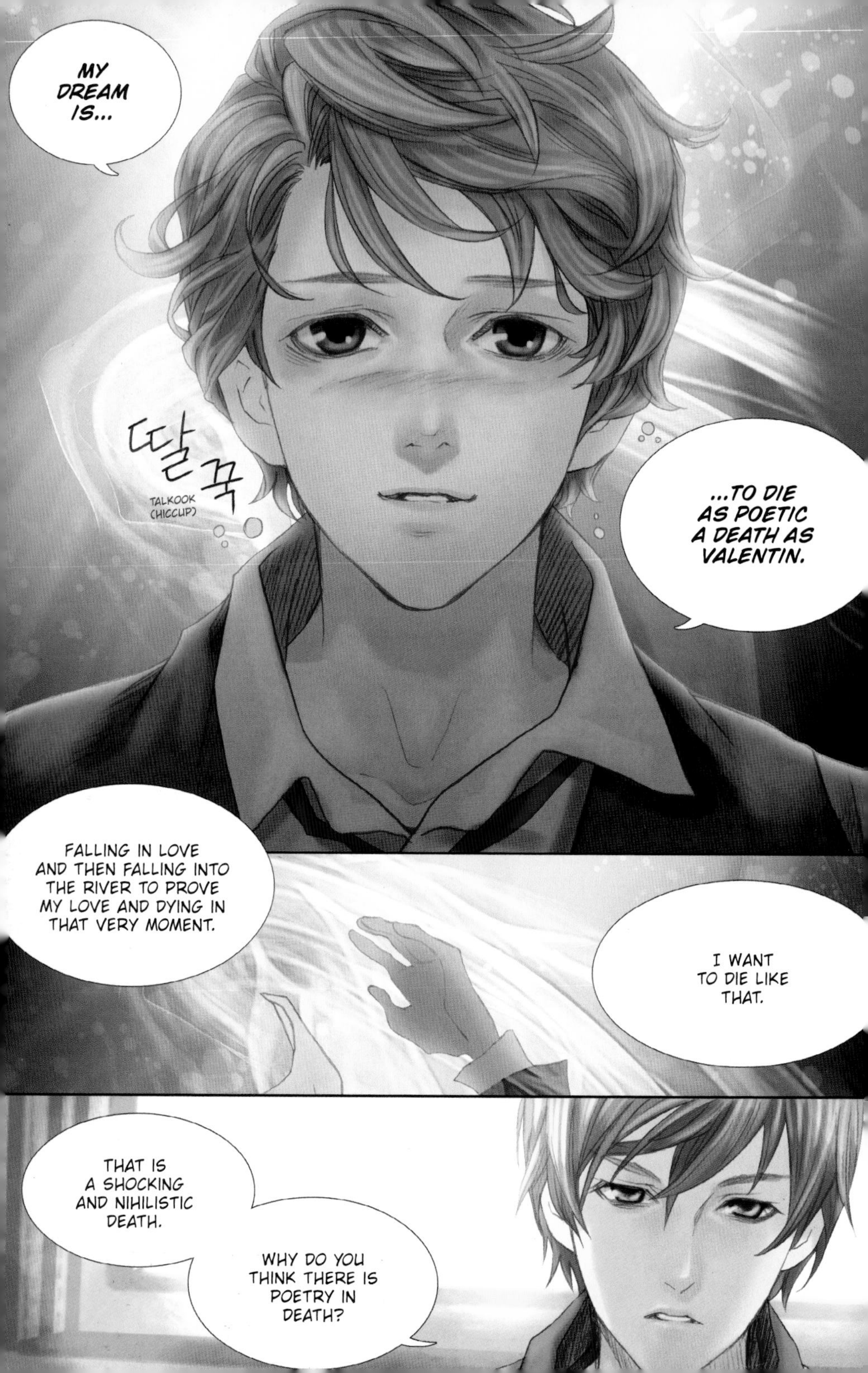
MY DREAM IS...
또딸꾹
TALKOOK (HICCUP)
...TO DIE AS POETIC A DEATH AS VALENTIN.
FALLING IN LOVE AND THEN FALLING INTO THE RIVER TO PROVE MY LOVE AND DYING IN THAT VERY MOMENT.
I WANT TO DIE LIKE THAT.
THAT IS A SHOCKING AND NIHILISTIC DEATH.
WHY DO YOU THINK THERE IS POETRY IN DEATH?

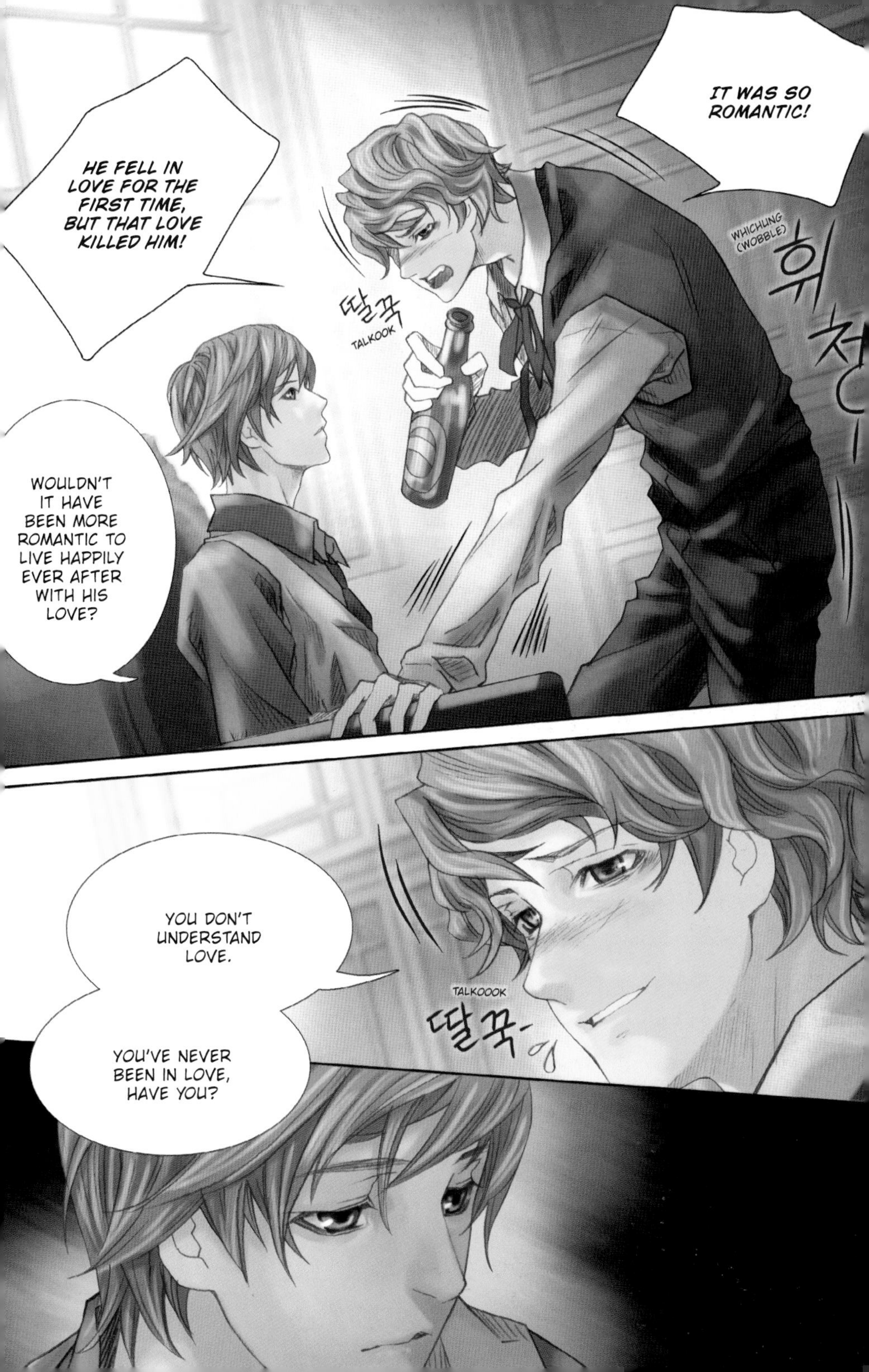
HE FELL IN LOVE FOR THE FIRST TIME, BUT THAT LOVE KILLED HIM!
IT WAS SO ROMANTIC!
딸꾹
TALKOOK
WHICHUNG (WOBBLE)
휘청
WOULDN'T IT HAVE BEEN MORE ROMANTIC TO LIVE HAPPILY EVER AFTER WITH HIS LOVE?
YOU DON'T UNDERSTAND LOVE.
TALKOOOK
딸꾹
YOU'VE NEVER BEEN IN LOVE, HAVE YOU?

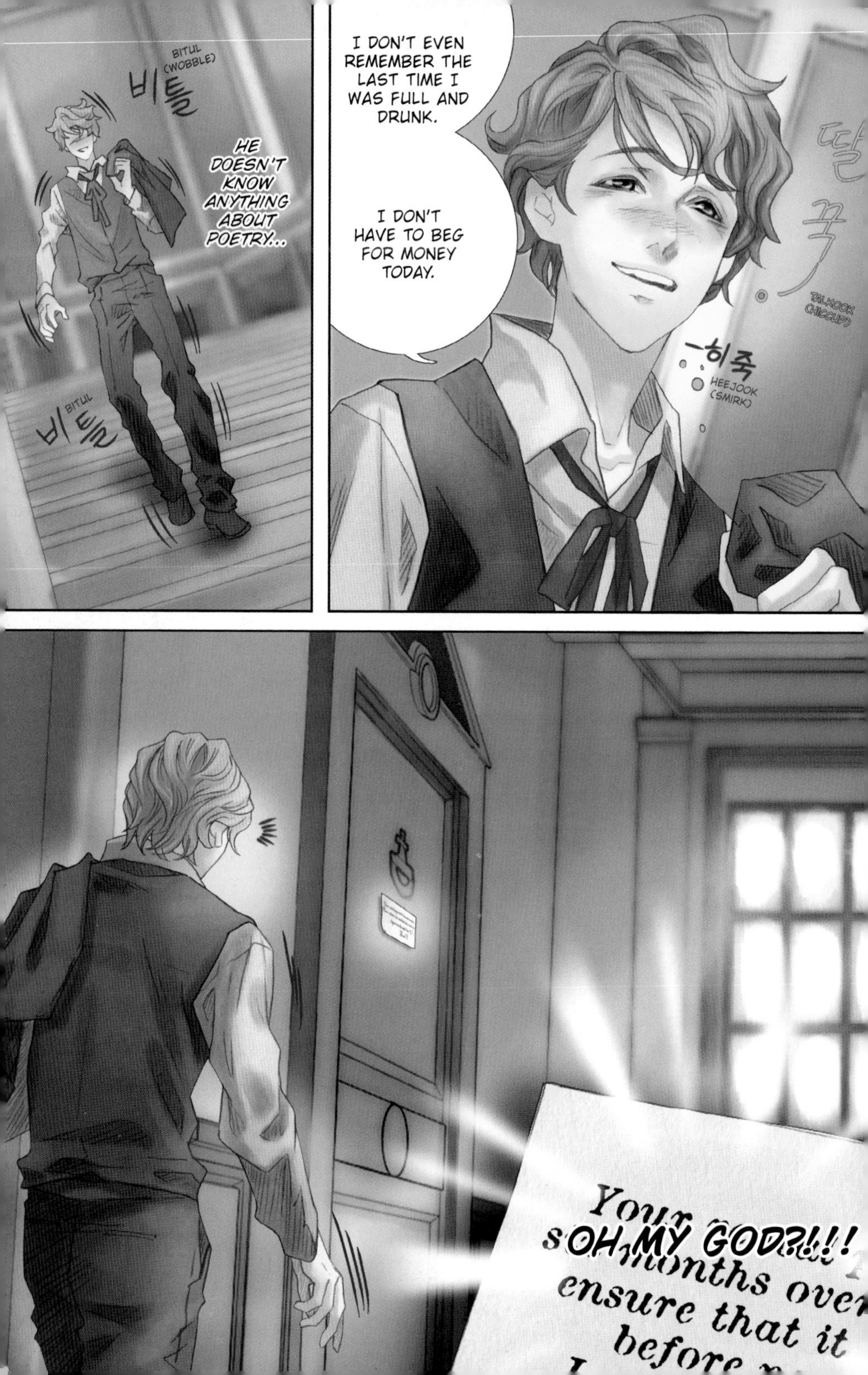
BITUL (WOBBLE)
비틀
HE DOESN'T KNOW ANYTHING ABOUT POETRY...
BITUL
비틀
I DON'T EVEN REMEMBER THE LAST TIME I WAS FULL AND DRUNK.
I DON'T HAVE TO BEG FOR MONEY TODAY.
딸꾹
TALKOOK (HICCUP)
히죽
HEEJOOK (SMIRK)
Your
months
ensure that it
before
OH MY GOD?!!!

Void's Enigmatic Mansion

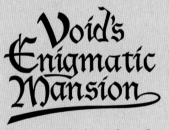

To be continued in volume 2...

Void's Enigmatic Mansion

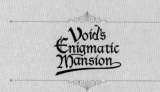

Visit artist HeeEun Kim's blog at http://blog.naver.com/kimnoran!

CAN'T WAIT FOR THE NEXT VOLUME?

Read the latest installments on the same day they are released in Korea!

CHAPTER 9

Void's Enigmatic Mansion

ART & ADAPTATION BY HEEEUN KIM
ORIGINAL BY JIEUN HA

To become the ultimate weapon, one boy must eat the souls of 99 humans...

...and one witch.

Maka is a scythe meister, working to perfect her demon scythe until it is good enough to become Death's Weapon—the weapon used by Shinigami-sama, the spirit of Death himself. And if that isn't strange enough, her scythe also has the power to change form—into a human-looking boy!

www.yenpress.com

Soul Eater © Atsushi Ohkubo / SQUARE ENIX
Yen Press is an imprint of Hachette Book Group

WELCOME TO IKEBUKURO, WHERE TOKYO'S WILDEST CHARACTERS GATHER!!

AS THEIR PATHS CROSS, THIS ECCENTRIC CAST WEAVES A TWISTED, CRACKED LOVE STORY...

AVAILABLE NOW!!

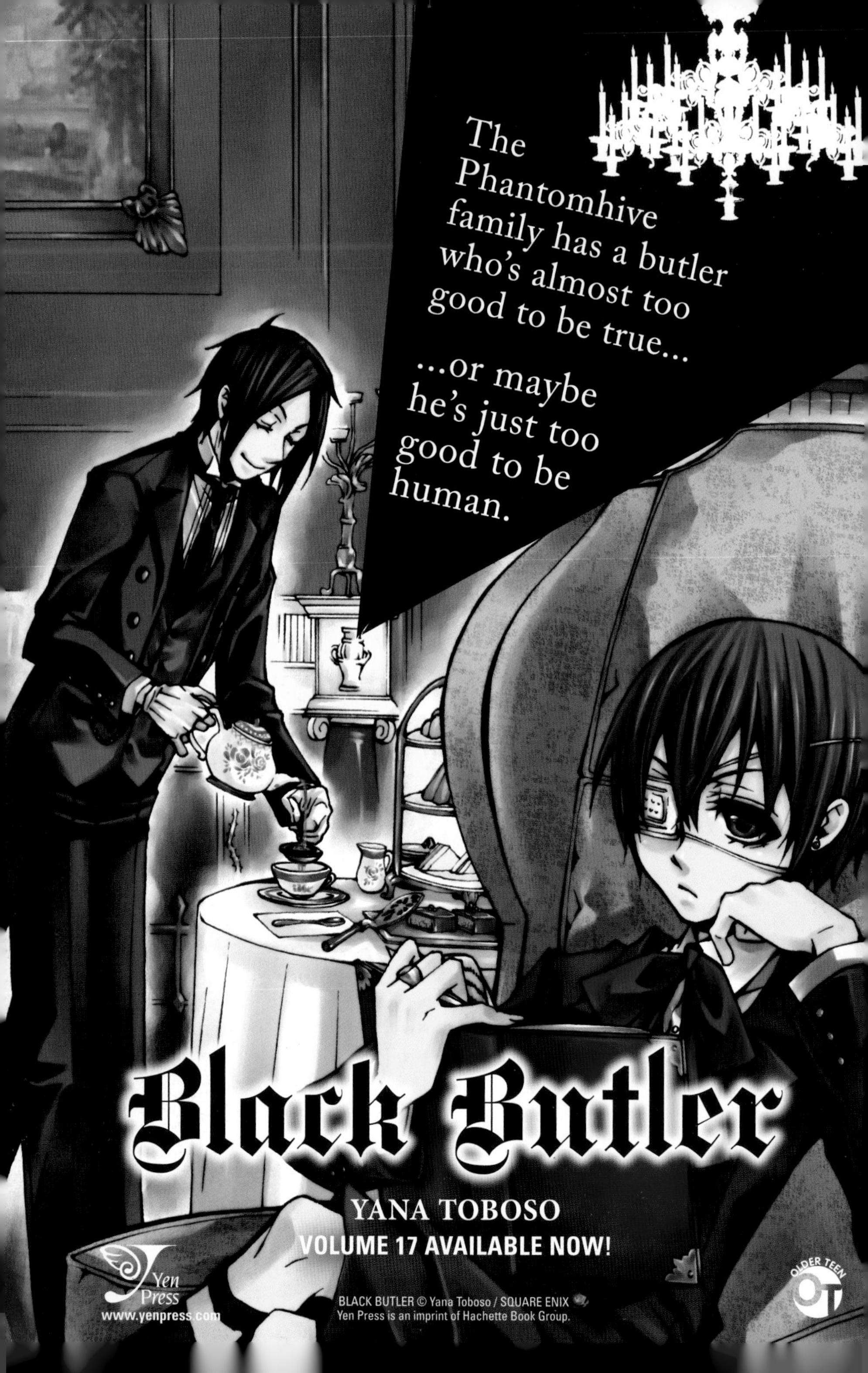
The Phantomhive family has a butler who's almost too good to be true...
...or maybe he's just too good to be human.
Black Butler
YANA TOBOSO
VOLUME 17 AVAILABLE NOW!
Yen Press
www.yenpress.com
BLACK BUTLER © Yana Toboso / SQUARE ENIX
Yen Press is an imprint of Hachette Book Group.
OLDER TEEN
OT

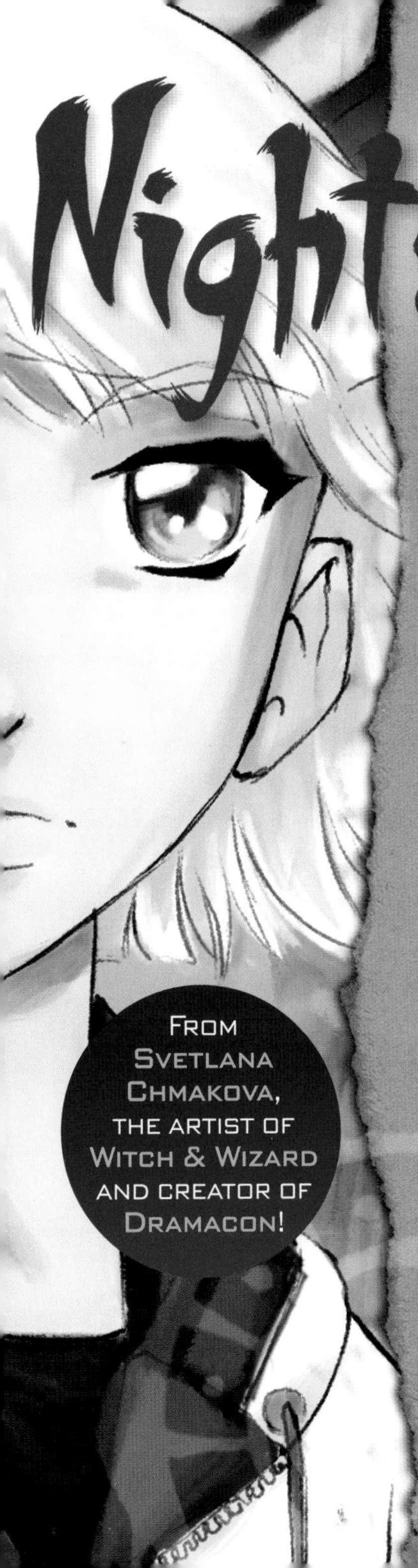

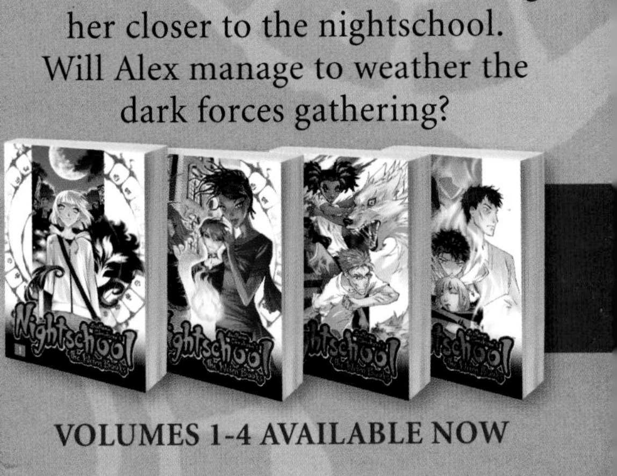

VOID'S ENIGMATIC MANSION 1

HeeEun Kim
JiEun Ha

Translation: HyeYoung Im
English Adaptation: J. Torres
Lettering: Stephanie Lee

VOID'S ENIGMATIC MANSION, Vol. 1
©2014 HeeEun Kim
©2014 JiEun Ha
Supported by KOMACON
All rights reserved.
First published in Korea in 2014 by Haksan Publishing Co., Ltd.

English translation rights in U.S.A., Canada, UK and Republic of Ireland arranged with Haksan Publishing Co., Ltd.
English translation © 2014 by Hachette Book Group, Inc.

Yen Press
Hachette Book Group
237 Park Avenue, New York, NY 10017

www.HachetteBookGroup.com
www.YenPress.com

Yen Press is an imprint of Hachette Book Group, Inc.
The Yen Press name and logo are trademarks of Hachette Book Group, Inc.

First Yen Press Edition: September 2014

ISBN: 978-0-316-41099-1

10 9 8 7 6 5 4 3 2 1

WOR

Printed in the
United States of America